Complete Guide to Digital Photography

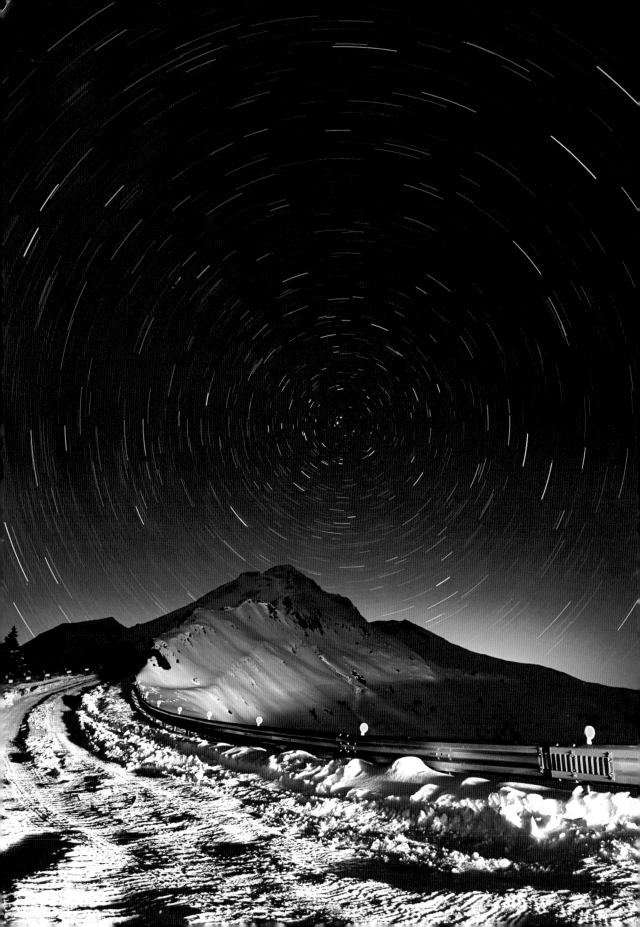

Complete Guide to Digital Photography

Ian Farrell

Quercus

Contents

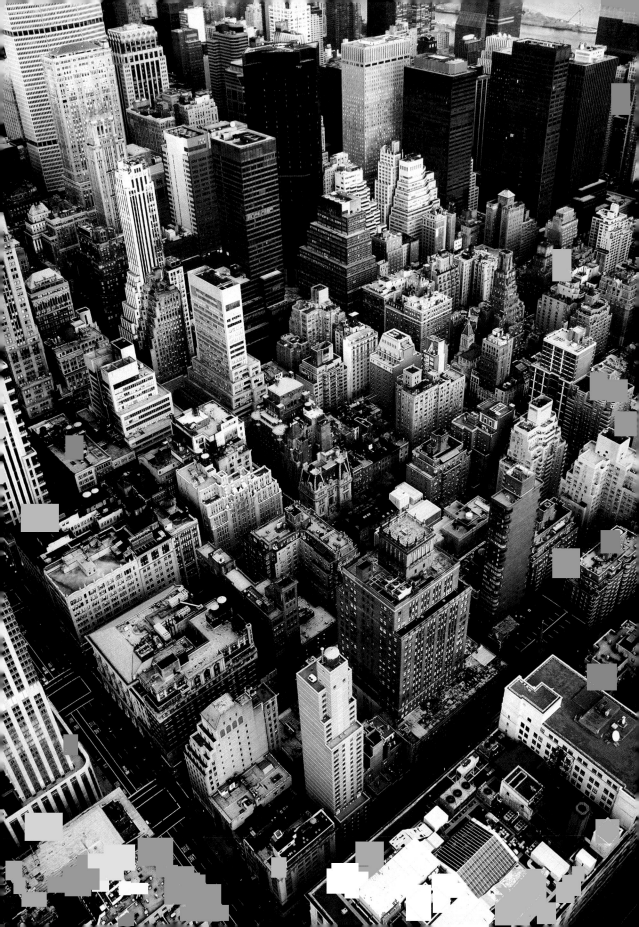

Introduction

These days we are all photographers: we all own a camera, and we all enjoy taking pictures. That said, the types of cameras we own differ wildly from each other, as does the subject matter we shoot with them. Some of us take pictures on holiday with pocket-sized compact cameras, or use their images as a record of our lives over the years. You might enjoy snapping everyday scenes with your cameraphone, or posting pictures of parties and nights out on social networking sites. But there is another reason for shooting photographs: for the sheer fun of it.

This book is about learning how to enjoy photography, and how to express yourself through the images you take. I hope it will inspire you with new ideas for photographs, as well as give you the technical skills to do them justice.

Indeed, photographers must blend together these two very different skill sets in order to be successful: the ability to be creative with compositions and concepts, and the technical expertise to capture this on camera. While the technical side of photography can be automated to a large degree, it is still useful to know about the science of photography so that you can judge whether the technology is getting things right or not. The more creative side of picture making, of course, has no such automation behind it, and this is where you can enjoy yourself with new ideas, or by paying homage to photographers that have gone before you and whose style you admire.

Only half of the picture-making process happens in-camera, of course. With some specialist photo-editing software running on a standard home computer, you can achieve all manner of adjustments, edits and special effects. This might involve fairly standard tweaks to exposure or colour, or outlandish composites that result in a photograph that would otherwise have been impossible to capture.

The rise of such digital editing over the last ten years has stopped photographers from being so reliant on commercial photo labs and given them back the creative power they once had in traditional, wet-chemical darkrooms – minus the smell of the chemicals and the headaches associated with them, of course. The new 'digital darkroom' comprises computers, screens, scanners and printers, instead – which bring with them a whole new learning curve.

As technology improves, so imaging software can do more and more, and photographers must learn new tricks. Indeed, you'll soon discover that there is no end to your photographic education, no point at which you suddenly realize that you are a qualified photographer. The learning process goes on, both technically and creatively, and there will always be someone who knows more than you do and whom you can learn from.

It is this that makes photography such a compelling pastime, and I hope that you enjoy learning from this book. Digest the information and tackle the assignments in it, and keep it by your side as a reference as you grow and develop as a photographer. And remember the golden rule: whatever you photograph, have fun.

Left: Black and white photography is as powerful today as it has always been. Free from the distraction of colour we can better appreciate textures, shapes and tone, as in this view over New York City from the top of the Empire State Building.

Ian Farrell,
Cambridge 2011

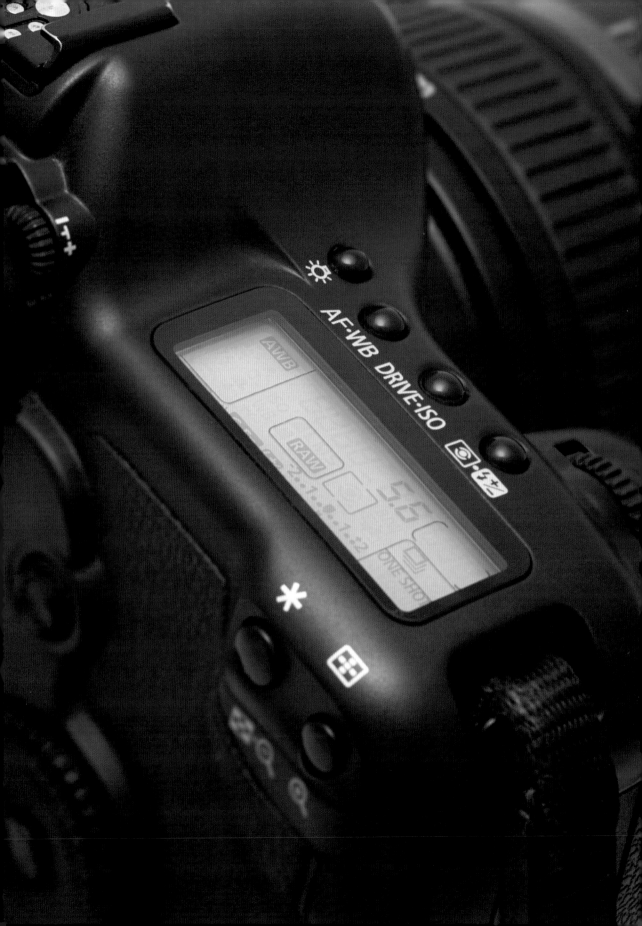

your
camera

If you're new to digital photography
(and even if you're not!) the amount of choice
available for everything from cameras and lenses
to bags and accessories can be utterly baffling.
But by thinking carefully about your needs and
requirements, you can pinpoint the perfect
equipment to get you started.

Introduction to **your camera**

Although there are hundreds of different digital cameras on the market, there are some fundamental things that they all have in common. At its heart, every camera is really a light-tight box with a hole in it. When you press the shutter button, light is let in through the hole (passing through some glass we call a lens) and falls onto a photo-sensitive electronic sensor, where an image is formed and recorded onto a memory card. This is how digital photographs are made.

Of course, there are many differences between different digital cameras. Some compact cameras cost little more than a restaurant bill, fit in a short pocket and provide easy auto-everything photography. Others cost more than a new car and can capture incredible detail and picture quality, or track and shoot moving objects at high speed. Which camera you use will depend heavily on what you want to do with it, and what kind of photographer you are. You may even decide you need more than one picture-taking machine to satisfy your needs. Let's have a quick look at what's available.

Compact cameras

Every family has one. The humble compact camera gets thrown in a bag, taken all around the world on holidays and is expected to perform as well at parties as it does shooting majestic landscapes. The compact camera is a jack of all trades, coping well with each of these scenarios while never excelling at any of them. However, where it does score is in being small enough to be taken along in the first place: other bigger, cameras may deliver better pictures, but if they are so hefty that they always get left at home, then the compact wins every time.

Compact cameras aim to provide everything you could want in a single package. They will have an integrated flash for low-light photography, plenty of auto-everything modes so you don't have to think too hard about technical aspects, and a motorized zoom lens to change your angle of view at the touch of a button. The power of this zoom lens is a major selling point in compact cameras, and is usually expressed as a multiplication factor: 5x, 10x or even 40x. This means that at the telephoto end, the zoom is magnifying objects by (for instance) ten times more than at the wide-angle end. When contrasting different cameras, however, do make sure that you are comparing like with like. Two 10x zooms may not have the same telephoto power if one has a broader angle of view in the first place. Look for a 35mm equivalent focal length and compare these instead – we'll discuss this more on page 20.

When buying a compact camera, also look for how many pixels the camera has on its sensor. This will determine the size of the prints you can make from each file, as well as dictating picture

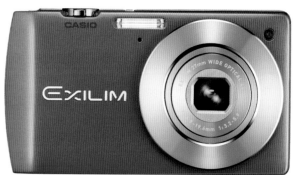

Right: You can take a compact camera everywhere with you, but it won't produce the image quality of a DSLR.

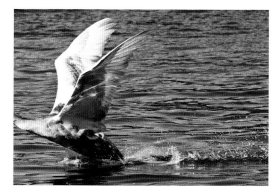

Above: *A compact or bridge camera may exhibit shutter lag, meaning the perfect moment is missed.*

Overcoming shutter lag

One of the biggest problems encountered by compact camera-users is the lag between pressing the shutter button and the camera recording the picture. Most of this delay is due to the camera focusing, meaning you can substantially improve your camera's reaction time by getting this focusing operation out of the way before the moment to take the picture arrives. You can do this with your camera's AF-lock feature: half-pressing the shutter release tells the camera to focus on the subject and hold this focus until the shutter release is pressed down further and the picture is taken. By locking focus on the subject (or the place where it will be) before you take the picture, you'll find the delay when you come to actually capture the image greatly reduced.

quality. A sensor with 12 million pixels on it (a '12 megapixel' camera) will capture more detail than a sensor with only 6 million pixels (a '6 megapixel' camera). We'll talk about pixels and resolution more on page 18.

The limitations of a compact camera include slow reaction times when shooting pictures, and limited control over depth of field (the amount of the picture that is in focus – see pages 84–87). Image quality is also limited by the small size of compact camera sensors, which are usually around 8mm across. As a general rule, the bigger the sensor, the better the image quality.

Bridge cameras

If the features of a compact camera are a little too primitive or automated for you, but you still want a camera that is small and lightweight, then a bridge camera (so-called because they bridge the gap between compacts and DSLR cameras) could be what you are after. Often styled like a DSLR, bridge cameras have the same kind of sensor and electronics as a compact, but usually have more advanced features, giving the photographer more creative control over factors such as focusing and exposure.

The same limitations regarding small sensor sizes and slow reaction times apply to bridge camera design, however, so those wanting to step up to truly creative photography should consider a DSLR.

Below: *Bridge cameras have more advanced features than a compact, including an extended zoom range.*

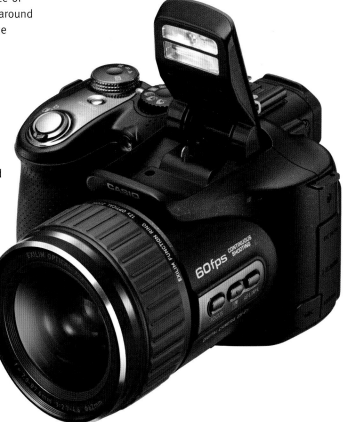

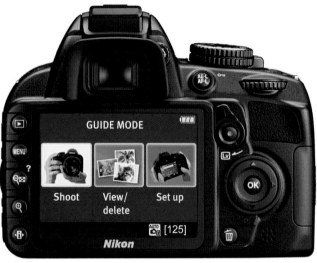

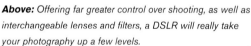

Above: Offering far greater control over shooting, as well as interchangeable lenses and filters, a DSLR will really take your photography up a few levels.

Digital SLR cameras

While a compact is great for slipping in your pocket and taking everywhere, a DSLR offers better picture quality from a larger sensor, faster handling, and increased flexibility with an interchangeable lens system.

SLR stands for 'single lens reflex', and refers to a design of camera that uses a mirror to enable the user to look straight through the main lens using the camera's viewfinder, meaning what you see is exactly what you capture. When the shutter-release button is pressed, the mirror swings up out of the way and the shutter opens to let light through to the sensor. At the end of the exposure the mirror comes back down again. This all happens in the blink of an eye; the only way you'd ever know what is happening is the momentary blacking out of the viewfinder for a fraction of a second while the mirror is moving.

Sensor sizes in DSLRs starts out at 17.3 x 30mm (Olympus) and ends at the same size as 35mm film (24 x 36mm) in so-called full-frame cameras. There are plenty of 'cropped sensor' sizes in between these extremes: 22.2 x 14.8mm (Canon), 23.6 x 15.7mm (Nikon, Pentax, Sony) and 20.7 x 13.8mm (Sigma) are all commonly found, and all give substantially better image quality than the tiny sensors used in compact cameras.

All DSLRs have interchangeable lenses, meaning photographers have access to a wider zoom range and better optical quality than they do with compact cameras. Most DSLRs come bundled with a standard lens – often an 18–55mm zoom, or similar – that is more than fine for general landscape, portrait and travel shooting. Other lenses are available that give extreme wide-angle views or highly magnified telephoto images. Specialist lenses are available that allow close-up shooting, or that let in lots of light for low-light photography without flash. When buying a DSLR you are really buying into a system of cameras, lenses and accessories that will grow as your photography develops, and could be with you for many years to come.

Don't forget your camera phone

They may offer the worst image quality of all digital cameras, but camera phones are something you can take everywhere with you. Recognize their limits and use them properly, and you'll find you can use them very artistically, especially with some of the more feature-packed models on the market, or those that allow downloadable photography 'apps' (application software) that simulate creative effects.

- Camera phone lenses are fixed; any 'zooming' on offer is really only cropping into the middle of the picture. Better to move your feet and preserve image quality.
- Look for abstract shapes and compositions, or patterns and colours that just look interesting; objects don't need to be instantly recognizable.
- Avoid low-light situations. Small sensors, like those found in camera phones, are not great in the dark, and flashes are typically very underpowered.
- Explore settings that simulate photographic effects such as toy camera, film grain or fisheye.
- Try shooting from the hip, without looking through the viewfinder. You can be very subtle and shoot candid photos without anyone knowing.

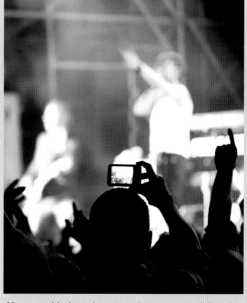

Above and below: A camera phone may not deliver the best image quality, but it's portable enough to take with you wherever you go.

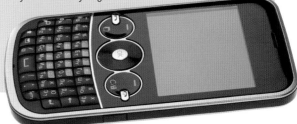

Microsystem cameras

In an attempt to unify the small size of a compact camera with the flexibility and image quality of a DSLR, some manufacturers developed what have become know as microsystem cameras. These are essentially DSLRs without the reflex mirror and optical viewfinder. Although this means that the photographer has to compose images on the camera's viewscreen, the camera can be made much smaller and lighter. Microsystem cameras still offer the flexibility of interchangeable lenses, and their large sensors deliver the image quality and depth of field-control associated with DSLRs.

Below: The portability of a compact camera meets the picture quality of a DSLR in a so-called microsystem camera.

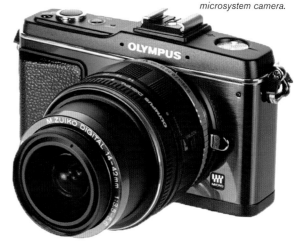

MAKING A PINHOLE CAMERA

A pinhole camera represents photography at its most basic. This very enjoyable, and undeniably cool, way to create images can be yours with some basic DIY skills and a digital SLR.

You often hear it said that a camera is really nothing but a light-tight box with a hole in the front. While today's digital cameras are about as far away from that concept as a laptop is from a typewriter, it can be fun to revert to first principles by converting your DSLR to a pinhole camera.

A pinhole camera does away with glass lenses and relies on a very small hole to form the image on the sensor. Being so small (around f/150 in aperture terms), depth of field (see pages 84–87) is huge, removing the need for focusing altogether. General image quality, on the other hand, is not so great, with images taking on a fuzzy look. What's more, you'll need to use very long shutter speeds. But this is all part of what gives pinhole photography its charm!

Making the pinhole
To make your pinhole camera, the first thing you need is the body cap that came with your camera. This is designed to protect it from dust and dirt when in storage, but we'll use it to hold our pinhole aperture. Clamp it securely in a vice or similar apparatus and drill a hole in the centre of the cap with an electric drill. This is not the hole we'll be using to shoot with (it's too big) but it will let us form a proper pinhole.

Tape a small strip of aluminium kitchen foil over the back of the hole. Next, with a small pin put a tiny hole dead in the centre of the body cap. This will be your working aperture. Ensure there is no dust or debris on the rear of the cap that could get stuck on the camera's sensor. A quick blast of compressed air should do the job.

Measuring and using the pinhole
The exposure metering systems on your DSLR won't work with the pinhole, but we can compare the amount of light let in through the pinhole with the amount of light passed through a normal lens, and use this for metering instead.

With the pinhole body cap fitted to the camera, shoot pictures of a test scene until you get well-exposed results. Start with a shutter speed of 10sec or so. When you are happy, replace the pinhole attachment with a conventional lens and meter the same scene at the smallest aperture. Divide the pinhole shutter speed by the normal lens's shutter speed to get a conversion factor. When shooting any other scene, you can meter this with the normal lens on at its minimum aperture, and find the right shutter speed for your pinhole by multiplying the metered value by the conversion factor. It's worth labelling your pinhole body cap with the multiplication factor so you don't forget.

Properties of a pinhole camera
It's a lot of hassle making a pinhole camera, but the results can be worth it. Long shutter speeds mean that movement blurs in the frame, while static objects stay sharp. What's more, the depth of field given by such an aperture is enormous, rendering objects in focus at distances from a few inches in front of the camera to infinity.

You'll need a tripod to keep the camera still. If your DSLR doesn't offer long enough timed shutter speeds use its B setting, which keeps the shutter open for as long as the shutter release (or remote release) is depressed.

ESSENTIAL KIT

- DSLR
- Body cap
- Kitchen foil and tape
- Drill and small drill bit
- Vice or workbench
- Tripod
- Remote release

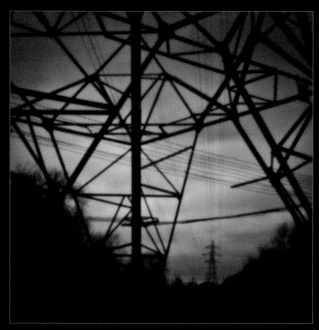

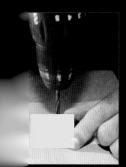
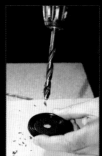
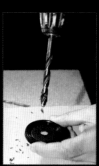

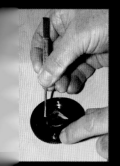
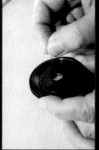

Above, clockwise from top left: (a) Drill a hole in the body cap; (b) expand the body cap with a larger drill bit; (c) tape a piece of foil over the drill hole; (d) prick a pinhole in the foil with a needle or pin.

Right, top and bottom: The results of a home made pinhole on a digital camera. The images have been turned to black & white and noise has been added.

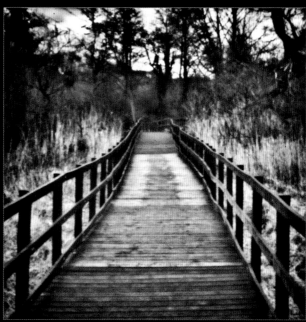

Anatomy of a **camera**

Some features are common to nearly all cameras. Let's have a look at the anatomy of a typical compact and a top-end DSLR, and investigate some of the other ingredients you should look for in a digital camera.

TOP OF THE CAMERA

Shutter release The all-important control that is used to capture images. This is usually a two-stage control, with a half-press causing the camera to autofocus and a full press capturing the picture.

Top-plate display DSLRs have a great many settings, even if they are being controlled for you in an automatic mode. The top plate gives you a summary of all these settings at a glance, showing exposure and focus information as well as battery status, drive mode and metering pattern.

Mode dial DSLRs often have dedicated dials for switching modes. It's a faster way of working, although it takes up more space.

Zoom and focus controls The two rings on a DSLR lens control the zoom position and manual focus.

Hotshoe Principally for high-power external flashguns, although a camera's hotshoe can also hold other accessories, such as microphones for video work or GPS location devices.

On/off | Shutter release

μ-5010   14 MEGAPIXEL

FRONT OF THE CAMERA

Lens cap

Manual focus

Changeable lens

Manual zoom

On/off | Shutter release

Exposure compensation

Lens release button

Exposure mode dial

Lens Built-in to most compacts, and interchangeable in DSLRs, a camera's lens is essential for forming an image on the sensor. Look for a good zoom range, but don't just concentrate on the telephoto end; the wide-angle part is just as important. Pick a zoom lens that has the same angle of view as a 28mm lens on a full-frame digital camera. An 18–55mm lens is often included with most cropped-sensor DSLRs. Some lenses include image stabilization and faster AF.

Hotshoe (for flash gun) | Top-plate display | Metering pattern button

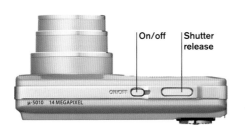

Built-in flash When conditions get dark, you'll often want to bring in a camera's built-in flash to shed more light on the scene. These units are not usually very powerful, having a range of 4–6m, but they can get you out of a tight spot at parties. You can also use the camera's flash on sunny days, to brighten up shadowy areas and reduce contrast – a technique known as fill-in flash (see page 96).

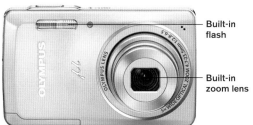

Built-in flash

Built-in zoom lens

Built-in flash (closed)

Shutter release

Control wheel

Changeable lens

REAR OF THE CAMERA

Viewscreen This is what you'll use to review and compose pictures with, as well as navigate the camera's menu systems. Better quality viewscreens contain more dots and show higher-resolution images. Others pivot and rotate, letting you shoot more comfortably from alternative angles.

Control dial Commonly a four-way controller that navigates through menus, selects focus points and scrolls around a magnified image. Command dials control aperture and shutter speed (see page 73).

Zoom controls and image playback Looking at pictures on a digital camera is as easy as pressing the 'play' button. You can then zoom in with the + and – zoom controls to see detail and check for sharpness. On compact cameras these zoom controls also control the position of the zoom during shooting; with DSLRs this is achieved by turning the zoom ring on the lens.

Viewfinder Few compact cameras have a direct optical viewfinder, but this is a key feature in a DSLR, allowing the photographer to look straight through the lens for very precise framing.

Image delete | Viewfinder | Autofocus control

Control dial

HD Video record

Control wheel

Playback

Control menu

White balance

ISO

Playback zoom control | Viewscreen | Focus-point lock switch | Multi-function dial

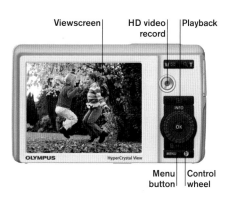

Viewscreen | HD video record | Playback

Menu button | Control wheel

Video record button HD video capture is a relatively new feature in digital still cameras, although it is quickly becoming the norm. A dedicated record button is usually found on the back of the camera.

Megapixels and image quality

The resolution of a digital camera – that is, the number of pixels on its sensor – dictates how much detail it can resolve in a photograph, and how large a picture can be printed.

Resolution underpins much of digital photography. It largely defines how good the picture quality will be, including how much detail a camera records and at what size a picture can be printed. We use it as a label (rightly or wrongly) when we are comparing cameras against each other, but how much do we really know about resolution? How much does it matter? And what is it anyway?

Resolution in this context is the number of pixels on the camera's light-sensitive sensor, and hence the number of pixels used to make up a picture. Much like high-definition televisions, the more pixels that are packed onto a camera's sensor, the sharper an image will be and the more detail it will record. A few years ago camera manufacturers were falling over themselves to offer higher and higher resolutions. Today, things are more stable, with most compact cameras offering between 8 and 14 megapixels, and consumer-level DSLRs sporting between 10 and 18.

Outside of the camera, it is more useful to talk about resolution not just in terms of the total pixel count, but in the number of pixels that are present in a fixed physical size. For this reason, resolution in 'pixels per inch' (or ppi) tends to be used to describe the resolution of a photograph when it is printed or viewed on-screen.

When printing a picture, there needs to be around 200 pixels in every inch to retain decent image quality. Any less than this and you start to see the individual pixels and the picture looks 'blocky' or out of focus. A picture from a 6 megapixel camera measuring 2,816 x 2,112 pixels can be printed no larger than 14 x 11 inches (dividing the number of pixels in one dimension by the desired resolution of 200 ppi). However, the same image shot on a 12 megapixel camera will print at 21 x 14 inches.

When cropping images on a computer, we are effectively throwing away some pixels and making the image smaller. In order to still be able to print at large sizes at around 200 ppi resolution, it's essential to have a lot of pixels in the first place, meaning high pixel-count cameras score again.

When looking at photographs on-screen you are seeing them in much lower resolution than if they were printed. Most displays have a resolution of between 72 and 96 ppi, so a photograph doesn't need to have as many pixels to be viewed on-screen as it does at the same size on paper.

Can you have too many pixels?

It is good to buy as many pixels as possible, but do use some common sense too. If the choice is between a 14 megapixel camera and a 10 megapixel model that has other useful features (high-speed shooting, tougher build quality, etc), then it may be worth foregoing the extra megapixels. Ask yourself how often you will want to print at such large sizes, if at all. Some users will only ever view images on-screen, making 14 megapixel resolution overkill.

Because compact cameras use such small sensors, there comes a point when adding more pixels to it becomes counterproductive. To crowd more pixels onto a sensor requires them to be made smaller and squeezed more closely together – two factors that negatively affect image quality. On larger sensors found in DSLR cameras, the maximum practical pixel count is 20–24 megapixels. For higher resolutions (30–80 megapixels) it is necessary to go to medium-format cameras that have enormous sensor sizes and are very expensive.

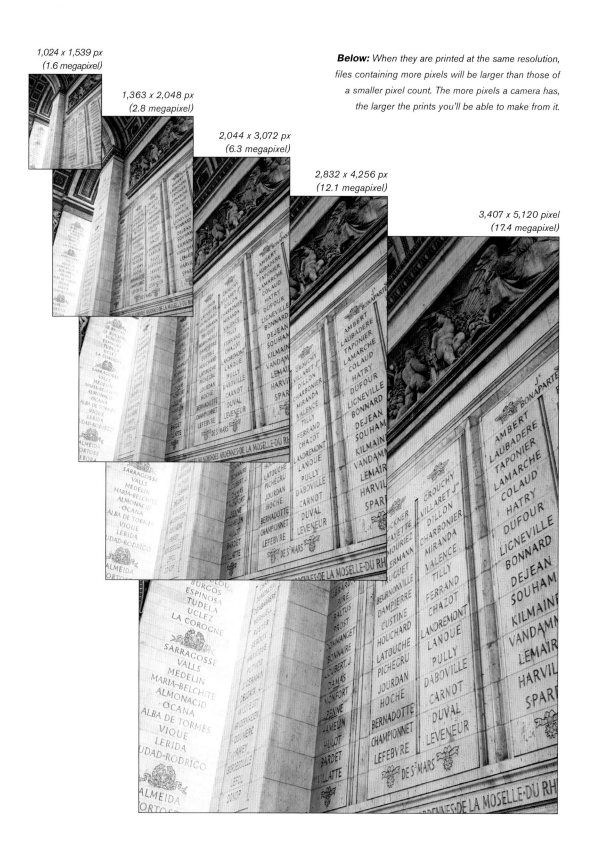

1,024 x 1,539 px
(1.6 megapixel)

1,363 x 2,048 px
(2.8 megapixel)

2,044 x 3,072 px
(6.3 megapixel)

2,832 x 4,256 px
(12.1 megapixel)

3,407 x 5,120 pixel
(17.4 megapixel)

Below: *When they are printed at the same resolution, files containing more pixels will be larger than those of a smaller pixel count. The more pixels a camera has, the larger the prints you'll be able to make from it.*

Types of **lens**

One of the joys of a DSLR is the ability to change lenses. Although the standard zoom lens that comes with a DSLR is great for most tasks, there are benefits that come with the various different options.

Other lenses allow a different angle of view, allow low-light shooting or deliver better image quality. The angle of view of a specific lens is dictated by its focal length, quoted in millimeters. However, focal lengths can be compared against each other only for cameras of the same sensor size.

Telephoto lenses

Longer focal length lenses – that's more than 35mm on most DSLRs, or 50mm on full-frame cameras – magnify objects at long distances. They are great for getting you a bit closer to the action, especially if you are shooting sports or wildlife. A telephoto zoom lens (known as a 'telezoom') is a great addition to your camera kit, and usually the extra lens that new photographers buy first. Something like a 70–300mm is good, and some units even include vibration reduction or image stabilization technology to reduce blur from camera shake. This is especially prevalent with telephoto lenses, as the same magnification that brings your subject closer also magnifies camera movement, no matter how still you are holding your DSLR.

Overcoming camera shake and freezing subject movement need fast shutter speeds, but to do this you will also need a wide maximum aperture. Unfortunately you'll pay handsomely for this in a telephoto lens. A budget 70–200mm optic may have a maximum aperture that varies between f/3.5 at the wide-angle end to f/5.6 at the more telephoto end, meaning you'll struggle to get

a shutter speed above 1/500sec in normal daylight conditions. Comparable lenses are available with a wider f/2.8 maximum aperture at all zoom settings, but you might pay four times the price.

Wide-angle lenses

The wide-angle end of the standard zoom that comes with your DSLR is usually enough for most situations, although there are some fantastic 'ultra wide-angle' lenses that give landscape and architectural photography a dramatic lift. Where standard zoom lenses offer a 18–55mm focal length range, ultra wide-angle lenses are typically in the region of 10–20mm or 12–24mm. Distortion with such lenses is quite severe, but this can add to the effect. Some cheaper wide-angle zooms can suffer from excessive darkening at the edges of the frame ('vignetting', or fall-off), and chromatic aberration (purple fringing along high-contrast edges).

Standard zoom lenses

The standard zoom lives on your camera for most of the time, and offers focal lengths from wide-angle (18mm) through to short telephoto (55mm). You may already have a cheap 'kit' zoom lens if one came with your camera, although it might be worth considering upgrading to a slightly more expensive option at some point. A better standard zoom will offer much better picture quality than the lenses that are bundled with cameras. More sharpness, higher contrast and more punchy colour rendition are also all on offer. You'll also notice less distortion and fringing.

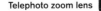
Telephoto zoom lens

Wide-angle zoom lens

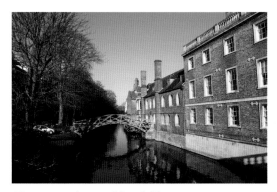

18mm cropped sensor, 24mm full frame

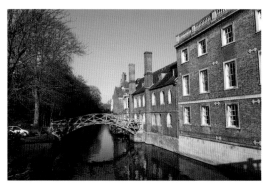

23mm cropped sensor, 35mm full frame

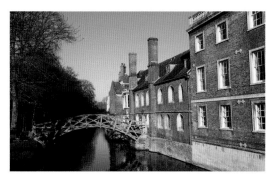

33mm cropped sensor, 50mm full frame

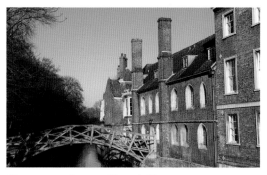

46mm cropped sensor, 70mm full frame

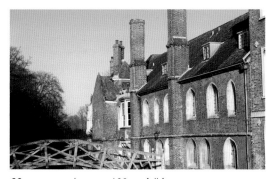

66mm cropped sensor, 100mm full frame

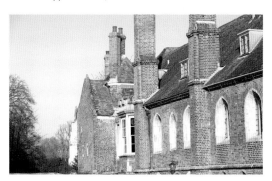

80mm cropped sensor, 120mm full frame

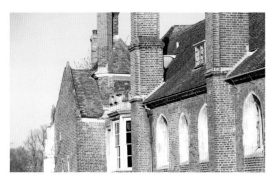

113mm cropped sensor, 170mm full frame

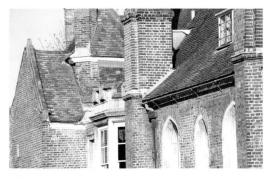

133mm cropped sensor, 200mm full frame

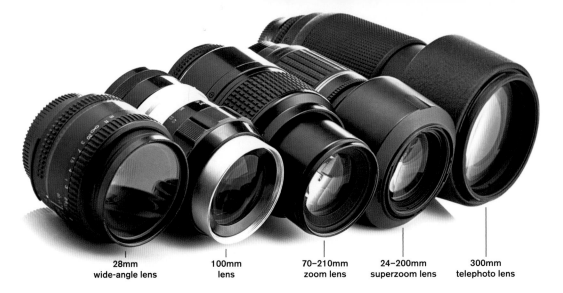

| 28mm wide-angle lens | 100mm lens | 70–210mm zoom lens | 24–200mm superzoom lens | 300mm telephoto lens |

Buying a quality standard zoom can often be a more cost-effective way to improve picture quality than buying a new camera. And when the time to upgrade your DSLR does come around, you can buy only a body, safe in the knowledge that you already have a good quality standard lens.

Superzooms

On the face of it, superzooms seem to offer the best of both worlds. An enormous zoom range (typically 18–200mm or more) covers everything from wide-angles for landscapes, to telephoto for sport or action. It's a good option for travel photographers, who might be trying to pack a minimum of equipment.

That said, there are drawbacks. To achieve such a huge zoom range, some optical compromises are made in the lens design, meaning image quality is not as good as you can expect from lenses with more modest zoom ranges. Superzooms are also very heavy and tend to focus slowly because the AF motors have such large pieces of glass to move around. Maximum apertures are also quite small (as little as f/6.5), making it hard to use a shutter speed that prevents camera shake.

Prime lenses

In more ways than one, prime lenses are the complete opposite of superzooms. They are far less convenient, only having one focal length and no ability to zoom at all. They do deliver excellent image quality and wide maximum apertures (f/1.4–2.8), however, and are smaller and more lightweight.

Not having a zoom range means that prime lenses are more difficult to use, but in the same way that a fountain pen can improve your handwriting, prime lenses can improve your photography. Without the facility to zoom, you must move your feet to change position, and in doing so photographers often consider other things they can do to change composition, such as getting down lower.

Specific prime lenses often have a specific job. For instance, a 35mm f/1.4 lens used on a full-frame camera is superb for documentary photography, being slightly wide-angle and having a very fast aperture for low-light work. Similarly, an 85mm f/1.4 has long been the portrait photographer's lens of choice, thanks to its slight telephoto nature and large maximum aperture, allowing depth of field control.

Below: Superzoom lens, giving wide angle to telephoto zoom range.

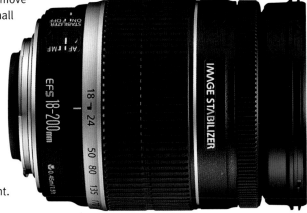

Lenses and sensor size

When comparing the angle of view of different lenses, we tend to talk in terms of focal length – the distance from the middle of the lens to the sensor. Lenses of shorter focal length have a wider angle of view than those with a longer focal length, but we can only compare focal lengths against each other accurately when we are using sensors of the same size.

This is best understood by thinking of the circle of light projected by a 50mm lens, for example. We capture images from this circle by putting a rectangular sensor in it, with the corners of the rectangle touching the edges of the circle. But using smaller sensors means that not as much of the image circle is captured in a photograph, and the angle of view becomes more narrow.

With different types of digital camera using slightly different sensor sizes, the only way that lenses can be compared against each other is to convert focal length back to a standard. For historical reasons, this standard is the size of old 35mm film, or a full-frame digital sensor. Multiplying a lens focal length by a 'crop factor' (the degree to which the sensor is smaller than full-frame) lets us compare a lens's angle of view with full-frame lenses. For example, when using a camera with a sensor that is 1.5x smaller than 35mm film/full-frame, focal lengths should be multiplied by 1.5 to convert them to a full-frame equivalent. For lenses used on cameras with sensors half the size of 35mm/full-frame, focal lengths should be multiplied by two. This means that our 50mm lens has the same angle of view as a 75mm lens when used on a Nikon DSLR, or a 100mm lens on an Olympus camera. Some common cameras, and their lens crop factors, are shown below.

Camera	Focal length crop factor (compared to full-frame digital/35mm film)
Canon EOS 1100D, EOS 450D, EOS 550D, EOS 60D, EOS 7D	1.6x
Canon EOS-1D MKIV	1.3x
Canon EOS-5D MKII, EOS-1Ds MKII	1.0x (full-frame)
Nikon D60, D90, D3100, D5100, D7000, D300s	1.5x
Nikon D700, D3s, D3x	1.0x (full-frame)
Olympus E- and Pen-series cameras	2.0x
Pentax DSLRs	1.5x
Panasonic G-series cameras	2.0x
Sony a-450, a-290, a-390, a-550, a-580	1.5x
Sony a-900, a-850	1.0x (full-frame)
Samsung GX-series cameras	1.5x

For those types of photography that require telephoto lenses, a cropped-sensor DSLR (i.e. one with a smaller sensor size than full-frame) can be a bonus, as the same lens gives a more magnified view than it would on a full-frame digital camera. On an Olympus DSLR, for instance, a 300mm lens has the same angle of view as a 600mm lens on a full-frame camera, but is much smaller and lighter.

By making lenses with an image circle smaller than a 24 x 36mm sensor, it's possible to create lenses that are much smaller, lighter and cheaper than their full-frame equivalents. Such lenses are usually identified by a DG, DX or EF-S initial somewhere in their name, or with the cunning marketing phrase 'designed for digital', which actually means 'doesn't work on full-frame cameras'.

Accessories

There is an accessory for everything in photography, from special-effects filters and remote shooting to tripods and image storage devices. And don't forget a good bag or case to transport and store your gear, too.

Filters

Filters are pieces of glass or resin that are fixed over the camera's lens in order to create special effects or enhance parts of a photograph. In the days of film photography there was a filter for everything, although the plethora of digital camera settings, and the possibilities afforded by computer retouching, mean that most filter effects can now be created digitally. This doesn't mean that filters are redundant, though. There are still several effects that are best created using traditional, in-camera filter techniques.

Polarizing filter

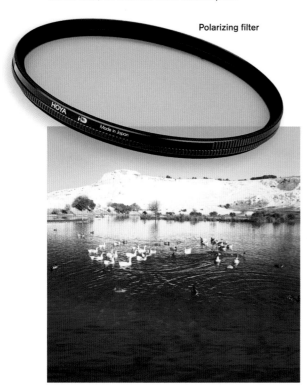

Polarizing filters

Polarizing filters reduce reflections in non-metallic surfaces and, as a consequence, make blue skies and green foliage appear to be more saturated in colour. As such, they are used heavily by landscape photographers.

Sunlight is composed of light waves oriented (or polarized) in different directions. A polarizing filter allows only one orientation through to the camera's sensor, acting like a sieve that blocks other light rays. This has the effect of reducing reflections from surfaces such as glass or water.

A polarizer has the most effect when you are shooting at 90 degrees to the sun, and you can adjust its intensity by rotating it on the front of the camera. The filter absorbs 1–1.5 stops of light, meaning you'll be using a shutter speed of 1/30sec instead of 1/90sec. This means that camera shake can creep in and spoil sharpness, so you may need to use a tripod to keep things steady.

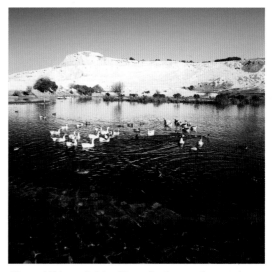

Above: Without a polarizing filter, the scene appears slightly flatter and contains distracting reflections.

Above: With a polarizing filter, reflections on the water's surface are filtered out and colours are more saturated.

Neutral density filters

Neutral density (ND) filters don't affect a picture in terms of colour or focus, but just absorb light, meaning you'll have to use a slower shutter speed (or wider aperture) than usual. You may wonder why you might want to do this, but as we'll see (on page 73) there are plenty of creative things you can do with slow shutter speeds (blurring movement in water or crowds) and large apertures (restricting depth of field). The problem comes when you can't achieve this because the lighting conditions are too intense, for instance in bright sunshine. Here an ND filter will absorb three or four stops of light, reducing a 1/125sec shutter speed to a blurry 1/15sec or 1/8sec.

The power of an ND filter is sometimes expressed in many different ways, which can be confusing. Some are labelled with optical density, some with the number of f-stops, and some with an ND number that relates to the fraction of light transmitted through the filter. Here are some common ND filter powers.

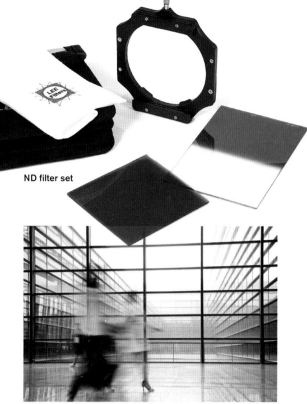
ND filter set

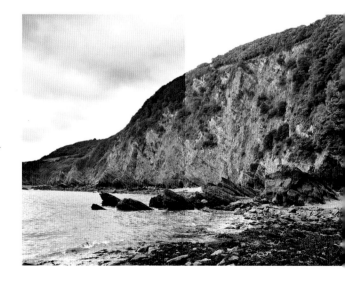

Above: An ND filter enables you to take long exposures even in bright daylight.

ND number	Percentage of light transmittance	Optical density	F-stop reduction
ND 2	$\frac{1}{2}$	0.3	1
ND 4	$\frac{1}{4}$	0.6	2
ND 8	$\frac{1}{8}$	0.9	3
ND 1024	$\frac{1}{1024}$	3.0	10

Graduated neutral density filters

As their name suggests, graduated neutral density (grad ND) filters have a clear part and a neutral-density part, which comes in various strengths. The abruptness of the transition from clear to ND also varies from hard to soft. Grad ND filters are used when one part of a picture is much brighter than another, such as a bright sky and a dark foreground. By positioning the ND part of the filter over the sky, and the transition over the horizon, the extremes of brightness can be brought closer together, so both can be recorded on camera.

Right: A graduated neutral density filter reduces the brightness of half the picture (left) – usually the sky – bringing it into the same brightness range as the foreground.

Tripods and supports

Sometimes it's necessary to support your camera when shooting. Most commonly this is on a tripod (since three-legged structures are the most stable), although monopods, clamps and bean bags are all used too. Support is usually necessary when long shutter speeds are needed. Hand-holding a camera under these conditions can lead to camera shake – blurring of a picture due to camera movement. As a rule of thumb, camera shake will be a problem with shutter speeds slower than the reciprocal of your lens's focal length. For instance, when shooting with the 55mm end of a zoom lens, you'll need a shutter speed of at least 1/60sec. At 18mm, you'll need a shutter speed of at least 1/20sec.

Manfrotto tripod

Tripods

When choosing a tripod, consider the material it is made from, its size (both open and closed), and the head that will support your camera. Traditionally tripods have been made of aluminium, which is lightweight and strong enough for most uses, especially if you don't take it out with you very often. Landscape photographers who are trekking across large distances should consider a carbon fibre model, as these are lighter still, if more costly. Other features in a tripod include retractable foot-spikes for more grip

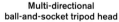

Multi-directional ball-and-socket tripod head

and a reversible central column, so the camera can be positioned near to the ground for close-up work. Some units even allow the column to be positioned horizontally – useful for studio work.

When considering a tripod also think about the head that will sit on top of the legs and support your camera. While budget tripods will come with a head included, more advanced models do not and you will need to budget for buying one separately. Heads come in one of two varieties: ball-and-socket or pan-and-tilt. The first of these allows quick and easy positioning of the camera: simply unlock the joint, move the camera into position and lock it back up again. They are also lightweight and compact, making them ideal for travel photography. Pan-and-tilt heads offer movement in each direction separately which is a more accurate way of working, especially for those shooting in a studio, although such a head is larger and often weighs more. Good tripod heads also feature a quick-release system for attaching cameras quickly. Instead of screwing the camera onto a tripod, a metal plate is screwed to the bottom of the camera, which attaches securely to a tripod head with a simple click.

i Table-top tripods and beanbags

Three legs might be the most stable way to support a camera, but it's not always the most practical. When space is limited, or you want something you can move around with more easily, it's time to consider another option.

For telephoto shooting at shutter speeds down to 1/30sec, a monopod is a good idea. As the name suggests, a monopod features one leg instead of three, so isn't self-supporting. But it will give you enough support to avoid camera shake at much lower speeds than if you were hand-holding the camera.

Alternative steadying devices include beanbags, which let you rest a long lens on car doors, tree trunks, etc., or miniature table-top tripods that let you position your camera on a handy brick wall. Some miniature tripods even have bendable legs that can be used to hang your camera from structures.

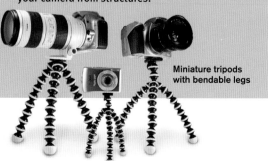

Miniature tripods with bendable legs

Reflectors

Light is reflected from almost all surfaces in some way, and we can use this to our advantage when shooting photography. Using a reflector it's possible to bounce light around in a scene, usually back towards a subject to fill in shadow areas, and lighten the darker areas of a picture.

While almost anything can be used as a reflector, it's worth thinking about which material is going to work best in a given situation. Reflected light takes on some of the colour of the material that is doing the reflecting, therefore you'll want to avoid greens, reds, etc. and stick to neutral materials.

White reflectors reflect more light than grey ones, and silver is even more productive. For this reason, when shooting portraits it's good to use a silver reflector on dull, overcast days, and a white one in bright sunlight. Bouncing sunlight off a silver reflector can really dazzle your subject and make them squint – not a good look.

Commercially available reflectors often have one side in silver and the other gold, with the gold side being used to 'warm up' skin tones. They are also lighter and have features such as built-in handles to make using them on location easier, and the ability to fold them away in a smaller case. You can also make your own reflector, of course. Suitable materials include large sheets of paper or mounting board, aluminium kitchen foil and large polystyrene boards – available from DIY stores for a fraction of the price you'll pay in a photographic shop.

Black reflectors

Because black surfaces don't reflect any light, a black board can be positioned next to a subject when you don't want any reflected light bouncing back at it. For instance, if you are shooting a portrait in a white room, using a light source positioned to one side means that you will get some light bouncing back from the walls, making the light seem less directional. Position a black reflector next to your model, just out of shot, and this will block the reflected light completely.

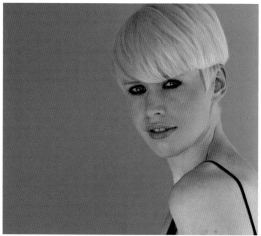

Before

Anti-clockwise from left: A reflector has been used to bounce some light back on to the face in this window-light portrait, producing a much more dramatic result.

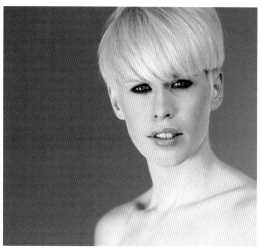

After

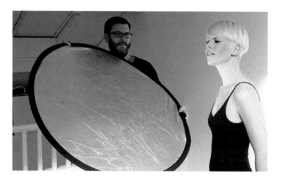

Other accessories

Memory cards

You're not going very far in photography without a memory card in your camera. There are various physical types, that differ in size, but these days most cameras take either SD (secure digital) or CF (compact flash) cards.

The first of these is much smaller, and so is used in consumer-level DSLRs and compact cameras. The humble SD card has had a few tweaks over the years to enable larger capacities to be created: SDHC (HC stands for high capacity) and SDXC (XC stands for extra capacity) have offered maximum capacities of 8GB and 64GB respectively, but note that these technologies are not backwards compatible, so an SDXC card won't work in a compact designed for SD or SDHC before SDXC was released. Compact flash cards are much larger than SD, but they are also more robust, operate more quickly and offer even higher storage capacities. They tend to be found in more advanced DSLR cameras that may be shooting at high frame rates or resolutions.

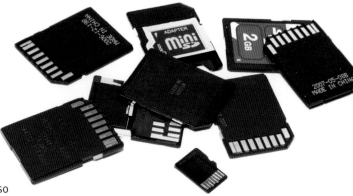

Above: Memory cards for cameras come in a few internationally standardized sizes.

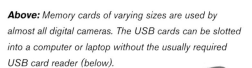

The two things to look for when buying a memory card are capacity (measured in gigabytes, GB) and the speed at which files may be written to it, measured in megabits per second (mbps). Many card manufacturers use a multiples system to express the speed of a card, eg. 60x or 133x. (1x is the speed of the original CD-ROM drives from the 1980s, which is 150kbps). A very fast card can cost a lot of money, and may be a false economy unless you shoot a lot of high resolution images or HD video content. On the other hand, a very slow card can lead to frustration when shooting sequences or transferring files to your computer. Aim for something in the middle: a 100x speed card, for instance.

It's also not always a good idea to buy the largest card you can afford. If something goes wrong with a huge card, you will lose all of the pictures on it, but if you split your image files across four smaller cards then losing one of them doesn't mean you lose 100 per cent of your photography.

Above: Memory cards of varying sizes are used by almost all digital cameras. The USB cards can be slotted into a computer or laptop without the usually required USB card reader (below).

Below: Most memory cards require some kind of card reader in order to transfer the data onto your computer – which type depends on your memory card.

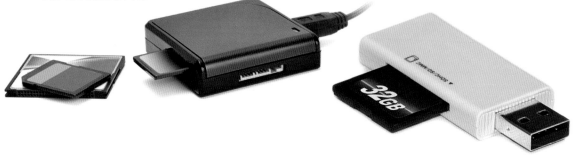

Storage devices

Backing up image files when away from home is a sensible thing to do. If the worst happens and your equipment is damaged or lost, then insurance may cover the cost of the hardware, but it won't replace your images for you. A portable storage device is the easiest way of backing up on the move, and doesn't require you to lug a laptop around with you. Essentially a cross between an external hard drive and a card reader, a storage device has a slot that you plug a memory card into. The contents of the card are then transferred to the drive, either as a backup or so the card can be wiped and used again.

Some storage devices are basic, simply acting as a container for your files until you get home and can transfer them to your computer. Others are more advanced, having a viewscreen, primitive editing facilities, and slideshow and printing functions.

Batteries and power

Running out of battery power halfway through a great shoot is what digital photographers dread most. How long a single charge lasts depends on lots of variables: how much flash you use; if you are focusing manually or automatically; even how much the display screen is used to access menus and review images.

When on longer assignments, or even on holiday, it's best to have a spare battery with you in case the worst happens. This doesn't have to be made by the camera's manufacturer – there are many third-party battery manufacturers that will make you a second battery that is just as good for a fraction of the price.

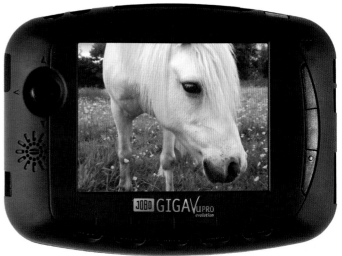

Above: An 80GB photograph storage device from Jobo that can store thousands of images, as well as play MP3 audio and MPEG video files.

Rechargeable battery packs

White balance accessories

White balance is often referred to as the temperature of light, i.e. how warm or cold it is. You may have noticed this when comparing indoor electric light to outdoor daylight. Indoor light is much more orange (warmer) than daylight, which is more blue (colder). A digital camera detects this and tries to compensate with its automatic white balance (AWB) function.

AWB gets this job right around 90 per cent of the time, although it can be confused in some situations, for instance when there is no actual white in the scene to refer to. This is when to use one of the myriad white balance accessories that are on the market. Some require you to put them over the lens and fire off a blank frame using the camera's custom white balance preset function (see page 70), while others can be used as a reference when white balance is set retrospectively in raw processing (see page 288).

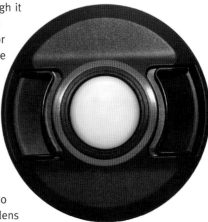

White balance lens cap

Underwater housings

Shooting pictures underwater is one of the hardest, most technically demanding areas of photography, and requires a significant investment in expensive underwater camera housings and flashguns to get professional-quality results. That said, there are underwater housings available for compact cameras at a fraction of the cost, and as long as you are aware of the limitations of such a camera, you'll get some great results while snorkelling or scuba diving.

Each underwater housing is dedicated to a specific model of camera, meaning that if you upgrade your camera, you'll have to upgrade your housing, too. Housings work by encasing the camera in a tough plastic shell, with rubber O-rings making the whole thing watertight. A duplicate set of controls on the outside of the casing allows operation of the camera.

O-rings can be fragile, and they need looking after to prevent leaks. Occasional cleaning and maintenance involves carefully removing each O-ring, cleaning it to remove any small particles of dirt or sand, then re-greasing it with a very small amount of silicon grease, usually supplied with the housing.

Underwater housings usually provide protection against water to depths of 40m, which is beyond the safe depth limit for a recreational scuba diver,

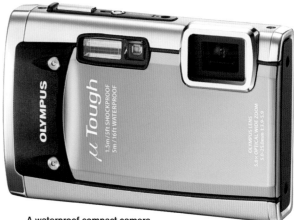

A waterproof compact camera, able to survive depths of up to 5m.

and so should be plenty for your needs. Some compact cameras are built to be waterproof without any need for an extra housing, although only to depths of 5–10m, making them more suitable for snorkelling rather than scuba diving.

An underwater housing, or a waterproof compact camera, is not just a good idea for the snorkellers and divers among us, however. It is a useful accessory whenever you are shooting pictures in a harsh environment. You might be using a camera on a boat where there is spray coming over the deck, or in a family swimming pool to photograph the kids. A housing can even protect your camera against sand and dust on the beach or in the desert.

Below: Underwater photography is difficult, but very rewarding.

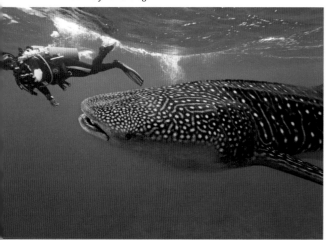

Olympus underwater housing, providing protection to 40m depth

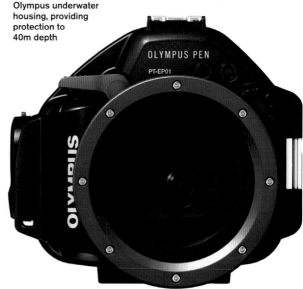

Remote releases

Triggering the camera without touching it is very important in photography. It may be that you physically need to be some distance from the camera, in which case you'll need a wireless remote, or a trigger with a long length of cable. More likely, though, is that you'll be trying to fire the camera without wobbling it. Doing so can blur pictures when you are using long shutter speeds, even with the camera on a tripod. You can use a camera's self-timer to get over this problem, but a remote release is less frustrating to use and will make timing easier.

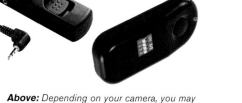

Above: Depending on your camera, you may be able to use either a cable shutter release or a even a wireless control.

Right: A lens blower brush will let you clean your equipment when you're away from home.

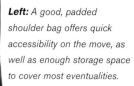

A camera bag

This is perhaps the most important accessory of all. A good bag is vital for storing your valuable equipment and providing a safe way of transporting it around with you. Your bag will need to protect your camera from the the weather, from dust and dirt, and even from those sticky-fingered folk who would like to steal your kit. But it needs to do all of this at the same time as making sure you can access your camera quickly and easily when you need to.

There are two main types of bag – backpacks and shoulder bags – although you'll also find hybrids and variations on these themes. Backpacks are great when you are carrying a lot of gear around all day. They distribute the load evenly across your body, making them more comfortable. Some larger backpacks even have space for a laptop computer, making them perfect for the location photographer. Where they fall down is accessibility: to get your camera out of a backpack you'll have to take it off and put it down on something, which is slower to do, and not always practical. A shoulder bag, on the other hand, provides easy access to your camera while on the move. You should be able to find your camera, take it out and use it, and even change lenses all without putting your bag down. Since shoulder bags are usually carried on one shoulder, or diagonally across the body, make sure you alternate which side you are carrying it, so you don't end up with backache.

Left: A good, padded shoulder bag offers quick accessibility on the move, as well as enough storage space to cover most eventualities.

Flashguns

Flash is used to inject more light into a photograph when the conditions are too dim for hand-held photography, or when contrast in bright daylight is too extreme. A burst of flash light lasts for a few thousandths of a second, making it a light source specific to photography, and totally useless to the human eye. Being so brief, it also has the ability to freeze motion. Flash can also be mixed with daylight for almost limitless creativity.

Nearly all digital cameras have a small flash built-in to them, which is fine for short-range pictures, and when a small blip of flash is required outdoors to lighten the shadows caused by harsh sunlight – a technique known as fill-in flash (see page 96). Such flashes are fully automated, meaning the only input required from a photographer is whether to use it or not. The complicated mathematics necessary to calculate an accurate correct exposure for flash photography is taken care of by sophisticated metering systems that measure flash intensity through the lens (known as TTL), using pre-flashes and distance information from a camera's AF to ensure accurate flash exposure.

Built-in flashes are limited by their relatively short range (typically 5–8m), fixed position on-camera and inability to accept light-modifying accessories. For this, an extra flashgun is needed, which connects to the camera through an accessory port known as a hotshoe. Messages sent through the hotshoe not only trigger the flash, but also pass information regarding flash exposure back and forth, ensuring images are neither too bright nor too dark.

External flashguns offer lots more power than their built-in equivalents, having guide numbers of 20–50 (see box, below). More power means the ability to shoot things with flash that are further away, as well as work with smaller apertures and

What are guide numbers?

When looking at flashguns, you will come across guide numbers as a way of comparing power between various units. A guide number is used to describe the power of a flash's output in terms that are understandable, and comparable to other models. In the times before TTL exposure and auto-flash control, guide numbers were also used to calculate flash exposure.

When shooting with a manual flash (or TTL gun in manual mode), dividing the guide number by the flash-to-subject distance will give you the aperture needed for the correct exposure. For example, if you are photographing an object 4m away using an on-camera manual flash, with a guide number of 32, you'll need an aperture of f/8 to expose it correctly. Because distance can be measured in different ways, and ISO sensitivity affects exposures, modern-day flash numbers are quoted in meters and at ISO100. You may also sometimes see a focal length quoted, even though a guide number is actually independent of the lens in use. This is actually for flashguns with a zoom head that narrows or broadens the beam of light to match a lens's angle of view. Narrowing the beam concentrates the light and makes it brighter, hence the increase in guide number.

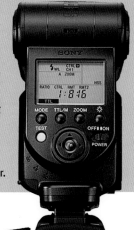

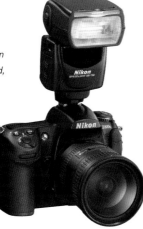

Right: A sophisticated camera-mounted flashgun with multidirectional head, wireless control for off-camera shots and numerous exposure modes.

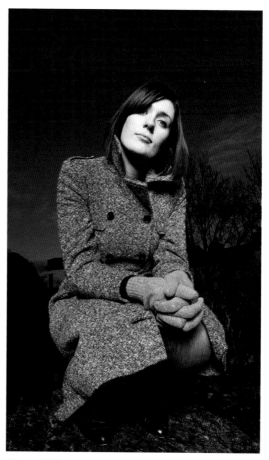

Above: Taking portraits in dramatic, near-dark conditions often requires an off-camera flash to lighten the subject.

use light-modifying accessories such as diffusers and softboxes. Many flashguns also allow you to bounce flash off walls and ceilings, generating much softer light than direct flash for shadowless pictures and no 'red-eye' (see box, below right).

A more recent technological development is the ability to use flash off-camera wirelessly. Multiple flashguns can be positioned anywhere in a scene and triggered by a signal from the camera. This can be from a DSLR's built-in flash, or from a special infrared or radiowave trigger. Either way it's a great way of using flash creatively, lighting a subject from specific angles. TTL flash metering still functions, letting a photographer specify the aperture that they want to use, confident in the knowledge the flashgun technology will take care of the rest.

The creativity doesn't stop there, either. A separate flashgun can perform tricks such as 'second curtain' flash (where the flash fires are at the end of a long exposure, not the beginning) and even stroboscopic bursts, for multiple exposures of fast-moving subjects.

Such is the popularity of flash photography, since off-camera wireless flash was developed, that a whole new trend in photography has been developed: strobism refers to the practice of using multiple flashes, often fitted with light-modifying accessories, to control all of the lighting in a scene, often mixing flash output with daylight for hyper-real effects. Light-modifying accessories include softboxes, domes and umbrellas, which diffuse light, making it softer, as well as grids and 'barn doors' that give light direction and focus it in one place.

Getting rid of red-eye

Red-eye occurs when the flash is positioned very close to the lens, which allows it to light up the retina of your subject, making it glow bright red. Although red-eye is now easily eliminated using software such as Adobe Photoshop Elements (and sometimes through in-camera processing, too), it's possible to avoid it in the first place by positioning your flash properly. Using an external flash will let you position the gun away from the lens, or bounce its light off a ceiling or wall – either approach will eliminate red-eye completely, and give you a more natural-looking light, too.

MAKE YOUR OWN REFLECTOR

The humble reflector is not the sexiest of photographic accessories, but it is one of the most useful. In still-life and portrait photography, a reflector is sometimes the only way of bouncing some light back into shadowy areas, or smoothing out contrast.

You can buy all manner of reflectors: gold ones to warm things up, silver ones for a natural look, or matt white ones to use in sunny conditions when you don't want to blind your subject. Some reflectors are designed to be portable and fold away in a tiny case, while others are huge and designed to be left out in the studio. However, you can also make your own reflector, and achieve results that are so good you won't be able to tell them apart from an off-the-shelf model.

A reflector does a very simple job, so it only needs a few basic qualities. Firstly, and most obviously, it needs to be reflective, so the surface will bounce light back into a scene. Secondly, it needs to be sturdy enough to stand up under its own weight, while remaining light enough to be easily moved around. Thirdly, it should be durable enough to take some knocks and not break or be damaged easily. And finally, it should be a neutral white to avoid introducing colour casts into the picture.

Your reflector can be as basic as a large piece of white card – the type of mounting board you find in art shops works best. This comes in sizes up to A0, and is sturdy enough to support its own weight when propped up by something. Alternatively, for something a bit larger, the sheets of white polystyrene foam board that are used for insulation in building projects make excellent reflectors. You often find these in photographic studios in sizes up to 200cm tall,

but don't pay the prices you see in photographic shops. A trip to your local DIY store is much more cost-effective.

For some extra reflective power, you can cover a white board with cooking foil, taping or stapling it in place around the back. It's best to avoid a perfectly flat, mirrored surface though; scrunch up the foil then flatten it out again before attaching it to the board. The creases will scatter the reflected light more, and soften it slightly.

Black reflectors

It may sound odd, but black 'reflectors' are sometimes just as useful as white ones. You can use them to eliminate reflections that may be coming from elsewhere in a room – a white wall or ceiling, for instance. Position a black reflector (more accurately a non-reflector) next to a subject when you are deliberately trying to deepen shadows or emphasize side lighting.

The same options are available to you for homemade black reflectors. Mounting board in matt black is very effective, and you can cover such a board with black velvet to improve its effectiveness. It's very common for studios to paint their polystyrene boards black on one side, so they can be turned around and used to eliminate reflections rather than cause them. If you do this, use black spraypaint, which is easier to apply than conventional brush-on emulsion. You may also want to run a layer of gaffer tape around the board to protect its edges during use.

ESSENTIAL KIT

- Reflective surfaces, such as cardboard, aluminium foil or polystyrene board
- Digital camera
- Window as a light source

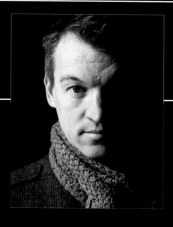

Right: *With no reflector, the right side of our subject's face is in shadow when he is lit from the left by window light.*

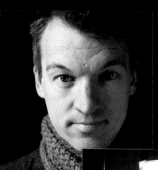
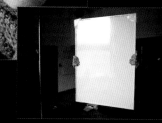

Left: *A sheet of mounting board, housed in a picture frame, reflects some light back into the shadowy areas.*

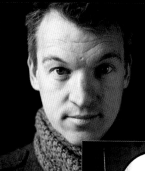
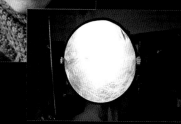

Left: *A commercially available reflector does much the same job, though folds up smaller to be more portable.*

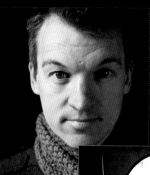
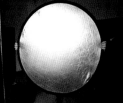

Left: *The reverse side of this commercial reflector is gold, not silver, and reflects a warmer kind of light.*

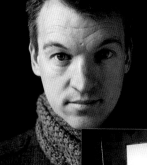
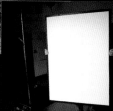

Left: *A sheet of polystyrene board is an effective reflector, too, and has the advantage of being lightweight and self-supporting.*

Care and cleaning

Digital cameras might be automated and (almost) idiot-proof, but they are also very intricate, complicated and fragile machines that need looking after. Taking care of your camera will increase its lifespan hugely. Even small things, such as always keeping your camera in its case, or being careful of the environment in which it's used, will help.

Your camera should always be kept in a good bag or case when you are out and about taking pictures, as well as for storage at home. Such a bag should be padded inside to protect against knocks and bumps, and have zip closings that exclude dust and dirt. It should be made of a material tough and waterproof enough to withstand a good shower of rain.

A camera's main enemies are water, sand, dirt and dust. As well as interfering with a camera's mechanical operation, water will instantly ruin a camera's electrics, too. Sand is a threat because a couple of grains will jam motors, gears and cogs, and can scratch glass elements. Dirt can have the same effect, and if dust makes it onto the camera's sensor it will leave black marks on your photographs. DSLR cameras are most prone to sensor dust – removing and exchanging their lenses allows dust into the camera, which can require the sensor to be cleaned.

Lenses are also prone to wear and tear as a camera is used. The front element of a lens is the most vulnerable, and should be protected in normal use with a skylight or UV filter. This way, you only have to clean a cheap filter, not an expensive lens. Some lenses come with a lens hood, which shades it from direct light and prevents flare, but it's worth using the hood all the time. It acts as excellent protection from knocks and bumps to the front elements and, like a skylight filter, is cheaper to replace than a whole lens.

Cleaning your camera

Even the best looked-after cameras need cleaning sometimes. The easiest part to take care of is the exterior of the camera body, including the viewscreen and controls. Usually this is best taken care of with a dry microfibre cloth, perhaps slightly moistened with the type of screen cleaner used for cleaning computer monitors. Never use anything like petrol, thinners or other solvents, as these can damage a camera's plastic body.

Cleaning the front of a lens element requires a more gentle approach. A soft microfibre lens cloth is often all that's needed. Resist the urge to breathe on the glass before wiping it; lens cleaning fluid is better. When cleaning a lens, it's best to start at the outside and work your way inwards to the centre – this avoids pushing grease and dirt out to the edges of the glass, where they are difficult to remove.

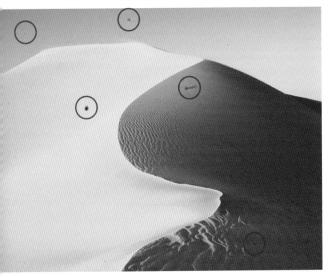

Above: Even the finest dust particle on the sensor will leave unsightly dark marks.

Sensor cleaning

Unlike compact cameras, where the sensor is sealed off from external elements, the sensor inside a DSLR can attract dust during normal use. This can occur when changing lenses, or by using zoom lenses, whose zooming motion sucks air into the camera. Once dust is in a DSLR's mirror box, the action of the the mirror flipping up and down quickly transfers it to the sensor. The electrical charge running through the sensor when it is in use also helps to attract dust particles.

You can minimize the need for sensor cleaning by keeping your kit clean at all times. Always keep either a lens or a body cap on your camera, and regularly clean the rear of your lenses' body caps; putting a dirty one on your camera is the perfect way to introduce dust. When changing lenses, do so with the camera mount facing downwards so that dust is less likely to fall into the opening.

To check for the presence of dust on a sensor, take a picture of a bright, even surface such as a white wall, or even the sky. Use a small aperture, such as f/22, and you should see dust show up as black or grey smudges. To get rid of this, you can either use a commercial cleaning service, or have a go yourself with one of the many sensor-cleaning products on the market. These come in the form of swabs dipped in a cleaning fluid and wiped back and forth across the sensor; CO_2 cartridges that blow dust off its surface; miniature vacuums that suck it up; and sticky pads that lift off dirt and dust.

All of these methods involve accessing the sensor through the lens mount, with the shutter opened and the mirror raised to give access. Done properly and with precautions this is a perfectly safe thing to do, but mistakes can cause damage, meaning a costly repair bill. Always use the camera's sensor cleaning mode to lock the shutter open, never the 'B' (or 'bulb') mode, which is intended for long exposures when taking pictures – if your finger slips off the shutter release, the shutter will close onto the device you are using to clean the sensor, causing a lot of damage. Similarly, always clean a sensor with a fully charged battery. If your battery fails halfway through the procedure, the shutter will close, causing damage.

Cleaning a DSLR sensor with swabs

Although this will require a little patience and care, it will be rewarding to achieve a clean and dust-free sensor again.

1 Detach the lens from the DSLR and clean both the rear of the lens, the lens mount and the camera mirror box with a soft brush.

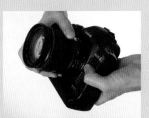

2 Dip the swab in the alcoholic cleaning solution. Don't over-saturate the swab – excess fluid will leave smears behind.

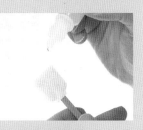

3 Access the sensor cleaning mode, which will raise up the mirror and open the shutter. You will now see the sensor.

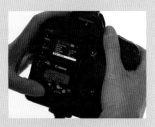

4 At an angle of 45 degrees, wipe the tip of the swab across the surface of the sensor from one side, before reversing direction.

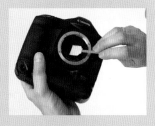

5 Shoot a test picture of a white surface. If dust persists, repeat the process, or use a CO_2 cylinder to blast it off.

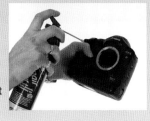

Which **computer?**

The home computer plays a central role in photography, along with peripherals such as inkjet printers, scanners and monitors. Together with the right imaging software, this makes up your digital darkroom, where your snaps can be transformed into masterpieces.

With the humble home computer now more powerful than it's ever been, more or less any PC or Mac can be used to edit, manipulate and output photographs from your digital camera. This kind of digital editing has put creative control squarely back in the hands of photographers, and ensures that you can stay in control of what is happening all the way through the picture-making process, from capture to output. What happens on your computer is a central part of what photography today is all about.

Almost any home computer is capable of editing photographs, although there are several ways to upgrade your set-up that will make life easier. These don't have to happen all at once, of course. Building a digital darkroom is modular in nature, and you can take your time getting things exactly right.

Storage and memory

Perhaps the first thing to look at is how much memory and disk space there is in your computer. The first of these (often called RAM in computer specification) dictates how many applications can be running at once, and how many picture files you can have open at any one time. Disk space, on the other hand, is used to store applications and image files when they are not running, as well as to hold the system files that make your computer work in the first place.

When it comes to memory, the general rule is that you can never have enough. Most computers come with 3–4GB these days, which is enough to get you started on most things. When a computer runs out of RAM it starts to swap information between memory and hard disk, slowing it down. This can happen when you have a lot of applications open at the same time when you are editing pictures (and have music, email, etc. running in the background) or when you've made a lot of edits to a big file. Each edit is remembered in the computer's memory so that you can undo the current action and go back to it if you make a mistake. RAM is inexpensive, and upgrading it to 8GB is a good way to future-proof your system.

Hard disks generally double in capacity and halve in price every 12 months or so, meaning it's always worth looking to see if you could benefit from more. What sounds like a roomy 500GB drive may only offer you 250GB of storage by the time you have applications and an operating system (Windows or Mac OSX) installed. For this reason, a separate hard disk for your picture files is a good idea – or even two so that you can back them up, in case one drive fails.

Hard drives come in two types, internal and external. Internal drives are installed inside a desktop, tower-type computer and offer much

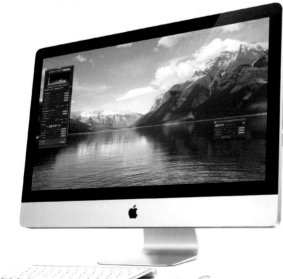

Apple iMac

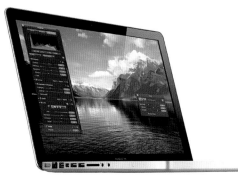

Apple Macbook Pro

better value. External drives connect via a USB or FireWire connection and are best for those working from a laptop, or who want to swap drives between computers.

Screens and graphics cards

One of the most important parts of a digital photography set-up (and often one of the most overlooked) is the screen you'll be working on. Budget screens, and those built-in to laptops, have a restricted colour gamut (i.e. the number of shades of each colour they can show) and the images they show can look different from different angles. You don't have to pay much more for a screen that doesn't suffer so much from these issues, and that gives you some extra space, too. Specifications to look for include:

Contrast ratio

A screen with a contrast ratio of 700:1 will give deeper blacks and brighter whites than one rated at 400:1. When comparing contrast ratios, don't use the 'dynamic contrast ratio' figure, which refers to the ability of the screen to shift its brightness according to what is being displayed.

Response rate

Aim for a screen boasting a response rate of around 8–10ms (milliseconds). Any longer than this and you risk seeing 'ghosts' as you scroll around the screen.

Resolution

The resolution of a screen is given by the number of pixels along each dimension of the screen, at its native settings, with the size of each pixel defined as the pixel pitch. The finer the pixel pitch the sharper the image will look, but the smaller the menus, etc. will appear.

PC or Mac?

It's an argument that has raged almost since personal computers were first invented: go for a Windows-based PC, or an Apple Mac computer? After decades of debate, the definitive answer is – it doesn't really matter. The choice between PC and Mac is completely down to personal preference. Some like the more user-friendly nature of a Mac, others like the extra control over their computer that they get with a PC. Virtually all imaging software is available for both platforms, and there is no compatibility issue when it comes to connecting cameras.

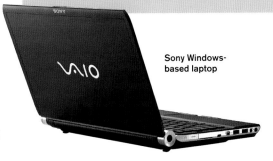

Sony Windows-based laptop

Brightness

Contrary to popular belief, brighter is not always better when it comes to a monitor. An over-bright display gives a false impression of what a picture looks like when printed. Brightness is measured in candelas per square meter (cd/m^2), and a value of 80–100 cd/m^2 is fine. Any more (eg. 500 cd/m^2) is overkill.

Connection types

These days a digital connection (DVI) is pretty much the standard for photography. Don't go for a screen sporting the older VGA connection.

Graphics cards

In order to be able to connect to a display, and perform the complicated calculations necessary for today's sleek-looking graphics, most computers need graphics cards. It's not necessary to spend a fortune (as it would with, say, game-playing or 3D work), but a card that has its own memory, rather than sharing system memory that could be used for other things, will give a performance boost.

Imaging **software**

In digital photography, capturing an image in-camera is only half of the photographic process. Processing images on your computer, using specialist digital imaging software, unlocks a multitude of creative options.

Although there are hundreds of imaging applications on the market, one name dominates it. Adobe Photoshop is so well-known among digital photographers that the verb 'to photoshop' is now commonly used as a euphemism for digital retouching. Although it costs as much as most DSLR cameras, Photoshop is so fully featured it is probably the only piece of imaging software you will ever need. It is used extensively by professional retouchers and photographers all over the world. To say it is an industry standard is almost an understatement.

Enthusiasts do have another choice, though: Photoshop Elements is Adobe's way of catering to a market that doesn't require Photoshop's most advanced features, and it costs about a fifth of the price, too. In this book we will focus mainly on Adobe Photoshop and Photoshop Elements, because of their ubiquitous nature with digital photographers, although many features are also found in rival applications, such as Corel PaintShop Pro or Gimp. Apple-users should also check out the excellent iPhoto that comes with every new Mac computer.

Where other software-makers score is producing applications for more niche uses. There are applications out there for stitching many pictures together into one, mapping multiple exposures together to reduce contrast and producing convincing black and white conversions, to name but a few. We'll be looking at all these topics (and more) in the pages to come, where we'll also explore the best applications that are available.

File management and workflow

Digital photography has got us taking many more pictures than we ever shot with film, and this can lead to an organizational nightmare. A weekend away can result in hundreds of images, a two-week holiday over a thousand. Add all this up and you are looking at a serious amount of photography in a year. Soon you'll reach a point where, if you are ever to find any of your images ever again, you'll need a filing system to stay organized. In the trade, this is known as a 'workflow'.

A workflow can be as simple as individual folders marked 'portraits', 'landscapes', 'weddings', etc., or 'Jan', 'Feb', 'March', but there are specialist applications that make this much easier. With Adobe Photoshop comes an application called Bridge, that lets you not only browse files on your hard drive with full-size previews, but allows you to keyword them ('New

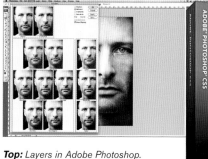

Top: Layers in Adobe Photoshop.
Above: Colour variation.

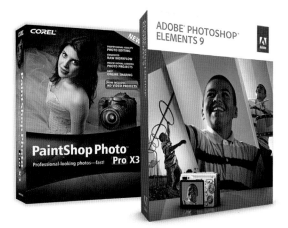

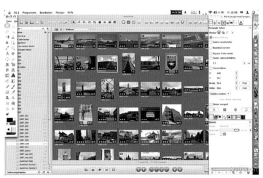

Above: *Corel Draw's PaintShop Photo and Adobe Photoshop Elements, the simple version of Photoshop.*

Above: *Windows-based image programme Gimp.*

York', 'London', 'Paris', etc.) so that you can search across multiple directories and find images you are looking for automatically. Photoshop Elements also includes such functionality in its file browser.

Taking this concept further is Adobe Lightroom, which builds a database of your images, allowing collections of images to be assembled as well as keyworded. What's more, you can edit JPEG and raw images in the application non-destructively (see page 42) and output files as prints, websites and slideshows. Apple-users should also check out Aperture, which follows a similar formula, and offers features such as face recognition and geotagging for cataloguing images according to who is on them and where they were shot.

Right: *Lightroom, Adobe's focused image-managing and output system.*

Below: *Lightroom's user-friendly develop adjustment screen.*

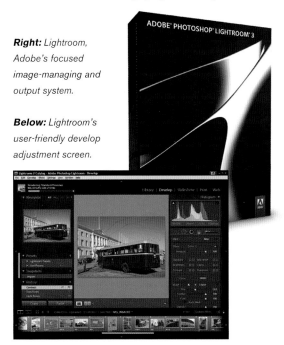

Plug-ins

Recognizing that Adobe have the software market sewn up, many smaller software manufacturers now produce their applications in the form of a plug-in – a small application that is run from within Photoshop. The great thing about plug-ins is that they can be called into action at any time while you are working on an image with Photoshop's other tools, and without leaving the programme, too. Most are installed into Photoshop's 'plug-ins' folder, and then appear in the main programme's filter menu.

Plug-ins are available for all manner of tasks, from converting an image to black and white to performing sharpening and selective blur effects. A Google search will uncover thousands (some free, others paid for) available for download.

Below: *Some of the many Photoshop plug-ins from third-party developers.*

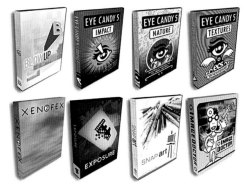

Files and formats

The images that come off your digital camera, and that you save from applications such as Photoshop, come in various formats. Each differs in terms of image quality and in the space it takes up on a memory card or hard disk. These days there are fewer file types to worry about, with the more esoteric formats falling by the wayside as standardization has come into force, but each of today's file types has its own strengths and weaknesses. Let's have a look at each one, when to use it and when not to.

JPEG files

The most common format in digital photography, JPEG files (JPEG being an acronym for Joint Photographic Experts Group, who created the standard) are small thanks to clever compression algorithms that describe areas of continuous tone with less data. Unfortunately this compression has a slight impact on image quality, although not to the point where you'll notice until you get to large print sizes. Users can even select how much compression they want. This is usually in the form of 'fine', 'good' and 'basic' settings in-camera, or a sliding 1–10 scale in applications such as Photoshop.

Lossy compression works by removing repetitive data and replacing it with an approximation. If there are 1,000 pixels all of roughly the same blue colour, a JPEG file describes this as 'blue for the next 1,000 pixels', instead of saying 'blue, blue, blue...' 1,000 times. Obviously this removes some subtle variations, but the drop in quality is not often noticeable.

JPEG files (sometimes also called JPG) are so commonly used because they can do everything. They are great in a camera because their small size means you'll get many of them on a card. As long as you are shooting at the best-quality setting, you'll make great prints from them, too, and they are the de facto format for showing photography on webpages and sending by email. If you don't want to have to think about file formats too often, stick with good quality JPEGs and you won't go too far wrong.

TIFF files

If JPEG files sacrifice some image quality for size, then TIFF files do the opposite. They might use 25MB to describe what a JPEG can do with 2MB, but there is no lossy compression involved, meaning you retain every bit of image quality. It's rare that a camera can capture files directly to TIFF format (though some can), and capturing as JPEG then converting to TIFF gives you no real quality advantage over leaving the file as a JPEG in the

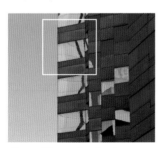

Above: *The quality of an image can depend on the level of compression used when saved.*

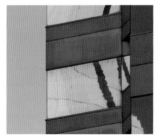

Above: *Saved at compression level 8, the image is of high quality.*

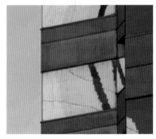

Above: *At compression level 3, the image becomes pixellated.*

Bit-depth and file formats

JPEG files are known as 8-bit. For ordinary people, this means that each of the red, green and blue colour channels are composed of 256 shades (2^8=256). Since all three channels are mixed together, 256 x 256 x 256 produces 16,777,216 possible colours in a single picture. That may seem like a lot, but only some of these will be blue, for example. So when trying to reproduce the subtle variation of tones in a blue sky, an 8-bit image doesn't always cut it.

Most digital cameras these days actually record 14-bit images (2^{14} shades per channel), although this is reduced down to 8-bits of information when a JPEG file is written – this is all the JPEG format can handle. To preserve all of the 14-bits of information you must shoot raw files and either process these into 16-bit TIFF files, or open the raw file into Photoshop in 16-bit mode.

Editing 16-bit images means you can make more extensive corrections to exposure and colour without introducing unsightly artefacts. You'll also be able to 'rescue' detail more easily (see page 238).

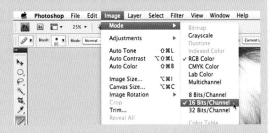

first place. To get the most from a TIFF file, you'll need to start with a raw file from the camera, or be saving image files from a scanner.

Some applications do support a type of loss-less compression for TIFF files, reducing their size by anything up to 50 per cent. This is a good choice when archiving files on disk for the future.

Raw files

When you take a picture with a compact camera, information from the sensor is processed according to in-camera settings such as saturation, contrast and sharpness. During this process, information that the camera thinks is not required for that particular shot is discarded and the rest is saved to the memory card as a JPEG file.

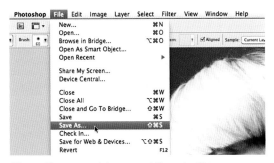

Above: *The very useful command 'Save As...' lets you save a file in a different format and/or a different location.*

In contrast to this, a raw file contains all of the information from the camera's sensor, meaning you have control of the image processing yourself on your computer afterwards, using special raw-processing software. A raw file has been likened to a digital negative that needs printing (processing) into a JPEG file before it can be viewed.

Raw files must be converted to JPEG or TIFF files with the software that accompanied your camera, or opened into an application such as Photoshop using a plug-in. Each raw file is different, being specific to a particular camera, so it's worth keeping such a plug-in up to date with downloads from the internet.

DNG

DNG, standing for Digital NeGative, was developed by Adobe as an open-standard raw format that is not dependent on hardware. It is only supported by a handful of cameras, but is useful for archiving files (as film photographers would for negatives).

PNG

The PNG (Portable Network Graphics) file format was designed for use on the internet, replacing the older GIF format. It's not useful for photographers, being up to ten times larger than an equivalent JPEG with little gain in quality. Hence PNG has not been picked up by camera manufacturers and you rarely come across it in your digital darkroom.

Scanners
and **scanning**

Film photography may be a specialism these days, but scanners are a great way of resurrecting those old prints, negatives and slides, and letting film photographers take advantage of digital editing.

A scanner is a device that can be used to digitize hard copy images, turning them into image files that can be edited and outputted using a computer. Hard copy images come in the form of prints as well as strips of negatives and slides (also known as transparencies). Since most photography is now digital, the demand for scanning as part of a digital workflow is not what it once was, but having a scanner still opens up some interesting possibilities for today's digital photographer.

Most of us have lots of old images from our film photography days, even if these are just holiday snaps. Scanning them allows you to create reprints from a desktop inkjet printer, archive your memories onto disk to save for the future, and even edit them with the full power of modern-day editing software, such as Photoshop. You can even restore old images that have faded or been damaged. In fact, for those photographers who still like to shoot film, a good quality scanner offers a way to combine traditional capture techniques with digital editing, for a different way of working.

Broadly speaking, three types of scanner are used by photographers: the flatbed, the film scanner and the all-in-one. Each is suitable for a different type of photographer, and does a slightly different job. Let's have a look at each in turn.

Flatbed scanners

The most common type of scanner is the flatbed – sometimes called a reflective scanner as this design captures light reflected off the original document to create an image. The document is placed face-down on a glass surface called a platen, underneath which a long, thin CCD sensor moves on a motorized arm down the length of the machine. At each tiny step along the way, the CCD captures a view of the document, with these slices being reconstituted at the end to make up the final image. Depending on the scanner, the quality at which the document is being scanned and the size of the document, such a process can take from between ten seconds to a couple of minutes.

As well as scanning in reflective mode, some of the more advanced flatbed scanners have a light source built-in to their lid that enables strips of film and mounted transparencies (slides) to be scanned, too. The light from this transparency scanning unit (TSU) passes through the originals and onto the CCD sensor.

Because of the relatively small size of such transparent originals, compared to the entire scanning area, the quality of 35mm film or transparency scans from a flatbed scanner will never be as good as those from a dedicated film scanner. That said, they will be fine for use on the web or in email, or even for making small 6 x 4 inch prints.

Flatbed scanner

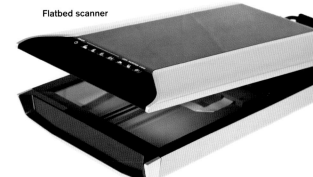

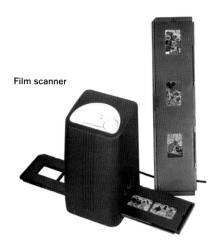

Film scanner

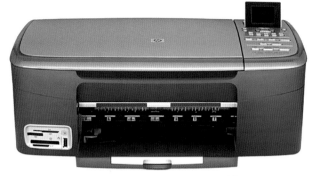

All-in-one scanner

Film scanners

For better scans of negatives and transparencies, a dedicated, good-quality film scanner is the best option. These units work in the same way as a flatbed scanner, although the film is usually drawn inside the unit, with the scanning happening internally. Being designed expressly for this purpose, film scanners are able to offer exceptionally high quality scans, with enough resolution to make the film's own grain structure the limiting factor in how much image detail will be resolved. Files measuring 860mm x 550mm are not unusual, meaning prints up to A2 in size can be made comfortably.

A good film scanner can be expensive, and you may struggle to justify the outlay if you don't shoot a lot of images with film, or you don't use them at very large sizes. Cheaper film scanners are available that operate on a different principle, using a small camera to essentially photograph the original against a backlight. The quality of the output from these machines is not as good as their more expensive cousins, though, being roughly similar to a flatbed scanner in film-scanning mode.

All-in-one scanners

Commonly, a flatbed scanner is built-in to a unit that can also print, and perhaps even fax and photocopy. These all-in-one units offer excellent value for money and save desk-space, although sometimes the quality of the scanning and printing is not quite as good as individual units. That said, the all-in-one is the best choice for a photographer doing a little bit of scanning and home inkjet printing (see pages 50–51) up to A4 in size. Some units offer wireless networking (WiFi) so multiple users can print from anywhere in the building, and connect to a telephone socket to offer faxing capabilities.

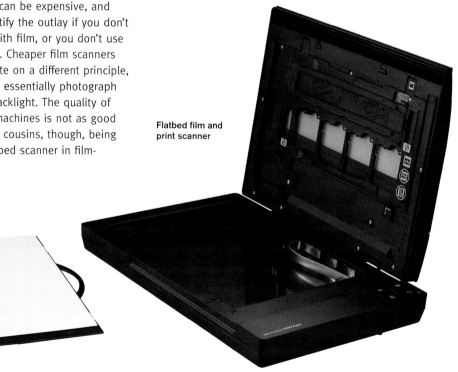

Flatbed film and print scanner

Scanning technology

One of the biggest problems with scanning is the presence of dust and dirt on the original, especially in the case of film scans, but also on prints. When a scanned image is enlarged, the dust is, too, meaning a speck measuring two millimeters can suddenly ruin a good image. These specks can be removed using software such as Adobe Photoshop or Photoshop Elements (see page 40), but the process can be laborious.

To make life easier, automatic dust-removal technology is often found in film scanners and flatbed scanners with a film-scanning capability. This works by scanning the original with an infrared (IR) lightsource at the same time as it scans with visible light. The IR detects what is dust on the film and what isn't, and this information is used to digitally remove it from

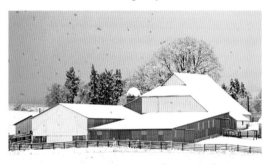

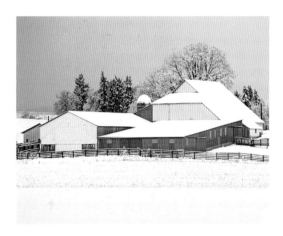

Above: A photo as the dusty original, and with reduced dust and scratches after being scanned with Digital ICE.

the scan. The most popular anti-dust technology is Digital ICE, developed by Kodak (you might see the logo on scanners), although other rival technologies are also out there. Be aware that anti-dust features of this type do not work with black and white film, which is totally opaque to IR light. This is a shame, because it is when scanning scratched and dusty old black and white film that such technology is most needed.

As well as anti-dust technology, some scanner software also features grain-reduction and colour-fixing algorithms. The makers of Digital ICE call theirs GEM (grain equalization and management) and ROC (restoration of colour); again alternatives are available.

Grain reduction is useful when a scanner is resolving the grain structure of the film itself, which can look ugly at high magnifications and print sizes. Be aware that in smoothing out such fine structure, grain reduction can also blur fine detail in the photograph, so it may take some experimentation to get the level just right.

Colour restoration is often useful when scanning old transparencies that have faded somewhat with age. You can achieve the same correction by making manual colour adjustments in your scanning software, although this is difficult to get right and time-consuming. It's worth seeing if an automatic process can take care of it for you.

Scanning software

All scanners need software in order to function properly, and for your computer to capture the images that they make. There is usually a device driver that does the first of these tasks, and a scanning application that does the latter. Both are made by the scanner manufacturer and should be included on the CD or DVD that came with your scanner.

It is usually possible to use scanner software in one of two ways: either as a stand-alone application, saving the scanned image to disk as a JPEG or TIFF file; or as a Photoshop plug-in, whereby the scanned image will open directly into Photoshop at the end of the scan. Direct import into Photoshop is often handled by software known as TWAIN – standing for 'technology without an interesting name'. You may see this in Photoshop's image or filter menus.

Scanner drivers are specific to an operating system, and problems can occur when photographers try to use an older scanner after upgrading their computers. In this case it's vital to get an updated driver, usually from the scanner manufacturer's website, to carry on using your hardware.

With scanning and film photography in decline, however, it is sometimes just not viable for manufacturers to update their software every time a new version of Windows or Mac OSX is released, meaning some older scanners now do not work with brand new computers. If you find yourself in this position, the only option is to use a third-party scanning application. Two such options currently exist: Vuescan (www.hamsoft.com) and SilverFast (www.silverfast.com), both of which are available to download as trial demo versions so you can see which you prefer.

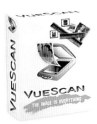

Right and below: *Vuescan and SilverFast are both good solutions to bridge system software updates.*

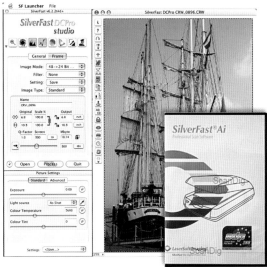

Scanning tips and tricks

Keeping your scanner free of dust and dirt will save a great deal of time at the retouching stage. Use a soft, microfibre cloth to clean the glass platen, and handle originals with white gloves to avoid fingerprints.

Don't always scan straight into Adobe Photoshop. Doing so ties up the application for the duration of the scan. Running the scanner

Below: A good quality multipurpose scanner can be a great way to rediscover or archive old negatives.

software as a stand-alone application means that you can still work on other tasks while scanning; running a scan takes very little of your computer's processor power.

On a flatbed scanner, scan in the middle of the glass and stay away from the edges. Optical quality is best towards the centre of the platen.

Choose a scanning resolution that is high enough for you to print at big print sizes, even if you don't intend to do this straight away – you might change your mind later. That said, don't go over the top and produce a file so big that your computer can't handle it.

All scanning software has a black and white mode, but it's best to scan monochrome originals (prints and negatives) in colour, then convert to black and white afterwards in Photoshop or Elements. This way you are capturing more information, and can take control of the monochrome conversion process (see pages 268–269).

ASSIGNMENT
SCANOGRAPHY

Your scanner isn't just a tool for digitizing film images – you can put it to good use scanning real-life objects, too, for close-up and still-life photographs that have a different look and feel to those captured with a camera.

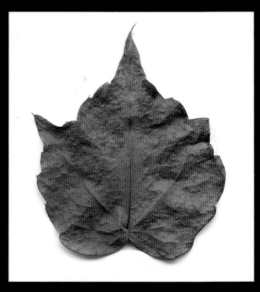

You may not have considered it before, but flatbed scanners are great for scanning three-dimensional objects, as well as flat prints and negatives. Put a handful of small change or your set of keys (carefully) on the glass and hit the scan button, and you'll soon see why: scanned images of objects are packed with detail and enlarge to enormous sizes. They can also have a very ethereal look, with focus being sharpest where the object is in contact with the glass, dropping off for regions that are further away.

As with any form of photography, you can make changes to the image with subtle changes in technique. Use a black cloth over the object you are scanning to avoid crushing it, or try deliberately squashing it on to the glass. Experiment with moving the object as the scan progresses – scanning your own hand, while moving along with the scanner unit for a moment, results in some bizarre effects.

Translucent, flat objects, such as leaves, petals or pressed flowers, make stunning fine-art prints, and if your scanner has a mode for transparency scanning, you can try using this to pass light through the object, instead of reflecting light off it. Scanography, as this technique is known, is all about experimenting and trying new things out. This type of photography is really only limited by your own imagination.

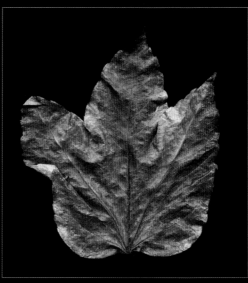

Above and top: Leaves, scanned against different backgrounds, make excellent fine-art images and can be printed at huge sizes.

ESSENTIAL KIT

- Flatbed scanner
- Computer with scanning software
- Cleaning materials
- Black cloth
- Coloured paper or card for alternative backgrounds

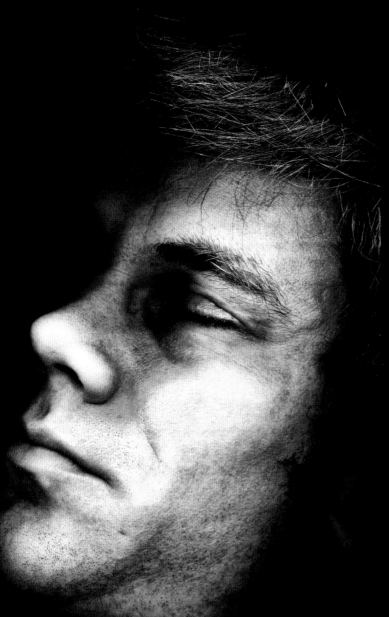

TIPS & TRICKS

Keep it clean
It's easy to get fingerprints, dust and dirt on the scanner glass while you are arranging the objects to be scanned. Use white cotton gloves to minimize this, and clean the scanner glass between images.

Change backgrounds
Try scanning objects with the lid up, the lid down, covered with a black cloth, etc. Excluding other light means you'll get a dark background. A painted shoebox can be used, and won't squash things, either.

Go transparent
Autumn leaves and dried flowers look great when scanned in transparency mode. Passing light through them reveals the fine structure of their veins.

Self-scanning
Scanning bits of yourself is good fun, though be aware that the scanner light is very bright, so you should avoid looking at it close-up.

Left: You can scan everything, even yourself, though for the sake of your eyes, be careful not to look at the bright scanner light.

Printers and printing

The decline of film photography means that we're far less likely to actually print out copies of our photos. This is a shame, because it's a great way to show off your photography – and with a home inkjet printer, you can stay in complete charge of the process.

You could be forgiven for thinking that printing photographs has fallen out of fashion. After all, we all look at our snapshots on-screen now, and share them using social networking websites, such as Flickr and Facebook. However, on-screen viewing really only showcases the 6 x 4 inch 'enprint' that we used to pass around family and friends. The type of large prints that you want to hang on the wall or put in your portfolio are still going strong, and have never looked so good.

When it comes to making prints, the first decision is between printing at home, or having a high street or internet printer make prints for you. Printing at home offers the distinct advantage of being in control of the process at all stages, meaning no nasty surprises. You can also be more selective about what image size you are printing, and the type of media you're printing on.

Inkjet printers

A home office inkjet printer is available for very little money, and even those that are meant for photographic-quality output are very affordable. It is worth doing some homework before taking the plunge, though. The cost of a printer off the shelf is often subsidized by the cost of ink cartridges, which can be exorbitantly expensive. When considering a printer, try to consider the total cost of ownership: how much does a full set of cartridges cost? How often will you need to replace them? Can you buy and replace them individually, or do they have to be changed all at once?

Home inkjet printers usually come as A4 or A3-size units. Larger printers are available (A2, A1 and larger), but these are expensive and really meant for professional output by photo labs. Although many of the bargain printers are A4 units, an A3 print has much more impact, especially when

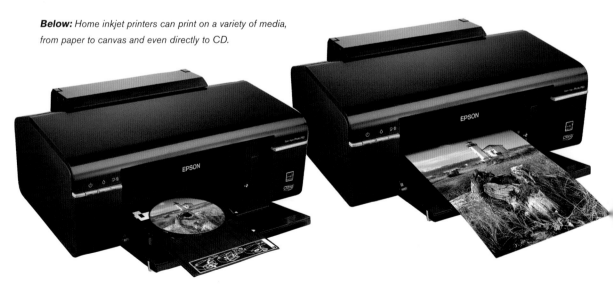

Below: Home inkjet printers can print on a variety of media, from paper to canvas and even directly to CD.

How long do prints last?

In its infancy, inkjet technology was criticized for the lifespan of the prints that it produced, with images sometimes fading over the course of a few months in direct light. Thankfully, things have got much better since then, with independent tests and simulations showing modern-day inkjet prints to be stable for over a hundred years.

To achieve this, though, there are a few basic precautions you need to take. Keep prints in acid-free, archival quality sleeves when they are being stored, and if they are on display, ensure that they are framed behind UV-resistant glass and hung out of direct sunlight.

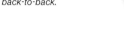

framed and on the wall, and could be worth the extra investment.

Inkjet printers work by squeezing out very small droplets of ink on to the surface of a sheet of paper. These droplets are so small (in some cases just a couple of picoliters) that, to the human eye, they appear to mix together to form an image. For this trick to work, we need four ink colours: cyan, magenta, yellow and black, and indeed this is the minimum ink set you'll find in an inkjet printer. Those designed for photographers often contain more than this in order to expand the gamut of colours they can reproduce on paper – a light cyan or red, for example – and as a general rule, the more inks a printer has, the better quality its prints will be.

There are two types of ink in use today: pigment and dye. Dye-based ink systems consist of dye molecules dissolved in water. Small droplets of this solution are deposited on the surface of the paper, where they are absorbed. The water then diffuses away and the ink is left in place. Dye inks offer slightly more vibrant colours than pigments, and are often more affordable. Pigment inks, on the other hand, are liquid in nature and do not have to be dissolved in water. They sit on top of the paper and are not absorbed, meaning a single dot of pigment ink is smaller than a corresponding dot of dye ink and can be laid down with more precision. Being water insoluble, dye ink prints are more resistant to deterioration over time.

The type of ink system used in a printer will be laid down in its specification. You may find that some advanced photographic models use a hybrid ink set, with dye and pigment inks working together.

Right: *Archival sleeves are the best way to store prints back-to-back.*

Paper and media

Ink is only half of the secret behind a good inkjet print. The other half is media. One of the main advantages of inkjet printing is the huge variety of paper and canvas available. The digital photographer can choose between glossy and matt finishes (or an intermediate), different weights of paper and different image qualities, meaning the right paper can be chosen for a particular task.

For example, a heavyweight glossy paper is good for framed prints, under known lighting conditions, whereas a portfolio print might need to be on lighter paper, with a semi-gloss or matt finish to avoid distracting reflections from overhead lights. Canvas is also available for a more classic fine-art look. This can either be framed or stretched over a wooden block frame for a contemporary feel.

It's important to set the right printer driver settings for the paper in use (we'll talk more about this on page 376). The quantity of ink the printer puts down, and the method it uses to do this, depends on the paper's coating, weight and other characteristics. Getting the settings wrong can seriously affect print quality. For papers made by the same manufacturer as the printer, this is easy – just pick the appropriate paper in the printer driver. For third-party papers, you'll need to read the instructions carefully and pick the right settings for your computer. Or use a custom colour profile (see page 290).

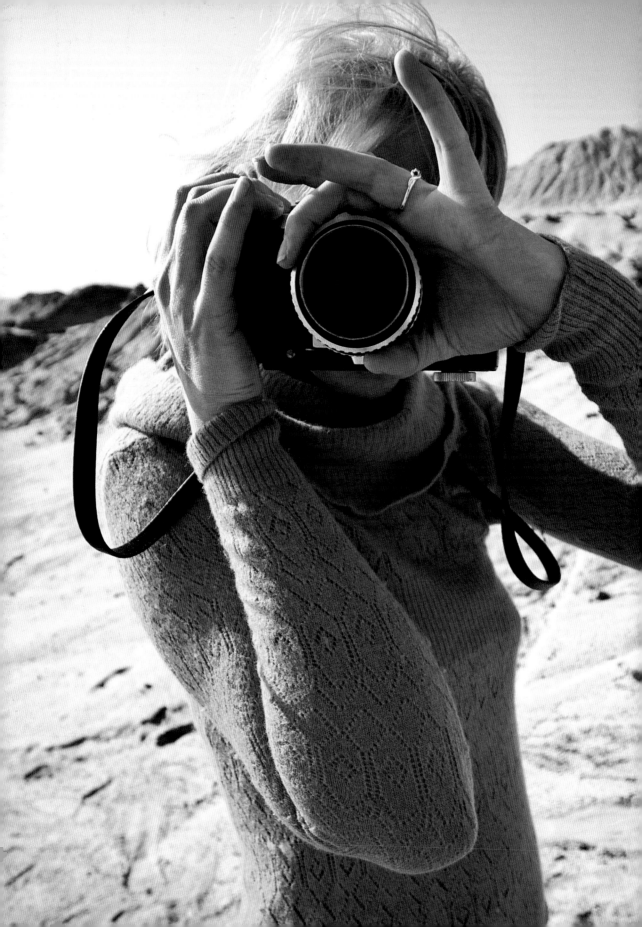

using your
camera

Now that we have discussed the basic equipment you'll need or may already have, it is time to look at your camera and start taking photographs. As you get to grips with your camera's controls, working with its different functions will become second-nature to you. You will be amazed at how quickly your self-confidence grows as you approach each subject or different light condition with the right tools and knowledge.

Using your **camera**

The current crop of DSLRs are so easy to use that you can get them out of the box and start straight away. But take some time to explore their many functions too, and you will start to take control over your photography.

Upgrading from a compact camera to a DSLR will do wonders for your photography. Better picture quality, faster response times and more creative control are just a few of the advantages on offer. That said, a DSLR can appear intimidating and complex to the first-time user, having so many functions and controls. Thankfully, modern-day DSLRs are far more friendly than they look, and many entry level models have user-friendly functions that allow you to take control over a picture without compromising on ease of use.

Automatic and program modes

Look on the mode dial of a DSLR and you will always find an exposure mode marked 'P', standing for 'program'. In program mode, the two main exposure variables of aperture (how much light is let in through the lens) and shutter speed (how long it is let through for) are controlled for you, so you can give your full attention to other things. This is the ideal starting point for those with some experience in compact-camera photography, and using program mode will still

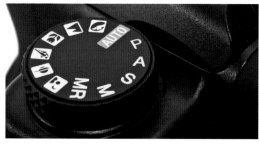

Above: On most cameras the mode dial is located at the top and includes these standard scene modes:
Automatic modes: auto, action, portrait, night portrait, landscape and macro.
Manual modes: program (P), aperture priority (A), shutter priority (S) and manual (M).

give you control over what ISO sensitivity you select, which focus mode to use, and any other features the camera has to offer.

On the other hand, if all this choice still fills you with dread, there is usually a more simple mode that automates more than just exposure. A full auto mode (often denoted by a green symbol, for some reason) does precisely what it suggests, looking after everything from exposure to focusing, ISO, flash and a whole lot more. It's perfect for those who want to get shooting with their DSLR as soon as possible, with a minimum of fuss.

Scene modes

Unfortunately, with a minimum of fuss comes a minimum of control. To really make the most of the technology in a DSLR, at some point every photographer has to be brave and take a step away from full auto mode. This doesn't mean going from one extreme to the other, though. Many cameras have 'scene' modes, which are like the 'green' full-auto mode, except they are tailored towards a specific type of photography. You may have even used them on a compact camera.

For example, setting a sports or action scene mode when shooting a football game or a runner on a track tells the camera to use fast shutter speeds to freeze action, and continuous AF to track moving objects as they come towards the camera. You could do the same thing yourself manually, but when you are starting out, scene modes are a great way of doing this with a minimum of fuss. Similarly, landscape or outdoor mode makes the camera use a small aperture to make sure that both near and far objects are in focus (see depth of field on pages 84–87), and night portrait mode will use flash and a long exposure to make sure a foreground subject and a dark background are both exposed properly.

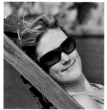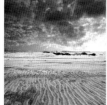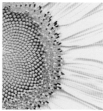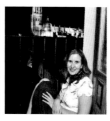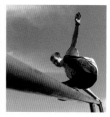

| Portrait setting | Landscape setting | Night portrait | Macro setting | Sport setting |

A more recent development is more intelligent full-auto modes that attempt to analyze a scene according to exposure, movement and the presence of faces and then either pick the appropriate scene mode, or custom-build a scene mode for that shot.

Holding your camera

Holding your camera properly is important when it comes to maximizing image quality. Perhaps the biggest source of soft, or unsharp, photographs is camera shake, caused by the camera moving during the time the shutter is open. Supporting your camera properly minimizes camera movement, and results in drastically sharper results.

For those new to DSLRs, it's tempting to hold the camera by the sides, as you might a compact, but this is not very stable. Instead tuck your left hand under the camera, cradling both the body and the lens. Your right hand then only really operates the controls; you should be able to take it away at any time. For extra stability, brace your elbows into your body as you hold the camera to your face. And get into the habit of breathing out as you gently squeeze the shutter release. For vertical compositions, rotate the camera so your right hand is on top. Your left hand should still be cradling the camera and lens, with your left elbow tucked into your body.

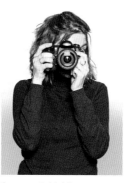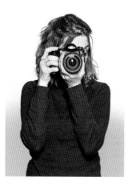

Incorrect: *Holding your SLR by the sides is not stable and can cause blur.*

Correct: *One hand supports the camera body; the other hand controls.*

Connecting your camera to a computer

Once you've taken a set of pictures, you'll want to transfer them to your computer so you can edit, view, archive and print them. You can do this with the supplied connection cable that came with your camera. Simply plug one end into your camera and the other into a USB port on your PC or Mac. Once the camera is switched on, the memory card inside the computer will be accessible like any memory stick or hard disk.

While this method of transferring pictures is fine for occasional use, having your camera connected all the time tends to drain power from the battery rather quickly, and transfer speed can also be quite slow. All these problems can be solved by using a card reader, a device that stays attached to your computer into which you can simply plug cards. This way your camera can still be used even when you are transferring files, and you won't flatten the battery.

Some card readers are specific to only one card type, while others read many types of storage media. Most units connect to USB ports, although some top-end card readers make use of Fire Wire technology for very fast transfer speeds.

Autofocus and focusing

When light rays reflected from a distant object pass into a camera, they must be focused onto the sensor for the object to appear sharp in the final photograph. Objects at different distances must be focused differently, so making sure one object is sharp may mean that another is blurred.

Most cameras have good autofocus (AF) systems that tend to get the focus accurate most of the time, but this isn't a reason to forget that the need to focus exists. It's important to take control of a camera's AF system, and make it work for you. An autofocus target or 'point' is indicated by a small square either in the camera's viewfinder or on the viewscreen, and it is the positioning of this point that decides where in a scene a camera will focus. Some cameras have multiple focus points spread out across an area, to increase the chances of locking on to the right part of the scene, but this is still no guarantee that good focus will be achieved every time without some common sense being used, too.

Virtually all digital cameras have a two-stage shutter release. A half press on this button activates the autofocus system, with the camera then locking onto whatever is underneath the active AF point. A green LED or symbol in the viewfinder will confirm this, or sometimes an audible beep. After this, the shutter release can be pressed down further to actually take a picture.

Allowing a camera time to focus in this way will result in properly focused pictures. Trying to press the button all the way down in one go may not give the camera a chance to focus, meaning you'll either get a blurred picture, or a long delay while focusing occurs, meaning you'll miss the action.

Two types of autofocus mode are commonly found: single and continuous. In single AF mode, once focus is achieved it is locked until the shutter button is either released or depressed completely to take the picture. Furthermore, a picture cannot be taken until good focus lock has been achieved. This is the best AF mode for general everyday use, as it allows you to select where the camera should focus by pointing at an object, then recompose the image after focus lock has been achieved but before the shutter is pressed down fully. This is an approach especially useful for off-centre subjects, or scenes where the main point of interest doesn't coincide with a focus point.

Off-centre focusing

A classic mistake: you photograph two people standing next to each other, but the camera's central AF point focuses on the scenery behind them instead, giving you an out-of-focus portrait. Off-centre subjects can be tricky to deal with using AF, but there are ways to ensure you get the right part of the picture sharp.

• When in single AF mode, use the central AF point to focus on the subject you want sharp by half-pressing the shutter release. The focus distance is now locked at this point. Without letting go of the shutter release, move the camera to recompose the picture, so the subject is no longer in the middle of the frame. Now take the picture.

• If your camera has more than one AF point, make an off-centre point active instead of the usual central point and place this one over the subject instead.

• A camera sporting more than one AF point also lets the photographer activate all points at once. In this 'wide-area' mode, the camera will automatically select the focus point that is covering the object nearest to the camera, which is usually (but not always) the main one.

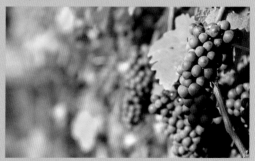

Above: *Focusing on the grapes on the right, locking the AF, and then shifting left to press the shutter release has resulted in this soft fade of focus.*

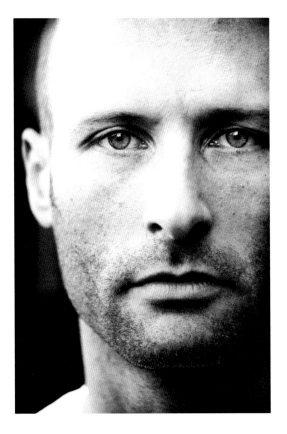

Left: Using a large aperture helps achieve a very shallow depth of field to filter out unwanted background and tighten the focus on the facial features.

its focus range in an attempt to get close to the right focus point. Some cameras also have a focus-assist light that tries to illuminate the scene a little more and enable the AF system to lock on.

But eventually there comes a time when it is much easier to just focus manually. While many compact cameras lack the ability to do this, DSLRs all have a manual focus mode, where focus is altered by turning a ring on the lens. You can judge whether you have accurate focus simply by looking at the scene through the viewfinder, or by watching for the electronic focus confirmation green circle that the AF system normally gives.

Manual focus isn't as difficult as you might think, and many photographers use it as their default mode. After all, it saves on batteries, and if you are shooting landscapes, still-life or slow-moving scenes, there is no real need for AF. On the other hand, autofocus is great for sports, wildlife and people photography, when you might need to focus more quickly than you could by hand.

The second AF mode – continuous – is used for tracking moving subjects. Rather than locking AF when the shutter release is depressed, a camera in continuous AF mode focuses all the time, readjusting constantly in order to track subjects that are moving around. The shutter release can be tripped at any time, even if the moving object isn't quite in focus, though hopefully your camera's AF system will be fast enough to make sure enough sharpness is there. Some continuous AF processing systems are sophisticated enough to follow very fast, erratically moving objects, using multiple AF points and artificial intelligence to track movement across the frame.

When AF goes wrong

Even the most sophisticated autofocus systems get it wrong occasionally. If a focus point overlaps a plain surface that is devoid of detail it won't be able to judge how far away it is. Low light also makes focusing more difficult. You'll know when a camera's AF is struggling as it will 'hunt' through

i Dos and don'ts

Do consider autofocusing as something you have to think about: selecting something to focus on and consciously doing this with a half press of the shutter release.

Don't forget about focusing and assume everything will be OK.

Do use only the central focus point, for more accurate selective focusing, combined with the AF lock.

Don't change your subject-to-camera distance when recomposing after using the AF lock. This will cause the camera to use the wrong focus distance, and your main subject could appear blurred.

Do make sure focus is locked before you take the picture. Look out for the focus-confirmation light or audible beep.

Don't forget manual focus mode; it can help when AF is struggling, such as in low light.

Composition

When we discuss composition, we are really talking about what makes an image visually appealing. What makes one photograph more attractive than another? How can the arrangement be used to convey different moods?

The importance of composition in photography cannot be overstated. Poorly composed photographs are confusing – it's not clear what we are supposed to be looking at, and what exactly the photographer is trying to say. Getting composition right is the clearest way of distinguishing your work.

Unlike the more technical aspects of photography, it's not possible to rely on automation and technology to get the basics of composition right. There is no one single, correct way to compose a picture – although there is always an incorrect way, of course. While there are some basic rules of composition, selecting which rule to use in any particular situation is entirely up to you, and it is this aspect of photography that most lets you put your own creative stamp on the picture-making process.

How you position yourself, your camera and the objects you are photographing can speak volumes about your mood and personality, what you are trying to say in your pictures and how the viewer will connect emotionally with the scene. Composition can also dictate how we relate to a photograph over time. Those images that make a dramatic first impression on us often become boring more quickly than those that we grow to love more slowly.

With so many ways to compose a photograph, and with each way effectively producing a different result, gaining experience in how to compose a photograph is key to that most sought-after aspect of photography: developing a recognizable, unique photographic style. Some compositions are classics, used by painters for centuries. Others are more contemporary, designed to jar or shock the senses for artistic effect.

A few simple rules will get you started, then we can look at some of the more outlandish compositions used by today's photographers. After all, rules were made to be broken.

Framing, aspect ratios and orientation

When we photograph a three-dimensional world using two-dimensional photography, we create relationships between objects and shapes that often don't otherwise exist. We can alter this relationship – and the composition of our photographs – by changing how we frame a scene. The vantage point we take, the viewing angle we use, and the subject-to-camera distance we adopt are just some of the framing tools at our disposal as photographers – as is the size and shape of the frame itself.

Deciding whether to hold your camera horizontally or vertically is one of the first choices to be made when approaching a scene. Traditionally, these orientations are known as 'landscape' and 'portrait', respectively, but there is nothing etched in stone saying that you have to use the camera horizontally to shoot scenic scenes and vertically to photograph people. Landscapes containing close-up foreground detail, leading off towards a distant horizon, often benefit from the vertical, upright frame that allows more depth. Similarly, portraits featuring the subject looking across a horizontal frame into empty space are very effective.

There are no hard and fast rules regarding which way up you should hold a camera, and it's almost impossible to predict this before you've raised your camera to your eye. Once your camera is out of the bag, though, always turn it through 90 degrees as you are exploring possible compositions. It's a good habit to get into and may just reveal a picture you hadn't seen before.

As well as the orientation of the frame, also consider its shape. Most sensors (and therefore viewfinders and screens) have an aspect ratio of 3:2, i.e. their physical width and height dimensions are in the ratio 3:2. But you shouldn't feel restricted to this. In the same way that a painter would choose a canvas shape that suited the task in hand, so photographers can pick an alternative aspect ratio that suits the scene being photographed. Some compacts and DSLRs allow you to do this in-camera, but it's also possible (and in some cases preferable) to change the aspect ratio after shooting, by cropping the image with software such as Adobe Photoshop (see page 264). This way, you get to try out different aspect ratios and see which fits best. You'll also get to choose from an infinite range of shapes, as opposed to the two or three that are built into cameras.

In addition to the standard 3:2 aspect ratio, you'll also find 4:3 and 5:4 rectangular sizes useful, as well as the 16:9 and 17:6 sizes beloved by landscape photographers, and even the square 1:1 format, which is great for portraits.

Below: *The same scene cropped to three very different aspect ratios: the traditional landscape orientation, the upright portrait format, and a long, thin panoramic crop. Be sure to experiment when composing pictures, and don't just stick with convention.*

Framing

Always pay attention to the edges of the frame. Get into the habit of going through a mental checklist before you press the shutter:
Does everything you've included help or benefit the photograph? Does anything detract from the composition? Is the horizon straight? How could a small movement reposition the frame to improve these factors? Should you change your vantage point?

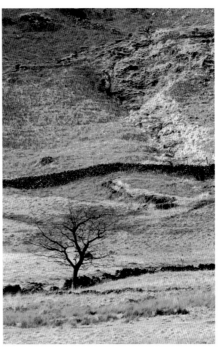

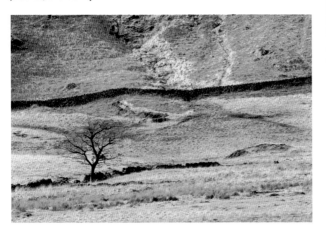

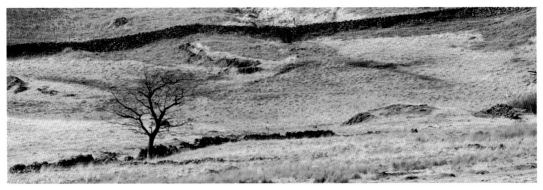

Rules of composition

There are numerous rules and guidelines that can help with composition. With time, knowing which of these to use in what situation will become intuitive, and you'll even be comfortable breaking the rules for extra creativity when you get more confident.

Until then, let's have a look at some classic ways to compose a picture, that can be used for everything from standard holiday photography to fine-art projects. Once you have internalized these rules, you will be able to play with them.

Fill the frame

The most elementary mistake made by those new to photography is to leave far too much room around the subject. This problem comes from looking only at the subject, and paying no attention to the edges of the frame. Scan around the image borders before you take the picture – how much space do you have?

A small subject in the middle of the frame surrounded by space is a very dull way to frame a picture, particularly in portrait photography. While you should avoid that all-time classic mistake of chopping off someone's head, it is perfectly acceptable to chop off a person's legs to create a three-quarter or half-length image. In these situations it's best to crop between joints, not over them.

Bull's eye composition

It's sometimes hard to resist centering the subject in the middle of the frame, especially for scenes containing a high degree of symmetry. Such 'bull's eye' compositions can be very powerful, creating impact straight away, although they also tend to tire quickly, too. Nevertheless, this compositional technique works well with faces, architecture or still-life subjects, particularly flowers. It also lends itself to a square format, as opposed to the more common rectangular 3:2 or 4:3 frame.

The rule of thirds

Perhaps the compositional aid most commonly used by photographers, the rule of thirds relies on the photographer imagining the frame split up by lines into thirds, both vertically and horizontally. Placing people, objects and even horizons along these lines will produce a composition that is more engaging and interesting than simply placing them in the middle of the frame. Furthermore, positioning objects on one of the four hotspots, where vertical and horizontal lines cross, will give emphasis to these objects in your composition.

Above: Filling the frame with a symmetrical, bull's-eye composition creates instant impact and drama.

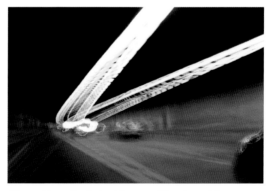

Above: Use a line to lead the eye of the viewer into a space or to emphasize the path of a moving subject.

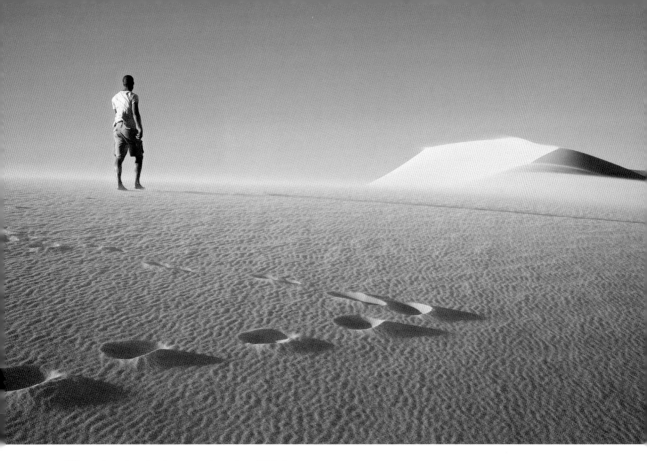

When shooting landscapes, the rule of thirds is most obviously applied by lining up the horizon with one of the two lines running horizontally across the frame, with foreground detail, such as a tree or rock, being positioned on an intersection. In portraiture, it's not uncommon to find the subject's body aligned along one of the lines running vertically, with their head on a hotspot at the top of the frame.

The rule of thirds is an extremely well-established technique. Its use by painters can be traced back over centuries, and its origins lie in an approximation of the golden ratio – a mathematical relationship found naturally in everything from sunflowers to spiral galaxies, and used by man for aesthetic reasons in architecture, music and art.

Negative space

Although we've looked at the perils of leaving too much space around your subject, caused by not getting close enough, such 'negative space' can be put to good use, especially when following the rule of thirds. In portraiture, having

Above: *Leading lines guide the eye into the picture towards the focal point, which is situated on a third.*

a subject looking into an area of empty space is very effective, with a left-to-right arrangement often working better for those who also read text in this direction. In landscape and architectural photography it's also possible to use empty space for dramatic emphasis in simple compositions.

Using leading lines

Some of the most striking compositions in landscape photography use lines and shapes in the foreground to guide the eye into the picture, eventually arriving at a focal point in the distance. Seeing these lines, and the relationships between them, is often very difficult without the camera to your eye, but this is a skill that comes with experience.

In countryside landscapes, the lines seen in ploughed fields or mapped out by dry stone walls are excellent compositional tools, as are the shapes seen on sandy beaches and in rock formations at the coast.

ASSIGNMENT
USING THE RULE
OF THIRDS

The rule of thirds is a traditional and powerful tool that will give your photographs more energy and impact, as well as making them interesting for longer.

There is a good reason why the rule of thirds is as popular as it is – it helps improve compositions hugely in virtually every area of photography, from landscape and architecture to portraiture and still life. Look at many of the pictures in this book (and indeed in magazines, adverts and galleries) and you'll see the rule of thirds in action again and again, with the focal point of a photograph positioned over one of the four hotspots prescribed by the intersections of imaginary lines carving up the frame into thirds, both horizontally and vertically. Horizons, buildings and people should be placed along these edges too, instead of centrally in the middle of the frame.

Some cameras offer the facility to superimpose gridlines on the viewscreen or viewfinder, and these can often be useful for showing the position of the rule of thirds' lines. If your camera doesn't show this, however, you shouldn't have much difficulty in imagining where they appear.

For this assignment, use the rule of thirds to shoot one portrait and one landscape photograph. For the portrait, try to make your sitter's head the focal point by placing it on a hotspot, or if you are shooting a tighter 'headshot' image, try placing emphasis on one of their eyes, instead. Don't worry if you crop off the top of their head when shooting this close up – this is not such a problem as when shooting from a distance, and is often used in fashion photography to make people look larger in the frame than they really are.

When it comes to the landscape image you will have many more options for what to put along a compositional line or on a hotspot. The horizon should follow one of the third lines, no matter whether you are holding the camera horizontally or vertically. Use the bottom line to give more emphasis to the sky and the upper line when you want to incorporate more foreground detail in the shot.

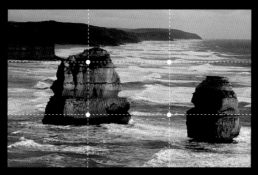

Above: Here, the larger stack on the left is the main focal point and is positioned on the two left hotspots.
Panasonic Lumix DMC-FP1, 70 mm, automatic metering

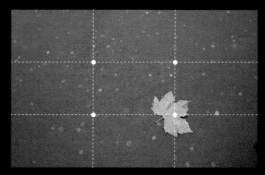

Above: Even though the leaf is small, it commands attention because of its position in the frame.
Leica M9, 28mm f/2 lens, 1/60sec, f/5.6, ISO160

ESSENTIAL KIT

- Camera
- Zoom lens
- Tripod can help with consistent camera positioning

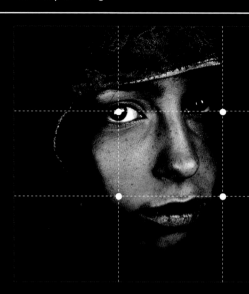

Left: *The eyes being on the first horizontal line create a strong impact on the viewer.*
Canon EOS 60D, 18-135mm, 1/100sec, f/5.6

Below: *The low horizon divides this composition into clear visual thirds.*
Canon EOS 20D, 24-105mm, 1/60sec, f/11

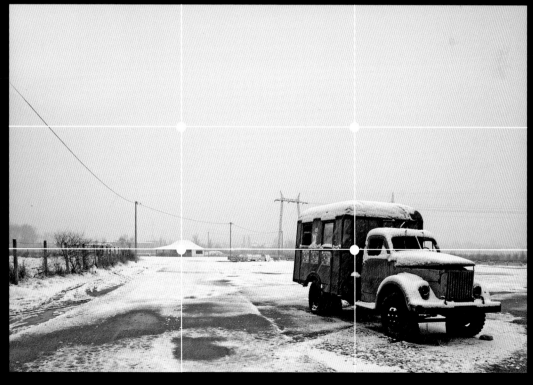

Lenses and composition

We've seen already how lens focal length can affect angle of view (see page 21). Telephoto lenses bring objects closer to us while wide-angle lenses allow us to include more of the scene. But lens choice can also change perspective, with objects appearing closer together when seen through a telephoto lens than they do when viewed with a wide-angle.

You can try this yourself with the standard zoom lens that came with your camera. Line up a couple of objects, one near the camera and one further away, and photograph them at the widest zoom setting. Now zoom to the most telephoto zoom setting and shoot the picture again, stepping back so the foreground object is the same size in the frame. You should notice that the background object now appears closer to the camera.

Below: Shooting with a long focal length telephoto lens has compressed perspective, giving this architectural study a more two-dimensional feeling.

The exaggeration of perspective when using wide lenses is a welcome bonus when you want to emphasize foreground detail in a landscape composition, or add a feeling of space when shooting reportage photography up-close. It's less welcome when it exaggerates features such as big noses in portraiture, which is the reason that portrait photographers tend to use slightly telephoto lenses (85–100mm) and stand back. This de-emphasizes large features and 'flattens' the face slightly for a more complimentary effect. The compression of perspective can also be used to good effect in architectural photography and far-off landscape scenes.

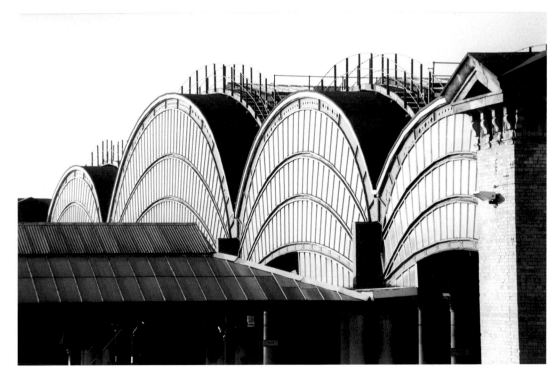

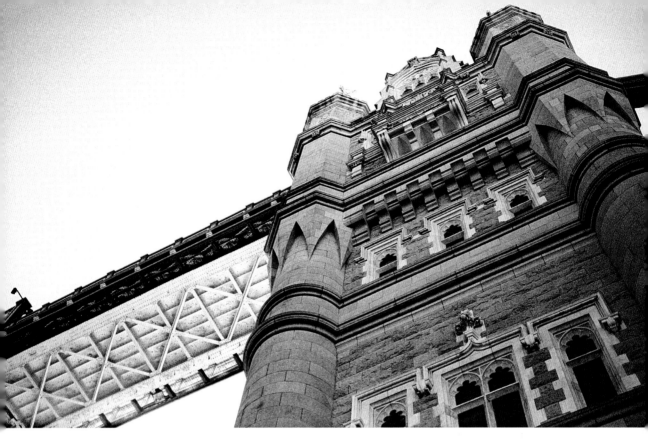

Lens choice and viewpoint

It's hard to talk about selecting the right lens or zoom setting for a composition without talking about the viewpoint from which you are shooting. If you are trying to create the feeling of looking slightly up or down at a subject, then using a wide-angle lens will exaggerate this effect, and can be used to inject some drama into your pictures. Look upwards at a building through a wide-angle lens to see the effect for yourself: the exaggerated perspective will make the building look much taller than it is, and angled steeply backwards. This is something of an all-or-nothing technique, though, with the drama of the low-down, wide-angle approach looking a bit odd in more normal scenarios. Looking up only slightly at a building through a wide-angle lens makes the structure look like it's about to fall over backwards – a problem known to photographers as 'converging verticals'.

The issue can be avoided by keeping the camera completely level, although this presents us with the problem of how to look up at the building in the first place. Professional architectural photographers use (expensive) specialist tilt-and-shift lenses (sometimes also

Above: A short focal length and a wide-angle lens exaggerate perspective, often adding drama and impact.

called perspective control lenses) but you can achieve a similar result by moving backwards until the top of the structure is visible in the frame with the camera still held vertically; you'll have to crop out the empty foreground you'll also capture as a result (see page 264). Alternatively you can angle the camera upwards and remove the offending converging verticals with software such as Adobe Photoshop (see page 40).

Below: This wide-angle Venice scene clearly shows the technique taken too far, resulting in converging verticals.

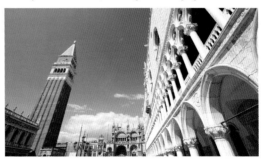

ASSIGNMENT
UNDERSTANDING LENS PERSPECTIVE

Perspective is an important aspect of photographic composition, and is affected to a great extent by the focal length of your lens. Deciding which to use at the right time is crucial to getting your photos looking their best.

Your standard zoom lens is a very versatile piece of kit. Covering focal lengths from wide-angle to short telephoto, you might find it never comes off your camera. But selecting which end of the lens to use is important: standing close to a subject and using a wide-angle lens gives a very different result from keeping your distance and shooting with a telephoto.

Wide-angle perspective exaggerates distances between objects and emphasizes the foreground in landscape compositions. Telephoto lenses, on the other hand, flatten perspective, making objects seem closer together and compressing the length of lines moving away from the camera.

For this assignment we'll explore how these effects manifest themselves in your images by comparing how landscape and portrait photographs respond to different zoom settings. Firstly, with your standard zoom, shoot a simple head and shoulders portrait at the widest setting (approximately 18mm) and then at the longest setting (usually between 50–60mm), moving back and forth as necessary to keep your subject at a constant size. What are the differences between these images? Which is the more appealing?

Secondly, find a landscape scene with some prominent foreground interest and repeat the exercise – shooting close-up with the wide-angle zoom setting, and from further away with

a more telephoto focal length. This can be a rural countryside or beach scene, or simply a townscape with the white line in the middle of the road leading your eye into the picture. Again, how does each picture differ? Did you find it easier to include the foreground detail with one approach more than the other? How does changing your viewpoint help? Try crouching down by the ground instead of shooting from eye level. And don't forget to turn the camera on its side and try a vertical composition, too.

If you have a compact camera you can perform the same exercise, although since the lens will probably have a more powerful telephoto setting, you may want to experiment with a few of these settings and note the difference between them. For those DSLR-users that have a telephoto zoom lens, there is no need to stop the exercise at the longest focal length offered by your standard zoom lens. Why not carry on and take pictures at 100mm, 200mm and 300mm settings too?

When comparing these sets of pictures, do you notice anything about the parts of the picture that are not in focus? You might notice that those shot with wide-angle focal lengths are more in focus than those shot at telephoto zoom settings. The amount of a picture that is acceptably sharp is known as depth of field and we'll be looking at this in more detail on pages 84–87, including how zoom settings affect how much of a scene is sharp.

ESSENTIAL KIT

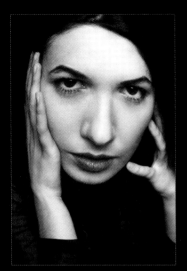

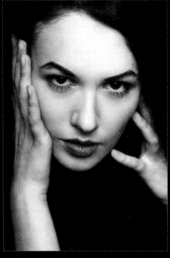

TIPS & TRICKS

- When shooting portraits in this way, standing back with a telephoto lens also means you won't crowd your subject, which will ensure they stay relaxed.

- Landscape subjects that suit the telephoto treatment include distant 'layers' of overlapping mountains, or buildings lined up along a street.

- Wide-angle lenses have a place in portraiture too, when photographing someone from down low or up high, when you want to emphasize perspective for added drama.

Above: A wide-angle lens distorts the facial features, giving it a quirky, yet intimate look.
Canon EOS 40D, 18mm, 1/125sec, f/8

Above: An 80mm lens pulls the facial features together and gives this portrait its naturalistic feel.
Canon EOS 40D, 55mm, 1/60sec, f/11

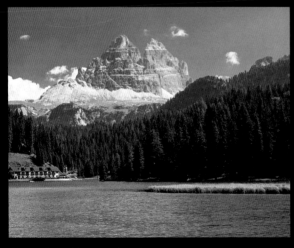

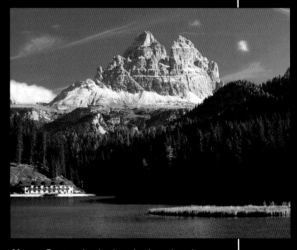

Above: This wide-angle shot allows for too much detail cluttering up the foreground.
Canon EOS 5D Mk II, 24-105mm at 35mm, 1/250sec at f/8, ISO200

Above: By stepping back and using a long lens, the mountain becomes the main focus.
Canon EOS 5D Mk II, 24-105mm at 100mm, 1/250sec at f/8, ISO200

Light

The language we use to discuss light can be very descriptive. We talk about its direction, brightness, how soft or hard it is, even its temperature. These characteristics have a huge influence on the look and feel of a picture.

One of the most obvious characteristics of light is the direction from which it is coming, relative to both the photographer and the subject. For outdoor photography, the type of omni-directional light that comes from an overhead midday sun will never deliver the best results. This type of light is often described as being too flat, meaning that its high angle in the sky prevents it from casting shadows. Shadows give a picture texture and depth, and are crucial for bringing out the best in an outdoor scene. Landscapes look much better towards the end of the day, just after the sun has risen, or just before it has set. The light is less intense, and its low angle means shadows are at their most pronounced. Shooting in this

type of light is the reason why most landscape photographers tend to be early birds, getting up before dawn to be in position as the sun comes up.

The direction of light in portraiture and still-life photography is also very important, though more easily manageable if the photographer is working with adjustable light sources. Don't be frightened of introducing shadows across the face of a subject when shooting their portrait; lighting someone from a 45 degree angle is often preferable to lighting them front-on. You could even try positioning a light behind them to create a silhouette. Experimentation really is the key here.

Soft or hard?

When we talk about soft or hard light, we are really talking about the type of shadow cast by the light. Hard light throws shadows with sharp edges – an abrupt transition from light to dark. Soft light causes shadows with blurred edges, and hence a more feathered, gradual transition. A good example of hard light is that emitted from a bare light bulb, which falls on the subject from one direction and without being bounced off anything else. These light rays can be thought of as all travelling in the same direction, which is why the resulting shadows are so well defined. Soft light is just the opposite: arriving on the subject from slightly different directions, or from a single, very large light source positioned close to the subject. For example, a subject lit by a single light bulb in a room with white walls, ceiling and floor will be lit with soft light, because of all of the light bouncing off the surrounding surfaces. Soft light exists naturally, too: sunlight on a bright summer's day is very hard, producing shadows across the

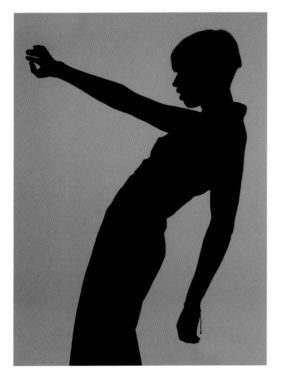

Left: *Shooting this profile in front of a brightly lit background resulted in a silhouette.*

face, but stepping into the shade makes these shadows disappear, because you are now being illuminated with soft light. You can also soften hard light yourself, by bouncing light around with reflectors (see page 27) or reflective surfaces.

When it comes to portraiture, soft light is the most useful. This can still be directional, if the light source is fitted with the correct accessory. Diffusers and so-called softboxes soften light by bouncing it around inside a large, reflective silver box.

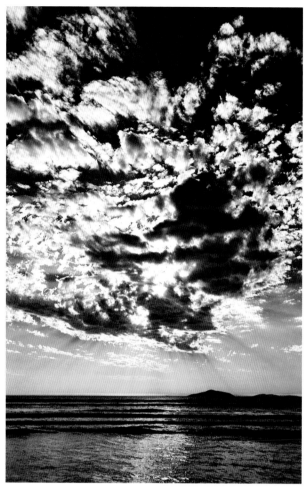

Right: *The almost black sky above the clouds perfectly counter-balances the shadow in the waves in the strong and low evening sunlight.*

Below: *Here, the diffuse early evening light creates a subtle pink haze, softening and pulling together the various focal points.*

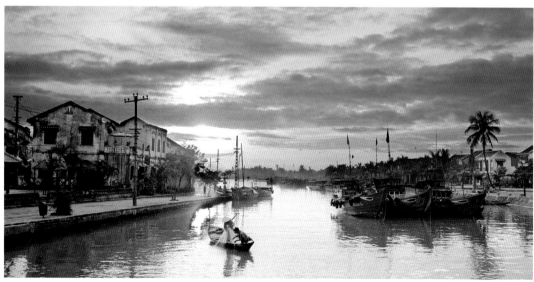

White **balance**

An often-forgotten property of light is its colour temperature. You've probably noticed this if you've ever thought that the artificial lighting inside a room is more orange than the daylight you find outside.

This extra 'warmth' is described in terms of a colour temperature, with warmer light being more orange/red than cooler light, which has a blue tint. Other types of light have different colour casts: fluorescent tubes emit a light that is slightly green, while modern halogens emit a steel blue-white light.

Much like the human eye, your digital camera can account for all of these variations when recording photographs. A feature called auto white balance aims to adjust the colour temperature of a scene so that it appears to be like daylight, no matter what light source you are shooting under.

To carry the analogy with heat a little further, colour temperature is measured in Kelvin (K), the absolute unit of temperature used by scientists. Daylight is approximately 5,200K, while the

temperature of light from a tungsten light bulb is more like 3,200K. Once your camera knows the temperature of the light you are using, it is very easy to adjust a photograph to make it appear as if it were shot in 5,500K daylight. But as with all automatic processes, it is this measurement of the ambient light colour temperature that can sometimes go wrong and cause problems.

For those tricky situations where your camera just isn't getting it right, you can take control of white balance yourself, setting one of a number of presets, such as shady, sunny, flash or tungsten (indoor). Often these presets can be fine-tuned to get exactly the result you are looking for. Mixed-lighting situations often cause the most confusion, where daylight and artificial light are both present, for instance.

 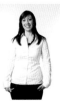 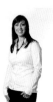 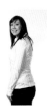   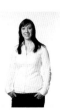

Left to right: Different white balance settings affect the colour temperature of an image. This flash-lit picture was shot with (left to right): auto white balance, daylight, flash, tungsten and fluorescent settings.

i Creating your own white balance preset

The manual white-balance presets programmed into your camera often don't have the precision for fine adjustment of colour temperature. A more accurate way to set white-balance manually is to create a custom white balance preset. Most digital cameras offer this facility, which involves photographing a white or grey surface under the lighting conditions being used for the shoot. This provides a 'neutral' frame of reference for the camera and tells it how much to adjust each subsequent frame by.

There are neutral targets on the market for colour balancing, but a single sheet of white paper costs substantially less and achieves the same results.

Select the 'custom white-balance mode' and shoot the neutral target, i.e. a sheet of white paper, to produce your white-balance preset. Your colour results will be far more natural.

Preventing overcorrection

Be aware that there are times when you may not want to adjust the colour temperature of a scene to make it look like daylight. Shooting a sunset is a good example: you may have waited a long time to see those fiery red and orange colours stretched out across the sky, so you certainly don't want your camera correcting them back to daylight. In this situation it's best to set a 'daylight' manual white balance setting (see box, below left), and capture the colours as they are.

You can also use this principle when shooting interiors, where you want to preserve the colour of light sources such as candles, for instance. Or when you want to use a strong colour cast for creative effect.

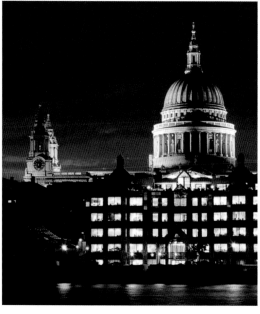

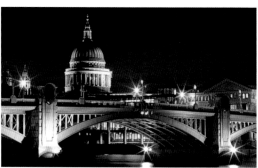

Creative white balance

There is nothing to say that you have to strive for realistic photography all of the time. Using auto white balance, or the appropriate white-balance preset, may make your images appear as if they were shot under daylight conditions, but what about using the 'wrong' white-balance setting to deliberately give your images a colour cast? Shooting grimy urban landscapes with an indoor white balance setting will give images a steely-blue hue that often suits this subject well. You may have to reduce colour saturation slightly if the effect is too strong.

Alternatively, try creating a custom white balance profile using a coloured target, instead of a neutral one. This can come in the form of a coloured piece of paper, or any other plain, coloured surface you can find. Also try taking a reading from the back of your hand (you may have to de-focus slightly to make it look like a plain surface). In portraiture this can have the effect of rendering skin as a milky neutral colour while sending other colours off the scale.

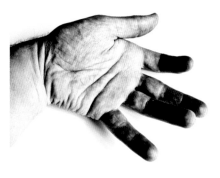

Above: *Using the 'wrong' white-balance preset – in this case the fluorescent setting – has given this image a green cast, which suits its strange and eerie character.*

Left, above and bottom: *Night-time urban photography reveals a riot of colour, with different types of lighting all taking on different colour temperatures. Experiment by shooting with different white-balance settings on your camera and see what the effect is.*

Exposure

Perhaps the most fundamental aspect of photography is exposure: how much light passes into the camera and reaches the sensor. More light falling onto the sensor means lighter pictures; less light means darker pictures.

Since the world we are photographing differs in brightness from scene to scene, the amount of light coming into the camera needs to be varied accordingly. This is done by changing one of three variables: aperture, shutter speed or ISO sensitivity. In automatic exposure mode, the camera takes care of this for you, measuring the intensity of the light in the scene with its built-in exposure meter and selecting an appropriate combination of aperture and shutter speed (ISO is usually, but not always, user-selected). Semi-automatic exposure modes, such as aperture priority and shutter priority, allow you to set one of the variables and the camera will pick the other. In manual mode you can choose both shutter speed and aperture, and compare your choice with what your camera thinks you should be using via the metering display in the viewfinder.

No matter what exposure mode you are using, though, it's important to have an understanding of what shutter speed, aperture and ISO actually are, and what influence they have over your photography.

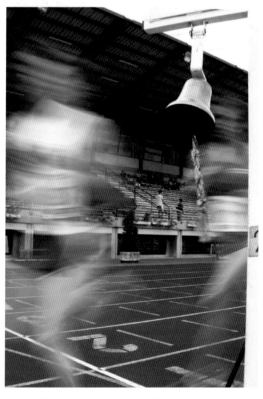

Above: A longer shutter speed of 1/30sec has blurred the passing runner but kept static objects sharp.

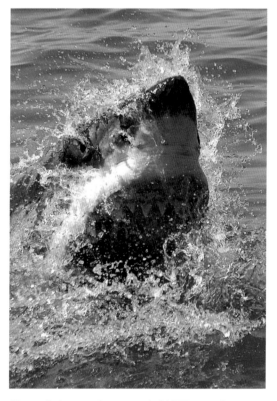

Above: Patience, a shutter speed of 1/500sec and an indulgent skipper all helped to achieve this shot.

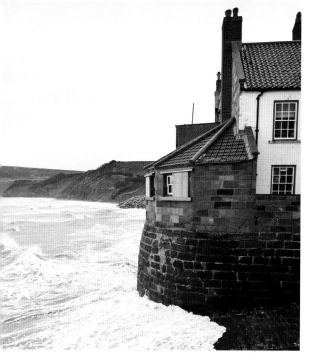

Above: With a shutter speed of 1/1000sec, the moving water is frozen sharp.

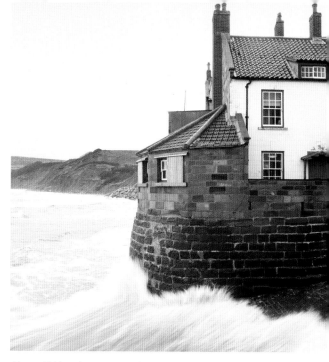

Above: With a shutter speed of 1/15sec, the water blurs as its motion is recorded on camera.

Shutter speed

Light is allowed to pass through the camera and onto the sensor by opening a shutter inside the camera for a moment. How long this shutter is opened for determines how much light passes though, and hence how light or dark the image will be. This is known as the shutter speed.

Shutter speed is measured in terms of fractions of a second, for example ½sec, ¼sec, ⅛sec, etc. These values tend to (almost) halve in length as the shutter speed is shortened – an adjustment known as a stop. Half-stops and third-stops are also common on almost all cameras. The shortest shutter speed you'll find on modern DSLRs is 1/4000sec or 1/8000sec, which is short enough to freeze most fast movement, so objects appear completely stationary. At slower shutter speeds, such as 1/30sec or 1/60sec, if an object has time to move while the shutter is open, it will appear blurred in the direction of movement. This can spoil an otherwise good picture, or can be used for creative effect to convey movement.

Right: This picture of flying fire sparkles was exposed for 3sec, capturing the heat visually radiating from the campfire. A log was moved around the fire to cause the on-going eruption of sparkles.

Do watch out for your own movement, though. If the photographer moves the camera while the shutter is open then everything will blur, an effect known as camera shake. Typically, you only need to be concerned about camera shake when the shutter speed is longer than the reciprocal of the lens's focal length – although this is an approximate rule of thumb. (Telephoto lenses magnify the effect, as they magnify everything else.) So for a standard 18–55mm zoom used at the 35mm setting, you might expect camera shake at shutter speeds longer than 1/30sec – in this case, it would be best to move up to 1/60sec.

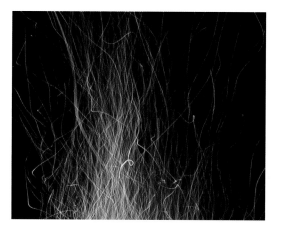

Aperture

We can also change the amount of light passing into the camera by adjusting the size of the hole that it comes through. This hole is known as the aperture and it is also adjusted in stops (sometimes called f-stops when distinguishing aperture and shutter speed adjustments). Decreasing the size of the aperture by one stop halves the amount of light coming through it.

The sizes of aperture available to the photographer depend on the lens in use, and different lenses may offer different sizes. They are marked in a more confusing fashion than shutter speeds, using f-numbers. An f-number is the physical size of the aperture divided by the lens's focal length. Although you don't need to remember this, it does help explain why things appear to be the wrong way around: physically large apertures have small f-number values (eg. f/2.8, f/4, f/5.6), while small apertures have large f-number values (eg. f/16, f/22, f/32). Just to make things even more confusing, each number increases by a factor of 1.4x – the square root of two.

This confusion is best bypassed by forgetting about the origin of f-numbers, and instead committing them to memory. Starting at f/1 (though you won't find many lenses with an aperture this big), the sequence goes:

and so on. The range of your own lens's values will be shorter than this, as it's unfeasible to build a lens that covers all values. Each f-stop lets in half the amount of light as the previous one, meaning you'll need to lengthen the shutter speed by exactly one stop in order to get the same amount of light through to the sensor and achieve the same brightness in a photograph. Third- and half-stop aperture values are available on all lenses, too.

ISO sensitivity

The third variable is the sensitivity of the sensor itself. This is more of an electronic cheat: rather than varying the amount of light entering the camera, altering the camera's sensitivity changes the power of the tiny amplifiers that magnify the signal as it comes off the sensor. So that all camera manufactures and photographers work to the same values, a standard amplification has been agreed, hence why sensitivity is referred to as ISO sensitivity (International Standards Organization), or even just 'ISO' for short. ISO sensitivity is also varied in stops. Again, a doubling in ISO value means the sensor is now twice as sensitive to light as it was. Different cameras offer different ISO sensitivities but a typical scale, in whole stops, goes something like:

| f/1 | f/1.4 | f/2 | f/2.8 | f/4 | f/5.6 |
| f/8 | f/11 | f/16 | f/22 | f/32 | f/45... |

| ISO50 | ISO100 | ISO200 | ISO400 |
| ISO800 | ISO1600 | ISO3200 | ISO6400... |

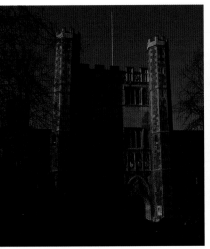

-3 underexposed

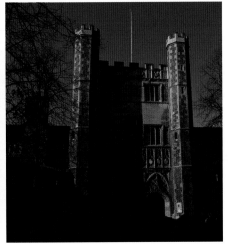

-2 underexposed

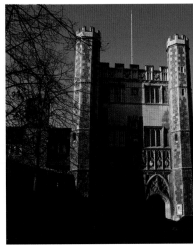

-1 underexposed

Third- and half-stops are also available. As the ISO value increases, so picture quality worsens, with something known as digital noise being evident in photographs. Noise is always there, but is exacerbated by the increased amplification that comes with high ISO settings. It takes on the form of white or coloured speckles in your images, and while it can be tackled with software in post-processing, it's best to avoid it as much as possible in the first place.

Putting everything together

Shutter speed, aperture and ISO have all been designed to work together. By varying each by a stop, the amount of light entering the camera is either doubled or halved (or the sensitivity of the sensor is doubled or halved). This means that opening the lens's aperture from f/8 to f/5.6 has the same effect on the brightness of a picture as lengthening a camera's shutter speed from 1/250sec to 1/125sec. Both actions let in twice as much light.

Likewise, lengthening the shutter speed while closing down the aperture by the same amount of stops will have no net effect on the brightness of the picture. At constant ISO, taking pictures at 1/250sec at f/8, 1/125sec at f/11, and 1/60sec at f/16 will produce exactly the same brightness. Equally, at 1/125sec, pictures taken at ISO200 and f/4, and ISO400 and f/5.6, will be identical in brightness.

This raises the question: why bother changing aperture, shutter speed and ISO, if changing just one of them is enough to influence exposure? The answer is that, while the brightness of a photograph remains unchanged in the above examples, the image taken at a higher ISO will suffer more from noise, and the picture taken at a slower shutter speed may show subject or camera movement. If we want to avoid these problems, we need to take control of ISO and shutter speed.

Even using different apertures has an effect on a picture: with small apertures (eg. f/11 or f/16), more of the picture will be in focus than just the object that has been focused on. Conversely, at large apertures (eg. f/4), focus will be more limited to the area on which you have focused, with objects behind or in front being blurred. This concept is known as depth of field (see page 84).

Below, left to right: The effect of varying exposure on image brightness. Changing either shutter speed, aperture or ISO sensitivity while keeping the other variables fixed will change the brightness of the image. Doubling the shutter speed or ISO brightens or darkens the image by one stop. An equivalent effect is achieved by changing the aperture by 1.4x.

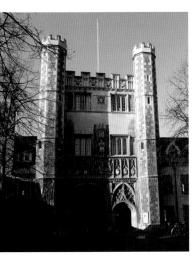 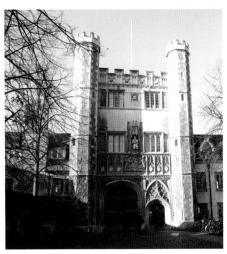 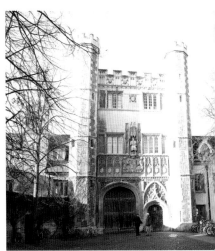

0 correct exposure   *+1* overexposed   *+2* overexposed

SHOOTING THE PERFECT SUNSET

We've learned how to use your camera's exposure metering, white balance and exposure settings, and now it's time to bring all this together to create the perfect sunset photograph.

There is nothing like being in a great place when Mother Nature decides to throw us one of her magical sunsets. Amazing skies and stunning scenery will have you reaching for your camera, and by taking control of white balance, exposure and metering you will be able to do justice to the view with your photography.

Exposing for a sunset is when spot metering really comes into its own. An average metering pattern, such as centre-weighted or evaluative, will try to expose for the foreground and, as a result, over-expose the sky and lose all of that wonderful cloud detail. Using your spot metering, take a meter reading from a patch of sky just next to the sun itself, but not actually on the sun. (Never look directly at the sun through a lens, as you could damage your eyesight.)

Lock this meter reading in using manual mode on your camera. If you don't have a tripod with you then you'll want to pick an aperture and ISO that allow you to hand-hold the camera – so a shutter speed faster than one divided by the film speed. If you do have a tripod, use a smaller aperture to get the best from your lens, and give you more depth of field. Using manual mode will save you having to go back and retake the exposure reading every time you want to shoot a picture. Although, that said, it's worth doing this from time to time because light levels change quickly at either end of the day.

Take a test shot and look at the histogram. You'll see some information right at the white end of the scale (the sun itself) and some peaks at the black end (anything silhouetted). The rest of the tones in the sky should be in between. If not, adjust the exposure manually, or with exposure compensation.

The last setting you want to use for an image like this is auto white balance. The orange and yellow colours in the sky are precisely the reason you are taking the picture, so you don't want the camera trying to cancel this out with a white balance adjustment. Instead, start with a daylight white balance preset, and try using the flash setting to warm things up even more than normal. In fact, if your camera has the ability to set a manual white balance in Kelvin (K), then dial in a low value, around 2,000–3,000K to really warm things up.

Opposite, top left: Shooting with evaluative metering has resulted in a correctly exposed foreground and a bleached-out sky. We need to switch to spot metering and take a reading from a bright area of the sky.

Opposite, top right: Spot reading off the bright clouds has given a better result. But the auto white balance has corrected for the orange colour in the sky.

Opposite, bottom: Using a manual white balance setting has helped keep the natural colour in the sky. Here, a daylight preset has been used.

ESSENTIAL KIT

- DSLR or compact camera with spot metering
- Torch, so you can see what you are doing
- Remote release for shake-free results (or self-timer)
- Tripod for long exposures

TIPS & TRICKS

- Take a spot reading from just next to the sun.
- Use a wide-angle lens and look up to emphasize the perspective of the patterns in the sky.
- Use a telephoto lens to silhouette objects against the sky.

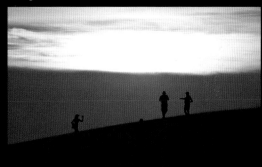

Too bright

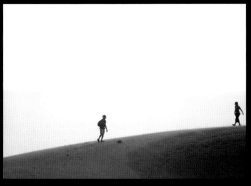

Wrong white balance

Correct settings

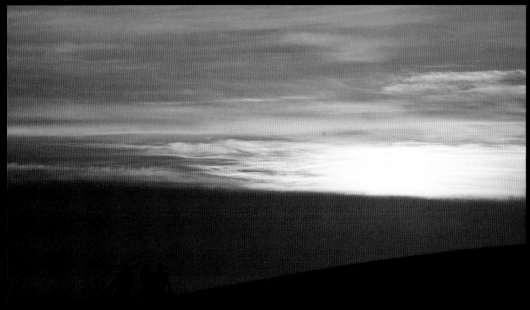

Measuring and assessing **exposure**

Now we know how to control the amount of light entering the camera, and hence the brightness of our pictures, but how do we know how much light we should use in the first place and if we have got the exposure right?

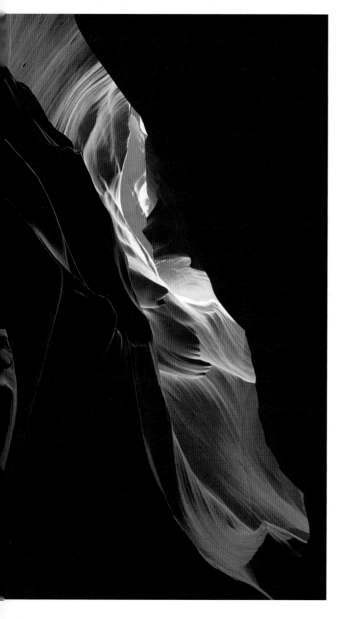

Picking the right combination of shutter speed and aperture is crucial to getting the brightness of a photograph correct. In an automatic or 'scene' exposure mode this is done for you, while in a semi-automatic mode, such as aperture priority, the photographer sets one variable and the camera picks the other. In manual exposure mode, the photographer controls everything. But in all of these cases the correct combinations of aperture and shutter speed need to be known first, either by the camera or by the person making the decisions. And this information comes from the camera's exposure metering system.

All digital cameras have some form of exposure metering technology that measures the intensity of light coming in through the lens. In manual exposure mode, this meter reading is often shown in the form of a graphical display that tells the photographer how far away (in stops) the current values are from the correct exposure. In automatic and semi-automatic modes, the information is used to set this correct exposure value for you.

As cameras have become more advanced, so exposure metering systems have become more and more sophisticated. Nowadays, the evaluative metering systems in DSLRs analyze a scene by splitting it up into dozens of different areas. It is intelligent enough to recognize the most complicated lighting conditions, and often what

Left: *Evaluative or average centre-weighted exposure metering would be influenced by the dark areas on either side of this picture, but by using spot metering to measure light from only the bright central section, we can tell the camera which part of the scene it should prioritize.*

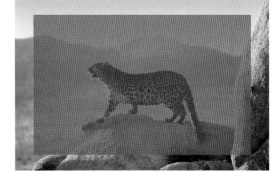

Right: Evaluative metering pattern systems assess a scene by breaking it up into many segments, analyzing the pattern to determine what type of picture is being shot.

type of photograph you are trying to take. You can also select other exposure metering patterns, including centre-weighted, which is an older, more simple technology, and spot metering, which only looks at a small part of the scene.

Spot metering

No matter how advanced exposure metering becomes, it can still make mistakes. Shoot a subject surrounded by black, and the camera will be influenced excessively by the dark surroundings and let in more light than it needs to, causing over-exposure. The same problem happens with light surroundings, for example snowy scenes, when under-exposure can occur. There are a few ways around this issue, but the most common is to use spot metering.

These days nearly all cameras have spot exposure metering. Instead of looking at the overall scene, as centre-weighted and evaluative metering patterns do, spot metering only looks at a small, central part of the frame. You can position your focal point over a part of the scene you think should be perfectly exposed, and the camera will tell you the aperture and shutter speed you need to get this result, regardless of the rest of the picture, which it will ignore in spot metering mode.

This is a useful technique when there is something of average brightness in the frame. All exposure metering is calibrated to mid-grey, which means it will only be 100 per cent accurate when it is looking at this shade, too. Skin tones, pavements, grass and brickwork are all average tones and can be used with a spot meter to obtain an accurate exposure. Put your camera in manual exposure mode and try it.

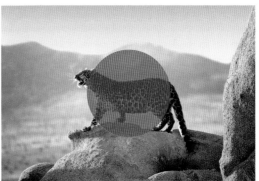

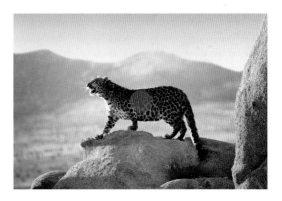

Above, middle: Centre-weighted metering is an older technology that takes an average reading of the whole scene, but emphasizes the centre of the frame. It can get confused more easily, though, and is not as sophisticated as evaluative metering.

Above, bottom: Spot metering only measures exposure from a very small, specific part of the scene, usually in the middle of the frame. This is useful when trying to bias an exposure to a certain part of the frame, which the camera won't recognize with evaluative or centre-weighted metering.

Exposure compensation

In manual exposure mode, correcting for under- or over-exposure is easy – you'll just have to change the aperture or the shutter speed. But is it different if you are using an automatic or semi-automatic exposure mode, where the camera is applying the results of its exposure metering for you? In this case you'll need to find your camera's exposure compensation facility.

Exposure compensation is measured in stops, and most cameras offer the ability to apply this in whole, half- or thirds-stop settings over a range of about two to three stops. Apply positive exposure compensation and the camera will open up the aperture or lengthen the shutter speed, depending on what exposure mode you are using. Apply negative exposure compensation and the opposite will happen.

Histograms and the right exposure

The joy of digital photography is that, once you have taken an image, you can instantly tell if the exposure is right or not by looking at the image on the back of the screen. But simply relying on a visual impression of the picture's brightness may not always give you the right answer. A camera's viewscreen is influenced heavily by the conditions under which you are viewing it. Images viewed in the dark can often look brighter than they really are, meaning you may have under-exposed the shot but don't realize it. On the other hand, bright sunshine makes viewscreen images look too dark, so you won't always see over-exposure.

It's much better to judge exposure from a histogram: a bar chart showing how brightness levels are distributed throughout the picture. You can see a histogram on the back of your

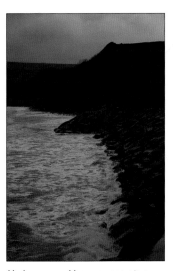

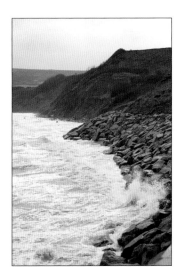

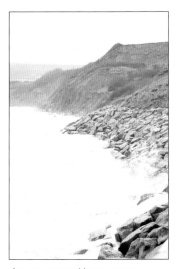

Under-exposed images generate a histogram that is biased towards the left-hand side, reflecting a dominance for darker tones.

For a correctly exposed scene comprising average tones, the histogram information is distributed evenly along the x-axis.

An over-exposed image causes histogram information to skew to the right-hand side, often pouring off the end of the x-axis.

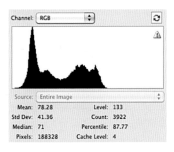

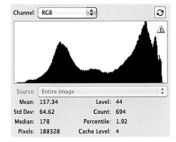

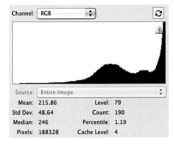

camera straight after the image has been taken – consult your camera's instruction manual for how to do this.

Although they look complicated, reading a histogram is actually very easy. Brightness is plotted on the x-axis, with absolute black on the left-hand side and absolute white on the right. Mid-shades are in between. For an average scene containing some blacks, some whites and a range of tones in between, you would expect to see a histogram reflecting this situation: most of the peaks in the middle of the graph, with some black peaks and some white peaks at the ends. If the information in the graph is skewed towards the white end, then this means you have over-exposed the scene (aperture too large or shutter speed too long). Likewise, if the information is biased towards the black end of the scale then you have

likely under-exposed the scene (too small an aperture, or too fast a shutter speed).

This has to be taken with a pinch of salt, though, as we are talking about an average scene. If you were to take a picture of a white rabbit in a snowy field, you would expect the histogram information to be mostly over to the right-hand (lighter) side of the x-axis, because the picture is dominated by white (or nearly white) tones. Similarly, photographing a black cat in a coal cellar would give you a histogram that is skewed to the left-hand side of the scale. The take-home message is that, when used in combination with some common sense, histograms are a powerful way of measuring the accuracy of an exposure. We'll also see how they can be used extensively in post-production in chapter four (see pages 244–245).

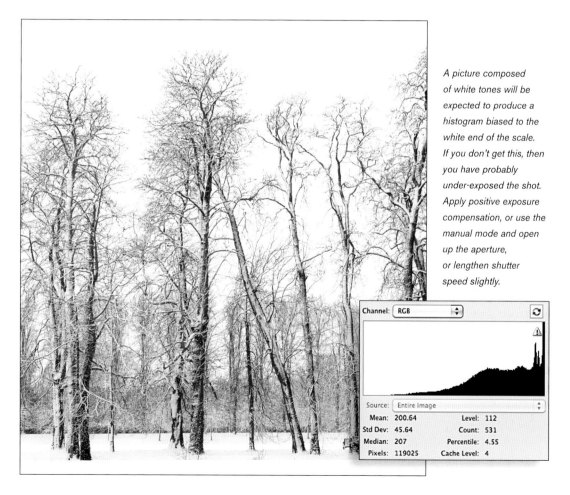

A picture composed of white tones will be expected to produce a histogram biased to the white end of the scale. If you don't get this, then you have probably under-exposed the shot. Apply positive exposure compensation, or use the manual mode and open up the aperture, or lengthen shutter speed slightly.

Channel: RGB

Source: Entire Image

Mean: 200.64 Level: 112
Std Dev: 45.64 Count: 531
Median: 207 Percentile: 4.55
Pixels: 119025 Cache Level: 4

ASSIGNMENT
SHOOTING LIGHT TRAILS WITH LONG SHUTTER SPEEDS

One of the most striking subjects to shoot with a long shutter speed is traffic racing along a road at night, capturing the movement of its lights as coloured streaks through the frame.

Shooting an urban scene at night on a tripod means you can really open your camera's shutter and record the movement going on, most notably the light trails left behind by cars and lorries moving through the frame. It's a common approach to shooting urban scenes, but also one that will let you familiarize yourself with working in manual exposure mode and how movement is influenced by shutter speed.

A tripod (or other support) is mandatory with slow shutter speeds; camera shake would spoil the image. Try using a remote release or self-timer to avoid wobbling the camera with your hand as you press the shutter release.

The best time of the day for this is the ten minutes following sunset, when there is still colour in the sky. Too late and the sky will look black, which is not as interesting as the patterns created by broken cloud against twilight.

Exposure can be hit and miss, but using your camera's manual exposure mode will help. As a starting point, adjust the aperture and shutter speed to the values indicated by the camera's metering system and take a test shot. You should be able to judge the brightness from the rear viewscreen and the histogram display (see page 80), and make any adjustments accordingly.

Once you have the right level of exposure, think about the right combination of aperture and shutter speed. Is the shutter speed long enough to register a complete light trail? A 1sec duration may only record a small streak of light; increasing this to 4sec or even 8sec will let you take in more light from the passing cars.

Composition and timing

Look for the traffic coming down the road and try to capture something interesting coming into the frame. Headlights will leave white trails, rear lights red trails, and indicators dotted yellow lines. A wide-load lorry or emergency vehicle with its warning lights flashing looks superb, as does an aeroplane tracking across the sky. Timing is tricky when firing the camera with a self-timer, so try and reduce the delay to 2sec. Most cameras offer this facility.

It's very hard to visualize these nighttime shots before they've been captured. Keep looking at the results as they come in and evaluate the composition of the scene. The light trails are perfect for leading the eye into the picture, perhaps to a visual treat placed on a compositional third. A cluster of lamp posts or a junction or building, perhaps?

Left: A 1sec exposure time gives light trails that are too short, and don't move through the frame properly.
Nikon D700 with 24–70mm lens, 1sec at f/4, ISO200

ESSENTIAL KIT

- DSLR, or a compact camera with manual mode and long shutter speeds
- Tripod
- Remote release (or self-timer)
- Torch, so you can see in the dark

- Working out exposure can be tough, but taking a spot meter reading from the dusky sky will give you a good starting point.

- If you have to get the exposure wrong, over-expose rather than under-expose. The glare from street lamps is very effective.

- Be aware that the light conditions change very quickly at this time of day. Evaluate exposure constantly.

- Go for a viewpoint that allows you to capture as many types of light as possible – each will be a different colour and add interest to the shot.

Below: Using a longer shutter speed has captured longer trails as the traffic moves through the frame, including the short orange trails of the indicator lights. Nikon D700 with 24–70mm lens, 8sec at f/11, ISO200

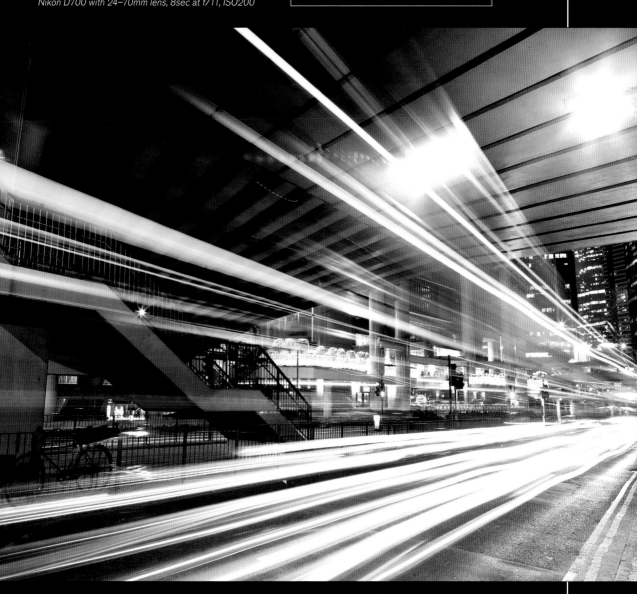

Depth of field

Controlling how much of a picture is actually in focus is a powerful creative tool that is surprisingly easy to get the hang of. Take control of this, and you'll be taking control of your photography.

When we are taking a picture, and we pick a spot to focus on, then, strictly speaking, the image is only in focus at exactly this point. In practice, however, sharpness drops off gradually either side of this focus point, meaning there is an area of 'acceptable sharpness' both in front and behind it. The extent of this as-good-as-in-focus area is known as the 'depth of field'.

The appearance of depth of field is dictated principally by the aperture in use and the lens's focal length. A picture taken with a small aperture will have a depth of field extending further beyond and in front of the point of focus than one taken with a large aperture. Wide-angle lenses also give the appearance of more depth of field compared with telephoto lenses. But when would you want plenty of depth of field? And when would you want to restrict it?

Landscapers tend to shoot at very small apertures (and with wide-angle lenses) precisely because they want to render everything in focus, from the rock in the foreground to the horizon in the distance. In doing this they have to use long shutter speeds to let enough light through to make an exposure of the correct brightness. This is why you always see landscape photographers with a tripod: hand-held shooting with such long shutter speeds would result in blurred images because of camera shake. Similar subject areas that need sharpness throughout the frame also require such an approach – architecture, and particularly still-life.

When it comes to maximizing sharpness, it's important to remember that depth of field extends behind the lens as well as in front of it. When shooting a landscape it's tempting to leave your camera's AF to focus on the horizon, or infinity, but by doing this you are wasting the depth of field behind the focus point. It's better to focus approximately one-third of the way into the picture, and let depth of field take the sharpness out to the horizon. You can check this is so with your camera's depth-of-field preview or 'live view' facility.

Restricting depth of field

There are times when only very little depth of field is required – mainly in portraiture, or when you are trying to draw attention to an object away from its background. For example, when a person is the focus of a picture, you can make them stand out from the background by ensuring they are sharper than what is behind them. Shooting with an aperture of f/4 or f/5.6 will do this, and using a telephoto lens will also help. Using very large apertures means you'll need to be much more accurate with your focusing, as there is less depth of field to cover up any mistakes. As you get closer, so the depth of field reduces further, although this can be used to great creative effect when shooting a portrait – focusing on the eyes and letting the other facial features, such as the ears, nose and mouth, become blurred.

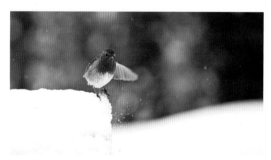

Above: A large aperture has limited depth of field, blurring the background. This often helps to emphasize the subject in the foreground.

Opposite: Large depth of field ensures that all parts of a scene are in focus, from just in front of the camera to infinity.

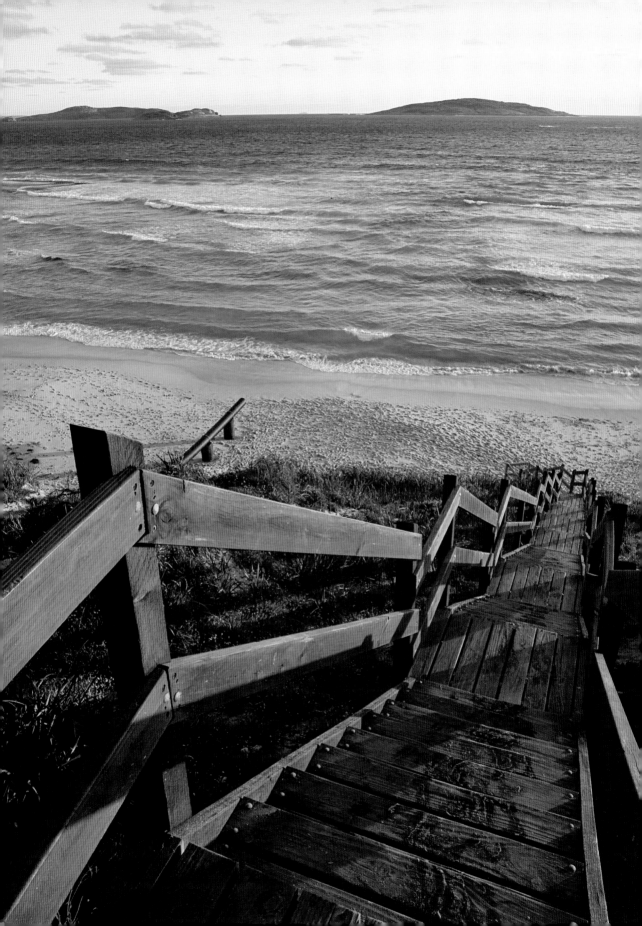

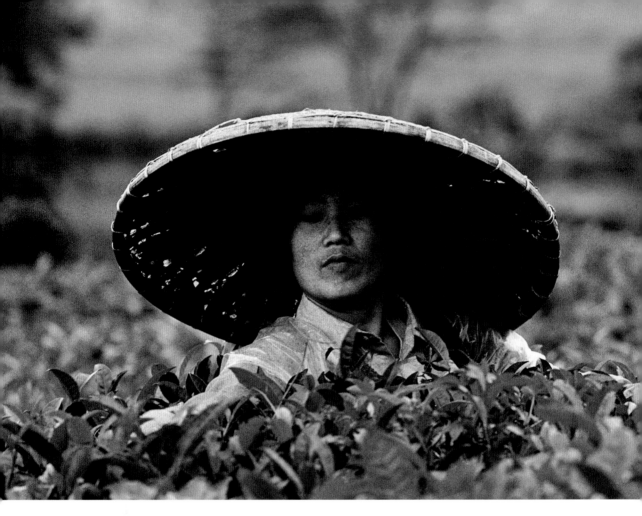

Previewing and calculating depth of field

When you look through the viewfinder of a DSLR, you are seeing the world at the lens's maximum aperture. This is to make the viewfinder image as bright as possible for convenience; when the photo is taken, the aperture quickly stops down to the set value before the shutter opens and the exposure is made. Unfortunately this makes it difficult to see how much depth of field a specific aperture is going to give you when you are composing a photograph, but there are a few features that enable you to preview what will be in focus and what will be blurred.

The oldest and most established of these is the humble depth of field preview button, which, when depressed, stops-down the aperture diaphragm from wide open to the size that it will be when the picture is taken. Looking through a smaller hole means the image in the viewfinder will be darker,

Above: Shooting in aperture priority or manual exposure mode allows you to take control of the size of the lens aperture being used. Here, a large aperture has restricted depth of field and let the subject stand out against a soft, blurred backdrop.

but you will be able to see the extent of depth of field, and predict what will be in focus and what won't. This is a very useful feature for landscapers who want to make sure everything is in focus, or portrait photographers who want to check that a background isn't too sharp, and distracting from their subject.

A more modern update of the depth of field preview is 'live view' mode, where the mirror inside your DSLR flips up out of the way and you can compose your image on the rear viewscreen. Some (but not all) cameras use the working aperture to do this, meaning you'll see for yourself the extent of depth of field in the picture. Consult

Right: Acceptable sharpness extends both in front of and behind the point of focus, so focusing on objects at infinity effectively wastes depth of field. To maximize sharpness in a scene, focus halfway into a picture.

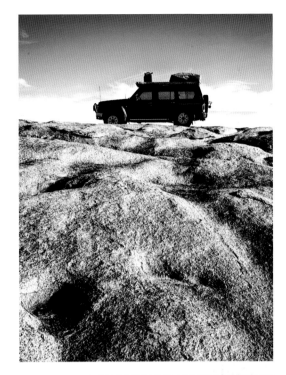

your camera's instruction manual to see if your equipment works in this way.

Some lenses have a depth of field scale, which tells you the distances between which the picture will be in focus. Markings for various apertures are shown either side of the central line that indicates where the lens is focused. Reading off distances at these two points indicate the near- and far-points of acceptable focus for that particular aperture. Not all lenses have this most useful of features, although alternatives do exist. Depth of field charts are available as laminated cards that you can put in your bag, and even in electronic form as calculators on smartphones and laptops.

Compact cameras and depth of field

Those shooting with compact cameras may struggle to notice any difference in depth of field when adjusting aperture manually. This is for two reasons. Firstly, many compact cameras do not have physical aperture diaphragms that change in size. Instead, internal neutral density filters are used to simulate the effect of an aperture. Secondly, in those compacts that do have a physical aperture, the tiny sensor size necessitates the use of very short focal-length lenses in order to get an equivalent angle of view to the human eye – less than 5mm in some cases. Such focal lengths give the appearance of having huge depth of field, which is great for landscapes, travel and general snapshots, but not so good if you want to limit depth of field for creative purposes, such as when shooting portraits.

This is one of the most significant limitations of a compact camera, and one of best reasons to upgrade to a DSLR if you are more serious about photography. That said, some of the newer microsystem cameras (see page 13) offer the sensor size (and hence depth of field control) of a DSLR combined with a much smaller physical size, by omitting the mirror and prism from the DSLR design.

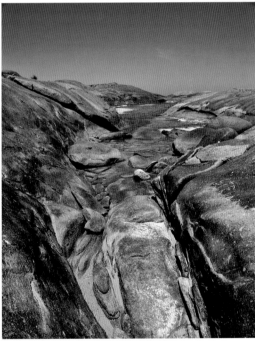

Above and top: Extended depth of field is a landscape photographer's best friend, but using small apertures can require long shutter speeds. Use a tripod and remote release to eliminate blur caused by camera shake.

ASSIGNMENT
SHOOTING A SHALLOW DEPTH OF FIELD PORTRAIT

Although we strive to get as much depth of field in landscape images as possible, when shooting portraiture the situation is different.

Restricting depth of field so the person in the foreground is sharp, but the background is out of focus, is a good way to draw more attention to your subject. An in-focus background competes with the subject for attention, but a blurred one makes them stand out, with an arresting and almost 3D-like quality.

Taking this principle a bit further, we can restrict depth of field even more, so that parts of your subject's face start to become blurred, too. This can be extremely effective, particularly when you ensure that the parts of the face that are in focus are the eyes – after all, it is said that they are the window to the soul.

Shallow depth of field is achieved by shooting with large apertures, and using a telephoto lens can appear to exacerbate this effect. For this reason, professional photographers using full-frame DSLRs or film cameras often shoot with

expensive specialist optics, which have a slightly telephoto focal length of around 85mm and a maximum aperture of f/1.8 or f/1.4. However, for enthusiasts using a cropped sensor DSLR (one with a smaller sensor than full frame), there is a much cheaper and equally effective option.

The humble 50mm lens is one of the cheapest optics out there, and also one of the best. Usually offering top-notch image quality, the 50mm gives almost the same slightly telephoto angle of view as an 85mm lens on a full-frame camera. Such lenses usually have wide maximum apertures, too (f/1.8 or f/1.4), making them ideal portrait lenses. Check both the secondhand listings and your local camera dealer – you'll be surprised at how affordable these lenses can be.

With a 50mm portrait lens fitted on your camera, try focusing on your subject's eyes with the camera's AF-lock function (see pages 56–57) before recomposing for the final picture. Try shooting as wide as f/2 and you'll see that while the eyes stay sharp, your subject's ears, nose and hair will pop out of focus. The background itself should be so blurred it takes on a sort of silky-soft appearance.

Lighting such a portrait is often best done with daylight, though be sure to pick somewhere in shadow rather than in direct sunshine. This can be outside, or indoors by a large window. Although the background will be blurred, try to pick something neutral in colour, or that is darker than the subject you are photographing.

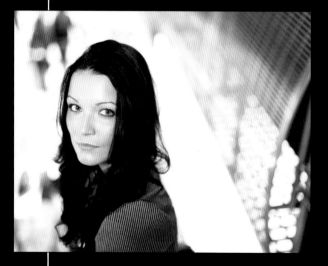

Left: Here, the shallow depth of field separates the subject from the busy background.
Nikon D700 with 85mm lens, 1/125sec at f/4, ISO200

ESSENTIAL KIT

- DSLR camera
- 50mm f/1.8 lens (or wider)
- Reflector to bounce daylight

TIPS & TRICKS

- To avoid having to refocus constantly on the eyes, keep the shutter release half pressed after taking the shot. This will hold the same focus lock.

- Your subject may feel on-edge with you being so near to them. Keep talking to put them at their ease, and show them the results on the back of the camera so they know what's happening.

- Try giving your portrait the black and white treatment (see page 268), which suits this approach very well.

Below: *The very shallow focus fixes the attention firmly on the eyes of the subject.*
Nikon D700 with 85mm lens, 1/250sec at f/2, ISO100

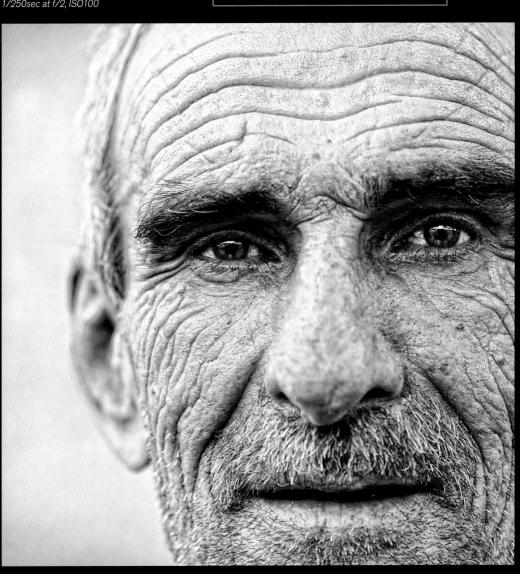

Macro photography

There are a number of ways to get up close and personal with your photography, ranging from specialist optics and other equipment to the macro scene modes found on digital compact cameras. All offer an amazing view on the miniature world.

Getting close up to objects reveals a whole new world of creative opportunities for photography. You can shoot still-life pictures created from objects normally too small to be noticed, or discover textures and patterns that work beautifully as abstract images. Everything starts to look different when you get really close to it – how different depends on how close you get.

The term 'macro' is often applied to close-up photography, although this word actually has a more technical meaning. In true macro photography, the object being photographed is reproduced as life-size or larger on the camera's sensor. For instance, photographing a coin that is 1cm in diameter would produce a 1cm-diameter image of a coin on the sensor – a 1:1 magnification. Most close-up facilities on standard zoom lenses don't come close to this magnification, although adaptors and accessories are available that can help. In this section we'll not be pedantic and will use 'close-up' and 'macro' interchangeably.

Compact cameras and macro

Close-up photography is an area where compact cameras score a victory over their more sophisticated DSLR cousins. Owing to the short focal length of the lenses used in these cameras, they can focus extremely closely, often down to as little as 2cm away from the subject. This closest focus distance is usually found at the wide-angle end of the zoom range, so you do have to watch out for distortion in objects that have a lot of depth to them. Even so, the results that can be achieved with a relatively basic compact camera in macro mode are astonishingly good.

Many compact cameras allow you to either set macro focus yourself manually, or use a macro scene mode, which usually also engages continuous AF to counteract any slight changes in focus distance due to camera movement. As with all close-up photography, the best results come from using a tripod to keep everything in one place.

i Depth of field and macro photography

Depth of field – the region either side of the focus point where a photograph looks sharp – is much less in close-up photography than it is with conventional subjects that are further away. Even at small apertures, such as f/16 or f/22, depth of field only extends a couple of centimetres in each direction, meaning you'll have to focus accurately and position your subject so the areas you want to keep sharp are (nearly) in the same plane.

Right: Because of the proximity to the lens, the flower easily separates from the background, even with an aperture of f/11.

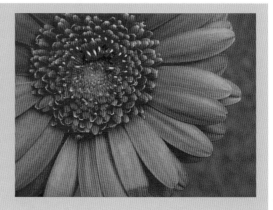

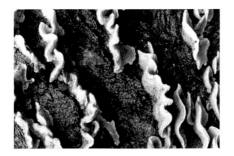

DSLRs and macro lenses

The conventional lenses that come with DSLR cameras do not focus to close enough distances to allow true macro photography. A typical 18–55mm f/2.8 standard zoom lens will focus down to 30cm, giving a magnification of around 1:3. To get any closer than this, you'll need to invest in some extra kit.

For the committed close-up photographer, a dedicated macro lens is a sensible purchase. Although these lenses can be expensive, they offer excellent image quality and a close focus distance that will give you genuine 1:1 magnification. They also focus out to infinity, as any normal lens would, making them excellent tools for still-life photography and portraiture, too.

Macro lenses are available in various focal lengths, from a standard 50mm right up to a reasonable telephoto 180mm. Telephoto macro lenses give 1:1 magnification at a greater distance, which can be useful if you are photographing wildlife: the increased working distance will enable you to work without scaring your subject.

Nowadays macro lenses come with fast AF motors and sometimes image stabilizers to help with camera shake, but these features are superfluous if you shoot macro correctly. The range over which a macro lens can focus is enormous, and it's better done manually than by relying on your camera's AF. A tripod is a must when using a macro lens – as well as preventing camera shake at slow shutter speeds, it will help maintain a constant camera-subject distance. Depth of field in close-up photography can be tricky.

Close-up on a budget

There are cheaper options than a macro lens for close-up photography with DSLRs. Supplementary close-up lenses screw into the

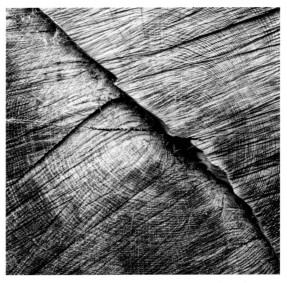

Above: A monochrome shot of a freshly-cut slab of wood, photographed in soft light with a macro lens.

Above left: An extension tube increases magnification and allows you to get closer to the subject.

lens's filter thread, and act as a high-quality magnifying glass, enlarging the image. These come in various strengths, labelled +1, +2, +3, etc., and while they don't offer quite the same image quality as a macro lens, they do cost around a tenth of the price, making them an excellent way to get started in close-up photography. Be aware that when a close-up lens is fitted, the lens won't focus to infinity anymore, and so must be removed for normal photography.

Extension tubes are another way of getting closer to your subject. Acting as a spacer between the camera body and the lens, an extension tube moves the lens elements further away from the sensor than the lens's own mechanism can do on its own. This enables closer focusing and gives a slight magnification, at the expense of a dimmer image, meaning each aperture on the lens is less than it was – making a tripod even more handy to avoid camera shake.

There are various types of extension tube, offering differing levels of automation. Some only act as a spacer, while others have electrical contacts to allow the same level of exposure metering and AF as normal.

ASSIGNMENT
CLOSE-UP EYESCAPES

Have you ever looked at someone's eyes? Really looked closely? The different patterns and colours in the iris make each one totally unique – and a great subject for some close-up fine-art photography.

To get the effect looking right (and not like something you'd see in a medical textbook), we'll need a combination of clever composition, good lighting, and some post-production work in Adobe Photoshop, or similar software.

The first thing to do is to work out how you are going to get up close and personal with your subject. Virtually every compact camera has a macro mode, although you'll have to get very close to your subject's eyeball with it to fill the frame. Be careful you don't block out all the light you need to get a good image. With a DSLR, there are a few options that will enable you to get in close. A dedicated macro lens is best, but also very expensive. Try a supplementary close-up filter that screws on the end of your camera's standard zoom lens, or a 2x extension tube. Position yourself as centrally as you can to the eyeball, and use a smallish aperture to get enough depth of field to help you with focusing.

Lighting this type of picture is difficult. We'll want to remove whatever reflection is in the eyeball later on at the post-production stage, so it's best not to have hugely complicated lighting reflections in the iris area. Instead, aim for a single catchlight in the solid black pupil, which you can create by setting up a small, single-point light source some distance away. Wrap a cone of black paper around a household spotlight or off-camera flashgun, for instance. If you use flash for a light source, watch out for your subject blinking. And don't make them hold their eyes open for too long – it's not very comfortable, and watery eyes don't look as good, either.

Post-production

Removing the reflections from a photograph like this may seem daunting, but it's actually simple enough. The Clone Stamp tool in Photoshop (and many other image editing applications) lets you copy one area of the image and paint it over another (see page 314), so all we need to do is paint over the reflected highlight in the pupil with some black pupil from elsewhere in the image. In chapter four we'll look at tips and tricks for effective cloning, including the Healing tool, which copies texture but leaves colour unchanged.

We only want the iris and pupil for our fine-art image, and we can crop away the rest of the image at the software stage, too. Draw a circular selection around the iris (done with the elliptical Marquee tool in Adobe Photoshop or Elements), then invert the selection (Select > Inverse) and feather (Select > Modify > Feather...), before hitting the delete key to clear away the rest of the image to the background colour, which is best set to white. Feathering removes the selection's hard, definite edge and replaces it with a smooth transition over a number of pixels – enter a value of 15–20 to get you started.

Output

If you shot the image with enough resolution, and didn't have to crop too much, then you should have a large enough file to make a nice big print. Why not check out the poster printing services offered by one of your local high street photo labs? Alternatively, you could turn the project into a collection, shooting an eyescape for everyone you know and arranging them in a grid.

ESSENTIAL KIT

- DSLR or compact camera
- Close-focusing attachment or macro lens
- Light source
- Computer with image editing software

TIPS & TRICKS

- Try to position the light so it is some way away, but shining over one of your shoulders. This means the small pin-point highlight reflection should be in the pupil, not the iris.

- When you are more proficient with post-production and editing, try increasing the saturation and contrast of the iris.

Below: The original image before Photoshop work.

Bottom: A selection of eyescapes cut out against a white background.

Nikon D700 with 105mm macro lens, 1/200sec at f/16 with flash, ISO200.

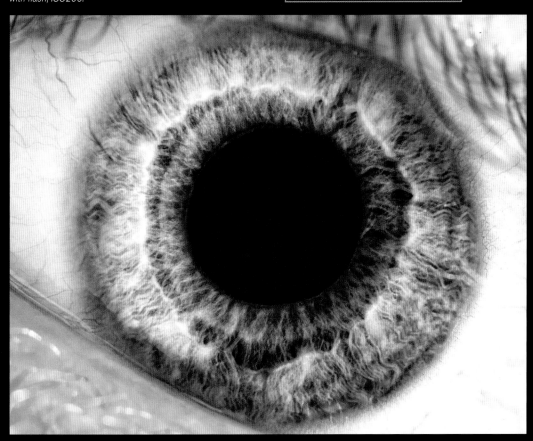

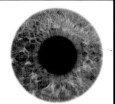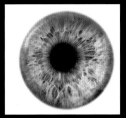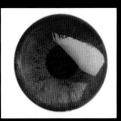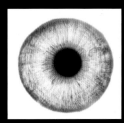

Long **exposures**

Photographers usually try to keep shutter speeds fairly fast, so we can hand-hold the camera without blurring the image with camera shake. But there is another way.

Put your camera on a tripod and you can use as long an exposure as you like. Moving subjects will blur, while static objects will remain sharp, with the extent of the blur dictated by the length of the shutter speed in use. A long enough exposure time may even render fast moving objects completely invisible!

Shooting at nighttime

For the blindingly obvious reason that there isn't much light around at nighttime, long-exposure photography is very popular in the hours following sunset. Cityscapes take on a new appearance when lit by electric lighting, with each type of light giving a slightly different colour. Moving objects,

Below: For moving subjects in front of static backgrounds use exposure times longer than 1/15sec.

like cars, leave trails through the picture where their lights move through the scene while the shutter is open. Headlights leave white streaks, rear lights red streaks and indicators dashed yellow lines, as they blink on and off.

The best time to shoot this type of photography isn't so much when the sun has set completely, but rather in the ten minutes just after sunset, when there is still a purple glow in the sky. This will lower the overall contrast level (which can be huge in night scenes) and will enable you to record some amazing detail in the sky.

Practical considerations

The biggest problem when shooting long exposures is camera shake. Even on a tripod it's possible to ruin an otherwise decent picture because of camera movement. Always ensure that

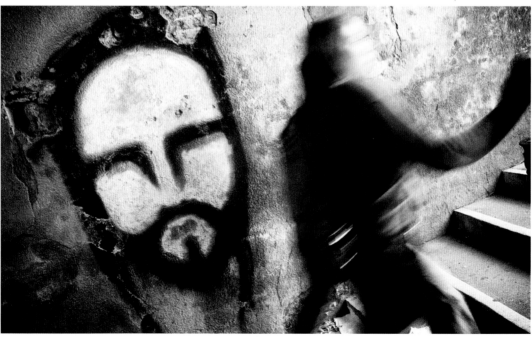

the tripod is on a sturdy surface that is free from vibrations. Don't touch the camera or the tripod during the exposure – an accidental kick with your feet will be enough to produce blurred results.

It's also important to trip the shutter release without wobbling the camera, which is difficult since doing this involves physical contact with your DSLR or compact. A simple solution is to use the camera's self-timer. This technique will let any vibrations from physical contact subside before the shutter opens and the exposure begins, with the only disadvantage being that timing the moment of exposure with another event (a passing car, a firework, etc.) is very difficult. For more flexibility use a remote release, which connects to the camera via a wire, infrared or radio waves.

To cut out vibration completely during long exposures, some DSLR cameras sport a mirror-lock feature, which aims to cut out the vibration (or 'mirror slap') caused by movement of the reflex mirror (that lets you see through the lens when looking through the viewfinder) before the shutter opens. The first press of the shutter release raises the mirror, while the second opens the shutter and records the picture.

How long is long?

The length of shutter speed you need in low-light situations depends largely on the type of effect you are aiming for. The longer the exposure time, the greater the blur. Too long and fast-moving subjects will disappear altogether and fail to register. But shutter speeds that are too short will just make objects look a bit fuzzy and not convey a sense of motion, which is what this technique is all about.

The key is experimentation – try a mixture of speeds, selecting the right aperture to match, until you get an effect you are pleased with. You'll see decent motion blur in most moving objects at 1/8sec or longer. Most DSLRs can time a long exposure up to 30sec in length, but if you want any more than this the 'B' setting (which stands for bulb) must be used. This will keep the shutter open for as long as you keep the shutter release depressed – although in reality this needs to be a remote release, in order to prevent the camera from moving during the exposure.

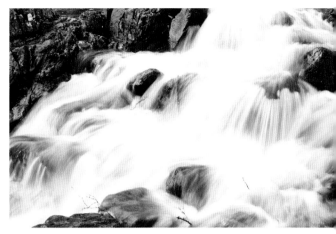

Above: *Moving water blurs when photographed with a long shutter speed, taking on a smooth, velvet-like look.*

Panning

Although a tripod is required for totally sharp pictures, hand-held long exposures can also be fun if a more abstract approach to photography is wanted. With your camera in shutter priority mode, experiment photographing lights at night with shutter speeds of 1–2sec, and you should get patterns that mimic the movement of the camera during the exposure. In fact, purposely waving the camera around will produce spectacular, if random, results.

With shorter shutter speeds of around 1/8sec, it's possible to follow a moving object so that it remains sharp during the exposure while the background blurs. This technique – called panning – is an excellent way to covey speed and motion in a photograph, and is used extensively in sports and action photography.

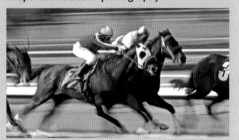

Above: *Panning at 1/30sec has worked well with these moving horses. Pan smoothly from left to right and gently squeeze the shutter release.*

Creative **flash** photography

In the past, the principal use of on-camera flash was to enable hand-held photography in dim conditions, although the huge improvement in image quality at high ISO sensitivities means that this is not always necessary nowadays. However, there are still many creative opportunities open to flash-equipped photographers, and the easy-to-use flash-metering systems in today's DSLRs mean these techniques are open to everyone.

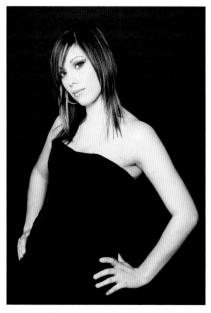

Above: Using off-camera flash means you can control exactly where light is coming from, as well as its brightness and character.

Bounce and off-camera flash

The light from any on-camera flash pointing straight at a subject is generally ugly and unflattering. It's harsh, and leaves hard shadows on both faces and background. The easiest way to avoid this is to bounce flash off the ceiling or a wall, which turns the hard, direct light source into a softer, indirect one, with bounced light from all directions filling in the shadows.

Taking the flash off-camera completely and positioning it elsewhere is also a great way of getting more creative with flash. Positioning the light source above and to the side gives portraits a more sophisticated look, and the flash can often be triggered using a DSLR's built-in flash as a wireless trigger.

Fill-in flash

It may seem odd to use flash on a bright sunny day, but this is when a blip of light from your camera's built-in flash unit, or an add-on flashgun, can really help your photography. The technique is often called fill-in flash because this is exactly what the light from the flash is doing: filling in the harsh shadows caused by bright sunlight. Natural daylight is still the dominant light source, but it's being supported by the flash.

Fill-in flash is easy to use. Simply use your camera in one of the normal exposure modes (aperture priority, program, manual, etc.) and set the flash to fire automatically with TTL (through the lens) exposure control. The camera's metering systems will balance the two types of light for you.

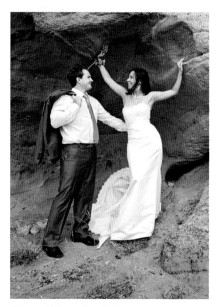

Above: Using a fill-in flash on a sunny day can brighten the darker lines and shadows created by direct sunlight and give a more even result.

Sync speed

The shutter in a DSLR camera is made up of two curtains. When the shutter release is depressed, the first curtain moves out of the way to expose the sensor for the required amount of time. The second curtain then moves across to block the sensor again and ends the exposure. The camera re-cocks the shutter mechanism by winding both curtains back where they came from, and the camera is ready to shoot again. This type of shutter is called a focal plane shutter and provides accurate shutter speeds from 30sec to right up to 1/8000sec with some cameras.

However, as speeds get increasingly fast, so the first curtain doesn't quite have time to reach the end of its run before the second one starts out. The net effect is the same, with the sensor being exposed for the correct amount of time, but as speeds get faster the two curtains can be thought of as providing a slit that moves across the sensor, exposing a little of it at a time.

This only becomes a problem with flash. Because the flash duration is so short, and there is only one flash to illuminate the whole exposure, we tend to see a band of flash exposure at high shutter speeds, instead of even exposure over the frame. The highest shutter speed with which we can use flash is the fastest shutter speed where the second curtain doesn't start moving before the first has completed its journey, and is called the camera's flash sync speed. Typically this is 1/200–1/250sec, although older cameras have sync speeds as low as 1/125 or 1/60sec.

Slow-sync flash

This follows the same principles as fill-in flash, but using flash as the dominant light source and natural, ambient light as a back-up. This technique is often useful at nighttime, when you want to expose the foreground with flash and preserve other details in the background. In bright daylight you can even dial down the daylight for a mean and moody look while leaving flash exposure set correctly.

High-speed flash

When using fill-in flash on a sunny day, it's not uncommon to encounter problems with the camera's shutter speed being too high. If the conditions are bright enough to cause the shutter speed to exceed the camera's flash sync speed, it's not possible to use fill-in flash without seeing a shadow-like band over part of the frame. The problem is particularly prevalent with large apertures, which necessitate the use of fast shutter speeds.

To get round this issue, some flashguns have a high-speed flash sync mode (sometimes also called FP flash) which uses multiple light pulses to illuminate your subject, rather than just a single flash. Some range is sacrificed, although most modern flashes should still be able to provide good fill-in flash in most situations using this method.

Stroboscopic flash

Firing multiple flash pulses in rapid succession is also useful for stroboscopic effects. Combined with a long shutter speed and dark background, this can be used to capture a moving object many times in the same shot as it moves across the frame.

This feature is available on many advanced flashguns. You'll be able to set the number of flashes and the frequency (in Hz) of the output.

Below: This photo combines a burst of flash with a long exposure to record the trails of light from the torches hidden behind the model's back.

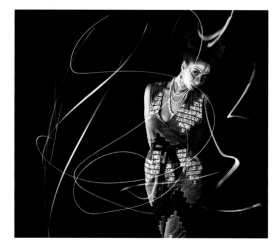

ASSIGNMENT
FLASH-LIT, SMOKY, STILL-LIFE IMAGES

You can create stunning abstract photographs with just some joss sticks, a piece of black background card and an off-camera flashgun.

The light from a flash gun is delivered in a very brief burst, making it ideal for freezing motion. It's also very directional when used off-camera. We can take advantage of both of these qualities with this assignment, which uses a burst of flash, at right angles to the camera, to create a stunning still-life image of smoke trails.

Most flash guns can be triggered off-camera by plugging them into your camera's sync socket, and you can buy the cables and accessories you need to do this at your local camera store very cheaply. That said, it's worth checking if your flash gun can be triggered off-camera wirelessly. Some require a special infrared or radio trigger to be mounted on the camera to do this, while others simply take a queue off the camera's built-in flash, which can be throttled back so it doesn't influence the picture at all.

To create the smoke in these photos, we've used a joss stick and put a black background behind the smoke so it stands out. This background needs to be some way behind the smoke to avoid the flash lighting this up too, and turning it grey. The flash should be positioned fairly near to the smoking joss stick, pointing up to illuminate it.

When it comes to exposure settings, choose a low ISO to maintain image quality and a small aperture to give you some depth of field, and ensure that the smoke will be sharp even if it blows around a bit. Set the shutter speed to the sync speed of your camera – usually 1/200sec or 1/250sec. Any slower than this and you run the risk of recording ambient room light, too, which will spoil the flash effect.

Focusing on a subject like this is difficult. You can't really see the smoke until the flash goes off, and this is too brief to allow you or the camera's AF to focus on it. A good trick is to include the glowing joss stick at the bottom of the frame and focus on this, instead. You can assume the smoke will be approximately the same distance away, and depth of field from the small aperture will take care of any difference. You can crop out the joss stick later with your image-editing software.

Once you are happy with your set-up, keep taking pictures until you fill up your memory card, or get bored. It's impossible to predict or influence what the smoke patterns will do, but it's fun to experiment by moving around the smoke trail, or blowing it gently, to make different shapes and patterns.

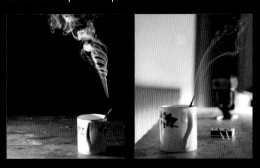

Above: A smoking joss stick was supported inside a cup and smoke illuminated with a standard flash gun used off-camera and positioned to the side.

Opposite, main picture: A swirl of smoke lit up brightly against the black, unlit background.
Nikon D700 with 24–70mm lens, Nikon SB900 flashgun, 1/250sec at f/8, ISO200

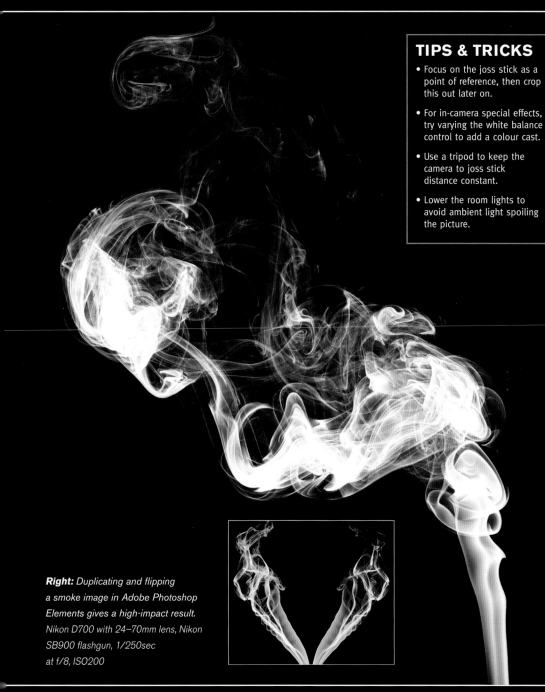

ESSENTIAL KIT

- DSLR with external flash socket, hotshoe or wireless flash facility
- Joss stick
- Cables and/or hotshoe adaptor for non-wireless cameras
- Flash gun capable of off-camera use
- Tripod
- Black background
- Memory card
- A bit of patience

TIPS & TRICKS

- Focus on the joss stick as a point of reference, then crop this out later on.

- For in-camera special effects, try varying the white balance control to add a colour cast.

- Use a tripod to keep the camera to joss stick distance constant.

- Lower the room lights to avoid ambient light spoiling the picture.

Right: Duplicating and flipping a smoke image in Adobe Photoshop Elements gives a high-impact result. Nikon D700 with 24–70mm lens, Nikon SB900 flashgun, 1/250sec at f/8, ISO200

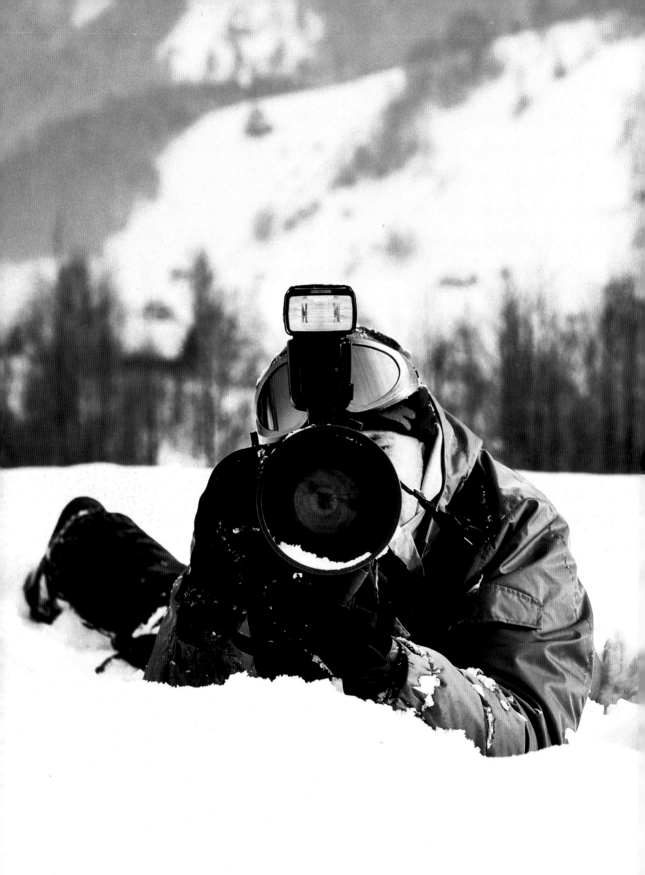

advanced
photography

When you start using your camera you'll quickly identify the kind of photography that you have a talent for. Taking pictures of people requires a very different approach to that used by landscapers, sports photographers or wildlife experts, and we'll look more at these techniques in this chapter.

Portraits and people

With the unstoppable rise of social media, portraits have become probably the most widely used shot taken nowadays, ranging from formal sit-down photographs to snaps of the family on holiday. And it's easy to improve the way we shoot these pictures, too, with a bit of thought about composition, posing and lighting.

You often hear people complain that they don't like having their picture taken, with many ranking the experience up there with going to the dentist or doing their tax return. And to be honest, given the mistakes that many photographers make when shooting portraits, it's not surprising they feel this way. If you don't show someone looking their best in a portrait, they are unlikely to enjoy the experience.

Poor composition and camera technique can lead to all manner of issues: trees and lampposts growing out of subjects' heads; emphasized double-chins and pronounced noses; distracting backgrounds that compete with your subject for

Below: A longer telezoom lens helps to take quick snaps that can quite often end up being much better than posed shots, especially if the subject is shy or self-conscious.

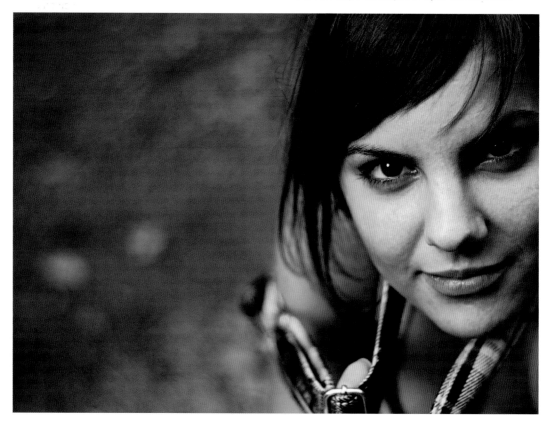

attention. But some simple technical fixes and the right gear selection can really help, as can developing a good rapport with your subject. After all, a portrait should bring over something of your subject's character, and the more they relax in front of the camera, the more likely this is to happen.

Above: *A telezoom, like this Nikon 55–300mm, is a great tool for portraiture, letting you keep your distance so you don't crowd your subject.*

Choosing the right gear

When selecting equipment for a portrait shoot, the first thing to think about is which lens you are going to use. Classic portraits shot on a short telephoto lens look better than those shot on a wide-angle. We have already seen that telephoto lenses compress perspective (see page 64), and when this is applied to a subject's face, the result is very flattering. Big noses and chins look smaller, and bone structure looks better. Depth of field is also more shallow with a telephoto lens (see pages 84–87), making it easier to blur the background behind your subject, making them stand out.

This means using the more telephoto end of your camera's standard zoom lens and standing back from your subject, rather than the wide-angle end and standing closer. This approach will also mean you don't crowd the person you are photographing, which should make them feel more comfortable. In fact, if you have a telezoom then using this may also yield good results.

Professional portrait shooters use specialist lenses for this type of work, such as an 85mm f/1.4 prime lens on a full-frame digital camera, but these can be very costly items. Fortunately, for those of us shooting on a cropped-sensor DSLR (APS-C-size, or Four-Thirds), the humble 50mm f/1.4 or f/1.8 will do an almost identical job and cost a fraction of the price. No portraitist should be without one!

Reflectors

Reflectors are mostly circular, collapsible and come with their own storage bag. Usually one side is silver and the other side white. You can also create your own out of anything that reflects light: aluminium foil on cardboard, white poster board, foamcore board: the only limits are your imagination and how much you can carry. A reflector shines additional light on your subject to fill in dark shadows cast by harsh light.

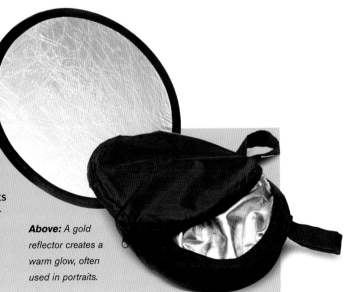

Above: *A gold reflector creates a warm glow, often used in portraits.*

Headshots and formal portraits

The most simple form of portrait, and possibly the most formal, too, is the headshot. This can be very basic indeed when a simple form of identification is all that is needed (think business headshot or passport snap), but the headshot can also be very creative, too. Shooting with as little depth of field as possible is a popular approach, maintaining sharp focus on the eyes and letting everything else fall gently out of focus. To do this you'll need to use as big an aperture as possible: f/2.8 or wider, ideally. If you can select the autofocus point that your camera uses, choose just one and use it to lock focus on your subject's eyes before you take the picture.

Your own position is as important as that of your subject when shooting a headshot. You'll want to be approximately on their level or slightly higher when shooting, so if they are sitting, then you should be too. Try positioning them centrally in the viewfinder to emphasize the symmetry in their face. Or position them over one side of

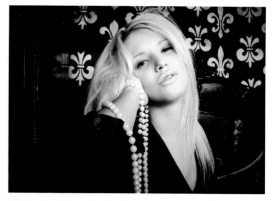

Above: *An interesting background can be an effective way to create an overall feel for your subject and the surroundings.*

the frame and have them turn their body away from you, with their head looking back to the camera. Don't forget profile pictures, either, where your subject is not looking at the camera but is positioned side-on. It's an often overlooked pose, but can be very powerful indeed.

Studio headshots

If you want to explore headshots in studio conditions but don't know how to start, the most important things to bear in mind are neutral backgrounds and a soft light. If you don't have professional lighting, expensive softboxes or indeed proper backgrounds, you can still achieve professional results if you keep it simple.

A few inches of duct tape and the largest sheet of coloured paper you can get hold of (or tape two or three sheets together) as well as a shady location on a sunny day, or out in the open on an overcast day, will give you everything you need.

Tape the paper sheets to a wall or ladder and attach it to the floor, and your seamless backdrop is installed. This will provide you with a cheap way to start exploring studio pictures. You will get good backgrounds for your pictures, with few shadows and good, even light.

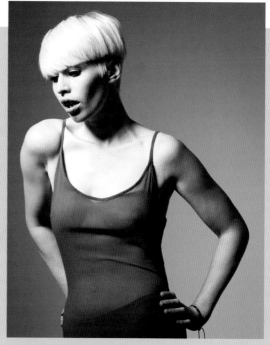

Above: *The soft light here was achieved with the help of a white reflector and off-camera flash.*

Lighting

When it comes to lighting portraits, it's best to rely on external light sources, such as windows or electric lights, rather than the built-in flash on your camera. Or move the shoot outside and use daylight, preferably from a bright but cloudy sky. Daylight is a great light source for people pictures, but try to avoid direct sunlight, which is too harsh and produces unflattering shadows on the face.

A popular approach is to find a large window indoors and sit your subject near it, either to one side or behind the photographer so it's directly facing them. If necessary, you can use a reflector (a large sheet of white card or silver foil will do) to lighten the darker side of the face.

Environmental portraiture

Virtually the complete opposite of the headshot is the environmental portrait, where your subject is shown in the context of their surroundings. Not only is much more of the person usually shown, but their surroundings and background are featured as part of the picture, too. The idea is to tell the story of your sitter – to bring across something of their character or profession into the picture. Here, you may find you need a wider-angle lens (a zoom will enable you to be more flexible) and while your sitter will still be the main focus of the picture, they won't be the only thing to look at.

Below: *Tell the story of your subject by including something about them in the shot. This could be a prop, or simply the location of the shoot.*

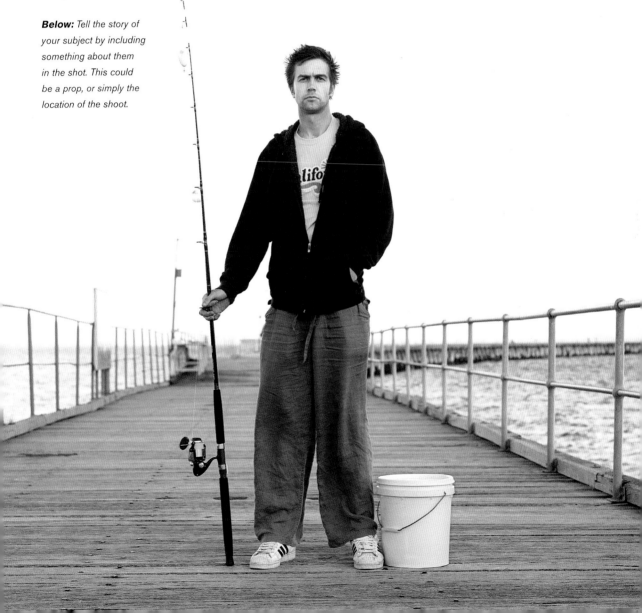

FOCUS ON
FORMAL PORTRAITS
WOLF MARLOH PEOPLE PHOTOGRAPHER

Born in 1971 in Germany, **Wolf Marloh** worked in new media before becoming a photographer in 2002. He assisted Clive Arrowsmith for three years and now works from his studio in central London as a portrait photographer.

What attracts you to portrait photography?
I love meeting new and interesting people and it seems a good excuse. Taking a portrait is like breaking into a safe. If you use explosives, you'll probably burn the contents. So you've got a stethoscope against the steel, and you're slowly going through different combinations. And then you hear a subtle 'clank' and you know you've got it. Now the door opens all by itself. You've got the shot. It's an exciting and rewarding process. Though sometimes, the safe is empty.

What path did you take?
I planned to be the new Ansel Adams and started shooting landscapes on 5 x 4. But as much as I loved trekking through the wild at 5am to catch the first light, I also love being with people. And I needed to make a living, which isn't easy as a fine-art photographer. So I assisted a fashion photographer for three years, and focused on portraits.

How do you relax your clients?
There's no magic trick. People relax on camera when they stop thinking about themselves. You take charge, and make yourself the centre of their focus. When I photographed Lord Norman Tebbitt, I was rather tense myself. He doesn't suffer fools gladly. He walked in and said, "I get nervous with these things. You'll tell me what to do, won't you?" He turned out to be most charming. I learned then that it was my responsibility to take control. It's you who sees the picture, so you need to know what to do.

How do you prepare?
With high-profile subjects, there's no margin for error. Arrive early. Double up on kit. What do you do if the camera malfunctions, the flash bulb blows, the memory card doesn't read? Be prepared. Think through everything, and be ready to throw it all overboard. I was promised ten minutes alone with Kofi Annan on a balcony with a semi-transparent cover for perfect light. I waited. He was in an important meeting and arrived three hours late. The sun had gone and he was in a rush. I had one minute. His whole entourage stood by as I drew a dark curtain behind him, used on-camera flash, bounced it off a wall, said something silly and took three shots: one surprised, one smiling and one serious.

How do you deal with celebrities?
A celebrity is like anyone else, just famous. I carefully researched my first high-profile clients, but it made it more difficult. What you read in magazines about people is generally either a PR version of themselves, or a bag of lies (or both). It just clogs up your mind. Treat them like you would treat anyone else. If you are yourself, they will respond by coming out of their shell.

Your dream subject, dead or alive?
The first man on the moon, on location. Failing that, Aung San Suu Kyi in a democratic Burma. And my parents in their twenties.

Kit list for urgent assignments
- 25-megapixel camera, and back-up body
- Apple MacBook laptop computer
- Two flash heads, plus stands and brollies
- 85mm f/1.4 prime lens
- Light meter
- Various sundries: gaffer tape, crocodile clips, extension leads, batteries, etc.

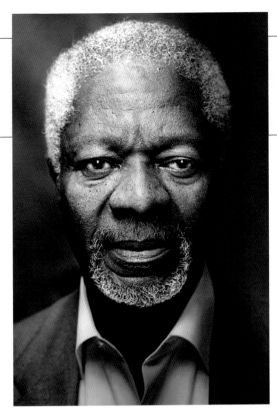

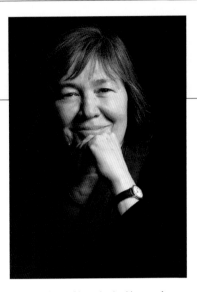

Above: Clare Short, in the House of Commons, London, 2006.

Left: Kofi Annan, in his hotel in Alexandria, Egypt, 2007.

Below: Philip Pullman, at home, 2006.

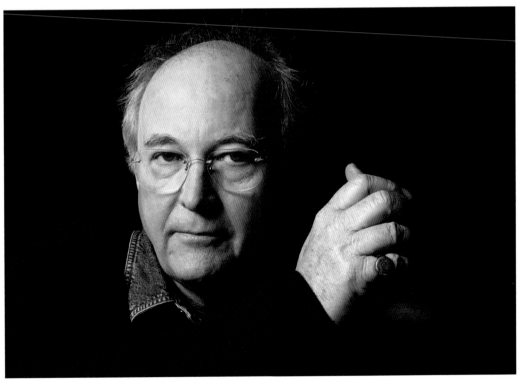

ASSIGNMENT
SHOOTING AN
ENVIRONMENTAL PORTRAIT

Tell the story of your subject by making use of their surroundings in your portrait.

I f a photographer is aiming to show something of their sitter's character in a photograph, they couldn't do better than shooting an environmental portrait. This could be in their place of work, or somewhere that is important to them in their personal life. It could tell the story of a sport or hobby that they are passionate about, or something that they are famous for.

When shooting this assignment, the first thing you need to do is identify your location and pay it a visit on your own, before the shoot date. Take your camera and explore the options for a picture without the pressure of anyone else looking over your shoulder. What does the scene look like through different lenses and at different zoom settings? What is the lighting like? Will you need a tripod to steady the camera?

This research will pay off when your subject is present, as you won't have to worry about technical factors and can give the person in front of the camera all your attention. Explain to them what you are trying to do (it might not be obvious) and watch how they interact with the environment when they are not being photographed; this will give you an idea of how to ask them to pose if they need some direction.

Right: Flash and ambient light were mixed in this location portrait, with the flash being positioned off to one side to cast shadows along the ground.

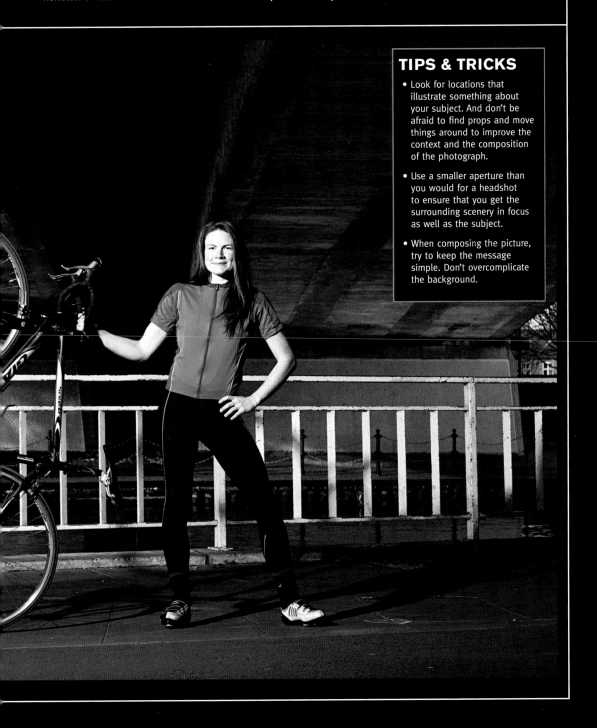

ESSENTIAL KIT

- Camera with manual control
- Wide-angle or standard lens
- Reflector or flash
- Tripod, to allow long exposure times
- Props if necessary

TIPS & TRICKS

- Look for locations that illustrate something about your subject. And don't be afraid to find props and move things around to improve the context and the composition of the photograph.

- Use a smaller aperture than you would for a headshot to ensure that you get the surrounding scenery in focus as well as the subject.

- When composing the picture, try to keep the message simple. Don't overcomplicate the background.

Self-portraits

Something all photographers should do from time to time is turn the camera on themselves and shoot a self-portrait. This can be any style you want (environmental, headshot, etc.) and in some ways is easier than photographing someone else. You certainly won't have any problems with photographer-subject communications!

What is tricky, though, is triggering the camera and getting the timing right. The most obvious way of doing this is to use the camera's self-timer to fire the shutter. All cameras have this facility: press the shutter button and you have a delay (usually ten seconds) to get back in front of the camera and into position. The only trouble is that you have to do this for every frame, so you'll be getting up and down all the time, and it can be hard to predict the exact moment when the camera will fire. Furthermore, the camera will autofocus when you press the shutter button, so if you are shooting with very little depth of field you'll be better off pre-focusing before you trip the shutter.

A better option is to use a remote release (either in combination with the self-timer, or on its own if you can keep it hidden from view). Also check if your camera has an interval timer – a feature that triggers the camera to take a picture every few seconds and is usually used for time-lapse photography. Setting up so the camera shoots every three to four seconds means you'll know exactly when it's going to happen, the camera will focus on you every time, and you won't have to run back and forth to the camera.

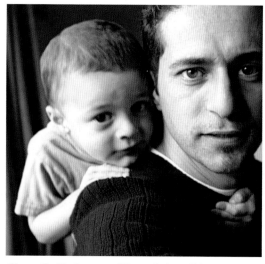

Above: Positioning yourself by a window will instantly give you interesting, soft lighting to play with.

Self-portrait with your phone

Everyone has seen the typical mobile phone self-portrait: the subject is holding the phone at arm's length and mostly they seem to pull faces. But you can achieve good results even with a simple phone if you first get accustomed to your phone's camera mechanism. For instance, some cameras don't take the picture until you take your finger off the button.

Right: It took a few attempts to get a result with this self-portrait, an homage to Andreas Feininger's iconic 1951 photograph 'The Photojournalist', a portrait of photojournalist Dennis Stock for Life magazine.

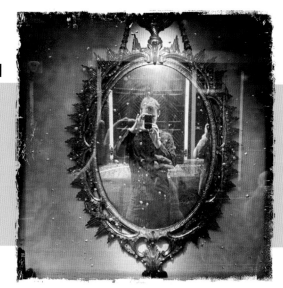

Mirror, mirror on the wall

An alternative approach to self-portraiture is to shoot your photograph in a mirror. You'll include the camera this way, but that is a good way of declaring your interest and passion for one of your hobbies – photography! Any writing will be reversed, but this can easily be fixed afterwards by flipping the image again using software such as Adobe Photoshop or Elements on your PC or Mac.

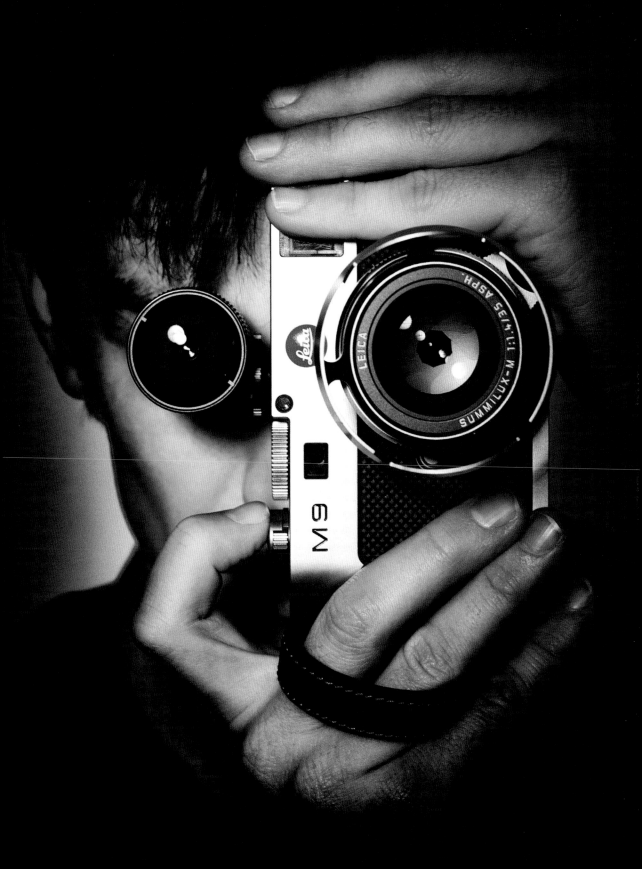

Fashion photography

It might sound obvious, but when photographing fashion, it's all about the clothes. Professional fashion shoots are lavish, over-the-top affairs with big budgets and even bigger egos. But that's not to say you shouldn't think about doing some fashion pictures of your own – it's a tremendously enjoyable thing to do for everyone involved, from photographer and model to stylist and make-up artist.

It's always better to use a model with bags of confidence who looks a bit quirky, than a classically pretty wallflower. Big, bold fashion pictures are all about confidence, and it needs to come from both behind and in front of the camera.

When planning a shoot, come up with a concept first through research and scrapbooking. Talk to the other people you'll be working with, who may have some great ideas too. Some locations may complement the clothes you are shooting; others may be more generic. Your concept can be as complicated as recreating the Mad Hatter's tea-party or as simple as shooting stylish images against a plain grey background. There are no real rules, which is one of the things that fashion photographers most enjoy.

Take advice on the clothes, too. What works well together? Is the main focus on one item of clothing, or an outfit, or perhaps just jewellery? Get help when deciding this if you feel unqualified. Your model will know what suits him/her. Make-up is crucial – the model can most likely help recreate the look you want, but if you have a friend who is good at this, rope them in as a make-up assistant.

The shoot

Getting your lighting right is of paramount importance. In professional fashion studios, this usually comes from powerful mains-powered studio flash units that can be fitted with light-modifying accessories. You can recreate the effect to a good extent by using a normal flashgun positioned off-camera (see page 96), or by using domestic light sources, such as a desk lamp or spotlight.

Your first studio lights

At first glance studio lighting can seem very complicated, but in actual fact it's quite simple to use. A basic kit perfect for occasional flash photography isn't too expensive, either, and should give you two flash heads, stands to support them, and light-modifying accessories such as umbrellas or softboxes that will soften or direct light. It's a versatile piece of kit, and something you should think about if you decide fashion and portrait photography is for you.

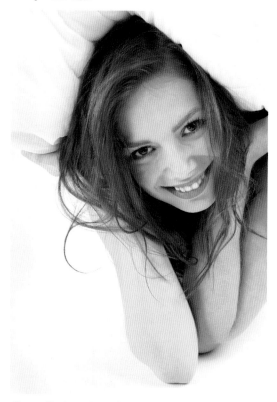

Above: *The best shots often happen as you talk to your model, creating a rapport that will be seen in the shot.*

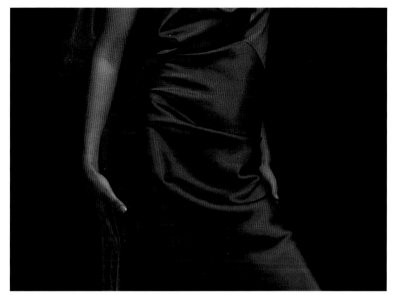

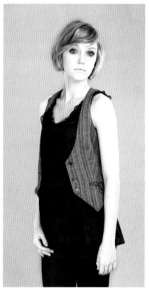

Above: *Focusing on shape, fabric and colour can tell an effective story all on its own.*

Above: *Here, colour styling brings out the model's eyes.*

You might have to soften its output by putting some diffusive material over the front (baking parchment is a good option) and correct for the warmth of household lightbulbs using your camera's white balance function (see pages 70–71).

When lighting a model, don't be afraid to take the light source away from the camera to the side to create shadows on the model's face. This gives the picture depth and feeling, as well as an edge. Perfect your lighting when your model is getting ready, or having make-up applied, using a stand-in in front of the camera if necessary.

When the time comes to shoot, it's important that no-one feels inhibited or awkward. Put some music on, and don't take things too seriously. Ask your model to move between poses every time you fire the shutter; it doesn't matter if some don't look great to start with: they will as things warm up. Give positive feedback all the time, especially so when you see something you like, and remember what is working so you can give some direction if the action stalls for a moment. Have regular breaks, too, and look at the images with your model, make-up artist, assistant and whoever else might be around. Above everything else, fashion photography is very much a team effort.

Finding a model

Finding a model for fashion can be as easy as asking a complete stranger if they would like to have some pictures taken. Alternatively, if you haven't got the nerve for that (and not many of us have), ask around your family and friends for willing volunteers.

You should also consider working with a professional model, which isn't as costly as you might think. Networking websites such as Model Mayhem and Net Model aim to bring together aspiring models and wannabe fashion photographers for mutual benefit. Arrangements known as 'time for prints' or 'time for files' (often collectively abbreviated to 'TF') are popular with models who are still wanting experience and images for their portfolios. The deal is that they will work with you for free and you provide high quality prints for their portfolio – everyone's a winner. Working with a professional model is a great way to improve as a photographer. They will be able to suggest ideas, help you with poses and give excellent feedback on images.

CHILDREN'S PORTRAITS
ANNABEL WILLIAMS LIFESTYLE PHOTOGRAPHER

Annabel Williams picked up her camera 25 years ago and quickly set about changing the face of modern portrait and wedding photography. Since then she has forged a highly successful career – not only as a portrait photographer but also as a sought-after photography teacher, distilling complicated topics into plain English.

How do you interact with your subjects?
To get the best out of people, you need to develop a relationship with them. Most clients expect me to turn up and start shooting straight away, but I never do that. I chat to them over a coffee, walk around their house and garden, look at areas that I could use for backgrounds, and go through their clothes looking for the most suitable and flattering items. It takes at least an hour, and during this time I'm getting to know them, and they are getting used to me and relaxing. You'll always get better results if you do 90 per cent of your work before you press the shutter.

> 'Photographing people is 90 per cent psychology and 10 per cent technical.'

Any tips for shooting children?
With children, I firmly believe that how you relate to them within the first five minutes of meeting them will determine how the rest of the shoot goes. When I walk into a client's house, I acknowledge any children kindly, but then ignore them unless they speak to me. It works every time! If you instantly start trying to win a child over, they will see straight through you. If a child is really lively and excitable, I might ask them to show me around the garden. Young children like nothing more than a project – and they love little boundaries, rules and games. I incorporate these into every shoot to make it fun for them.

What about lighting?
I always look for natural light – soft and flattering, not harsh. On a beach, the lack of shade can be tricky. Try shooting into the sun, so that your subjects' faces are in the shade. In other places I always look for topshade, either under a tree or in a doorway, because the light is consistent. A child can play or do anything within that area, and you know the results will be consistent, too. This works well for very young children, who just need to do their own thing while you take pictures.

How much direction should you give?
Unless you are shooting young children, you will need to give direction, as most people are self-conscious in front of a camera. I see everyone as a shape. To begin with, I ask them to stand in a certain place, but however they feel comfortable. Then I move the 'shape' around until it looks right – asking them to move their leg a certain way, lean over here, move their chin towards something, etc. Many of my shots look very natural, but they are actually set up. For example, this shot of a mum and her four children (see right) didn't just happen. I have chosen the order in which they are holding hands and told them where to run and where to look, giving them instructions and controlling what they are doing in order to end up with a natural-looking shot. I also got them to do it about six or seven times and took lots of different shots – some of which were out of focus or had the wrong expressions, which is inevitable with this sort of shooting. But some of the shots will be fantastic – and one fantastic shot is all you need!

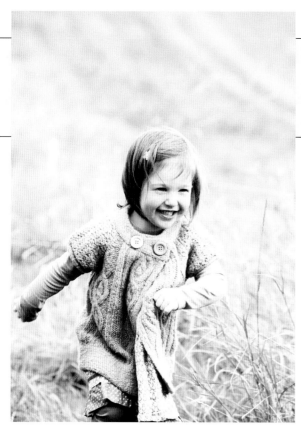

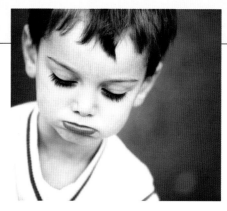

Above: *A telezoom, such as 70–200mm, will allow you to crop in close to your subject while maintaining a good working distance.*

Left: *Young children love playing games and running around, which makes for great shots.*

Below: *The beach is an excellent outdoor location for a set of family portraits and the sand makes a great impromptu reflector.*

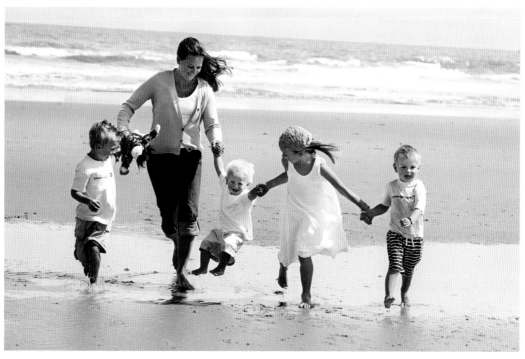

ASSIGNMENT
SHOOTING A WINDOW-LIGHT PORTRAIT

A window is one of the best light sources possible. Sitting your subject next to it bathes them in soft, natural daylight, for a more natural approach to portraiture.

A studio packed full of expensive flash lighting equipment isn't necessary for shooting beautiful portraits. A large window, a reflector and a bright but cloudy day will do just fine. In fact, it's an approach used by professional magazine and portrait photographers the world over.

What you don't really want is direct sunshine falling onto your subject – it gives far too much contrast for this type of shot. So when it comes to picking a location for a daylight portrait, a north-facing window is perfect for the job. Alternatively, shoot at times when the sun is elsewhere, or cloud cover is acting as a diffuser.

Start by placing your subject next to the window. You should notice that the difference in brightness is more extreme the closer they are sitting to the glass. You can also fill in shadows in the face with a reflector. Alternatively, if the window is big enough, try shooting with it behind you, acting as a front-on light source.

Pictures like this look good shot in black and white, or with colour saturation reduced. It's a look that complements the simplicity of the soft daylight. If you work in colour, achieving the right white balance is crucial for accurate skin tones. Try shooting in raw and using a grey card (or white sheet of paper) to set colour temperature manually on your computer (see page 70).

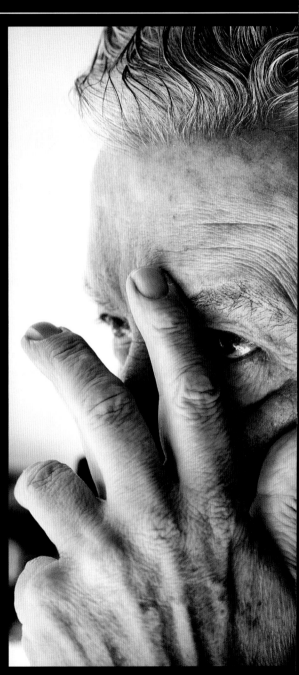

Right: A white table acted as a reflector here, subtly lighting the subject's face.
Nikon D700, 24–70mm f/2.8, 1/125sec at f/5.6, ISO200

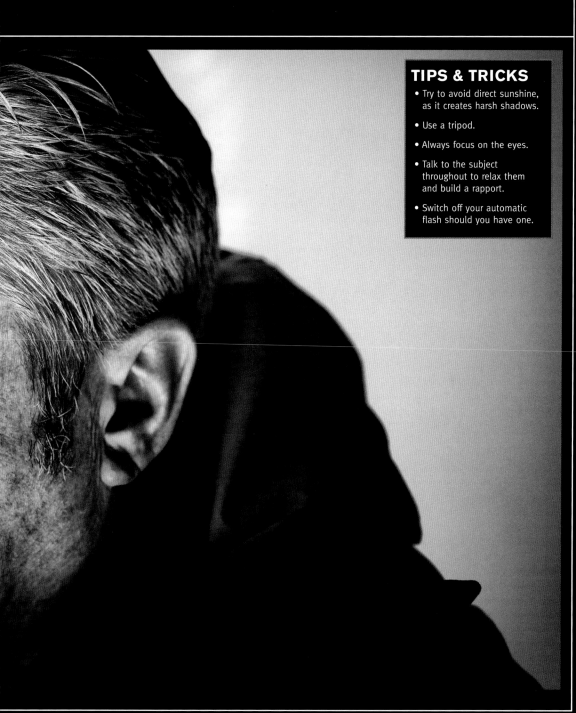

ESSENTIAL KIT

- DSLR or compact camera
- Tripod
- 50mm or longer lens
- Reflector

TIPS & TRICKS

- Try to avoid direct sunshine, as it creates harsh shadows.

- Use a tripod.

- Always focus on the eyes.

- Talk to the subject throughout to relax them and build a rapport.

- Switch off your automatic flash should you have one.

Still life

Still life is principally the photography of objects. This can be for a number of reasons, artistic and practical, and can take a number of forms. It can be used for sales and advertising purposes, as well as for fine art, and can take place in the studio or at home, as well as on location.

Some still-life images are carefully set up, with hours of preparation time going into the construction of a set and the lighting that accompanies it. Others are more spontaneous, found on location and shot without changing anything.

The pace of a still-life shoot is less rushed than shooting, say, fashion or portraiture images. Taking your time means you can get the small details and lighting just right, and concentrate on image quality, too. Although a compact camera is fine in theory, you'll find still life easier to shoot with a DSLR and a lens that focuses reasonably closely. A sturdy tripod is also a must, and you'll probably find a remote release useful when working with slow shutter speeds.

Below: Choose your still-life background carefully. Here the wood grain complements the colours of the spices.

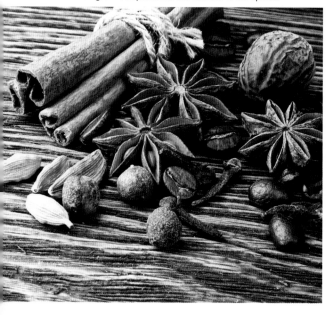

The composition of still-life pictures follows much the same rules as any other type of photography. The rule of thirds (see pages 60–61) can be a powerful creative tool, and negative (empty) space can also be used to great effect. A common artistic theme in still life is simplicity, and this is certainly an area where less is more. When shooting a photograph of a flower, for instance, try to let the beauty of your subject shine through, without anything competing too much for attention.

Backgrounds and the environment

A home still-life studio is easier to create than you might think. Window light is used extensively in the more artistic side of still-life photography, and a kitchen or utility room work surface near a large window can be used for all manner of projects. Walls and work surfaces often make a good backdrop for a photograph. If you want a completely plain, seamless background then try making a cove from a piece of white paper. A cove background (also used on a larger scale in portraiture) comprises a piece of paper curved gently through 90 degrees so that the front sits on a table top and the back is on the wall behind. With no visible horizon between background and foreground, the result is a seamless, 'invisible' backdrop. This approach is used extensively in product photography, as well as the more artistic side of still life.

Depth of field is important with still life, and can be difficult to handle when close-focusing. That said, if you are struggling to achieve complete front-to-back sharpness then try an alternative approach – using a large aperture to restrict focus to one area, with shallow depth of field.

Lighting

Typically, still-life lighting is soft and shadowless, although some directionality helps to avoid a boring result. If you have access to off-camera flash then this can be used to good effect if you have a way to soften the light. Try firing it backwards onto a large piece of white card, or using one of the many light-modifying accessories on the market, such as an umbrella or softbox.

Daylight is also a good option, though be aware that the character of the light coming in through a window can change through the day as the sun moves around. Reflectors can help fill in shadows, and semi-transparent tracing paper (or greaseproof kitchen parchment) doubles up as a very effective diffuser. Commercially available light tents let you encase a subject with soft light – using flash, daylight, or even electric light from domestic desk lamps (just make sure you correct for the warm colour temperature with your camera's white balance controls).

Finding still life

By its very nature, still-life photography is usually very contrived, being set up for the purposes of the photograph. However, it can be fun to go about 'finding' still-life pictures, too. Seek out images that already exist, and photograph them in their own surroundings. This could be something as familiar as the bowl of fruit you walk past every day, or as alien as the swirls and patterns made by water as it falls into the bath. Other fertile hunting grounds for naturally occurring still-life images include the garden shed or garage, where the passing of time and the presence of spiders' webs give objects a nostalgic look. Also approach the owners of antique or junk shops and ask if you can prowl around their store with your camera and close-up gear.

Finding still-life images is a good theme for a competition with some photography-loving friends. Each of you has a set time limit to find pictures in a defined space and shoot them, with a winner being judged by an impartial mutual friend. You can set rules to govern how difficult this is, for instance whether are you allowed to move the object within the room.

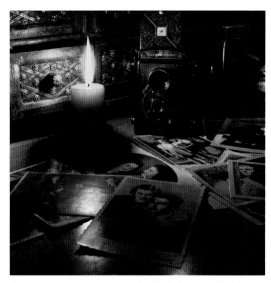

Above: *Sometimes incorporating the light source into the composition can add to the atmosphere, like this candle in a nostalgic composition of old photographs and cameras.*

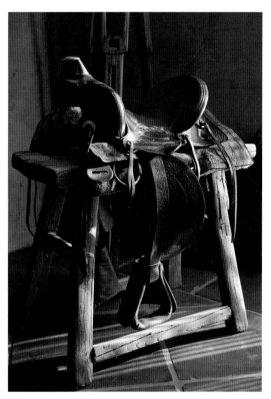

Above: *Objects that are used on a daily basis often make for great still-life subjects, especially if they carry meaning for the photographer, like this propped-up saddle in the corner.*

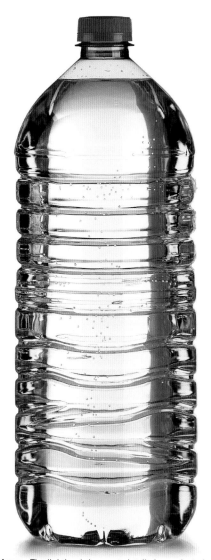

Above: Flat lighting brings out details in product shots, commonly used in advertising.

Below: Most product photography is shot with a white background, but if the subject is white, another colour may be more appropriate.

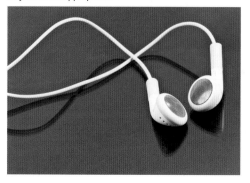

Product shots

Not all still life is shot for artistic reasons. Millions of pictures are shot every year for catalogues and adverts that try to sell us goods and services. While such pictures have to be visually appealing, their primary purpose is often to allow us to inspect something before we buy it, which requires more of a functional approach to still life.

Dramatic lighting and elaborate shadows are out, replaced by flat lighting that shows every detail of the object being photographed. While some advertising photography shows a product in the environment where it will be used, most catalogue shots will be against a plain white or black background, to avoid distractions.

If you ever sell things using online auction sites such as eBay, then a more considered approach to product photography could do you some favours. It's well established that better quality photography on an eBay listing results in more people clicking though to your sale, which in turn leads to more bids and a better price. Setting up a home studio for some basic product-shot photography is easy to do with just a few household items.

A scoop background with no visible horizon can be made from a large sheet of white paper and a dining chair – attach the paper to the chair back so it falls down and rests on the seat, curving gently through 90 degrees as it does so. For a bigger scale set, turn the chair around and put it up on a table, resting the paper on the table top.

Lighting a scoop background is simple enough, but ideally you need to somehow diffuse the light source you use. This can mean a flashgun fired off a ceiling, wall or piece of card, or even fitted with a specialist softbox-type diffuser. You can also use window light, but do ensure that you are using the right exposure to make the background appear white, not grey. Shoot the background on its own, inspecting the histogram (see pages 80–81) as you go along, and lock these aperture and shutter speed settings in using the manual mode.

If you shoot a lot of this type of photography then it could be worth investing in a light tent. Such devices consist of a cube of translucent material that acts as a diffuser, softening light whichever direction it comes from, and letting you use domestic light sources, such as a desk lamp. Just be sure to get your white balance right.

Food photography

The look of professional food photography has changed a lot over recent years. Gone are the stiff, formal images of the 1980s, which used cold mashed potato as ice cream and half-cooked, varnished pasta. In are more lifelike, gritty images of food that's so realistic you could eat it after the shoot has finished.

The vast majority of the skill in food photography is in the styling and presentation of the food. Pay attention to the balance and colour of the food on the plate – looking at how the professionals do this in cookbooks will help give you ideas. Having some oil on standby to make things glisten will help, as will shooting warm food when it is still steaming.

Unlike other still-life photography, it pays to be speedy when shooting food. A dish doesn't always keep its good looks for long, so try and plan things in advance. When the dish is ready you'll want to photograph it before it has a chance to melt, collapse or change colour. Try using a stand-in empty plate, with all the necessary props, so you can get your lighting just right, then substitute the real thing at the last minute.

When it comes to putting the food in context, props such as glasses, cutlery and table furniture are important. Don't clutter the shot with these, but do consider using them in the background, even if they are out of focus.

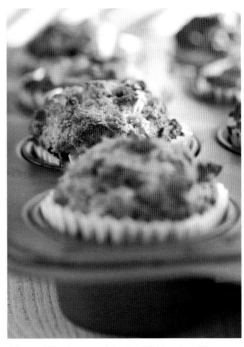

Above: Effective use of depth of field makes this tray of muffins, straight out of the oven, look good enough to eat.

Below: The white background and straight-on angle emphasize the colour, shape and pattern of these sweets.

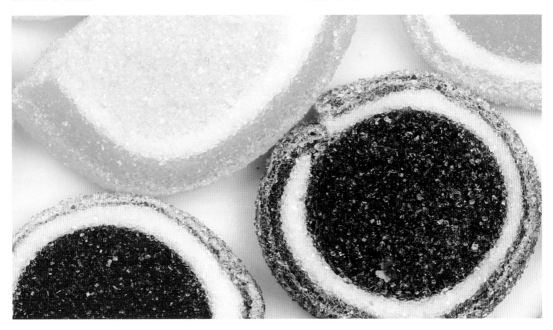

ASSIGNMENT
SHOOTING A
BACK-LIT STILL LIFE

Translucent objects look great when photographed with light coming through them. Use your imagination and you'll soon find plenty of things you can photograph in this way.

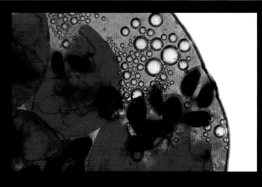

In still-life photography we usually light objects from the front to avoid them disappearing into silhouette, but thin, colourful, semi-transparent objects are perfectly suited to being lit from behind. This could be plastic toys, sweet wrappers or even – as shown here – slices of fruit and flowers.

A macro lens is great for this type of work, but if you don't have one then another close-up accessory, such as a supplementary close-up lens or an extension tube, will be fine. For your light source, there are many creative solutions.

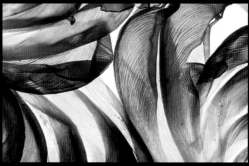

If you have one, the type of lightbox used for viewing photographic negatives or slides is perfect. It's flat, wipe-clean and pumps out a bright, evenly distributed light. If you don't, then these are the characteristics you need to recreate. Try making a table from a sheet of glass supported by books on either side (unless you already have a glass coffee table, of course). Under it, place a sheet of white paper on the floor and illuminate this paper with domestic desk lamps. Create a custom white balance preset from the blank white background to ensure accurate colour reproduction.

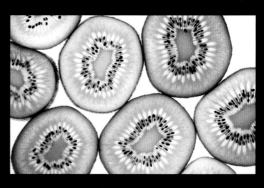

Now place the objects to be photographed on the glass and photograph them from above. Your camera's spot metering (see page 79) will give you the right exposure for the job.

Fruit makes a good subject, especially if you pick fruits of different colours. Try freezing the fruit before you slice it for a neater edge.

Above top: Lighting from beneath intensifies the colour of these whipped redcurrants.
Above centre: These tulip petals were shot with a macro lens, but a supplementary close-up lens or an extension tube works just as well.
Above: Choose your subject for this type of shot carefully. Colourful, translucent objects are the most effective.

ESSENTIAL KIT

- DSLR with macro lens or close-up accessory
- Compact camera with macro mode
- Tripod and remote release
- Lightbox – or a glass sheet, paper and desk lamp

TIPS & TRICKS

- Vary the subject-to-camera distance so that you explore the detail and patterns in one fruit slice, as well as the patterns made by tessellating them.

- Increase the saturation setting on your camera for a more punchy result.

- Stay square-on to your subject to avoid perspective distortion.

Below: For punchier colours in these petals, the saturation in-camera was increased.

All pictures: Nikon D700 with 105mm f/2.8 macro lens

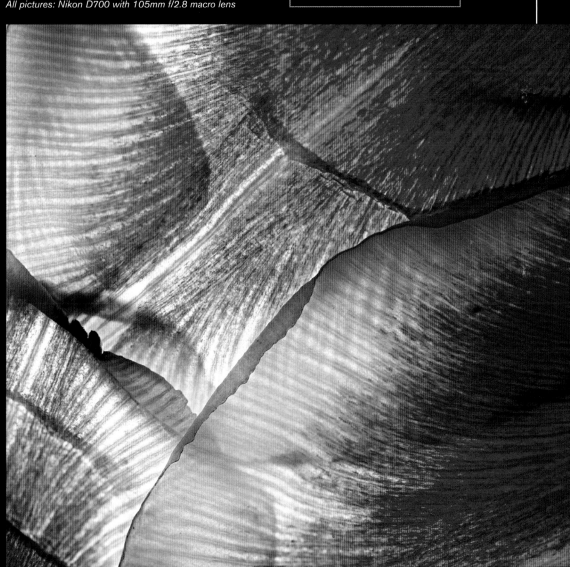

Urban landscapes

Most of us live around towns and cities, not rolling hills and countryside, but that doesn't mean there isn't a landscape to photograph. The urban jungle is every bit as photogenic as the real thing.

When it comes to comparing urban and rural landscape photography, there are perhaps as many differences as there are similarities. While the conditions that bring out the best in countryside landscapes often do the same in city scenes, the pace of change in urban landscapes makes shooting them more unpredictable. While you can be sure that the view down a valley in a national park will remain the same for centuries, townscapes are constantly changing from year to year. Old buildings are knocked down; new ones go up in their place. But this rapid pace of progress is one of the reasons that urban landscape photography is so intriguing as a subject.

Your cityscapes may not always be seen in isolation, but rather in the context of pictures

Below: Finding a high-up vantage point and shooting a panoramic picture by splicing together multiple frames has worked well in this night-time Parisian landscape.

taken beforehand, and afterwards. In this way, shooting urban landscapes is more than just fine-art or travel snapping – it's also reportage, documenting the state of a city at a certain moment in time, before the relentless march of progress alters it again.

There are many themes to explore when shooting in the city. Housing, transport, cityscapes, panoramic views, rivers and waterways all come under the umbrella of the urban landscape. Such photography isn't always pretty. While it's tempting to show the glamorous side of a city, the more run-down, gritty side of life is just as photogenic. And the contrast between the two is sometimes the best approach of all.

Contrasts are especially important in the architectural side of urban landscapes. In most cities the range and age of architectural styles is very varied, so there is little point in trying to concentrate on one style by excluding others. It's more effective to embrace this mixture and show the contrasting designs next to each other.

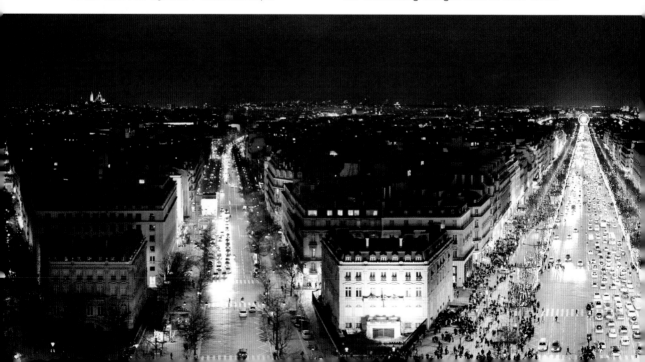

Timing, location and people

The time of the day has just as pronounced an effect on the urban landscape as it does on its rural counterpart. The light at either end of the day is more flattering, being softer and warmer, and often diffused by cloud. But in the urban landscape, other differences manifest themselves over the course of the day, too.

Morning is a great time to photograph streets, as they have usually just been cleaned. Furthermore, at 6am there are vastly fewer people on them than at other times of the day. Of course you can also wait until around 8am, when you could be seeing the height of the rush hour. Your urban landscape will now be packed full of commuters and there will be people everywhere.

The presence of people in urban landscape pictures is a controversial one. Just as a rural landscape wouldn't concentrate on animals in a field or birds in trees, urban scenes work best when people are not the sole focus, which is what makes it different from street photography (see pages 166–167). If you can't minimize the significance of people in the shot, consider returning to the scene on another day or at a different time to capture it people-free. Or investigate ways of editing the scene on your computer to remove the people altogether. That said, the presence of people – the things they've left behind, the buildings they live in, the cars they drive – is everywhere, and can often give your pictures context and meaning.

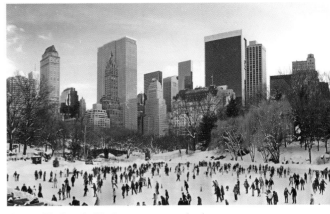

Above: Black and white is a great approach when emphasizing lines and shapes, even when the classic approach to a subject may be to shoot it in colour.

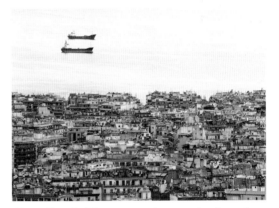

Above: Try to look for unexpected crops and angles, as in this view of lower Thessaloniki, Greece.

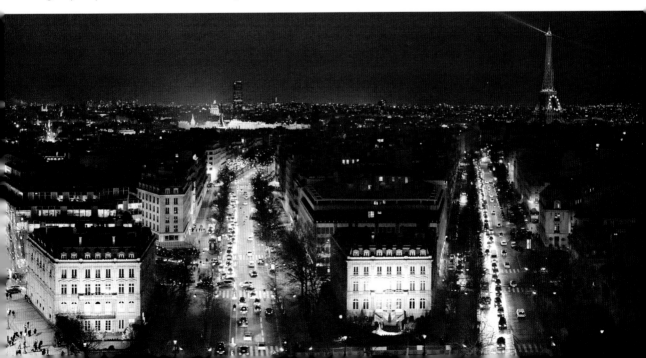

ASSIGNMENT
URBAN EXPLORATION

Not all landscape photography has to be of classically beautiful views. The run-down areas of town have a beauty all of their own, and are easy to find.

Open any city guidebook and the public face you'll see is that of clean streets, classic buildings and new, exciting developments. There's nothing wrong with that, but if this is all you photograph when shooting urban landscapes, then you are missing much of a location's character. The run-down areas of a city are worth a look, too. They are often rich in culture and history, and tell a different story of our society.

A different look requires a different photographic approach. Urban grime always looks good when photographed in black and white, and it can be a fun exercise to switch your camera into black and white mode, composing on-screen in 'live view' mode to let you see in monochrome. Colour has its place too, of course, but a more muted palette complements the melancholy character of the more run-down parts of town. You can create this in-camera, too, by turning down the colour saturation and slightly increasing the contrast to compensate.

Some cameras even let you save such settings as individual picture styles for easy recall later on.

Just as with rural landscapes, composition is of key importance when shooting this type of subject matter, but the approach is different. Just as muted colours are appropriate to a more sombre type of landscape, so a more deadpan composition can also help get the message across. Don't be afraid of photographing things square-on, and using empty space to draw attention to the decay in a run-down area.

Ruined or abandoned buildings are especially tempting. A whole new pastime dubbed 'urban exploration' (UE for short) has sprung up around photographing such buildings, with communities sharing tips with each other on the internet regarding new locations and methods of gaining access to them. Be careful if you are thinking of a spot of UE though; it is still illegal to break into a building, even if it is abandoned. This is an activity that is best approached with the permission of the owner.

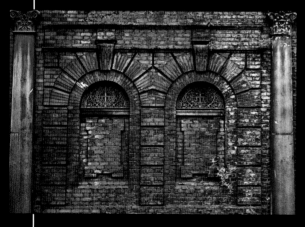

Left: The old red bricks and green weeds give this picture a lovely warm feel of fading grandeur.
Leica M9 with 50mm f/2 lens, 1/250sec at f/5.6, ISO200

Opposite top: Choose the time of day for your shoot carefully. Throngs of business people seeking lunch would alter this scene significantly.
Contax G2 with 35mm f/2 lens, 1/60sec at f/4, ISO400

Opposite bottom: Muted colours and a rule of thirds composition have been used to good effect in this view of Saigon, Vietnam.
Nikon D700 28mm f/2.8, 1/125sec at f/5.6, ISO200

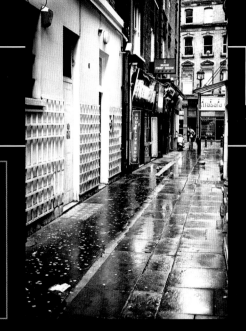

ESSENTIAL KIT

- Lightweight DSLR with standard zoom, or compact camera
- Inconspicuous camera bag

TIPS & TRICKS

- Look for frames within the picture; the urban world is full of them. Window and door frames, as well as tumbledown brick walls and barbed wire fences, all enhance composition and direct the eye around the picture.

- If you don't know whether you want to shoot in colour or black and white, shoot a colour raw file and a simultaneous black and white JPEG. Many DSLR cameras can be set to shoot both in this way.

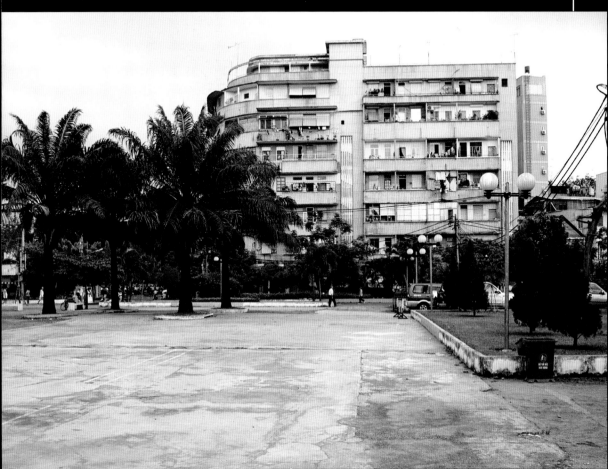

Landscapes

Landscapes are the most popular subject for most enthusiast photographers. They are the first thing we shoot when we are on holiday, a reminder of happy times and places. And when they are photographed properly, landscapes fill us with awe at the wonder of the natural world.

It's one thing to be surrounded by beautiful views, and something else to be able to record those views faithfully on camera. It's easy to render mountains as unremarkable blips on the horizon, waterfalls as boring and static, and seascapes as cold, grey and lifeless. To avoid such disappointments, successful landscape photographers generally follow a few basic rules that help them capture the atmosphere of a location, and convey its magic.

The location

The first thing to do with any landscape shoot is to get to know the location inside-out. Explore your favourite places on foot and look for all the possible vantage points, so you can be sure that you've explored every possible angle and composition. Don't be afraid to get low down next to the ground (if your camera has a swivel screen it will be useful here) or stand on a wall or rock for a higher viewpoint. For landscape photography

Below: *Snow makes for a dramatic landscape, but it's a challenge too, as in this magical shot of Monument Valley, Utah. Metering can be tricky so check your camera's histogram.*

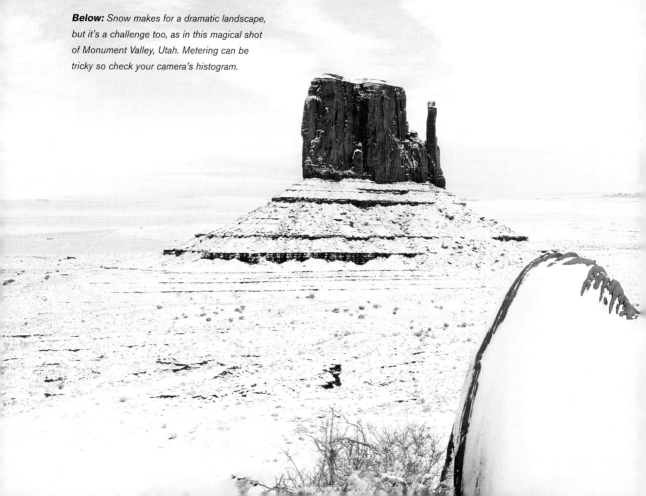

in your local area, keep a notebook or map and add notes on your favourite spots so you'll be able to return throughout the year, as conditions and seasons change.

Remember to take your time; landscape photography is all about the long-term goal. Getting to know your location involves knowing how the various viewpoint and lens combinations will work with the conditions that Mother Nature has thrown at you. If something's not quite right, make a note of it and come back another day. The perfect landscape photograph is elusive, but the subject matter isn't going to vanish overnight.

Although notionally static subjects, landscapes alter their appearance all the time – changing from minute to minute, day to day, and even year to year. Over the course of a day, the lighting in a landscape changes drastically, altering the look of a photograph as it goes along. If dramatic results are the name of the game, then avoid working in dull, overcast conditions when the light

is completely flat. The best light is to be found at either end of the day, so you'll need to be prepared to get up early or go to bed late. Monitor the weather forecast. If the next day looks like it's going to be fair, then get up early and head out before sunrise. As it comes up, the sun will warm the scene and give the sky a vivid pink or orange glow. The hours around dusk are equally inviting. Under these conditions, sunlight is not only warmer but also lower in the sky. This helps it to create longer shadows throughout the landscape and emphasize detail.

In the summer, when many landscapes are at their most lush, these conditions don't last long. As soon as the sun is higher in the sky, it's much harder to get a striking result, with harsh midday sunshine flattening detail. Although the winter months can mean fewer leaves on the trees, the sun stays lower in the sky for longer and rises and sets at more sociable hours, making it easier to capture that precious quality light.

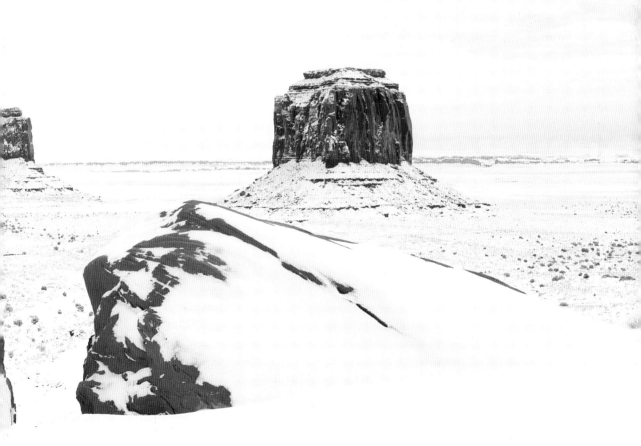

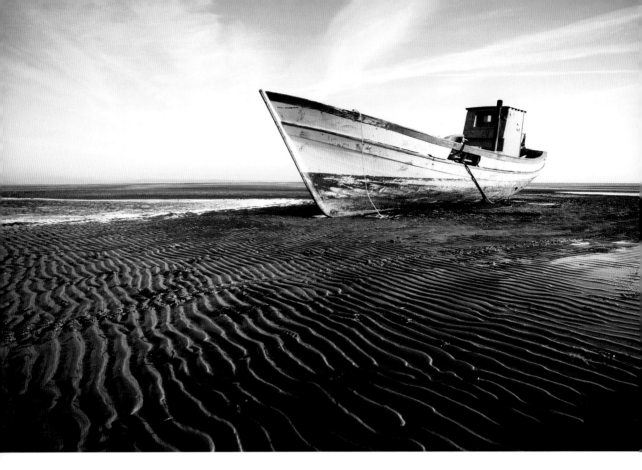

Coastal landscapes

There is something about being at the coast that makes us immediately reach for our cameras. Maybe it's the feeling of space, or the drama of the water crashing around on the rocks. Quiet bays, sleepy fishing villages and rugged rockpools are equally appealing. Seascapes look as good in the winter as they do in the summer, but they change their personality and appearance unpredictably. Here are five ways to take control and ensure that every trip to the coast is a recipe for photographic success.

Fill the foreground When composing any landscape, filling the bottom of the frame with foreground interest will do your composition a lot of favours, and at the coast you are spoilt for choice when it comes to options. Look for lumps of driftwood on the beach, lichen-covered boulders, dune grasses, even rock pools. Reflections in puddles are also interesting and can help balance the often bright sky. When you start looking, you'll see that the options are endless.

Above: Old boats or wrecks at low tide make for great subjects, but make sure to use puddles or ripples in the sand for interesting foreground.

Blur the sea Photographing a coastal scene with a long shutter speed results in the water blurring and everything else staying sharp. Use a long enough shutter speed (five to ten seconds) to shoot waves crashing over rocks and you'll find they look like mist, not water. The effect is haunting, and easy to achieve at dusk. Use a tripod and remote release to avoid moving the camera and blurring the image.

Freeze the waves Alternatively, go for a fast shutter speed and freeze waves in mid-air as they break over the rocks. It's an approach suited to stormy days, and best tackled from a distance with a telephoto lens.

Watch the tide The ebb and flow of the tides is responsible for the constantly changing character of the coast. What is covered with water now

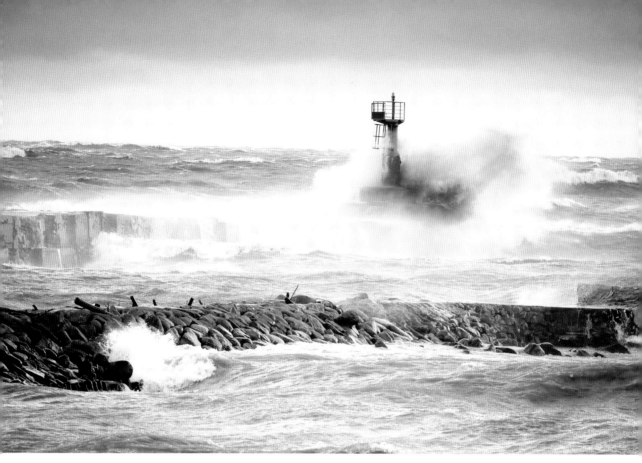

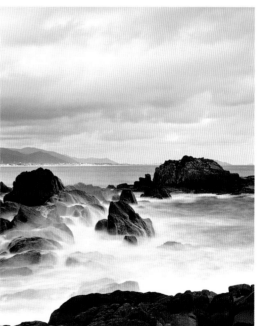

Above: On stormy days, head to a beach with cliffs or man-made structures such as this lighthouse in Camogli, Italy, for dramatically crashing waves.

might be exposed and full of rock pools in a few hours. With a little bit of research you'll find that you can easily predict tides and it should be possible to calculate when they are going to coincide with interesting lighting and weather conditions. Low tide is not the time to capture waves coming over the breakwater, just as you might be disappointed if you arrive to photograph ripples in a sandy beach and find half a mile of it covered with water.

Look for details You don't always have to focus on the big picture to capture the atmosphere of the coastline – keep an eye out for the interesting details, too. Lichen on boulders, patterns in the sand and the texture of the rocks are all legitimate subjects. Look out for man-made subjects too – lobster pots, old boats and colourful beach huts, for instance.

Above: A long shutter speed blurs the sea, while the rest remains in sharp focus. A five-second exposure has turned the waves into haunting mist in this shot of Florianopolis, Brazil.

FOCUS ON
LANDSCAPES
JOE CORNISH LANDSCAPE PHOTOGRAPHER

Joe Cornish got his first camera as an art student in the late 1970s. He has devoted himself to landscape photography since the mid-1990s and has been a National Trust freelancer for over 20 years. His book *First Light* is recognized as a classic. Joe divides his time between printing for his gallery, leading workshops, writing and making new images.

How did you get started?
While studying as a student – landscape was the subject I felt most comfortable with. I was also inspired by the 20th century landscape photography I saw, which all happened to be black and white. I soaked up the work of Ansel Adams, Edward Weston, John Blakemore, Ray Moore, Thomas Joshua Cooper and others.

What talent do you need to be a good landscape photographer?
Like most human endeavours it has more to do with hard work than talent. In my case I was good with a pencil as a kid, and I think a 'good eye' is important for any photographer. As for the landscape element, it is essential to be happy in your own company and have some tolerance for discomfort, but those are hardly talents!

Have digital photography and online stock libraries changed your way of working?
It has actually made my working life much, much harder. Previously I could concentrate completely on my photography, and always had a reasonable chance of making it pay. Now I develop my images from raw, archive everything methodically, and then when I need to prepare work for use, go through an additional printing stage. In essence I have to do three times as much work, compared to pre-digital. And due to the hugely increased competition from the

proliferation of picture suppliers, and the legions of talented non-pros out there, the value of stock has plummeted so it is no longer a source of steady income, as it once was.

On the positive side, printing my own work has elevated its quality to a level I could not have dreamed of before. And digital capture is opening up new ways of approaching photography that I hadn't previously considered.

As Yosemite is inextricably linked with Ansel Adams, is there a particular place that has shaped your work?
The North Yorkshire landscape on my back doorstep has been my 'Yosemite', including the perky summit of Roseberry Topping. I have walked these hills countless times, taking thousands of photographs. Many of my ideas about landscape have developed here.

What type of cameras do you normally shoot with?
I often choose a Canon EOS 5D MkII or a Nikon D700 for commissioned assignments. For my own work I generally take a Linhof Techno view camera with a Phase One P45+ back, and a Panasonic or Canon compact as a photographic 'sketchbook'.

What advice do you have for photographers just starting out?
Everyone will find their own way in their own time. But it probably goes without saying that developing an astutely self-critical, yet constructive eye is pretty important.

In composition, the key ideas are energy and balance. I like to think that these same ideas can apply elsewhere in life, at whatever level we choose to take them; they apply equally well to photographers just starting out.

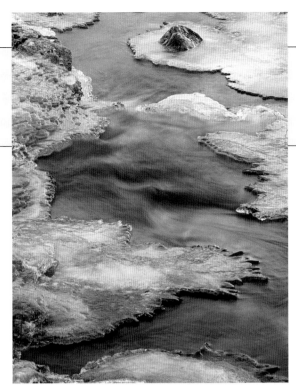

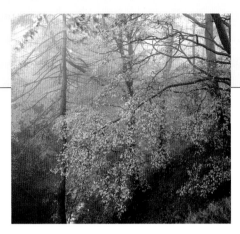

Above: *Mist and rain can be wonderful for the saturated colours of autumn.*

Left: *As an example of nature's art, delicate and often short-lived ice formations are hard to beat.*

Below: *Digital compacts are great for spontaneous and experimental photography.*

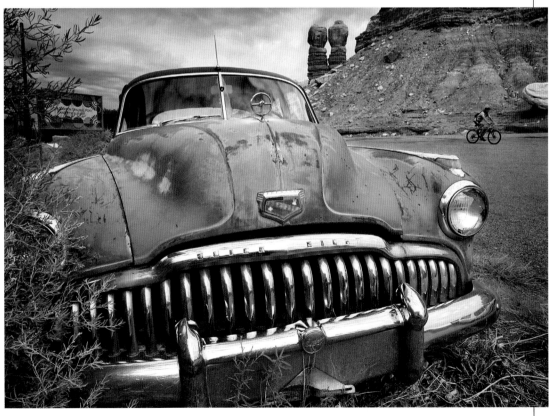

Landscape **composition**

Composition is everything when it comes to landscape photography. Where you stand and how you compose such a picture makes the difference between a simple snap and a great piece of photography.

A great location, perfect conditions and gorgeous lighting are all useless unless a landscape photograph is composed properly. It's tempting to shoot with wide-angle lenses to get more of the scene into the frame, but if this is done without care, then all too often the result is a boring composition with too much empty foreground space. It's a classic, common mistake.

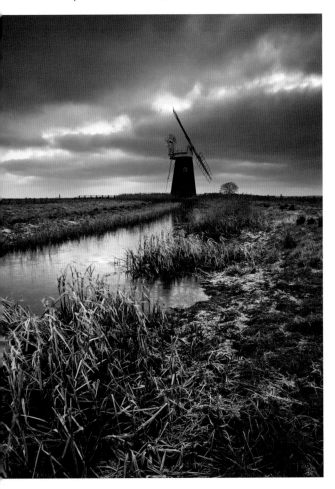

The answer is to fill that empty space. Foreground interest can be anything (rock, puddle, haybale, plant) but the approach is the same: get in close and use a wide-angle focal length to give the object some dramatic emphasis. The eye should be drawn into the scene and the photograph should take on more of a sense of depth and scale.

When composing a landscape, it's vital to consider what is really important and what is not. Be as picky and critical as possible, making sure your composition has an anchor – a focal point for the picture to hang on. There is little point in photographing an empty field, but include a lone tree, or a crumbling old ruin at the right point, and suddenly the composition will sing.

Where to put this focal point is one of the big decisions that you, as the photographer, will have to make when you are shooting. We've already explored the concept of the rule of thirds (see pages 60–61), and landscape photography is a discipline where this approach really works well. Divide the frame into thirds horizontally and vertically and put details on the points where these lines cross. The lines themselves will give you an idea of where to put the horizon.

It's not uncommon to see shapes in the foreground that tend to frame the landscape behind them, and this can be used as a powerful compositional tool. The overhanging branches of a tree or an ornate rose-covered archway are perfect examples, as is a window in an ancient castle ruin. With the focal point of the picture positioned in the right place, such devices will only serve to guide the viewer's eye even more strongly to the right place in the frame.

Left: Lead the eye into the scene and direct it to the focal point. Here the threatening clouds and creek effectively guide your eye to Mutton's Mill, Norfolk.

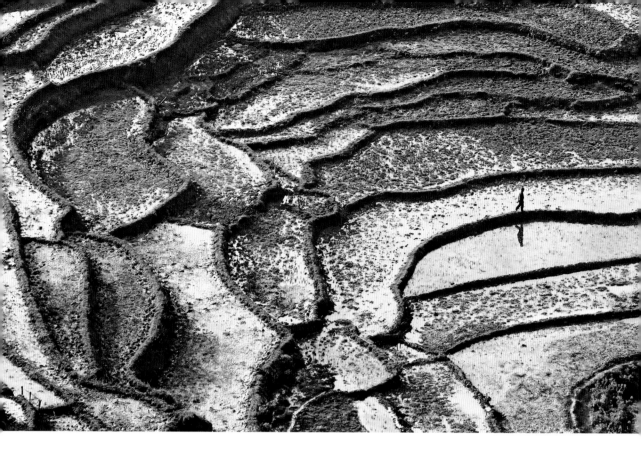

Making the most of colour

The natural world is full of colour, and using it properly will take your landscape photography to a new level, adding impact, drama and emotion. First, though, we have to understand how colours can work together, and how different combinations can invoke different moods and feelings.

Bright, vivid hues create a fresh, exciting feel. Contrasting colours (red/green, yellow/blue) create tension and add to the impact of the scene, while softer, more muted colour combinations impart a more gentle, tranquil feel, particularly when combined with a warmer overall atmosphere. Concentrating on a single colour is also a good approach to shooting landscapes. Green is the dominant colour in many landscapes and is the colour of spring, new life and freshness. Blue, however, is more ambiguous: forbidding and lonely in some situations, such as cold weather, but joyful and warming when the sun is shining.

Yellow and orange are warming colours, and always create a happy and positive feel. Red is the most potent (some would say passionate) colour of all, but doesn't appear so frequently in nature.

Above: In this shot, taken in Sapa, Vietnam, the interplay of reflections and rice crops on the organic shapes of the paddy fields make for an interesting, almost abstract pattern, with the lone figure of the farmer adding a sense of scale.

In fact when it does, it should be handled with care and not allowed to dominate the scene.

The boldness of colours is dictated as much by the ambient conditions as by the in-camera settings. Under bright sunlight, colours look much more saturated than they do on dull, overcast days. You can increase saturation further by fitting a polarizing filter (see page 24) to your lens, or increasing the colour saturation in your camera's picture-settings controls. That said, don't fight against the conditions: if it's a dull day then there isn't much you can do about it, and it's best to go for the more subtle approach afforded by softer, less saturated colours. Mist, haze and fog tend to cause colours to merge, giving a very soothing (almost magical) feel to a landscape. At dusk, this effect can become almost monochromatic, causing a landscape to be reduced to a series of warm shades that grow lighter in the distance.

ASSIGNMENT
SHOOTING MOVING WATER

The presence of water in a landscape offers up a raft of creative possibilities, but capturing the movement and blur in the water is a crucial part of shooting this type of scene.

In the form of a river or stream, water will always flow along a prescribed course, and often this course can be used as a compositional tool to draw the eye into the picture. This works so well because water flowing along a river is often the only thing moving in a picture, and it's this movement that guides us through the image.

Recording a sense of movement relies on using the right shutter speed for the job. A fast speed will simply freeze the water's flow, but a longer shutter speed will allow the flow of the river to be recorded on camera as a smooth, creamy blur. The longer the shutter speed, the more blurred the water's movement will be.

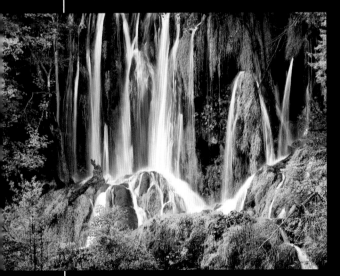

Above: Examine a scene from all angles before setting up your tripod. Don't let your tripod's position dictate your shot. Olympus E-3, 50–200mm f/2.8–3.5, 1/2sec at f/16, ISO200

Choosing your gear

Landscape photography can involve a lot of walking to find a good location, so limit the kit you take with you to the bare essentials. A tripod is a must, as you'll be working with long exposures. A telephoto lens is useful for isolating sections of the river, while the wide end of your standard zoom is good for taking a broader view with foreground interest.

Obtaining such slow shutter speeds can be tricky on bright, sunny days, when there is lots of light around. A neutral density (ND) filter can help reduce the amount of light coming into the camera so you can use a slower shutter speed. A polarizer also has this effect, as well as reducing reflections and glare from wet rocks and increasing colour saturation.

Compose and expose

Look for the best viewpoint before you set up your tripod. Don't be afraid to wade into the water to do this (as long as it's safe to do so). Your tripod will be waterproof.

The degree of blur caused by a particular shutter speed will vary according to how fast the water is flowing, and is hard to predict. To take control over shutter speed, shoot in either manual exposure mode or in shutter priority mode if you want some degree of automation. Start with a shutter speed of 1/2sec and go longer in one-stop increments (eg. 1sec, 2sec, 4sec, etc.). As you try to get longer and longer speeds, you may find you have reached your lens's minimum aperture and can't get a longer speed. This is when to add an ND filter.

ESSENTIAL KIT

- DSLR
- Standard zoom lens
- Telephoto lens
- Tripod
- Wellington boots for wading
- ND or polarizing filter

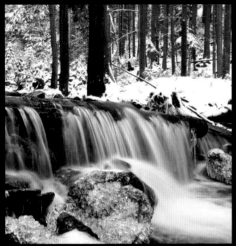

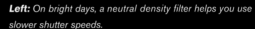

Left: *On bright days, a neutral density filter helps you use slower shutter speeds.*
Canon EOS 450D with 18–55mm f/3.5–5.6, 1sec at f/22, ISO100, with 2-stop ND filter

Below: *With a telephoto lens, you can focus in on a specific area of water. Here a shutter speed of two seconds gives a real sense of the water's fall over a weir.*
Nikon D700 with 70–200mm f/2.8 lens, 2secs at f/16, ISO100

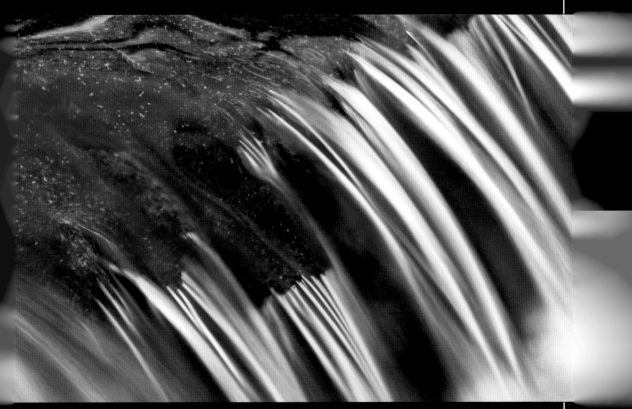

Dynamic **range**

The human eye can see a greater range of brightnesses than a digital camera, and this is a problem for landscape photographers.

The sky in a landscape scene is usually brighter than the foreground, sometimes so much so that detail in both of these regions cannot be recorded with just one exposure. There are several tricks used by landscapers to overcome this, involving filtration and the blending together of multiple exposures.

Graduated filters

The most established way of calming down a bright sky so it matches the exposure of the foreground is to use a graduated neutral density filter – sometimes known as an grad ND or a grey grad. Grad NDs come in various strengths, but the principle is always the same. The top part of the filter lets through less light than the bottom part, which is completely clear, and the transition between the two parts is graduated or blended. Such filters are usually square or rectangular and fit in a filter holder that attaches to the front of your lens. These filter holders can fit more than

one filter at a time, so you can stack up grad NDs if you need to, or combine them with a polarizer.

When setting up your grad ND, position the transition so it matches the horizon, then stop down to your working aperture with the camera's depth of field preview button or 'live view' facility. The softness of the transition area changes with aperture. You can buy hard or soft grad NDs, too, with hard types having a more abrupt transition than soft ones. Which is best depends on the scene being photographed, so it makes sense to have a few different types. Some manufacturers produce kits containing two or three examples, which represent good value for money.

Below: *Without the use of a graduated filter, the bright sky in this rural Wyoming scene would have caused the camera to under-expose.*

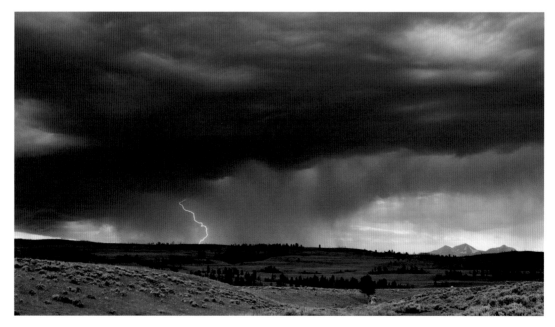

HDR imaging

The modern-day alternative to grad filters is to shoot multiple frames at different exposures and blend them together to form an image that contains all of the detail in the scene – a process called high dynamic range (HDR) imaging. We'll talk more about HDR in chapter five (see pages 336–341), but the advantages it scores over using grad ND filters is the ability to tackle situations where the boundary between light and dark areas is not separated by a straight line. The horizon is unobstructed in many landscapes pictures, so this is not a problem, but when rocky coastlines, trees or buildings overlap the horizon, HDR is a better approach.

The disadvantage of HDR is that separate frames must be shot at different exposures for the technique to work properly, and the camera and subject must not move between exposures. This requires the use of a tripod, and means that HDR will not work if you have movement in the picture – trees blowing in the wind, cars or people moving, etc.

Below: An HDR filter was used for this shot to tone down the brighter sky and increase texture and saturation on the rocks in the foreground. The slowed shutter speed causes the crashing waves to blur into a dreamy haze.

Polarizing filters

The polarizing filter has long been the landscaper's best friend. It can help to increase colour saturation and vibrancy, particularly in blue skies and green foliage.

Rotate the filter while looking through the viewfinder and you'll see the change, with the sky becoming darker or lighter as the saturation changes. The effect is greatest when shooting at an angle 90 degrees to the sun, with very little effect when positioned at 180 degrees or zero degrees. For this reason, polarizers don't always work well with wide-angle lenses, as they take in portions of the sky that deliver maximum and minimum polarizing effect. On page 24 we discuss the polarizer in more detail.

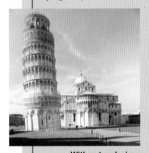
Without polarizer

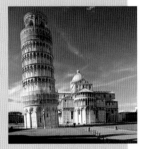
With polarizer

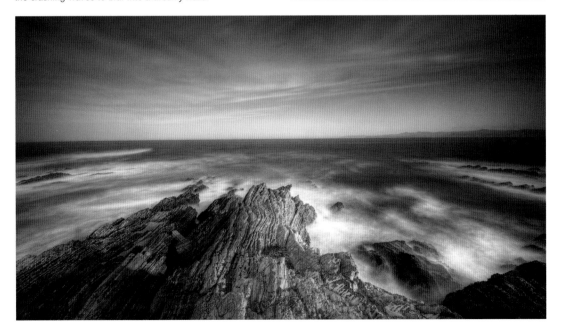

Travel photography

Everyone takes a camera on holiday with them, but next time you go away why not come back with some quality travel photography, rather than a set of holiday snaps?

A trip away always presents great opportunities for photography. New and interesting cultures, foreign landscapes and experiences – what passionate photographer could resist these great opportunities? Good travel photography is all about telling the story of your trip, or of a particular location. Photographing small details, local characters on the street and food in marketplaces is just as important as shooting more obvious landscape scenes. In order to tell the complete story, a good travel photographer must be a jack of all trades, able to photograph anything.

Local culture

Even the most touristy of locations has a 'real' side to it, where you can find some local culture. It might be an early morning market, or a district where residents work or shop. The key to finding out where all of this happens is research – and this starts before you've even got on the plane.

Back at home, guidebooks and internet research will tell you what is happening in the area you are going to, and will probably give you some good ideas for how to photograph it. Are there any local events, such as colourful festivals? What is your destination famous for – music? Food? Architecture?

Portraits and street photography

Although it takes some courage, walking up to someone on the street and asking if you can take their picture is something every travel photographer should do. Depending on where you are, you might have to part with a little small change in return for the photo opportunity, but it could be worth it.

Look for colourful characters in interesting places wearing clothes that are indicative of the location and culture. Don't be afraid to offer a little bit of direction to get the background and lighting as you want it; you might only get one opportunity to shoot the picture, so make the most of it. And don't forget show your subject the image on the back of the camera – it will always raise a smile!

Photographing people without their knowledge is a more difficult issue, and one that requires a combination of legal knowledge and common sense in equal measures. In most countries it is perfectly permissible to shoot pictures of people in public places without their knowledge or consent, although others, such as France, have introduced privacy legislation that forbids it. Regardless of the legal situation, however, it is polite and reasonable to stop shooting pictures if someone spots you and objects. If you are in a really sticky situation, show them the images and offer to delete them, if necessary.

Although it's tempting to stand off at a distance and shoot candid pictures with a telephoto lens, an alternative method is to get in really close with a wide-angle lens and 'shoot from the hip', i.e. don't bother looking through the viewfinder. Set your autofocus mode to wide-area, if your camera allows, to increase the probability of getting something in focus, and then just subtly click away while remaining inconspicuous. You can crop for accurate composition later (see pages 264– 265). It's a very enjoyable way to work, and you'll get some great images of life on the street.

Opposite: A small compact can be great for taking quick, inconspicuous photographs, like this snap of a boy on horseback in the Altai Tavanbogd National Park, Mongolia.

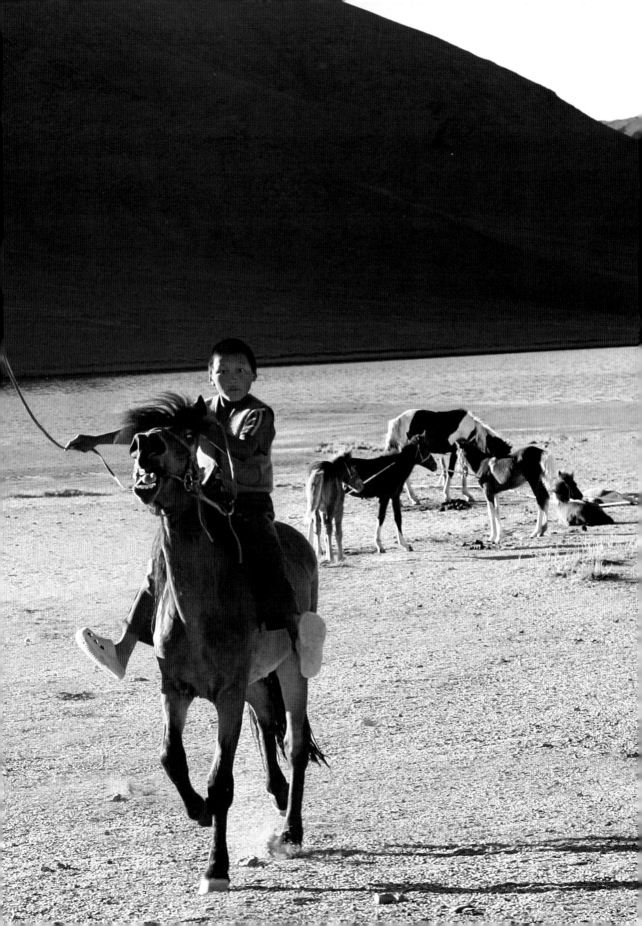

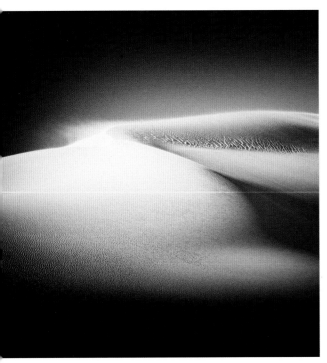

Above: *Landscape images don't have to be in landscape format. Try square, panoramic and portrait approaches.*

Landscapes

Landscape and travel photographers share a great deal in common – after all, photographing the terrain of a location is a vital part of telling its story. Landscapes often look better at either end of the day, so it's well worth getting up early and finding a location for sunrise. Or, indeed, you may have already identified a photogenic spot that would look good towards the end of the day. Tracking the sun's position in the sky during the day will help you to identify the best time to visit.

Every renowned location has its famous scenes, and these are a good place to start shooting. You'll probably be able to identify them from local postcards in tourist shops. But do make sure you go further than this and find pictures that aren't so famous, too. Always keep your eyes open, and if the light or time of day is wrong then take the picture anyway as a reference, and make a note to come back later on.

The usual accessories will come in useful when travelling: graduated neutral density filters (see page 25) for reducing the brightness of bright skies, a lightweight tripod and a remote release for shooting in low light.

Equipment for travel

At the planning stage of a trip, it's also vital to think about what equipment you are going to take with you. As you are going to be on the move all the time, it's important not to weigh yourself down, which may mean leaving some pieces of kit behind. On the other hand, you don't want to leave yourself without the tools you need to shoot stunning pictures. Try to reach a compromise between portability and functionality – for example, one or two zoom lenses covering a big range of focal lengths are better than half a dozen prime lenses that weigh too much and will need to be changed all the time.

If you can, take a spare battery with you, and don't forget that you may need an electrical socket adaptor to be able to charge your batteries. Also think about storage. Take enough memory cards with you that you won't have to clear any to keep shooting, and think about an option for backing up your pictures on the move. A portable storage device is great for this (see page 29), but you could even take a laptop if you can guarantee its safety – in your hotel room, for instance – and burn your pictures to a DVD. Alternatively, find an internet café and use their facilities to upload your photos to an online storage space.

Right: *Small and portable, storage devices often come in protective cases and are very affordable these days.*

Impromptu aerial photography

Before you've even arrived at your destination, there are opportunities for decent travel photography. The views from commercial airliners flying at 35,000 feet can be incredible, although doing them justice in a photograph requires a mixture of skill and opportunity.

The best place to sit on a plane if you plan to shoot pictures from a window is in front of the wing. Behind the wing, the heat haze from the jet exhaust causes very blurry distortion. If you aren't sitting there, you can always take a wander up the plane to an emergency exit at the front and shoot out of this window. Be sure to mention what you are doing to a member of the crew, though, and ask them if it's OK.

Reflections in the many layers of glass inside an aeroplane window are also a problem. To reduce them, it's best to get the lens as close to the glass as possible without actually touching it (vibrations from the engines will cause blur) and shield the area around the camera so light is not falling on objects that might be reflected. A lens hood helps with this, as does hiding the whole apparatus under a cloth or piece of clothing.

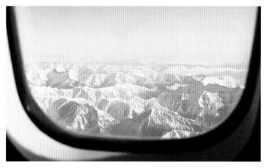

Above: Don't miss out on the opportunity to begin your travel photography before you reach your destination.

Underwater photos

Underwater photography has always been an expensive pursuit, but these days there are some more affordable ways to get below the waves with your camera. Some compact cameras are waterproof to depths of 5–10m, which is more than enough for snorkling on reefs and playing in the sea. If you are a scuba diver then another option is an underwater housing, which will protect your camera to depths of 40–50m. While these are hideously expensive for DSLRs, they are more reasonably priced for compact cameras, which have the added bonus of having good macro performance and easier handling, too.

When shooting underwater, the best pictures are always at shallow depths. This is because light cannot penetrate water very well, so conditions get darker the deeper you go. Pictures also look bluer the further down you venture, because red light is scattered more than blue by particles in the water. You can correct this with your camera's white balance feature, but only to a degree.

Always try to shoot in patches of sunlight, and with the light coming over your shoulder. Alternatively, look upwards and photograph silhouettes against the bright surface.

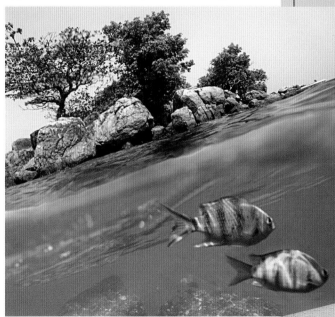

Above: For your first underwater photography you could just try using a simple waterproof compact camera – you'll be amazed by the results.

ASSIGNMENT
SHOOTING A
STREET PORTRAIT

Portraits don't have to be formal and structured, and travel photography doesn't always have to be fly-on-the-wall reportage. Blend the two by shooting the portraits of the people you meet on your travels.

While it's good to shoot reportage-style images on your travels, portraiture can also have an interesting role to play. If you see an interesting face, or someone dressed in exciting or unusual clothing, approach them and ask if you can take their picture. Nine times out of ten you'll get a positive answer. The advantage

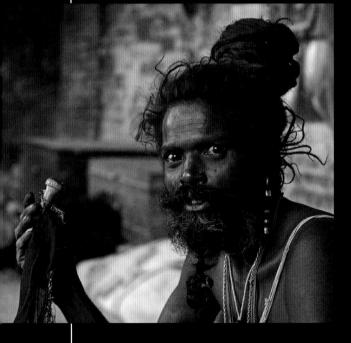

of digital cameras is that the results are instantly available. You can show your subjects the pictures, which often draws a giggle or two.

Obviously, with such spontaneous portrait photography, you don't have the time to arrange a background or mess about with reflectors. That said, you can try moving your subject to make sure they are in the right location: avoid direct sunlight (unless it's at the start or end of the day) by moving them into a shadowy spot. And if you are not using the background to show the person in their environment, try to make it as unobtrusive as possible by picking something neutral in colour and lacking in detail. You can also throw this out of focus by using a large aperture to restrict depth of field (see page 84).

Unless you are very comfortable with manual exposure mode, using one of the automatic or semi-automatic modes will let you give all your attention to your subject. You won't have much time to work, so thinking quickly is good. Use the long end of your standard zoom, or swap to a 50mm lens before you approach the subject – a perfect portrait lens for this type of work (see page 88). If you are using aperture priority exposure mode then select a wide aperture of f/4. If you'd rather use a fully automatic mode then choose the portrait scene mode, which should choose a large aperture for you.

Above: *Cropping closely blurs distracting background from this portrait of a holy man smoking his pipe in the Pashupatinath Temple near Kathmandu, Nepal.*
Nikon D700, 24–70mm f/2.8 lens, 1/250sec at f/4, ISO100

Opposite, main: *A Mongolian shepherd asked to have his picture taken with his horse in northern Mongolia.*
Canon EOS 5D MkII, 24–105mm f/4 lens, 1/250sec at f/4, ISO200

ESSENTIAL KIT

- DSLR and standard zoom,
  or a 50mm prime lens
- Digital compact set to telephoto zoom
- Small currency incentive

TIPS & TRICKS

- Colourful characters deserve colourful treatment. Choose vivid picture settings in your camera's menu to give the colours in the scene some power.

- Focus on the eyes, and let everything else drift slowly out of focus.

- Don't restrict yourself to a vertical frame – try a horizontal 'landscape' composition, too.

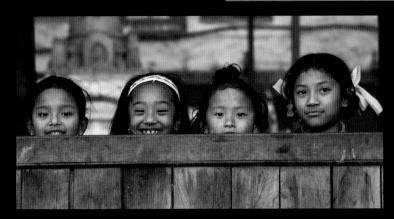

Left: Kids the world over like having their photo taken, and showing them the shots on the back of the camera will often have them giggling, like these girls in Bhaktapur, Nepal. Canon EOS 5D MkII, 24–105mm f/4 lens, 1/250sec at f/4, ISO200

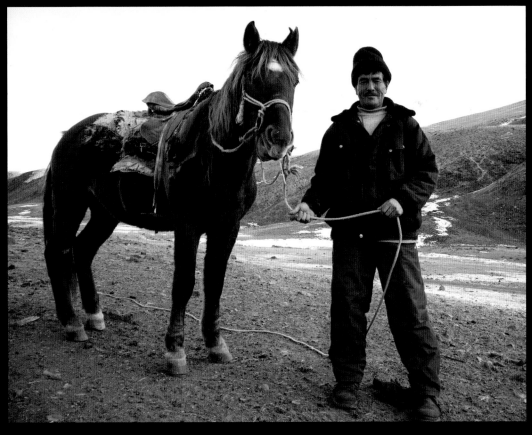

FOCUS ON
TRAVEL
CHRIS COE TRAVEL PHOTOGRAPHER

Chris Coe hated photography as a child. His father collected cameras and as a consequence one always seemed to be pointed in his direction when he was growing up. A working tour of the USA as a student provided the inspiration to take photography seriously, though, and after ten years working in medicine, Chris switched careers to become a freelance photographer. Some 40 books and many commissions around the world later, Chris not only pursues his career as a pro, but also runs the prestigious international Travel Photographer of the Year awards (www.tpoty.com). You can find him at www.chriscoe.com.

What brought you to travel photography?
Initially, a tour around the USA with an Olympus Trip. Latterly, inspiring places that challenge me to capture them in a more creative and imaginative way.

What talents do you need?
Versatility, enthusiasm, persistence, thinking laterally, good communication, confidence and friendliness/personability.

Is there a particular place that shaped your work more than any other?
There are obviously places I prefer to travel to and that inspire me more, but I always love seeing new places. It's not the places that shape my work but the light, so wherever the light is most interesting inspires me.

How much of your work is commissioned and how much self-generated?
Most of my work is commissioned. When I started I had to work really hard to generate and secure work but as you get established, more and more work comes by word of mouth and personal recommendation.

Do you work with online stock libraries?
At the moment I don't work with any online libraries but this is solely because I don't have the time to prepare many new submissions. My own libraries are all online though, which helps online sales.

What type of cameras do you normally shoot with? Does it depend on location?
The choice of camera mostly depends on the end use of the images. Most of my work is on medium format and 35mm, but I always try to use the format that will give me the highest-quality images within the time available. If I'm shooting a personal project then I'd always choose either my beloved Hasselblad XPan panoramic camera or the Linhof large format, unless I'm doing something experimental, in which case I'd probably try out techniques on a DSLR. I also tend to use it more for photographing people.

What advice do you have for photographers just starting out?
Take the time to learn the basics of photographic technique and composition. These are the building blocks that will always underpin your photography in the future. Don't be afraid to make mistakes but always work out how you could do it better next time – you should never be afraid to ask for help or advice. Be a perfectionist but don't be precious about your images – share them with others and print the best ones, but don't expect everyone else to like them. If you want to do photography as a profession then be realistic about what you can earn and how quickly you can establish yourself. Learn from the images of the best photographers, and above all remember that photography is supposed to be fun!

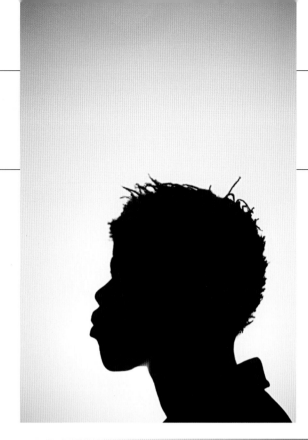

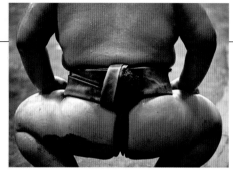

Above: A Sumo wrestler readies himself for the start of a training session in Tokyo, Japan, the only country where Sumo is practiced professionally.

Left: Cobra, a San Bushman of the Kalahari tribe, stands silhouetted in a Botswana sunset.

Below: Pacific rollers pound the coast at Marshall's Beach, San Francisco, as the iconic Golden Gate Bridge glows in the last evening sun.

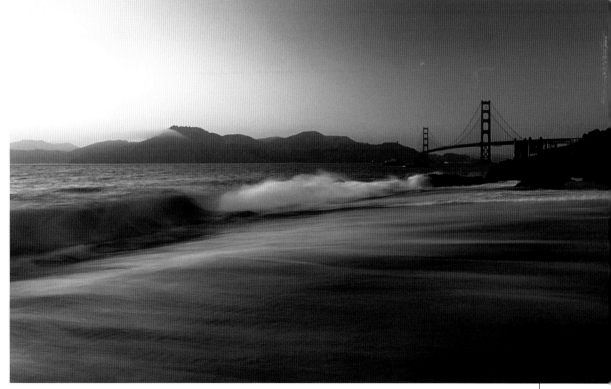

SHOOTING AN EARLY-MORNING MARKETPLACE

Markets are the cultural centre of any town or village, and a hive of activity where the hustle and bustle of everyday life provides amazing subject matter for the travel photographer.

Marketplaces have a lot in common, regardless of the country in which you find them. They are centres for trade and commerce, where people come to buy and sell anything from fresh fruit, vegetables and meat to flowers, electronics, movies and music. It is their function as a central meeting point that makes them a great place for street photography. Different types of people come from different walks of life – restaurant owners, farmers, mothers, traders – you name it. And, of course, tourists.

The best time to see a marketplace free from excessive numbers of holiday-makers is first thing in the morning; you will see the real side of even the most touristy locations in the hours around sunrise. Food markets especially are at their busiest at this time, because this is when boats of fish come ashore and business owners need to stock up for the day ahead. Because people are so busy, they are less likely to notice you wandering around with your camera, and there are some tricks that will make you even less conspicuous.

Try shooting 'from the hip' – that is, without looking through the viewfinder. Use aperture priority autoexposure mode if you can, and set a mid-range aperture of f/5.6–8, which is enough to give you some depth of field and also to generate a shutter speed fast enough to avoid camera shake. Tweak your camera's ISO sensitivity to ensure this. Wide-area autofocus will make sure you focus on the subject, and a wide-angle lens should mean you can get up close to your subject and shoot them without them realizing.

Compact cameras can be used for this type of work, but are more frustrating to use because of their shutter lag (see page 11). A DSLR responds more quickly to a press of the shutter release, particularly if you have already pre-focused by half-pressing the shutter release in the first place.

Wander around and use your eyes as much as you do your camera. You might see a stall that is perfect for a photograph, just not right now. Keep an eye on it and come back later on. Back home you will want to make good use of the Crop and Rotate tools in Adobe Photoshop, Lightroom or Elements to tidy up your 'from the hip' compositions (see pages 264–265). Hopefully this way of shooting will reward you with relaxed, natural-looking images of everyday life from the place you are visiting.

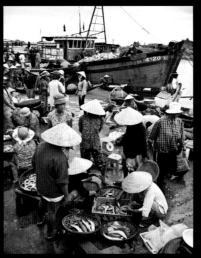

Above: Gaining a little height and looking down on the market gives a real sense of atmosphere at this busy fish market.
Nikon D700 with 50mm f/1.4 lens, 1/125sec at f/11, ISO800

ESSENTIAL KIT

- DSLR with wide-angle lens or standard zoom
- PC or Mac with image-editing software

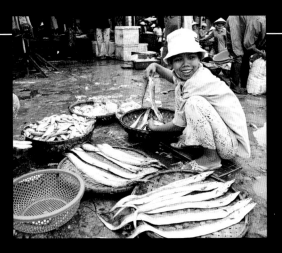

TIPS & TRICKS

- Practise shooting from the hip with your zoom at one setting, so you get an idea of what will be included in the frame from where you are standing.

- You don't always have to work this way: a smile and a polite request to take some pictures will let you stand and photograph someone as they work.

Left: *Get down to the same level for a feeling of involvement in the scene.*
Nikon D700, 28mm f/2.8 lens, 1/60sec at f/8, ISO800
Below: *Shooting from the hip is a useful technique for grabbing images. Make sure you set aperture priority mode and a mid-range aperture first, though.*
Nikon D700, 28mm f/2.8 lens, 1/125sec at f/5.6, ISO400

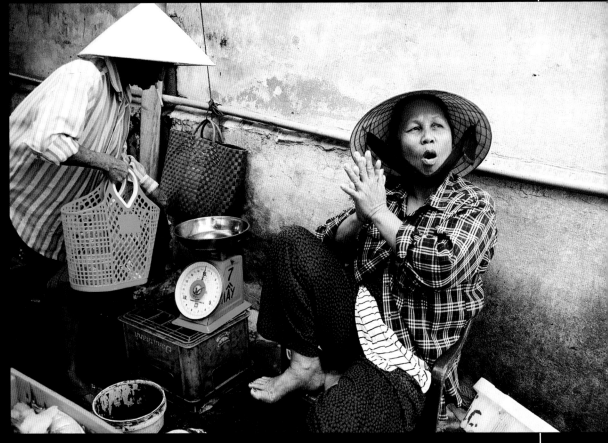

Architectural photography

Good architectural photography needs to show a building in its context, and bring across some of the beauty that the architect created when the structure was designed.

When it comes to photographing buildings, a pure, simple style works well. Professional architectural photographers almost never include people in their images, and go to painstaking lengths to record every detail just how they want it.

Familiarity with a location, and the available vantage points, is essential, as is the knowledge of where light will be at various times of the day. In fact, for static objects, buildings can be surprisingly complicated to photograph. Here are ten tips that are guaranteed to improve your images.

1. Be sensitive to the direction of light Whereas frontal lighting makes a building look flat and lifeless, side lighting (also known as relief) brings out detail and emphasizes texture. You can't control the direction and light as you can in a studio, but you can predict what time of day (and even what time of year) the sun will give you what you want. Also keep an eye on the weather – direct sunlight and light softened by layers of cloud give very different effects.

Below, left and right: *Two contrasting views of the same building. Standing back with a telephoto lens provides a very different image to up close with a wide-angle.*

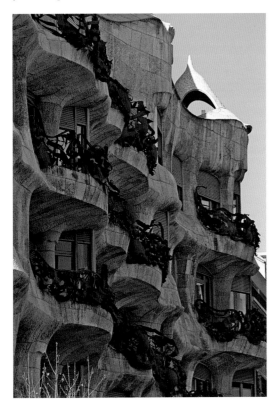

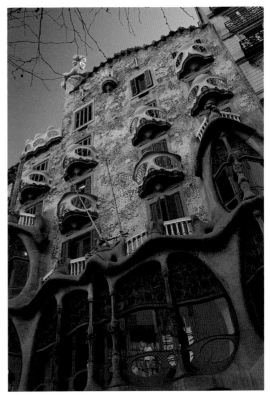

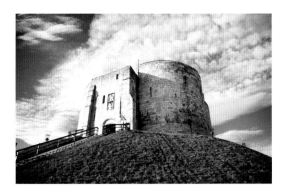

Left: *The black and white treatment of this old stone ruin emphasizes the lines and shapes of the building as well as of the mound and stairs.*

2. Experiment with lenses While a wide-angle lens is great for shooting a building in the context of its surroundings, it can create annoying distortions, especially when tilted upwards (the dreaded 'converging verticals' – see pages 154–155). Telephoto lenses tend to flatten perspective, whereas wide-angle optics exaggerate it. Use this to your advantage and shoot the same building in different styles to learn each approach.

3. Shoot at night Buildings take on a different personality in the dark to that which they have in the daytime. The direction, colour and character of light changes, as does the environment in which the structure is seen. Use long exposures and a tripod for the best picture quality, and take a meter reading from the dusky sky to start with; don't be afraid to bracket your exposures. The half-hour just before and just after sunset are the best times to shoot.

4. Always consider the details – the architect certainly will have. Find those parts of a building that have received special attention during its design phase and you'll be onto a winner. Explore these details with a telephoto lens, contrasting them with other parts of the structure if possible. Go for doorways, window frames, ornaments, roofs, etc. and concentrate on the patterns made by these lines, shapes and textures.

5. Take your time Architectural photography is a slow, considered discipline; it may take several visits to get the shot you are after. And when composing images, don't rush. Check around the frame carefully and decide if each element is helping the composition or not. If the answer is no, can you exclude it, or reduce its influence?

6. Look for repeating patterns Some of the most powerful compositions are those that feature the same motif repeating over and over throughout the picture. This could be the latticework of an old station roof, or the grid lines of a modern-day glass-walled office block.

7. Create impact with your composition Inject some drama into your architectural photography by adopting a dramatic viewpoint and looking upwards with a wide-angle lens. An angled composition also helps here, and if there are many lines within the scene, frame them so they run off into the corners.

8. Look out for contrast Some conflict and contrast really helps an architectural photo to sing. Throw a curved element into a picture full of straight lines and angles, break up symmetry or inject a small amount of bright colour into an otherwise muted scene. Sometimes the sky can supply a good counterpoint, too.

9. Colour or black and white? Although it's a subjective decision, the choice of whether to go for a black and white or colour approach to a shot can completely change the look and feel of the finished photograph. Monochrome works very well when you are trying to emphasize the lines and shapes of a building; colour is better when looking at a structure in the context of its surroundings.

10. Try to find a unique view Many buildings have been photographed countless times, and usually from the same spot in very similar ways. Always have a good look around a location and explore new vantage points with different lenses. Think about cropping to new aspect ratios, or using negative space for new and unusual compositions.

FOCUS ON
ARCHITECTURE
MORLEY VON STERNBERG ARCHITECTURAL PHOTOGRAPHEF

Morley von Sternberg trained, qualified, and began his career as an architect before establishing his name as one of Britain's most respected architectural photographers. He has photographed an extraordinary array of landmark buildings both in the UK and overseas, as well as portraits of some of their creators and patrons. His work appears regularly in *The Sunday Times*, as well as leading architectural and design publications. He has also been the sole contributor of photographs to a number of books.

How did you get started?
I originally trained and qualified as an architect, but along the way I discovered photography, and came to the realization that I enjoyed it more than architecture.

'Photographers are like Renaissance men – their expertise spans so many different subject areas.'

What talent, character traits and abilities are helpful in your field?
Problem solving is the number one skill a photographer requires. I always think of photographers as being Renaissance men – their expertise has to span so many different subject areas.

The hardest part of your job?
Waiting for the right weather, without a doubt. Architectural photography is all about capturing a mood, and weather plays a vital part in this.

Do you work with online stock libraries, and if so, do they make up a significant percentage of your income?
Yes I do, but they only contribute a small percentage of my income.

Is there a particular city you think shaped your work more than any other?
Rather than cities, I feel that it's other photographers that have shaped my work. My inspirations are people such as Julius Shulman, Morley Baer, Art Strieber and Tony Ray-Jones.

How much of your work is commissioned and how much self-generated?
My work is 99 per cent commissioned – it's the backbone of what I do.

What type of cameras do you normally shoot with? And what type of lens?
My tool of choice is a high-resolution digital SLR with shift lenses.

How do you keep your ideas fresh?
By looking at the work of other photographers. I was really impressed by a recent Muybridge exhibition – he solved many technical problems to create his images and is very inspiring.

What advice do you have for photographers just starting out?
Be passionate. Also, take loads of photographs and analyze and review them so you can reach the stage where you don't have to take so many photos to capture that one, magical shot.

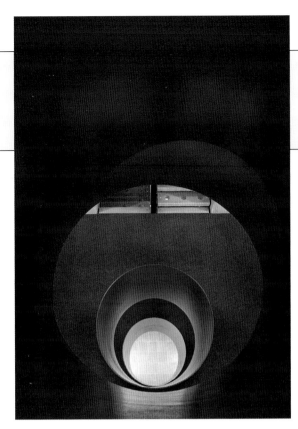

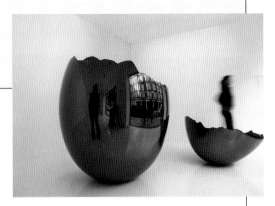

Above: *Unusually for architectural photography, this shot includes people. Here they help the viewer get a sense of the scale of this sculpture in the Gargosian Gallery, London.*

Left: *The powerful shape and colour of this seating area demand attention.*

Below: *Focusing on a single element of a building, in this instance the curve of the roof, creates impact in a composition.*

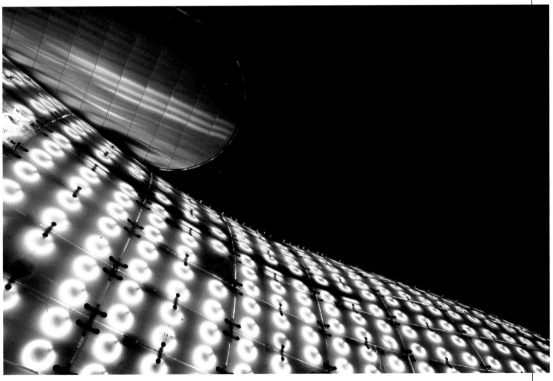

Converging **verticals**

Converging verticals are a peculiar quirk of perspective, and the bane of architectural photographers' lives. For a more natural result we can use some in-camera tricks or post-processing.

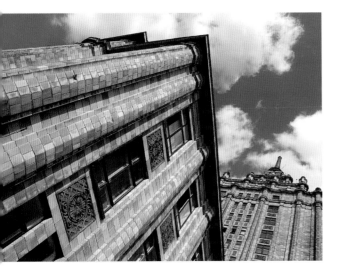

No discussion of architectural photography would be complete without mentioning converging verticals: a trick of perspective whereby buildings seem to lean backwards when they are photographed from below, appearing to be on the verge of falling over.

There is, in fact, nothing theoretically wrong with this – it's only the same perspective effect that makes railway lines appear to be getting closer together as they get further away from you. But our brains don't tend to register this in objects

Left: The wide-angle lens used for this picture of the Empire State Building in downtown Manhattan, New York, caused the vertical lines to seemingly converge.

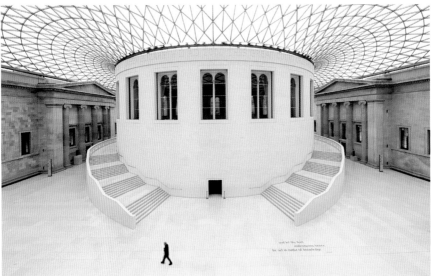

Above: Even though a very wide-angle lens has been used to shoot this image of the British Museum, converging verticals have been avoided by getting up to a high vantage point and shooting with the camera held vertically.

rising vertically from the ground, like buildings do, which is why it looks odd in photographs.

Converging verticals only occur when the camera is tilted upwards to look at a building, and the effect is exaggerated by wide-angle lenses. In order to avoid the problem, professional architectural photographers use specialist cameras or lenses that have perspective control movements. These allow the back of the camera to be kept completely vertical while the lens is pivoted upwards (a 'swing' movement). This equipment is phenomenally expensive, though, and well beyond the reach of most amateur photographers. Fortunately there are a few tricks – both in-camera and post-production – that can help tackle converging verticals in a more economical way.

If converging verticals only rear their ugly head when the camera is tilted upwards, then shooting from further back, keeping the camera vertical and cropping out the empty foreground space afterwards, will do the trick. You may even be able to get away with a little upward tilt if you are shooting with a telephoto lens.

In many imaging applications you can correct for converging verticals in a few mouse clicks. In Photoshop, use either a free transform of the image (see page 265) where you can expand the top of the image separately from the bottom, or the always useful lens correction filter, which is also available in Lightroom and Photoshop Elements.

There are times when this kind of perspective distortion can inject some drama into a picture, but to do this there has to be an abundance of it. As a general rule, either generate lots of converging verticals by using a wide-angle lens and looking upwards from a very nearby viewpoint, or try to eliminate the distortion completely. The middle ground can look scrappy and unprofessional.

Right: If you have the chance to see a city from above – in this case Hong Kong – and have a head for heights, take it. Set a large aperture to raise shutter speed and beat camera shake.

Aerial photography

A great way to see any city is from above. While best done in a helicopter or small plane, you can also get above it all by getting up a very tall building and looking down. If you take this approach, try to get outside to avoid the presence of reflections in glass windows, or use a polarizing filter to reduce their influence.

On the other hand, if you have the chance to take a flight over a city, you would be a fool not to grab the opportunity and take your camera up with you. Again, it's best not to shoot through a window if you can avoid it. Your pilot may let you open a small window, or even better a complete door so you can lean out slightly – if you have a head for heights. If you do this, you won't be able to have anything loose with you in the cabin in case it falls out, so make sure you have the right lens on. Your standard zoom should be adequate.

Engine vibration is a big problem and can cause camera shake even at shutter speeds that would normally be fine. Image stabilization technology doesn't work well in these situations, as it cannot compensate for such high frequency vibrations. And lens hoods make matters worse, as the wind buffets them around. Use a large aperture to increase the shutter speed to around 1/1,000sec, raising the ISO if necessary. You won't need much depth of field, as everything is more or less the same long distance away.

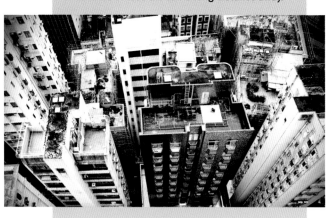

FINDING THE DETAIL IN ARCHITECTURE

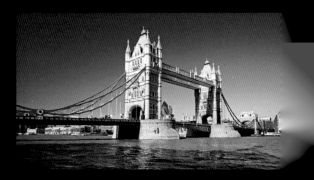

Photographing a building isn't always about shooting the complete structure. Capturing those recognizable architectural details is important, too.

Some buildings are recognizable from the smallest detail. The White House in Washington, DC in the USA, the Sydney Opera House in Australia, the Kremlin in Moscow, Russia and the Guggenheim Museum in Bilbao, Spain are all examples of architectural designs of such striking beauty that they are recognizable from the smallest detail – from spires and tiles to rooftops. Why not capture these details in the form of a visual essay to complement shots of the structure as a whole? Or even resort to such a technique when a building's surroundings make it difficult or impossible to get a decent wide shot.

Use a telezoom – or the long end of your compact's zoom range – to get in as close as possible from street level, or investigate what you can shoot from within the building, from windows or even from the roof if at all accessible. Good weather will give you strong, bright light to shoot in, although it's often worth waiting until the end of the day (or shooting at the start) to get more directional light that will let you play with shadows and enhance texture. Alternatively, wait for a cloudy day to provide you with flat lighting, which can work very well for architectural detail shot in black and white. Also consider using a polarizing filter to control how much reflection you are getting from the building's glass.

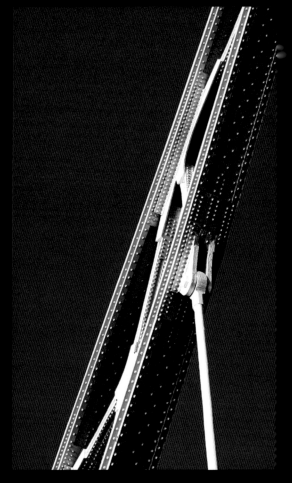

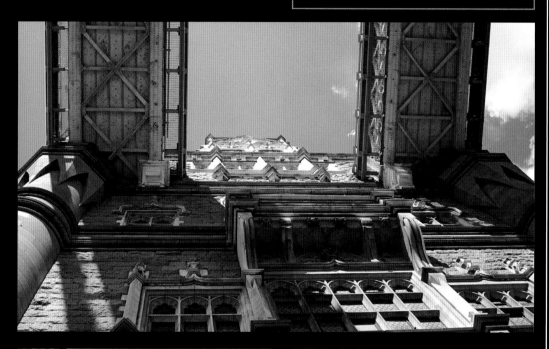

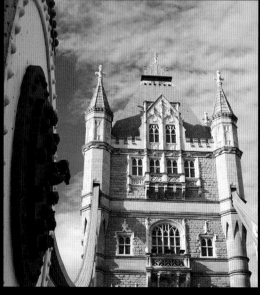

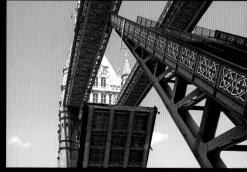

Clockwise from top left : The iconic Tower Bridge in London as seen from the river; the mighty north tower and walkways from below (above top); the opened bascule from below (above); a close-up of a suspension joint (left), and a close-up of the magnificent suspension (far left). Nikon D700, 24–120mm f/4 lens, 1/125sec at between f/5.6 and f/11, ISO400.

Reportage photography

You can't be selective about what a camera records in a scene – it's all or nothing – which makes photography a very good medium with which to document the world. Telling a story through your photographs is one of the most rewarding processes there is.

Reportage, also know as documentary photography, is film-making or photojournalism that tells a story entirely through pictures. Indeed, we all know that a picture is worth a thousand words, which makes you and your camera a potential master storyteller.

Documentary photography is truly accessible to all. Whether you are shooting with very expensive DSLR gear in the deserts of the Middle East, or with a camera phone on the streets of your home town, the success of a reportage project lies in your ability to tell a story, and document the world around you. The world is made of up many subjects, of course, but usually reportage photographers look at anthropology: people, and the effect they have on their environment.

Observing what is going on around you is more important in reportage than in any other area of photography. Walking around with your camera permanently glued to your eye will result in you missing opportunities; it's much better to observe with your own eyes and your attention fully on your surroundings. Don't be afraid of revisiting a location time and time again – as you do so, your familiarity with it will enable you to see new things that you missed the previous time.

It's important to research your subject, too. The history of a location, the customs and practices that go on there now, as well as its geography, are all important and can be researched from home.

The rewards of documentary photography are both instant and long-lived. When done well, reporting on contemporary issues can strike a chord with people, get them talking and or inspire action. It can tell the story of protests, sporting events and celebrations from your point of view. Even portraits can document people and their culture. The secret is in telling a good story.

That said, be aware of dangers at all times. The idea is that you can proudly show off your pictures afterwards, not get seriously injured or killed in the process of taking them.

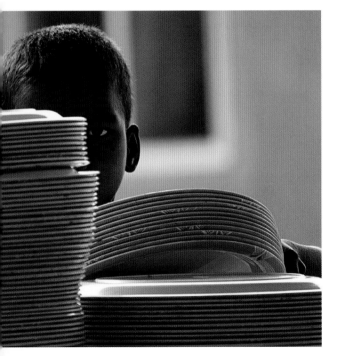

Opposite: *Reportage documentary is a powerful way to convey the reality of a situation. This image of a struggling firefighter during the forest fires raging on the Spanish island of La Palma in 2009 brings home the true horror of the catastrophe.*

Left: *This striking picture by Siddhartha Lammata shows a seven year-old boy stacking plates at a restaurant in New Delhi, highlighting the issue of child labour.*

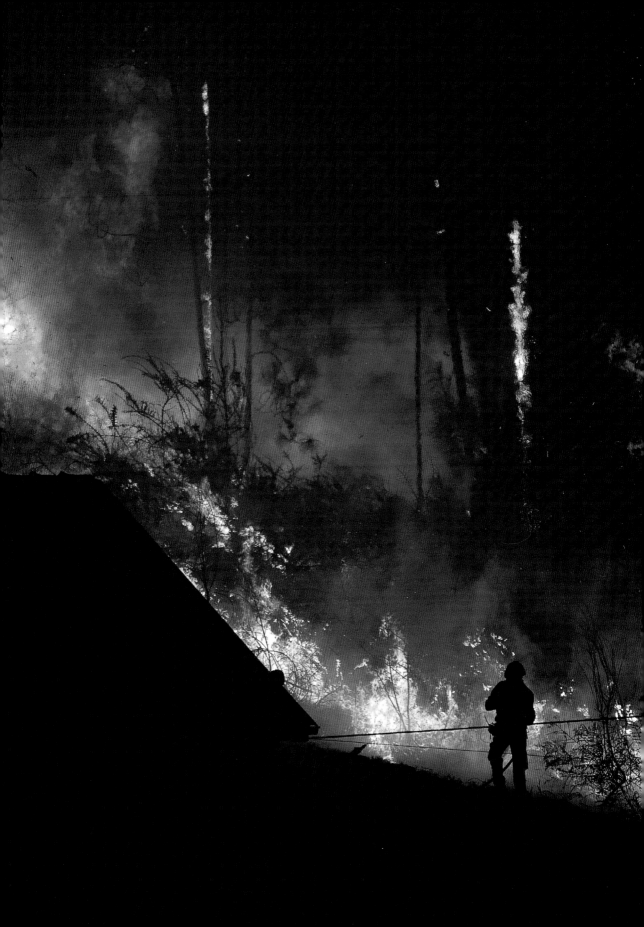

Different approaches

Reportage stands out as one of the areas in photography in which you can most develop a signature style. Looking at the work of modern-day photojournalists, as well as those who produced documentary images in the past, reveals a wealth of different approaches. Taking inspiration from the work of some of these famous names is a good way of developing your own photographic style. Below are some of the different approaches the aspiring documentary photographer can take, along with some names to research.

The storyteller

Working to self-assigned or commissioned briefs, the storyteller carefully researches the topic, then sets out to report on it with photography alone. Remaining passive, and observing without interfering with their subject matter, they are there as a neutral observer and not as someone who shapes the images in front of them. Projects can be at home, or on the other side of the world.

Below: Reportage photographers tread a difficult line between becoming involved in their subjects and remaining detached. In telling the story of Kosovo's Road of Death, photographer Tom Stoddart deliberately placed himself in the frame.

The collector

Often shooting as a side project, the collector seeks to identify common themes running through society by shooting pictures on a single topic. The location, style and subject matter can be different, but the theme is a constant. This can be an entertaining aspect of culture that will remind you of a location or time, or a serious comment on modern society.

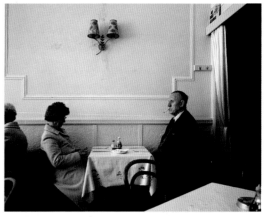

Above: A different approach to documentary could be to become a collector like Magnum photographer Martin Parr, with his project 'Bored Couples'. Pick a theme and 'collect' images to illustrate it.

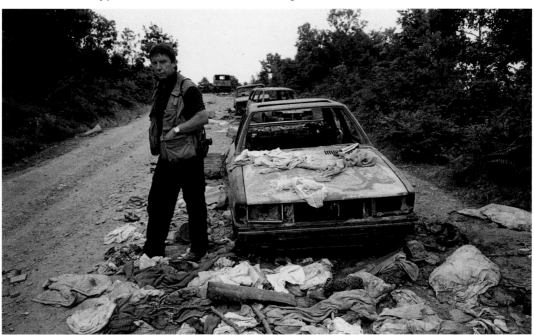

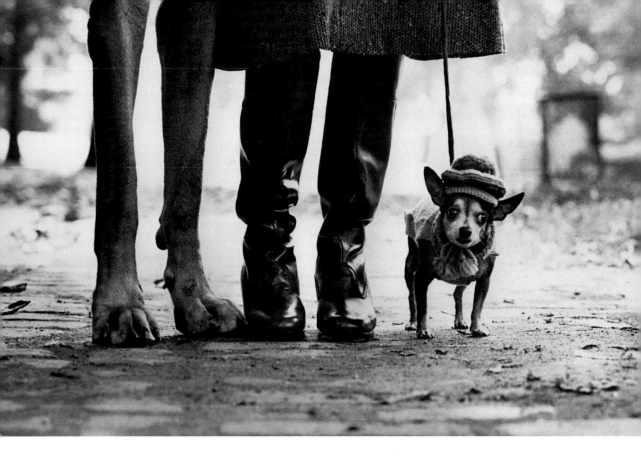

The humourist

Think of documentary photography and you may think of gritty but depressing images of war zones and conflict, but there is a lighter side to reportage. The humourist aims to comment on society through humour – either to entertain or to make a more serious political point through satire. Those with a dry sense of humour and a love of irony will be at an advantage here.

The portraitist

As much as we think of portraiture as something completely different to documentary, shooting portraits of people, particularly on location, is a great way to document their existence. This approach works best as a body of work – a group of portraits from the same 'clan'. They might be a local club, a group of war veterans or even strangers on the street, providing there is a common element to link them together.

Right: A shepherd and his flock in the Alpes de Provence, France, on a foggy autumn afternoon that made for very soft and even light, ideal for a roadside portraits.

Above: Elliott Erwitt's 1974 portrait of a chihuahua, accompanied by its female owner and a Great Dane, is a perfect example of Erwitt's eye for the humorous detail.

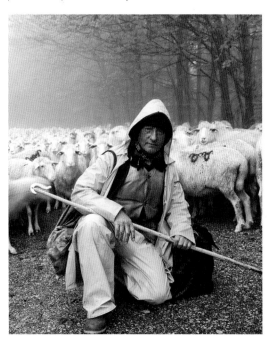

FOCUS ON
REPORTAGE
TOM STODDART DOCUMENTARY PHOTOGRAPHER

Tom Stoddart became interested in photography as a teenager and supplied his first pictures to local newspapers in northeast England aged 17. After moving to London he has since worked for countless international newspapers and agencies, including *The Sunday Times* and *Time* magazines. During his eventful career, he has witnessed the siege of Beirut, the fall of the Berlin Wall, the election of Nelson Mandela, the Balkan wars – where he was badly injured during the intense fighting in Sarajevo – as well as both wars against Saddam Hussein in Iraq. Tom is acknowledged to be one of the world's leading and most respected photojournalists. You can find him at www.tomstoddart.com.

Is there a particular city you think shaped your work more than any other?
While on commission for *The Sunday Times* in Beirut in 1982, when the city was under siege by Israeli forces, I graduated from press photographer to photojournalist: I recognized the power of a set of images over single images shot to accompany already-written editorials.

How much of your work is commissioned and how much self-generated?
At least 75 per cent of my work is self-generated and self-financed. I see something that interests me somewhere in the world and I travel there to document the crises as they unfold.

'Work hard and be interested in everything, and you'll soon realize you have the best job in the world.'

How did you get started?
I was always interested in political issues and documenting them was what drew me into reportage. Managing to get into local newspapers was an important first step.

What talents, character traits and abilities are helpful in your field?
You need to be very persistent, determined, and above all you need to be interested in the issues around you.

What's the hardest part of your job?
To keep going. The future is bright for photography, but it's getting harder for individual photographers to get paid for their imagery as there is so much of it around.

What type of cameras do you use? Do you always shoot in black and white?
My trusty Leica MPs. The most important thing is to use a camera you are comfortable with, and one that is small enough for you to work with very quickly and capture the important moments. I much prefer black and white over colour. I was once told, 'If you photograph in colour you see the colour of their clothes; if you photograph in black and white you see the colour of their soul.'

What advice do you have for photographers just starting out?
Most importantly, you need to be willing to work very hard and be interested in everything around you, and you will soon realize you have the best job in the world.

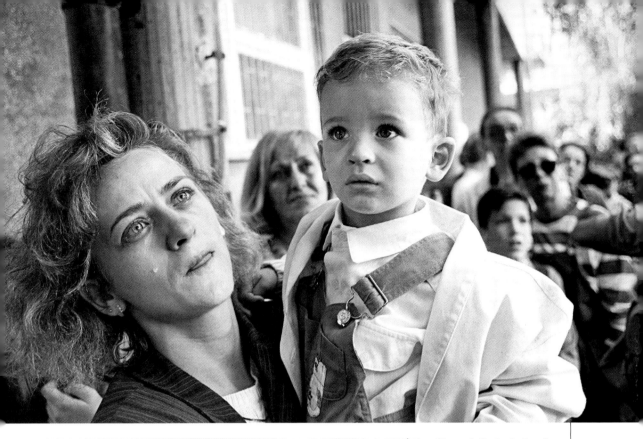

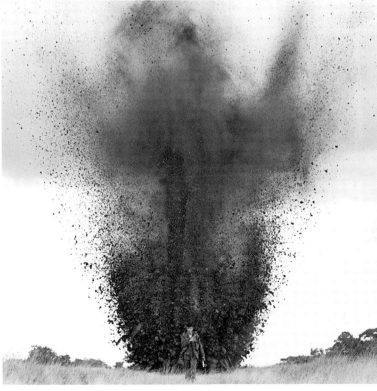

Above: *In the beginning of the Sarajevo siege in 1992, Serbian forces sometimes allowed children to be bussed out to escape the Serbian shelling. This particular scene was later re-enacted in the Woody Harrelson film* Welcome to Sarajevo.

Left: *Taken in 1996, this image shows Colombian special forces blowing up an airstrip used by the drug cartels to transport cocaine from a coca-processing lab in the Colombian jungle region of Guaviare. This is where more than half the world's cocaine is produced.*

ASSIGNMENT
DOCUMENTING EVERYDAY LIFE

Photography is the best way we have of keeping a visual record of everyday life. Record what you do each day and you'll have a fascinating set of pictures to look back on in years to come.

Ordinary life only seems humdrum when you don't really pay attention to it. There is plenty that we encounter every single day that is cool, interesting, disturbing, even newsworthy – and visually arresting. For the reportage photographer, documenting the ordinary is perhaps one of the biggest challenges there is, and, it could be argued, a prerequisite to documenting the extraordinary.

Carrying a small camera around with you everywhere you go is something that many enthusiast photographers do as a matter of course. Not the big, full-featured DSLRs used for more purposeful work, but a compact or microsystem camera that can tuck away in a bag. Even camera phones can be used, with certain limitations.

The idea is that next time you find yourself looking at a great piece of street art, a delicious-looking fruit and veg stall or a interesting pattern in the clouds, take a picture. Publish it on Twitter, Facebook or your blog. Document real life, and show other people what makes you smile every day.

To get you started, try photographing the following seven subjects. Limiting yourself to a certain number or theme can often help you find subjects. Also, juxtaposing your results afterwards will be both entertaining and rewarding if they all tie in together in a clear manner.

Over the course of the next day, photograph:
1. An animal.
2. Something that makes you smile.
3. Something that makes you sad.
4. A friend.
5. The place you work.
6. Yourself.
7. Your next meal.

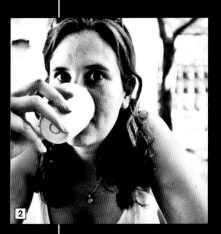

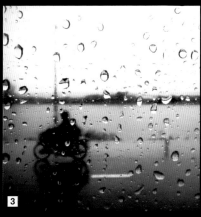

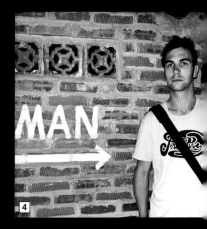

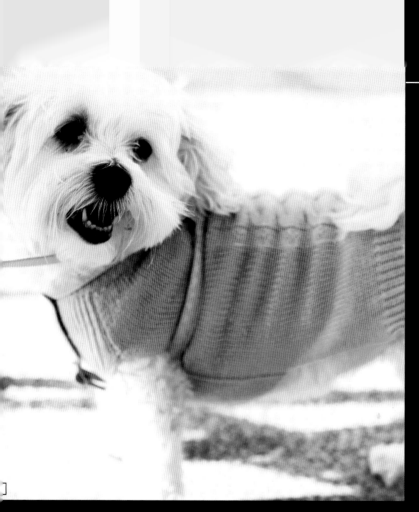

Left and below: *Seven pictures by the author documenting his day, shot with a camera phone for more convenience.*
Apple iPhone 3GS with the Hipstamatic app

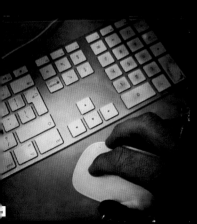

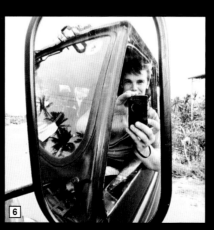

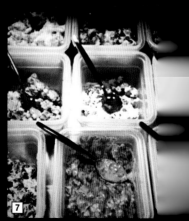

Street photography

Street photography has been around for decades, and provides a valuable record of how we live our lives at work, rest and play.

A subset of reportage, it has much in common with urban landscape photography (see pages 124–125) but is distinct and different from it; street photography deals with people and the effect they have on their environment as they go about their lives. It is an uncensored view of the societies we have created and live in, a record of the drama of everyday life.

Different approaches to street photography can cause different reactions. While some photographers go after humour, others explore the more difficult side of street life. But whatever your approach, there is plenty of subject matter deserving of your attention – from streetmarkets and graffiti to housing and transport.

You can shoot street photography with any type of camera. In fact, it's good to change the equipment you use often, as this will force you to change your shooting style as well as breaking unwanted habits you might develop. The way a picture is composed and framed is different with a compact camera and a DSLR, for example. Some street photographers even like to go back and shoot with a film camera. Changing lenses is like changing your point of view. Do this often, and you won't stagnate and get bored of photographing the same things. If you usually

Below: Look out for amusing ways in which your subjects seem to interact with their surroundings.

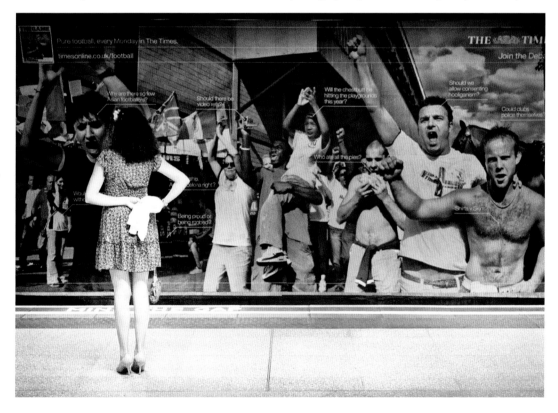

shoot with a standard zoom, try using a prime lens for example, and vice versa. When it comes to street photography, variety is most definitely the spice of life.

Approaches to street photography

Street photography is as much about expressing yourself as it is about documenting your subject. You put your own mark on street images by deciding how they are shot, and in what style.

Although you may think that photographing people anonymously without getting caught is the job for a telephoto lens and a distant viewpoint, many street photographers prefer to get close to the action, shooting with a wide-angle lens from close in. This up close and personal approach gives us a sense of being in the scene with the subject, and makes for very powerful compositions. You can also try shooting from the hip, i.e. without looking through the viewfinder. Using your camera's

wide area AF to ensure the autofocus finds the subject, you'll be surprised at the effectiveness of this technique. Wide-angle optics ensure that you'll be able to compose by aiming roughly, and shooting at high ISO sensitivity values means you'll get a small enough aperture to generate lots of depth of field to cover any focusing problems, while also maintaining a fast shutter speed to freeze motion.

Black and white works very well for street photography, so don't discount a colour picture without looking at in monochrome first (see pages 216–217). Sometimes black and white photographs free us from the distraction of clashing colours so we can concentrate on what else is happening in the frame, be it texture, shapes, lines or form. In fact, with many street scenes, keeping it simple is the best approach. If you are new to this type of photography, keep your camera in an auto exposure mode and concentrate on identifying good subjects, and composing them well.

Photographing people in public places

In most countries it is perfectly legal to photograph strangers in a public place, although there are exceptions. Make sure you are aware of the situation in your own country and any you are visiting before embarking on a street photography project there. As well as the law, it pays to stay on the right side of common sense and diplomacy. Not everyone is a fan of photography, and some people won't understand why you want to photograph them going about their everyday lives. In this situation, if you get rumbled and someone objects, it's always best to stop photographing and apologize. The last thing you want is to find yourself in an ugly street scene all of your own. Offer to delete images if things get really heated.

You can also identify yourself to people in the scene you are shooting and ask them (via

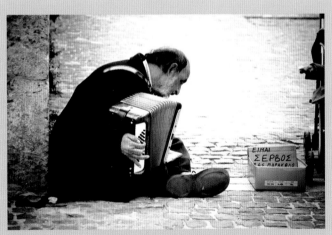

Above: Use some common sense when photographing people in public. It's not always possible to ask permission.

improvised sign language if necessary) if they mind you shooting them. Then wait for them to resume whatever they were doing; they will soon get used to your presence.

Sharing your photos

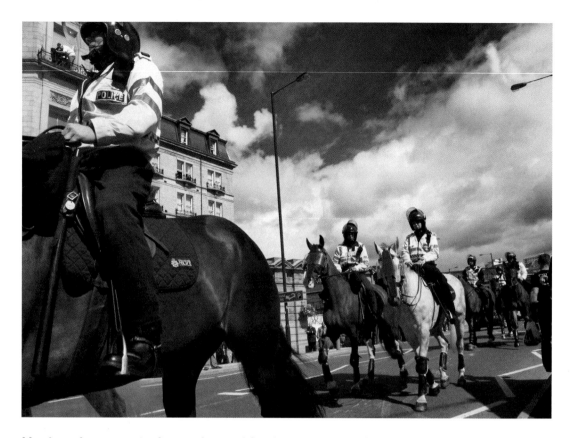

Having documented a project with photography, there are various channels you can use to showcase your work to a wider audience. This can even include selling your photos, if you've caught something truly newsworthy.

These days, the spiritual home of reportage is the internet. Whether it's a personal blog, a photo-sharing platform such as Flickr or a social media site such as Facebook, there are plenty of ways to broadcast your work to the world. And if your message is a powerful one, or your photographs are very good, your project can 'go viral', being passed from person to person until you have quite a following.

Above: Once hooked on reportage, you will probably want to carry a camera with you everywhere, to capture images you feel illustrate the day's news.

Photobooks (see pages 394–395) also lend themselves to documentary projects really well, and if you are working on a project that means something to your community, why not consider an exhibition of your images (see pages 398–399), supported by some coverage in the local press.

Citizen photojournalism
If you are the kind of person that gets hooked on reportage, then the chances are it won't be long before you decide to carry a camera everywhere with you, just in case. And a good idea that is,

too. If you are fortunate (or unfortunate) enough to get caught up in the middle of a news story, it could be your pictures that are seen by the masses in the news the next day.

In recent years, citizen photojournalism has been responsible for the images that have accompanied the unexpected news events of the day, from terrorist bombs to demos and riots. Even the humble camera phone can produce an image that is poignant and full of impact.

Depending on the event you've photographed, some images could be worth some money. If you want to make the most of an opportunity like this, you are best (quickly) contacting an agency that can syndicate the picture for you – that is, not sell it to just one newspaper, but rather licence it around the world. It must be emphasized that this is only worth doing if you witness something that is earth-shatteringly important and newsworthy.

Shooting in low light

Reportage tends to be shot in natural light, as flash can kill the ambience of a scene. This means being able to deal with a situation even when light levels get low. For this reason, documentary photographers tend to shoot with wide-aperture lenses that allow relatively fast shutter speeds to be used even when there is not much light around. A DSLR that performs well when the ISO sensitivity is increased is also a bonus.

Practise holding your camera properly (see page 55) and squeezing the release slowly, so you don't get any camera shake. Do watch for subject movement, though – and if you can't eradicate it, use it to good creative effect instead.

A photojournalist's kit bag needs to be as portable as possible, so don't weigh yourself down with excessive gear. Take only what you need.

Below: Pick a theme for a reportage project and subjects start to appear everywhere.

Reportage projects

Stuck for inspiration? It's always easier to work to a brief, so here are four projects for you to explore with your documentary skills.

Record a tradition
It could be an ancient marketplace or a colourful fiesta. The human race is a sucker for tradition, and you can find people meeting up to do all manner of strange things. It might be as crazy as running with the bulls or as traditional as a meeting of travellers. Photograph the action, the people and the details, and find new and interesting vantage points and perspectives.

365 project
Scan image sharing websites such as Flickr and you'll find plenty of people who have undertaken perhaps the most ambitious photographic project of all – to take and share a picture every day for a year. 365 pictures is a lot of work, but they can show whatever you want. This type of project lends itself to spontaneity, and is best shot with a camera phone or compact camera.

Changing places
Are there any areas of your city that are being developed, or that are about to undergo a transformation? If you can, get in there before the change starts, to record the way it looks now, then keep visiting at regular intervals to photograph the progress of change as it happens. Think about landscapes, details, and even portraits of the people working on the project.

Collect something amusing
What makes you laugh? The things written in the dirt on the back of cars? Missing apostrophes and bad spelling in signs? Amusing graffiti? Pick something you can photograph over a non-specific time period wherever you spot it.

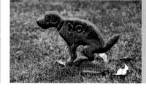
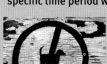

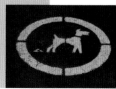

Wedding photography

As a guest at a wedding, you can produce a different style of photography to that of the official photographer, and a set of pictures that the bride and groom will be genuinely happy with.

Professional wedding photography is a very hard job. You need to be cool under pressure and remain creative, no matter what the venue, the weather, or the guests throw at you.

On the other hand, we all take cameras to a wedding to shoot pictures as keepsakes. And if you are known as a talented enthusiast, then what more special wedding present to give a newlywed couple than an album of alternative shots of their day, captured from your perspective as a guest.

Whatever your approach, there are a few different ways to shoot the big day, and some technical aspects to be taken into consideration. You might be taking a digital compact in a handbag, or a DSLR slung over your shoulder. Either is an equally valid approach, although the limitations of each type of camera tend to dictate the kind of photography you'll be shooting.

Be a fly on the wall

For a guest, the easiest type of wedding photography is reportage, often called a 'fly on the wall' approach. You'll blend in nicely as other people will be taking pictures, too, and you won't stand out as doing something a bit special. In the true style of reportage photography (see pages 158–161), the key here is to tell a story.

Above: Photos of the bride (and groom) getting ready can capture special moments, but don't get in the way. Don't use a tripod, up the ISO and shoot hand-held so you can stay in the background.

Not just any story, of course, but the story of the wedding as it unfolds. You can give yourself an unfair advantage here by swotting up beforehand, finding out the running order of the day from the bride and groom or the best man or ushers.

As you don't have to worry about being inconspicuous, try getting in close and shooting with the wide-angle end of your zoom lens. This will give your pictures a more intimate look, and give the viewer an impression of really being at the heart of the scene. Always try to shoot with the available light in the room, rather than engaging your camera's flash. Flash can be intrusive and tends to swamp everything, killing the ambient mood. If you are working indoors and are having trouble getting a shutter speed you can hand-hold, then increase the camera's ISO setting. If you are worried about image quality and noise then you can always go black and white at a later stage, which hides a multitude of high-ISO sins.

Without being obtrusive, try to get a few shots of each stage of the wedding – if you can, shooting when nobody else is around. This doesn't always have to be of the bride and groom, of course. If everyone else has their lenses trained on the happy couple as they are having their first kiss, but you are the only person that snaps a quick picture of the groom's mother having a little cry, then you've got yourself a scoop.

Posed portraits

At the other end of the spectrum to reportage images are posed portraits. The bride and groom may either love or hate these – everyone feels differently – but it's worth asking if you can borrow them for ten minutes during the day to indulge yourself. Do this after the official photographer has done their work. This way you won't be getting in the way, and the happy couple will be nicely warmed up and used to being photographed.

With only ten minutes to work in, you'll have to be fast. Prepare in advance, and know what you're doing. Stick to the plan so you can concentrate on creating a rapport with the couple. If possible, choose a location that is away from the other guests so they feel less intimidated and self-conscious.

Don't forget the details

The bride and groom have no doubt obsessed for weeks over the details. The colours of the place settings at dinner, the flowers, the champagne at the reception. They will thank you for including these in your pictures from the day. Your everyday zoom lens focuses close enough for most such photography, although you could always slip a supplementary close-up lens into your pocket in case there is an opportunity to photograph the rings, or a small piece of nostalgia such as cufflinks or a borrowed piece of antique jewellery.

Below, clockwise from top left: A lot of thought goes into the details that make a wedding special, so don't forget about them – the shoes, the place settings at the reception, the wedding rings, and of course the bride's bouquet.

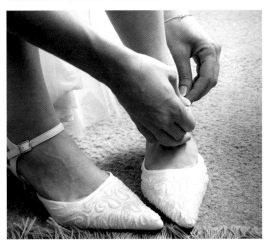
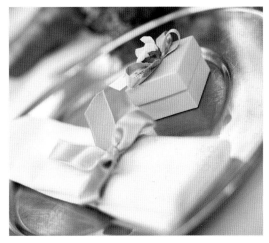
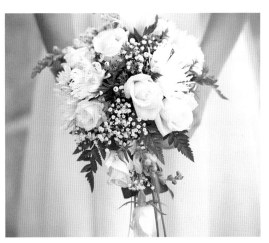
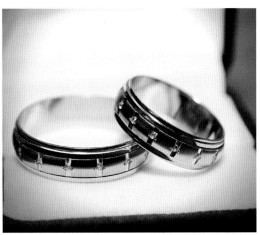

ASSIGNMENT
SHOOTING A WEDDING PORTRAIT

You may not be the official photographer at a wedding, but that doesn't mean you can't take an official-looking portrait.

Approach the bride and groom before the wedding and ask them if there will be a ten minute slot in the day when you can borrow them to shoot a portrait somewhere at their location. Make this a time after the official photographer has finished their work – never get in the way of someone who is being paid to photograph the wedding.

With only ten minutes to spare, you'll need to plan ahead and work quickly. If the wedding is local to you, why not have a walk around the venue before the big day and scope out some good spots? Search on the internet and see if you can find any other wedding photographs that have been shot there that can give you some inspiration. And pay particular attention to the time of day. This

will dictate where in the sky the sun will be, and what you have to work with in terms of light.

If you know the location beforehand, and can design the shot in your head, you can take only the minimum of equipment you need to shoot the picture. You are a guest, after all, and you don't want to be watching over an enormous bag of camera kit for the rest of the day. A standard zoom or 50mm prime lens on your DSLR should be fine. You may need fill-in flash from a flashgun, or a reflector to lighten shadows.

When you are shooting, work quickly to keep the attention of the bride and groom. Keep talking to them, and keep them engaged. If their facial expressions look forced, ask them to look somewhere else for a moment (or at each other) then back to you. Or tell them to relax for a moment while you fix a problem with your camera – there doesn't have to be a problem, of course.

If the weather is not looking great, or there aren't many good outdoor locations, don't be frightened to choose somewhere inside. Posing people right next to a window works well: the light is soft, and by exposing for the face you can often render the background so dark as to be nearly black. It's an approach that works well in black and white, too.

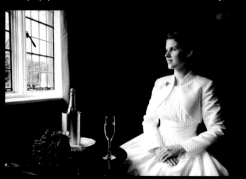

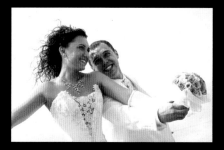

Above left: Light from the window creates a lovely soft ambience in this quiet image.
Nikon D700, 24–700mm f/2.8 lens, 1/90sec at f/5.6, ISO800

Left: Metering for white outfits on a white background can be a real headache. The histogram on your camera's display can help here.
Canon EOS 550D,18–55mm f/3.5–5.6 lens, 1/250sec at f/5.6, ISO200

ESSENTIAL KIT

- DSLR and standard zoom or portrait lens
- Flash or reflector for high-contrast conditions
- Tripod for low-light conditions

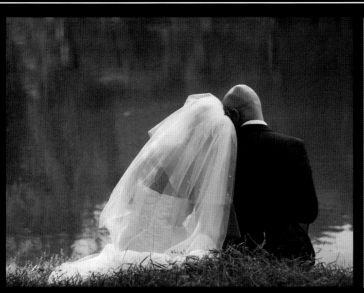

TIPS & TRICKS

- Look at professional photographers' work and try to figure out how they lit or composed the shot.

- Ask a friend to 'assist' you – holding kit when you aren't using it and helping to carry bags.

- Keep calm. Even though you need to work quickly, don't feel rushed. If the couple have said they are happy for you to shoot them, they won't mind you taking a moment to think about the shot and iron out any problems.

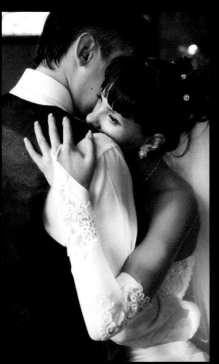

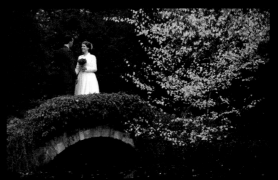

Top: *A moment away from the frenetic activity of the wedding day creates a serene image in soft evening light.*
Olympus E-3, 12–60mm f/2.8–3.5 lens, 1/60sec at f/4, ISO400

Above: *Visit the wedding venue beforehand to look for suitable spots – bearing in mind the time of day.*
Nikon D700, 70–200mm f/2.8 lens, 1/30sec at f/8, ISO200

Left: *Have a few poses in mind so you're not keeping the happy couple hanging around while you decide.*
Nikon D700, 24–70mm f/2.8 lens, 1/100sec at f/5.6, ISO800

Shooting your first **wedding**

Have you ever wanted to be the offical photographer at a wedding? It might just be the hardest thing you ever do, but if you are organized and prepared for what is to come, it could be the most rewarding, too.

The trouble with being an enthusiast photographer is that, sooner or later, one of your friends is going to ask you if you can photograph their wedding. They might not have enough in the budget to commission a full-time professional, or they may just like your style of photography, but whatever the reason you should think long and hard before you agree to take on the project. Don't ever say 'yes' on the spot.

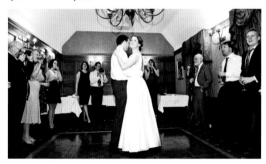

Above: *A must-have shot – the first dance.*

Covering a whole wedding as the main shooter is a huge task, and one that is loaded with responsibility. If a technical problem meant that the bride and groom ended up with no images of their big day, would you want to be the one who had to tell them? In addition, you won't be able to relax and enjoy the day in the way you normally would, which is something worth thinking about if they are close friends or family.

However, if you are sure you want to take on the biggest photographic challenge you may ever encounter, then with a lot of planning and some thinking on your feet, there is no reason why your talent as a photographer shouldn't shine through.

It's very common for the photographer to be as nervous on the big day as the couple themselves. To make the task at hand more manageable, break down the day into these five smaller parts.

The arrivals and preparations

As the bride and groom prepare for their big day, there are picture opportunities everywhere. The bridal party will no doubt be on their second glass of champagne and will have no problem with you photographing the bride as she is zipped into her dress. Adopt a fly on the wall approach here, and keep an eye out for details, too.

It's often a very tender moment when the bride and groom are with their parents just before the service – an impromptu portrait of the bride with her father will always work well. For the groom, try and rally the best man and any ushers and friends for a quick portrait outside, once everyone is ready.

The service

A photographer crashing around, while shooting with a powerful flash and a camera that beeps every time it focuses, can spoil what is the moment of a lifetime for the couple. Make sure this isn't you.

Not all registrars or ministers allow photography during the service itself, but if you go and introduce yourself before the event gets underway and politely ask what you can shoot and from where, there is no reason you won't be allowed to shoot at least something, even if it's from the back of the room with a long lens. If you do take this approach, you'll need a tripod. The light levels in churches and registry offices are not too bright, and a telephoto lens magnifies camera shake.

Once you have a good viewpoint, watch the service through the viewfinder and wait for the expressions on the bride and groom's faces, as well as members of the congregation. You only need a couple of shots here, but it's good to have a few to pick from. And don't miss the first kiss, whatever you do.

Opposite: *Scout out suitable locations for posed pictures. This jetty provides a beautiful image, complete with reflection.*

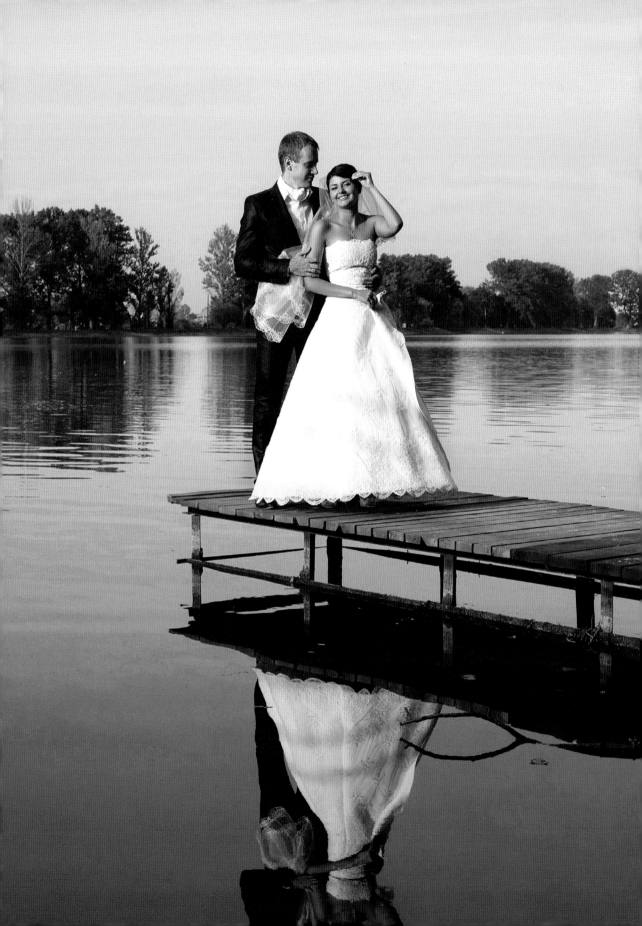

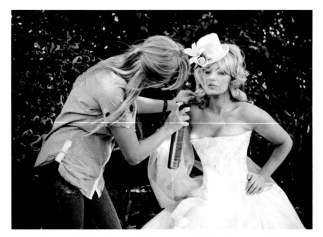

Above: *Don't miss must-have moments like this one of the bride being fussed over before her big entrance.*

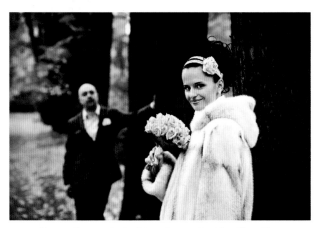

Above: *The couple don't have to pose together. Here, the shallow depth of field draws the attention nicely to the bride.*

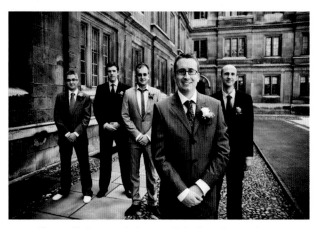

Above: *Be brave and place people in dynamic groupings. Straight line-ups rarely make for interesting photos.*

The portraits

If you are shooting posed portraits of the couple, then these can start with an impromptu picture as they are leaving the church or registry office; they will have smiles on their faces that nothing can wipe off! If you've skipped out before them then simply ask them to pause for a moment in the doorway (a particularly good approach in older buildings), and grab a couple of frames with shallow depth of field to blur anyone behind them.

For formal posed portraits, it's best to have worked out what you are going to shoot before you get to the big day. Look at the location beforehand (at the same time of day as you'll be shooting) and figure out what you want to shoot and where. Some assistance from an usher carrying your bags will help. Don't take more than 30 minutes – this is a wedding, not a photoshoot, and the bride and groom will want to be with their guests.

Bright, sunny days may be great for the guests, but the strong sunlight is far from ideal for wedding photographers. Use fill-in flash (see page 96) to even-out contrast in direct sunshine, or better still position people in the shade when they are having their picture taken.

The group shots

Group shots can take an age, but they don't need to with some organization and an assertive nature. Enlist the help of an usher or family member who knows most people at the wedding. They can be rounding people up for a picture while you are shooting. Traditionally, group shots begin with small groups of the families and expand, but you might want to start with huge shot of everyone and then gradually send people away – it can make life easier.

Large groups of 20-plus people are sometimes best taken from a height. Looking down from a balcony or upstairs bedroom window, for instance, means you'll see everyone's faces. Arrange everyone in a symmetrical shape, with the bride and groom and their families at the front.

The reception

When shooting the reception, it's often best to go back to a fly on the wall approach. Light levels will be getting steadily lower, and it may get to a point where you have to resort to flash. If you do, then try bouncing the flash off ceilings and walls to soften its output, while using a slightly longer shutter speed than the camera's flash sync speed to capture some ambient light, too (see pages 96–97). Using manual exposure mode and fixing the shutter speed at 1/60 or 1/30sec should do it. An aperture of f/4–5.6 is fine for most purposes. Open up for more range and stop down for more depth of field.

The reception is a good time to start concentrating on the guests, who will all have got used to you being there by now. Use a telezoom to shoot pictures of them talking and enjoying themselves – this is something the bride and groom will want to look back on.

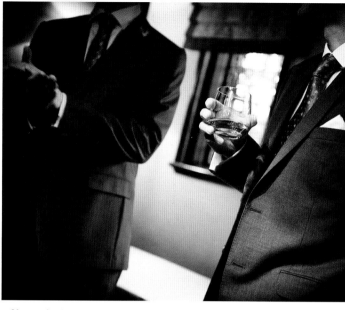

Above: As the light fades at the evening reception, use a flash, bouncing it off walls to soften its output.

Editing and producing albums

It's not uncommon to come back from a wedding with hundreds of pictures. Not all of these will be required, so an editing phase is necessary to sort the wheat from the chaff. Software such as Adobe Lightroom, or the Bridge and file browser applications that come with Photoshop and Elements, are excellent for this as they let you rank pictures, giving each one a number of stars between one and five. You can then filter so only five-star pictures are showing, for example, and give this final edit to the bride and groom.

Your newlywed clients will probably want to order prints and albums from you, and there are specialist companies that provide this service. Albums can be designed on your PC or Mac, and the pages uploaded over the internet to the printer. Prices vary according to the quality and finish of the album, and are designed to be marked up by the photographer to add to the profit margins.

Right: After an initial edit of the images, show the newlyweds the best shots and work with them to create an album.

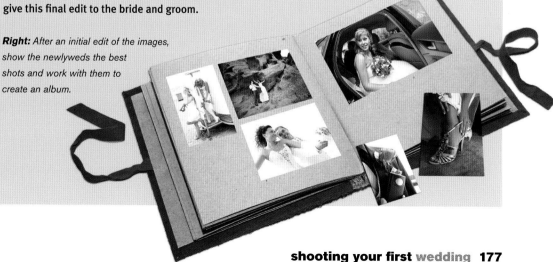

Sports and action

Still photography represents a moment in time, and when we apply this to fast-moving objects the results can be fascinating. We see details that are usually a blur in real life or on video. An object frozen in time causes us to imagine what happened beforehand, and what will happen next.

Action photography takes in many subjects, from sports and aircraft to active children and dogs chasing balls. In short, anything that is moving so quickly that it is difficult to photograph sharply.

It is shutter speed that controls the appearance of movement in a photograph. Control this by using your camera in shutter priority or manual exposure mode, and you'll control the look and feel of the action, too. A short shutter speed freezes fast movement completely, so it appears sharp. A longer speed allows movement to blur in the direction of travel. Bear in mind that no single approach is the correct one; these are simply different tools in your photographic armoury.

Freezing motion

Shooting with a short shutter speed to completely arrest moving objects is the most common approach to sports photography. To do this you will need to open up the lens's aperture to let plenty of light in, which means that depth of field will be shallow. Many sports photographers use this to their advantage, however, to isolate the subject matter against a soft background, making it stand out. If your lens can't open up enough to allow the shutter speed you need, raise the ISO sensitivity on your camera. How fast the shutter speed needs to be depends on the speed of the object being photographed. Start at 1/250sec and review the results on the camera's preview screen; you may have to go up as far as 1/1,000sec or 1/2,000sec to arrest movement completely.

Left: *A fast shutter speed freezes this volleyball player's action. To achieve this, experiment with the shutter speed, starting at 1/250sec.*

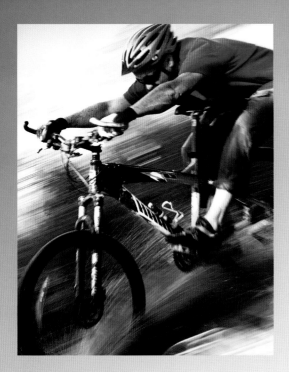

Left: Convey a sense of speed with a slow shutter speed. 1/30sec is a good starting point, then experiment with slower speeds.

i | Sports mode

We've talked a lot about how to select the settings needed for action photography manually. However, the chances are that your camera will have a sports scene mode. This auto setting will engage continuous shooting and autofocus as well as telling the camera to pick combinations of shutter speed and aperture that are biased towards fast shutter speeds and large apertures, in order to freeze motion. Perfect for those still learning the art of photography.

Blurring motion

The trouble with freezing fast motion is that it often doesn't give any impression of speed, unless the object being shot is off the ground at the time, or in a completely unnatural position. Sometimes a better approach is to blur the object slightly as it moves through the frame by using a slower shutter speed. Again, exactly which speed to use will depend on the situation in hand, but you could start with 1/30sec and get progressively longer. Too much blur will render the object unrecognizable, and too little will freeze its movement dead. You'll want a compromise between the two, which can only be arrived at with some experimentation, reviewing the results as you go along.

Note that sometimes you will want a combination of freezing and blur. A good example of this is photography of helicopters and propellor-driven planes. Shoot these with a shutter speed of 1/2,000sec and you'll not only freeze the aircraft but freeze the rotor or propellor blades, too, which looks a bit odd. Come down to 1/500sec, though, and you will still arrest the movement of the plane while allowing some blur in the rotors for a more natural look.

Flash and sports photography

While camera shutter speeds usually go up to 1/4,000sec (with some rare exceptions), the duration of a burst of flash can be as brief as 1/30,000sec, with the added bonus that this can be used in low light conditions too. In many sports, flash photography is forbidden as it can distract the players (tennis, badminton, golf, etc.), although there are some events where it is common to see professional sports photographers using a blip of on-camera flash to help freeze movement.

A good flash technique for action photography is to mix a longer shutter speed with a burst of flash. The flash will freeze the object, while the rest of the exposure will cause a blurred trail of movement. In a standard flash mode the flash fires at the start of the exposure, as the first shutter curtain opens (see page 97). This causes the trail of movement to appear in front of the frozen moving object. Engage 'rear-curtain' flash mode (sometimes called second-curtain flash sync) and the flash will fire at the end of the exposure instead, so the blurred trail is behind the subject, giving a much more natural effect.

MULTIPLE EXPOSURES FROM CONTINUOUS SHOOTING

Controlling the shutter speed when shooting moving objects determines whether a subject is captured as static but sharp, or blurred but dynamic.

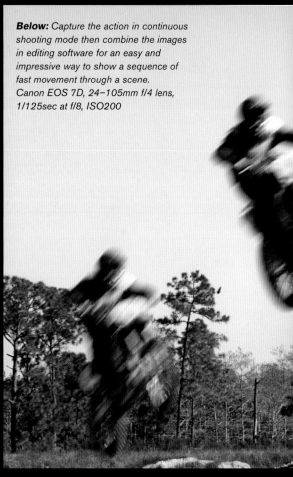

Below: Capture the action in continuous shooting mode then combine the images in editing software for an easy and impressive way to show a sequence of fast movement through a scene.
Canon EOS 7D, 24–105mm f/4 lens, 1/125sec at f/8, ISO200

However, with a fast, continuous shooting rate and some Photoshop trickery, we can have the best of both worlds: a sequence of multiple exposures tracing out the path of movement across the scene, with each image frozen sharp by a fast shutter speed.

The effect is impressive, but thankfully also relatively easy to achieve. You'll need a continuous shooting frame rate that is fast enough to capture a moving object multiple times as it moves through the frame – the faster the object moves, the faster you'll need to shoot. Many top-end enthusiast cameras can shoot at around five to six frames per second, which is usually plenty. You'll need to keep the camera on a tripod to make sure that the non-moving parts of the scene stay in the same place between shots, then as the moving subject comes into shot, start the shooting sequence by holding down the shutter release. It's best to prefocus using manual focus mode, as the object may not always be under one of the active focus points.

When you have transferred the image files to your computer, open up a sequence in your favourite image-editing software. You'll see each frame open in a separate window, but we want each to be an individual layer in the same window. The easiest way to do this is to use the clipboard, copying and pasting between windows until all the images are stacked above each other in the same file. We'll talk more about layers and what can be achieved with them in chapter five (see pages 344–347).

Align each layer perfectly with the one underneath it. You can do this by simply making sure that the corner of each layer aligns perfectly with the corner of the window. When this is done, start to remove parts of the upper layers that do not contain the moving object. You can do this with the Eraser tool (see pages 348–349) or by introducing layer masks (see pages 350–351) and masking off parts of each layer.

ESSENTIAL KIT

- DSLR or compact with continuous shooting mode
- Tripod
- Adobe Photoshop, or software that allows editing in layers

should match the speed of the moving subject. Vary both to get the right effect.

- Carry out rehearsals to ensure accurate framing.

- Try and pick a subject that describes a distinct motion through the air.

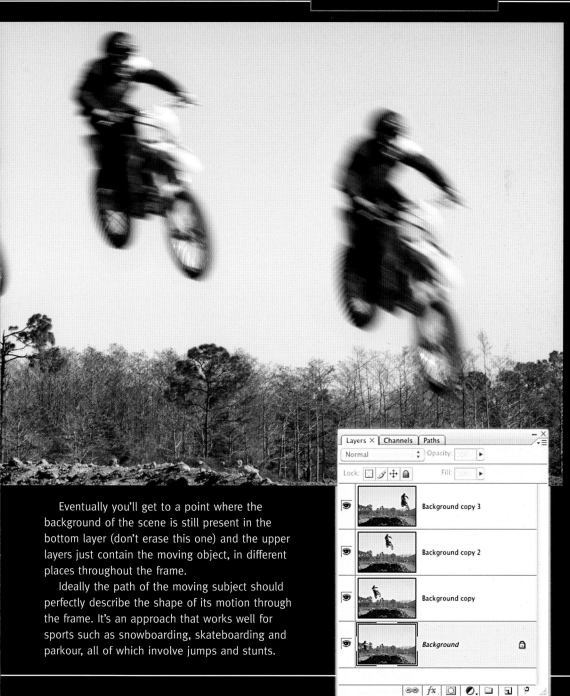

Eventually you'll get to a point where the background of the scene is still present in the bottom layer (don't erase this one) and the upper layers just contain the moving object, in different places throughout the frame.

Ideally the path of the moving subject should perfectly describe the shape of its motion through the frame. It's an approach that works well for sports such as snowboarding, skateboarding and parkour, all of which involve jumps and stunts.

Lens choice for sports

Out of practical necessity, much sports photography takes place from a distance. After all, it would be chaos if photographers were allowed to chase footballers around a pitch, or crouch in front of tennis players as they served. Hence the telephoto lens is a sports photographer's best friend.

When shooting with full-frame digital cameras (i.e. those whose sensor is the same size as old-fashioned 35mm film), telephoto lenses between 200 and 400mm are the most useful. But a 400mm lens is unwieldy and very expensive, which means that those shooting on so-called cropped sensor DSLRs (with sensors smaller than full frame) are at an advantage. Nikon, Canon, Pentax and Sony cameras, using APS-C-sized sensors, have a lens multiplication factor of around 1.5x. This means that a 300mm lens gives the same angle of view as a 400mm lens on a full-frame camera. Olympus and Panasonic DSLRs use sensors with a 2x multiplication factor, so a 200mm lens effectively becomes a 400mm optic.

Affordable 70–300mm optics are available, many with built-in image stabilization technology that attempts to compensate for camera shake. However, such lenses often have relatively small maximum apertures, f/4 or f/5.6 at the longest end, which limits the brevity of the shutter speed that can be used, and hence the ability to freeze motion. Telephoto lenses with a wider maximum aperture, say f/2.8, are available, but cost roughly three times the price of entry-level models.

For those needing to get even closer to the action, teleconverters, which fit between the camera and the lens, provide a cost-effective way to increase focal length by 1.4x or 2x. Be aware that you'll lose one or two stops, respectively, off the maximum aperture, however.

Focusing on moving objects

Most cameras have a continuous focusing mode. Instead of locking focus when the shutter release is pressed down halfway, the camera continues to focus, tracking moving objects around the frame and refocusing as they get nearer or further from the camera. This is the approach that is best used when photographing sports, or other action. Try using just one focus point for added accuracy, or possibly just a limited number of them. Engaging all focus points at once can slow down a camera's autofocus system, handicapping it when shooting fast action.

An alternative to autofocus is to engage manual focus mode and prefocus on a spot that you know the action will pass through. It's an approach that works well for predictable action, such as cars coming around a bend or runners sprinting down a track. You are guaranteed a sharp picture, as long as your reflexes are up to the job.

There is always a tangible delay between the photographer pressing the shutter release and the camera capturing an image. This shutter lag is worse in some cameras (compacts) than others (DSLRs) and can result in you missing the moment, and the point of focus if doing this manually. Focus lag can be minimized by half-pressing the shutter release in anticipation of taking the picture. Perfecting this kind of timing requires experience, and you'll get better at it as you shoot more action photography. Or you could try continuous shooting, capturing a sequence of frames at high speed. It is usually the first frame in every sequence that is the best.

Left: The sports photographer's best friend – a telephoto zoom.
Right, main: Continuous focusing mode can help capture the moment – like Thierry Henry in action for Barcelona.
Right, inset: Sports photographers focus on the action at the Australian Open.

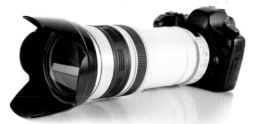

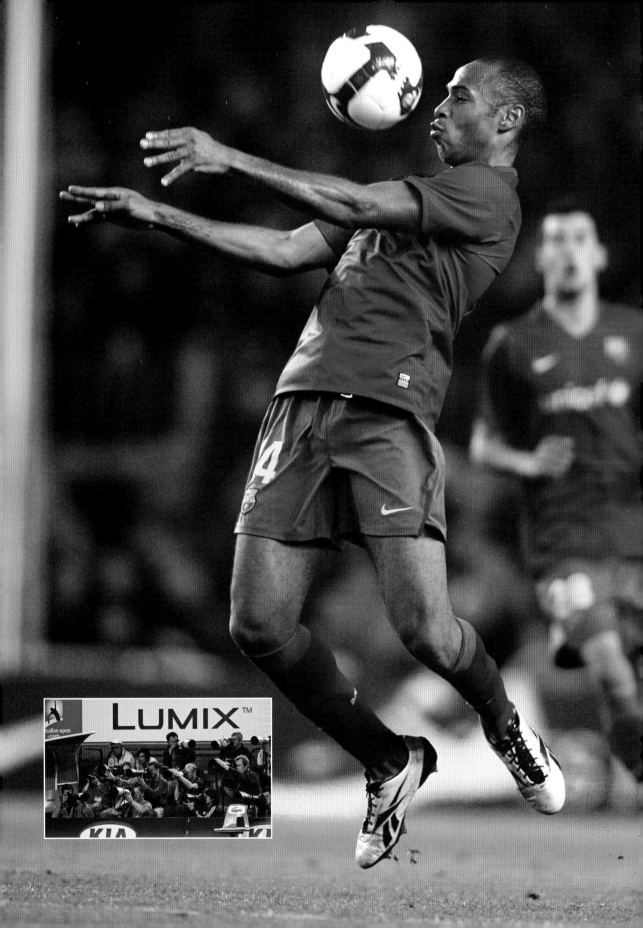

TRACKING AND SHOOTING A FAST-MOVING OBJECT

Long shutter speeds blur movement, but this doesn't aways mean it's the subject that blurs. By panning the camera, the background can give the impression of speed and movement instead.

Panning is a technique where a slow shutter speed is used to incorporate motion blur into a picture, but by moving the camera so as to track a moving object, it is the background that blurs and not the subject. By moving the camera to keep the subject in the same place, we effectively turn the background into the moving object instead.

A shutter speed of between 1/15sec and 1/4sec works well, although this very much depends on the speed of the motion involved. When tracking a racing car, a shutter speed of 1/60sec may be sufficient to generate background blur; a runner

or cyclist may need a slower speed than this for movement to register. Get the speed too fast and you'll see no blur; get it too long and you run the risk of blurring the subject, too, as you struggle to hold it in exactly the same place in the frame.

Practise the side-to-side panning motion so that you can do it smoothly and consistently. Stand with your feet about half a metre apart and pivot around your waist with the camera at your eye. Track the object so it stays in the middle of the frame, under the most sensitive autofocus point, and squeeze off two or three frames in continuous shooting mode. Don't snatch at the

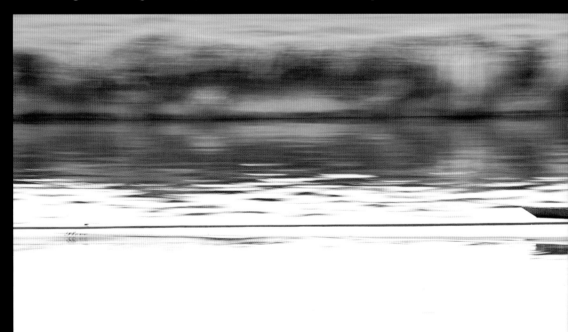

TIPS & TRICKS

• Experiment with different shutter speeds and review the results on the back of the camera. It's very hard to predict what will work and what won't.

• If the autofocus system is struggling to keep up with the action, try manually pre-focusing on the point where you will shoot the subject instead.

Right: *To achieve good results with panning, practise your stance and releasing the shutter gently.*
Nikon D700, 70–200mm f/2.8, 1/15sec at f/8, ISO400

shutter release or rush the panning motion. A softly, softly approach works better here.

To take control over the shutter speed, you'll want to shoot in manual exposure mode. Or if the light is changing quickly, shutter priority mode will let you lock the shutter speed and have the aperture vary according to current meter readings.

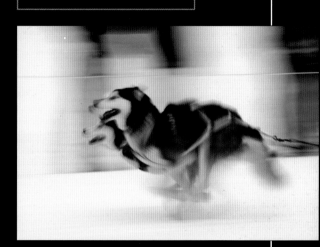

Below: *Panning the camera with the subject blurs the background, rather than the subject. Here the rower is in sharp focus, while the bank is blurred.*
Nikon D700, 24–70mm f/2.8, 1/15sec at f/8, ISO200

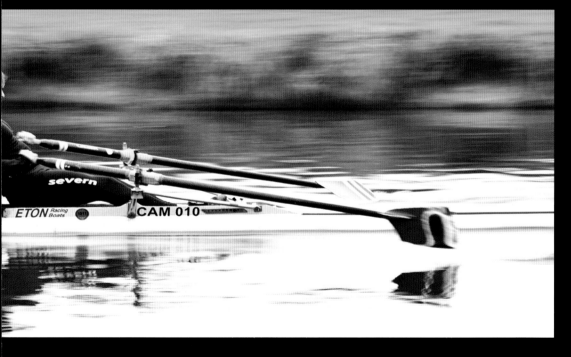

Garden photography

The array of wildlife in the garden outside your home is enough to get any photographer excited, once they know it's there. Go on a garden safari and explore your own urban jungle.

Life is frustratingly busy for the modern-day photographer. While it would be lovely to get out every day and shoot landscapes in the countryside, the reality of day-to-day life means that job and family commitments often come first. But there is a location much closer to home (literally on your doorstep) where you can take the occasional ten minutes out to shoot some stunning images.

Below: The early morning fog in the Japanese Garden in Portland, Oregon, helps separate background from foreground and brings out the vivid autumnal colours.

The humble garden is packed full of colour and wildlife. If you don't own one yourself, then public gardens are great, too. In the springtime they are bursting into life, with blossom and new flowers everywhere, while the summer months see plants in full bloom – a riot of colour. Autumn provides the opportunity to capture the warm, golden colours of the leaves as they begin to drop from the trees. And, of course, if you are even slightly green-fingered, then you have full control over the species you'll find in your garden. You can even choose to grow plants especially to photograph.

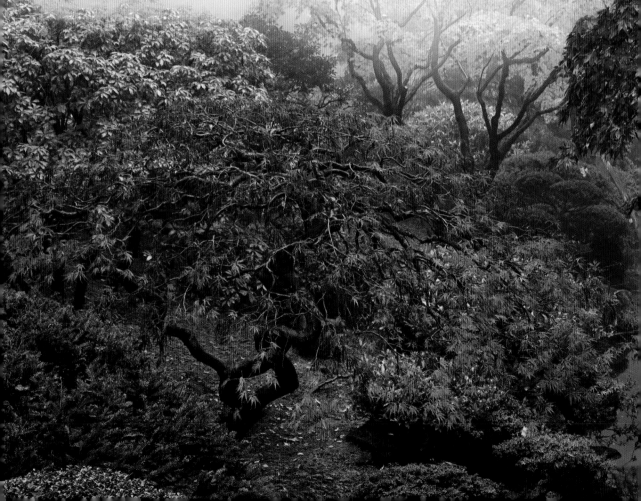

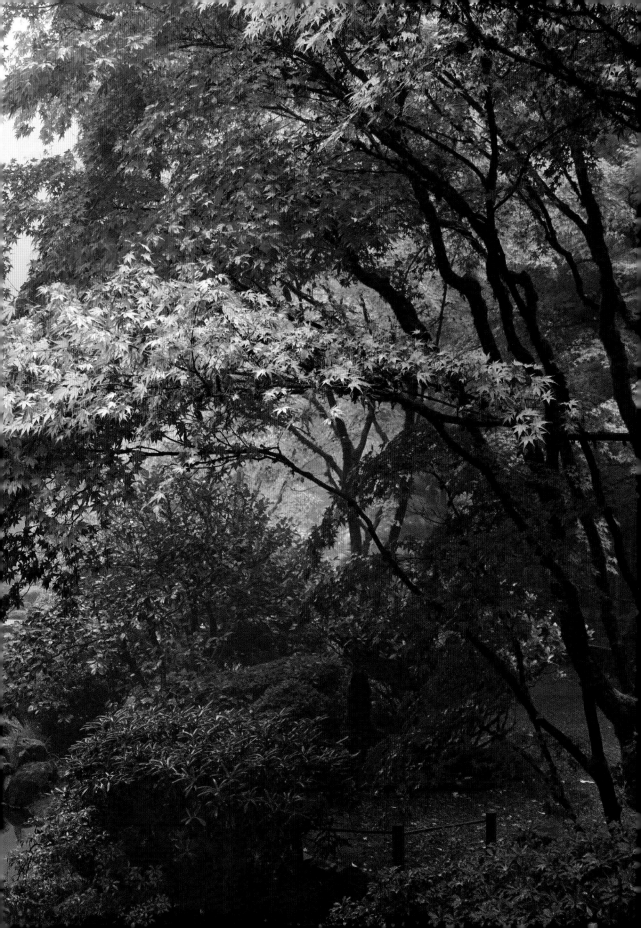

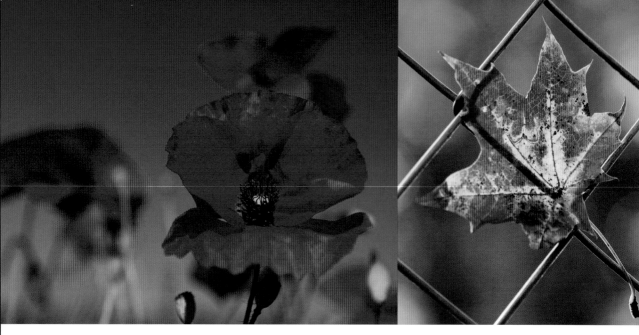

There are subjects all over a domestic garden. Flower close-ups are the most popular, although there are other, less obvious, subjects if you look a little harder. Back-lit foliage and the form and texture of wood and other materials are all good candidates. Also look for local wildlife. The number of insect species found in an everyday back garden is mind-blowing. And of course, birds and squirrels are usually frequent visitors, too.

Gardening equipment

The good news is that the humble DSLR or compact camera is more than capable of producing some stunning images around the garden. Most standard zooms offer a pretty good close-focusing distance, usually down to 0.35m, which is more than enough for most flower images. And you can get closer than this by adding a supplementary close-up lens, available very cheaply from your local camera dealer.

When photographing individual flowers, you'll probably want to use a tripod. Even in bright daylight this makes focusing and composition more easy by fixing the camera-subject distance. And when light levels do drop, a remote release (or your camera's self-timer) is a good way of tripping the shutter without causing camera shake.

There are also a number of non-photographic accessories that you'll find useful for this type of work. A pair of scissors or gardening secateurs are good for tidying up as you go along, removing

Above, left: Nature provides a stunning array of colours and shapes for you to photograph. Brilliant red poppies against a bright blue sky are a classic shot.

Above, right: Shallow depth of field renders this autumn leaf caught on a fence beautifully against the contrasting out of focus green background.

unsightly torn leaves or dead flowerheads, for instance. A small workbench with crocodile clips will be useful for holding things in place, or even out of the way. And a water spray is great for covering things in fine droplets of water, recreating the dew-soaked look of early morning at any time of the day.

Lighting is often difficult to work with in the garden environment. Bright sunshine is too high-contrast, so avoid shooting objects in direct sunlight if possible. Either wait for them to be in shade (you live fairly close by, after all) or create your own shade with a diffuser or piece of card. You can also use a reflector or some off-camera flash to fill in the shadows.

Viewpoints, composition and depth of field

When composing photographs in the garden, your first thoughts should really be about your viewpoint, and the background that this gives you. Gardens can be cluttered spaces, and a disorganized or untidy background is not what we

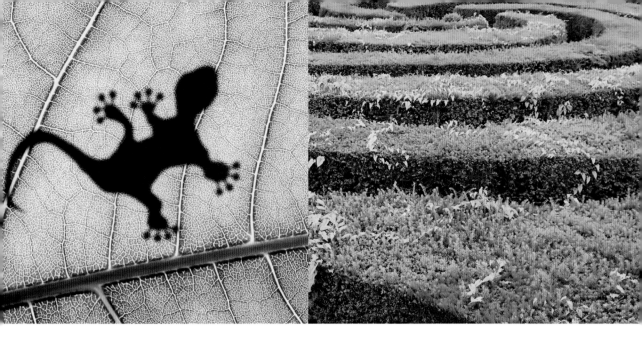

are looking for. Using your DSLR's depth of field preview facility (see page 86), or even live view on some cameras, you'll be able to see how out of focus the background really is at the current aperture. Try to pick something colourful that will complement your subject – or failing that, a hue that will contrast for a more dramatic result. When adopting a low-down viewpoint (see top left), the background could be a blue sky, whereas shooting a subject side-on it is more likely to be green foliage. That said, you can always create your own backgrounds with pieces of coloured card.

If you have a macro lens, or macro facility on your compact camera, also try getting over the top of a flower, and filling the frame with it. Focus on the stamens and let the rest of the petals drift out of focus to give you a soft, smooth background; you won't get much depth of field at such close focusing distances no matter what aperture you use.

Focusing on flowers in the garden can be more difficult than you might think. To be precise about exactly where you are focusing, you really need to use just one focus point as opposed to an AF area, but then this single point can easily be confused if it drifts over an area lacking in detail. The answer is manual focus, but if you go for this approach watch out for subject movement. If the wind is blowing things around, the camera–subject distance will be constantly changing. Wait for a lull in the conditions before checking focus and shooting the picture.

Above, left: *Back-lighting a subject is a wonderfully versatile technique. Here the direct sunlight through a leaf renders this lizard as a silhouette.*

Above, right: *Some public gardens are great for surreal topiary photographs, but make sure to catch either the early morning or late afternoon light that will best enhance the geometrical shapes.*

Public gardens

Those that live in garden-less apartments may well be thinking that this sort of photography is not for them. However, most towns and cities have some sort of public garden or park that is planted-out to look good all year round (sometimes better than we could achieve at home). Public gardens are larger than private spaces, too, so you'll be able to shoot more of the general landscape than you would at home. Those gardens belonging to stately homes or pubic buildings are good candidates for this approach, though be sure to check the terms and conditions regarding photography on-site. Some parks and gardens require special permission to be given in order to shoot with a tripod, for instance.

ASSIGNMENT
SHOOTING WILDFLOWERS

Wildflowers are a classic subject for photography, and as they come and go throughout the spring and summer months, so there is plenty of time for you to get out there and capture them on camera.

Flowers are nature's tarts, showing off their beauty for the sake of reproduction. But they do make stunning photographs, especially when shot up-close and printed at large sizes. Flowers are all over the place, too, in parks and gardens throughout the year. Springtime sees the first flowers of the year come into bloom, and with summer comes a riot of colour.

Photographing flowers outdoors presents different challenges to shooting them in a studio. We can't control the light as well, and are at the mercy of the elements. Direct sunlight is never good for this type of photography, so pick a time of day when you can find your blooms in the shade, or think about ways to diffuse the light – by holding something over the top of the flower when you are shooting it, for instance. Reflectors are also invaluable here, bouncing light back into shadow areas in order to even out excessive contrast.

That's quite a lot of equipment to hold at once, so explore one of the excellent photographic clamp accessories designed to help hold reflectors. You can also use them to keep back foliage that is obscuring your view.

The weather is a big factor when photographing wildflowers. Not only do we not want direct sunlight, but wind is a big problem as it tends to blow your carefully framed subject around, ruining your composition and making focusing very difficult indeed. Bad weather also tends to damage the flowerheads themselves, spoiling petals and leaving unwanted debris all over the place. If you can shoot a fresh flowerhead that has just had a day or so of peaceful weather, then this will look much better on camera.

When it comes to equipment, a DSLR fitted with a long-ish macro lens is perfect. A slightly telephoto macro lens lets you keep your distance from the subject, so you don't spoil the lighting with a shadow of the camera. Compact cameras have excellent macro capabilities, but because these operate at wide angles you will have to get very close indeed to the flowerhead. Be careful of shadows and try to minimize the distorting wide-angle effect.

Above: *Shooting against the sun, these dandelion flowers become almost translucent. Keep your distance to avoid your shadow interfering by using a telephoto macro lens. Nikon D700 with 105mm f/2.8 macro lens, 1/4sec at f/22, ISO200*

Left: Shooting raw and using a grey card to set white balance helps to ensure accurate colours in this lily image. Nikon D700 with 105mm f/2.8 macro lens, 1/8sec at f/22, ISO200

Nature and wildlife

Flora and fauna are some the most popular subjects for photographers, but also some of the most challenging to get right. Thankfully, though, you don't need to go on safari to get some stunning wildlife images.

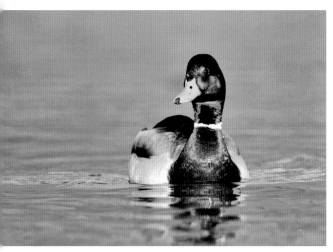

Above: Public parks are great for photographing ducks. Use a telephoto lens so you can fill the frame with your subject.

Photographing the natural world – and all of the amazing wildlife in it – is something we all try at one point or another, and it's not hard to see why. Ask anyone working in wildlife, from scientists to photographers, and they will tell you that there are more unanswered questions in the natural world than there are known facts. What more reason do you need to get out your camera and take some awesome images?

The secret to successful wildlife photos lies in understanding the behaviour of the subject you are shooting, from lions to doormice. The wildlife photography that gets the most exposure in the media is usually shot in a far-off exotic location, but that doesn't mean you can't produce some incredible results closer to home, too. The streets and gardens in our towns and cities are teeming with wildlife, and if you are near to a patch of countryside or coastline then you have even more options open to you.

Gardens and towns

A popular but challenging subject for the surburban wildlife photographer is the humble garden bird. Aside from a telephoto lens, specialist equipment is not a prerequisite, and some amazing species can be tempted into view by baiting your garden with food and giving the birds something to stand on. An added advantage of baiting for birds is that other cheeky critters, such as squirrels and foxes, may turn up too. Different baits attract different animals, so try tasty morsels of dog or cat food, which does a good job of attracting hedgehogs, and is more healthy for them than the traditional bread and milk.

Small animals and birds are easily startled, so you may want to take steps to make your presence less obvious to them. Covering yourself in branches or climbing up a tree is not always necessary; shooting from within a garden shed or conservatory is an easier option. If you use a tent or hide, give the local wildlife a few days to get used to it before spending hours in there waiting for a shot.

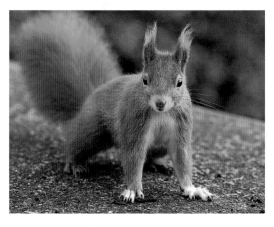

Above: A little bribery helped this red squirrel in a Budapest park to overcome its shyness – so don't forget the snacks!

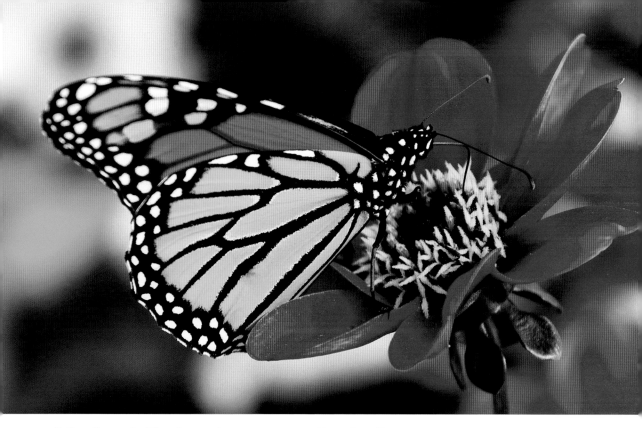

At the other end of the size spectrum are the millions of insects and spiders that live in our gardens. They are not to everyone's liking, but such animals are amazing to watch, and impressive when photographed. Early morning is a great time to go looking for spiders' webs, as they will often be covered with dew. In fact, the early part of the day is a good time to look for all other insects, as well. It is still a little colder from the lower night-time temperatures and they are less active and a little more docile, making them easier to stalk with your camera.

Above: Butterflies are still slow in the cool morning, so it's a good time to capture them with your macro lens.

This is especially true of butterflies and moths – in the morning their reflexes are slower. That said, watch your shadow. If it falls over a resting butterfly it will think it's about to be eaten and make a break for it. A macro lens is a must for DSLR owners attempting insect photography (or an accessory such as a close-up lens or extension tube). Digital compact shooters should engage macro focus mode and get as close as they can.

Equipment for garden wildlife

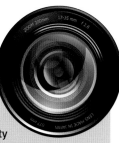

A telephoto lens is your best bet, as it will allow you to fill the frame with your subject from a distance. A 70–300mm zoom is ideal, though be aware that the maximum aperture of such a lens is often small. Raise the camera's ISO slightly to ensure you still get fast shutter speed.

A good tripod is essential. Nature photography can involve shooting from all angles, so aim for a model that has a reversible centre column.

A macro lens is great for close-up work and small details. Most standard zooms can focus pretty closely these days, but if you want quality images of small subjects, this specialist lens is the way forward. It will be useful for other subjects such as portraits and still life, too.

Above: A good macro lens is the best way to capture insects.

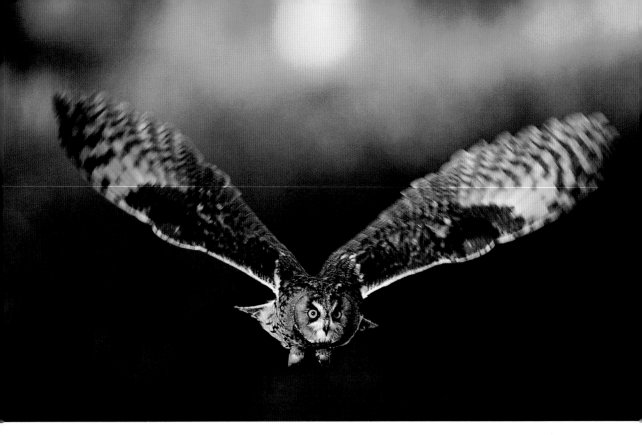

Going further afield

For those without access to a garden, or who are after a change of scene, public parks and botanical gardens are an excellent hunting ground for wildlife images. In seasonal climates, the transitions between the seasons often present a fascinating array of plant life. The onset of spring brings early flowers, as well as blossom and new foliage. Summer is often a riot of colour. And the autumn months can be a visual treat in those areas where deciduous trees are growing.

Botanical gardens are devoted to the culture of plant wildlife, with the overall aim of studying them for scientific or educational reasons. It's why the range of plants grown is so vast. Some species are quite rare and will make a good addition to your library of wildlife images. Most botanical gardens let photographers shoot pictures for non-commercial purposes without paying a fee, but it is worth ringing ahead and checking if they allow use of a tripod. Most do, but only with advance permission.

Other public green spaces allow access to birds and mammals that you don't usually see in the garden. Ducks, swans and other wildfowl can

Above: This wild tawny owl in flight was photographed in the late afternoon in Snowdonia, Wales. Falconry displays also offer fantastic opportunities to photograph birds of prey.

be very photogenic, as well as providing good practise for photographic techniques and giving you a chance to get to know your equipment.

Wildlife parks and zoos

Woodlands where the habitat is managed, or wildlife parks and zoos that are home to all manner of animal species, are all great places to graduate from squirrels and sparrows to something a bit more impressive.

Deer parks have their historical origins in hunting, although the only shooting you are likely to see there these days will be from fellow photographers. Deer themselves are notoriously shy, and their sense of smell allows them to detect you from a long way away. But it's worth persevering and learning one of the most important lessons in wildlife photography – the need for patience! Like every other animal, deer only tolerate strangers up to a certain distance. With experience, you'll be able to gauge what this

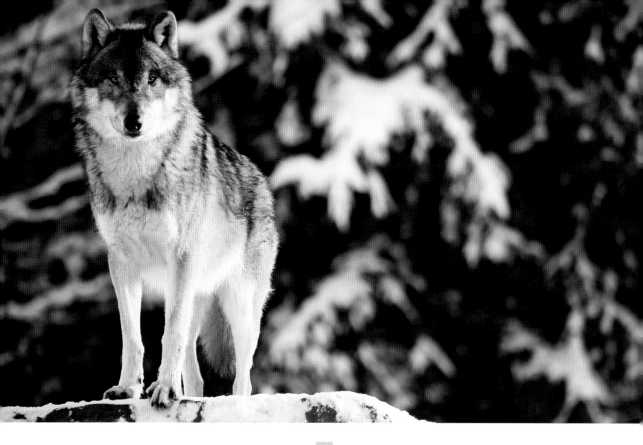

Above: *While wildlife parks can be controversial, they allow photographers to shoot animals they might not otherwise encounter. This grey wolf was photographed in Indiana, USA.*

distance is (for other animals too), increasing your chances of getting a good picture.

Thanks to the migratory nature of many bird species, their location at a specific time of year is quite predictable. Many nature reserves have been set up around these migration habits, and are perfect getaways for photographers looking for images of rare birds nesting, hunting or feeding. For the less adventurous, a falconry display offers a great chance to photograph some impressive birds of prey, both in action and at rest.

Zoos are a controversial subject – some think they are cruel; others see them as a vital part of the conservation effort. But whatever your point of view, zoos and safari parks offer a diverse range of animals that you won't see anywhere else unless you fork out for an exotic holiday. With clever composition and some attention to what is happening in the background, it is possible to get shots of animals that are pretty close to what you might see in the wild.

Basic wildlife technique

No matter where you are shooting, the rules of wildlife photography remain the same. Here's a run-down of some basic techniques that will help you get the best possible shots.

Use a long lens – a telephoto will not only get you close to the action, but will help you blur the background, too. And when it comes to picking an exposure, try to go for the fastest shutter speed you can. Not only will this freeze any movement by your subject, it'll also get rid of blur from camera movement, which is exacerbated by telephoto lenses.

A fast shutter speed means a wide aperture, which is handy as you want to restrict depth of field so your subject stands out. Don't forget that many species have evolved to look just like their native habitats! Use a tripod, monopod or bean bag to support your long lens, and engage image stabilization technology if your camera has it. Finally, think creatively. Try silhouettes or alternative camera angles, or contrasting black and white for a more artistic approach.

ASSIGNMENT
PHOTOGRAPHING SPIDERS IN THE MORNING

Some people hate them, others find them fascinating. Either way, spiders are nature's survivors and are strangely gripping to photograph.

Spiders' webs make for stunning pictures. Go out looking for them early in the morning, when the dew or mist has left them covered in water droplets. If you miss this time or the conditions aren't right, a very fine water cloud from a simple pump sprayer can create the effect for you, though be careful not to overdo it.

Get in as close as you can to the spider and fill the frame with a section of the web. Use the lines as a compositional device, putting the spider on a compositional 'third', or even dead-centre for instant impact. Using a long lens will let you isolate the spider from the background by restricting depth of field. A 105mm macro lens is perfect for the job. Use the camera's depth of field preview function to establish the fine balance between getting the spider in focus and keeping the background blurred.

Although this is not a fast-moving subject, a tripod can help you keep camera shake under control by holding the camera steady. This might sound like more hassle compared to hand-holding the camera and raising the ISO sensitivity, but you'll get better image quality by keeping the ISO low.

***Right:** Putting this Argiopa spider dead centre in the frame lends instant impact to this image. The camera's depth of field preview helped to keep the spider sharp against the blurred background. Canon EOS 7D with 100mm f/2.8 macro lens, 1/250sec at f/8, ISO400*

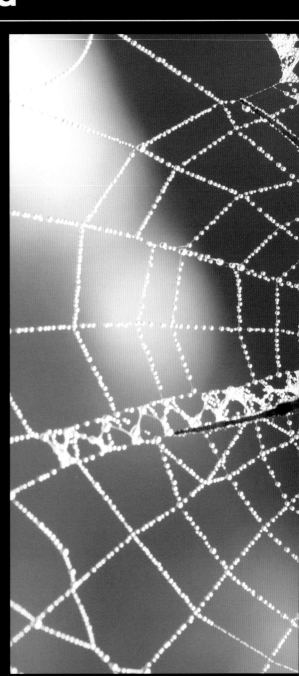

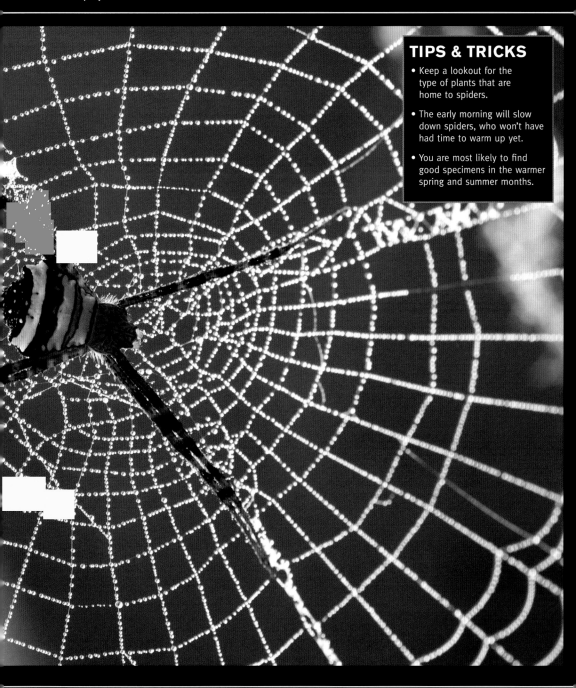

ESSENTIAL KIT

- DSLR and macro lens or close-up accessory
- Compact camera with macro mode
- Tripod and remote release
- Water spray

TIPS & TRICKS

- Keep a lookout for the type of plants that are home to spiders.

- The early morning will slow down spiders, who won't have had time to warm up yet.

- You are most likely to find good specimens in the warmer spring and summer months.

Going on a **wildlife holiday**

For the wildlife photographer who has well and truly got the bug (so to speak), going on safari has to be one of the ultimate things to do in life.

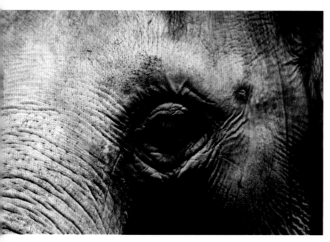

Above: Bag yourself truly wild wildlife shots, like this close-up elephant image, on safari.

These days it's fairly easy to get anywhere in the world in under 24 hours, and it's perfectly possible to slot a three- or four-day safari into your existing travel plans when going on holiday.

Top locations include the many African big game parks such as the Serengeti or Masai Mara, as well as locations in Uganda where gorilla-spotting is keeping the local economy alive. India is also a popular destination for tiger safaris. The best times of the day are early morning and late afternoon, just before the sun sets. The middle of the day is often so hot that all animals want to do is sleep, and overhead high-contrast sunshine isn't exactly flattering, either.

At the other end of the temperature scale, a visit into the Arctic and and Antarctic circles is also now possible via cruise ship, giving photographers a glimpse of the stunning landscapes of some of the most inhospitable places on earth, as well as the extraordinary wildlife that somehow manages to live there. Whales, birds, seals and penguins are all possible sightings.

Coastal safari

The sea covers about 70 per cent of the Earth's surface and is home to a staggering array of wildlife. For the amateur photographer, taking pictures underwater is difficult to achieve, this being a rather specialist discipline, but there are options available to those prepared to invest some time, effort and money.

For the snorkeller, one of the many waterproof compact cameras on the market is an affordable route into underwater photography. Such cameras can withstand depths of between 5–10m; ideal for casual use. Any deeper than this and you'll need a waterproof housing and a scuba diving qualification. The former option is safe to 40–50m, while the latter is good for 18–30m depending on the level you learn to.

Be warned that the deeper you go, the darker it gets, meaning that most decent available light restricts photography to the shallows anyway. At depth, think about an external underwater flash unit. This will be attached to an arm that lets you position the flash off to one side, which is important in underwater photography. Flash coming from the same direction as the lens illuminates particles in the water, causing backscatter.

Underwater housings are expensive. For a compact camera, expect to pay about as much as you did for the camera itself, and much more than the cost of the camera for a DSLR housing. But if you are already an experienced diver, it could be an investment worth making.

Opposite: A whale shark cruises lazily just below the surface. An amateur photographer spotted the creature while snorkelling just off the rocks of Bartolome Island, part of the Galapagos Islands, Ecuador.

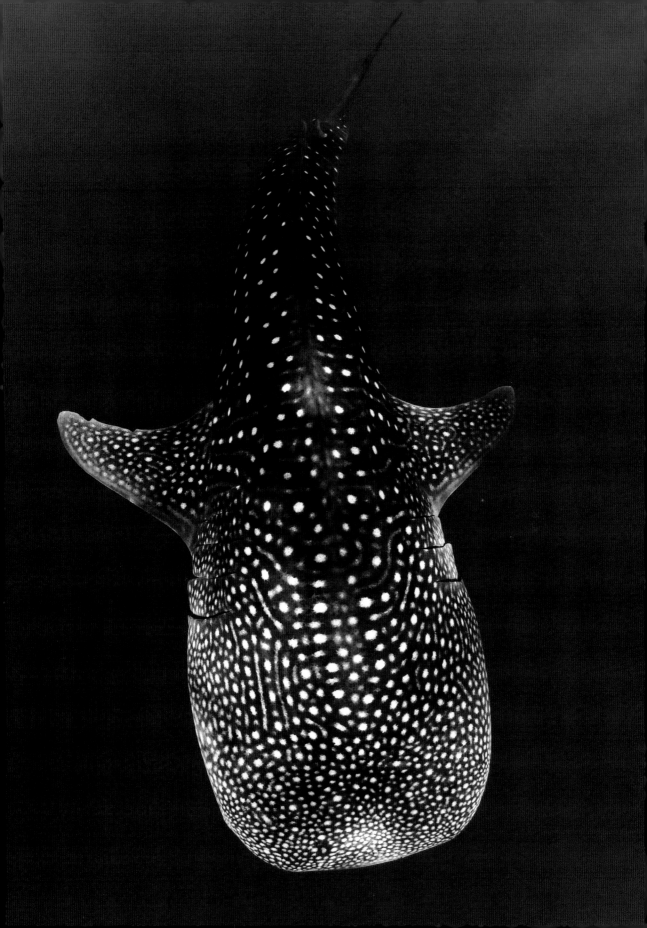

URBAN WILDLIFE SAFARI
LAURENT GESLIN WILDLIFE PHOTOGRAPHER

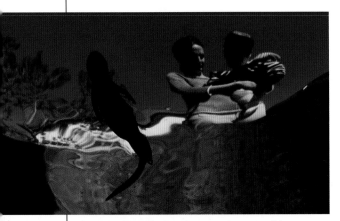

Left: *Shot from below the surface, this startling image shows an Alpine newt coming up for air in a garden pond in France.*

Laurent Geslin first became interested in photography while studying History of Art, and after working as a wildlife guide for several years he made the transition to professional photographer, specializing in wildlife. His pictures have been published in many newpapers, books and magazines including *BBC Wildlife* and *National Geographic*.

How did you get started with wildlife photography?
I started as a wildlife guide, first in France, then in Namibia and South Africa, and it seemed a natural progression to pick up a camera and start taking wildlife pictures.

Do you concentrate on urban wildlife?
I've worked all over the world: Australia, Brazil, India and frequently in Africa. The urban safari project is part of my work when I'm at home.

What sort of special equipment do you need?
I use a variety of fixed lenses, from 14mm up to 500mm, as well as wide-angle zooms. I also use flash and infrared triggers and other gadgets, and always use up to three different bodies.

Do you spend many nights outside? Do you need a lot of patience in your job?
Wildlife is mainly nocturnal – animals wake up late afternoon and go to sleep in the early morning, so you have to adapt to their schedule. Sometimes you can spend 18 hours in a small hide only to get one shot or sometimes none at all. For some particularly shy species you might have to sleep in your hide to avoid disturbing them. So yes, you need a lot of patience to be a wildlife photographer.

Has wildlife photography influenced the way you take other kinds of pictures?
I started off doing a lot of portraiture, press photos and fashion. As I gradually made the move, all these experiences informed my approach to wildlife photography. It doesn't seem to have worked the other way round, though. But whichever field you work in, having internalized the basic rules of composition and technical know-how will help you seize that crucial moment.

What has been your best wildlife experience so far?
I love being out in the bush, spending days and nights without seeing anyone, following herds of roaming elephants or stalking leopards. Those kinds of places are very rare now, but I have been lucky to live in southern Africa and those moments are etched into my memory. I also love working with urban wildlife. Watching a peregrine falcon in Barcelona or stalking a little vixen in London while the city sleeps – that is very cool.

Below: It took a few hours of waiting to get this shot of a red fox in London approaching a pile of discarded junk food under a car.

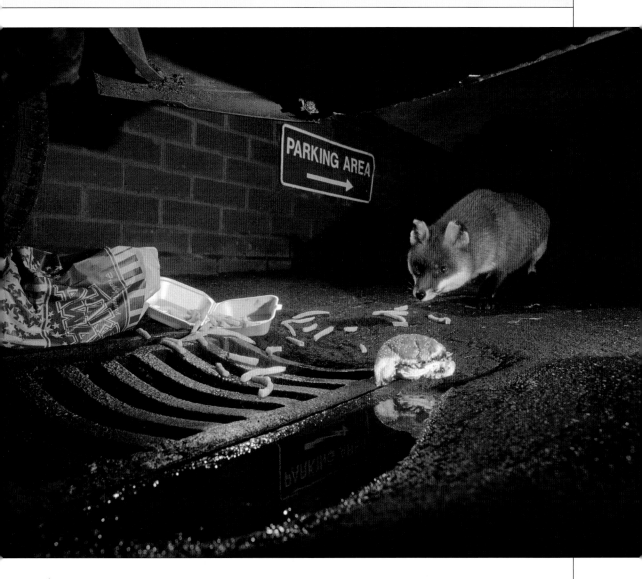

'Watching a peregrine falcon in Barcelona or stalking a little vixen in London while the city sleeps – that is very cool.'

PHOTOGRAPHING GARDEN BIRDS

Garden birds are great to photograph. Colourful, detailed and exhibiting interesting behaviour. And best of all, they come to you, so you can shoot them from the comfort of your own home.

There are lots of bird species that can be attracted into your garden with a few choice, tasty morsels on a bird table. However, bird tables and plastic feeders don't always make very good sets for a wildlife shot, so it's better to give them something else to stand on. A tree branch carefully clamped out of shot is ideal. Position it next to the bird feeder, and hopefully our feathered friends will use it as a hopping-off point before jumping onto the bird table.

The advantage of this approach is that you can effectively choose the background of the picture to suit the bird you are trying to photograph. Also think about where you will

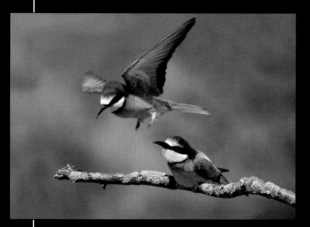

Above: *This branch, conveniently growing outside a cottage window in Bulgaria, offered these European bee eaters a perfect perch – and meant the photographer could set up indoors in the warm to wait for the shot. Canon EOS-1D MkIII with 100–400mm f/4–5.6 lens, 1/2000sec at f/5.6, ISO640*

be shooting from: if it's possible to shoot from inside your home through an open window, then you'll be a lot more comfortable than you will be sitting outside in a cold hide or tent.

Of course, to do this you'll need a decent telephoto lens – at least a 70–300mm used on a cropped-sensor DSLR for a little more magnification. A 1.4x or 2x teleconverter can also help greatly, although remember that this will cost you some light, and therefore a stop or two off your maximum aperture. This in turn restricts your ability to blur backgrounds and achieve a fast shutter speed.

A fast shutter speed is important, not only to freeze the action of your subject, but also to prevent loss of sharpness caused by camera shake. This is made worse by telephoto lenses, but can be lessened by putting the camera on a tripod and using any image stabilization that may be incorporated into your lens or camera body.

Your camera shouldn't struggle to focus too much on this type of subject. Try using wide area AF to catch the bird wherever it is in the frame, and if the camera struggles, switch to a mode where the selected single point is assisted by those around it.

The extreme telephoto lenses built-in to bridge cameras are often long enough to fill the frame with a small bird from a considerable distance away, but the shutter lag of such cameras may cause some frustration. Birds will not pause on the makeshift perch for long before hopping off to find the food, and if your camera takes half a second to focus and fire, you may miss the action.

ESSENTIAL KIT

- DSLR with telephoto lens and (optional) teleconverter
- Tripod
- Branch or makeshift perch
- Bird food as bait

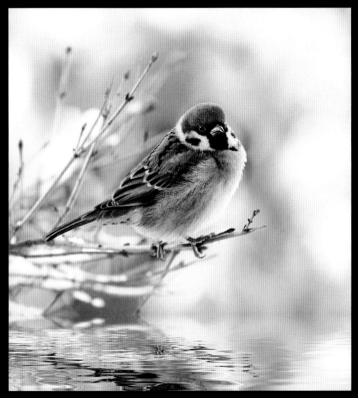

TIPS & TRICKS

- Many things can scare birds, but one thing that is sure to do the job is your pet cat. If you have one, try this assignment in an alternative location, such as a friend's house.

- Use continuous shooting mode to capture a series of pictures in quick succession.

- If your AF is struggling, try manually prefocusing on the spot where the bird will land.

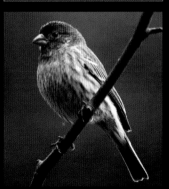

Above: A tripod and long lens were essential to get this shot of a house sparrow, complete with reflection in a garden brook.
Canon EOS 7D with 100–400mm f/4–5.6, 1/500sec at f/5.6, ISO400

Above right: While bridge cameras' telephoto lenses are suitable for shooting garden birds like this Eurasian finch, shutter lag means catching the moment can be difficult.
Fujifilm FinePix HS10, 1/500sec at f/4, ISO400

Right: This portrait of a male pileated woodpecker needed a fast shutter speed to render the bird sharp.
Canon EOS 40D with 70–300mm f/4–5.6 lens, 1/500sec at f/5.6, ISO400

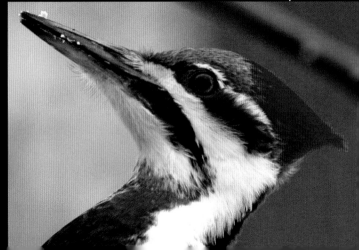

Shooting in **low light**

Some subjects look better when the sun goes down, but shooting pictures in low light conditions is far more of a challenge than it is in broad daylight.

To state the obvious for a moment, photography is all about light, and the images we can create with it. So when light levels fall, taking pictures can become difficult. At this point we can either put away our cameras, or change our approach.

There are three approaches to low light. We can open up the shutter to let more light in, and use a tripod for support. Or we can use wider apertures and more sensitive ISO settings to ensure that we can still hand-hold the camera even in dim conditions. Lastly we can shed more light on the scene with flash, either on- or off-camera.

Each of these approaches is different, and has its pros and cons. But with all three in your arsenal of skills, you'll be able to stay creative even when the sun goes down.

Tripods and long shutter speeds
One way of letting in more light to the sensor is to keep the camera's shutter open for longer. In low-light conditions, shutter speeds come down to 1/15sec or even longer. Such exposure times cannot be hand-held without incurring camera shake, and therefore we have to steady the camera with a tripod or similar support. If your subject is moving, it will also cause blur. This means that the long shutter speed approach is not suitable for subjects that are moving around – for instance at concerts. Where this approach does score, though, is when image quality is of paramount importance. By lengthening the shutter speed you can keep the ISO sensitivity – and levels of digital noise – low. Perfect when high-quality images of architecture and landscapes are required.

High ISO, fast-aperture photography

When long shutter speeds are not practical, because the camera must be hand-held or the subject matter is fast-moving, we have to find other ways. Making the camera's sensor more sensitive to light by increasing the ISO sensitivity is one way. Most cameras start at ISO100 or 200 and this is where you'll find the best image quality. As ISO is increased you can use faster shutter speeds, but image quality is compromised by digital noise.

So that ISO sensitivity doesn't have to be raised too much, it's a good idea to use this approach in combination with a fast-aperture lens, i.e. one with a large maximum aperture of f/2.8 or wider. The more light you can let through the aperture, the lower the ISO setting will need to be to achieve a hand-holdable shutter speed and freeze subject movement.

The high ISO/fast aperture approach is ideal for things like live music and stage photography, but can also be applied to parties and nights out. The benefit of this over flash is that the ambient lighting will be captured just as you see it, giving your photos far more atmosphere.

Flash photography

Flash is a versatile tool to fall back on. Anyone who owns a compact camera is familiar with it, although they will probably not have been overly impressed with the quality of the results. The problem with direct automatic flash is twofold. Firstly the front-on flash creates hard shadows, harsh reflections and other problems such as red-eye. Secondly, conventional automatic flash effectively replaces the light in the scene with the light from the flash. Any ambient light is not captured, and neither is the atmosphere.

But all this doesn't mean flash is a waste of time – we just have control it in order to overcome these issues. Positioning the flash off-camera means we can decide where shadows fall and avoid reflections. Opening the shutter for a longer period while triggering the flash means some of the ambient light will be captured, recording more of the natural atmosphere.

Below: Capturing the beauty and calm of the full moon over the ocean in Surfer's Paradise, Australia required a long shutter speed and a tripod.

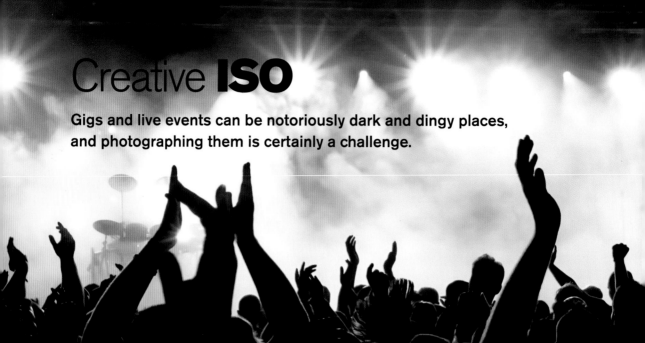

Creative **ISO**

Gigs and live events can be notoriously dark and dingy places, and photographing them is certainly a challenge.

Because of the need to change your shooting position all the time, and the subject's movement, a long exposure time is not practical. Flash is also a no-go: not only does it kill the ambience that was lovingly created by the lighting technicians, but it really gets on the nerves of the people watching the show, and event organizers usually ban flash. Much better to go to the ISO setting on your camera and select a wide aperture to let in lots more light. You'll be surprised at the shutter speeds you can achieve when shooting at ISO800 and f/2.

How wide?

Ultimately, your aperture size will be limited by the lens you are using. Most standard zooms do not fare well in this department, offering a maximum aperture that varies with zoom setting from f/3.5 to f/5.6. More expensive zooms of the same zoom range offer a widest aperture of f/2.8, which is two stops wider than f/5.6. A more affordable option is a 50mm standard lens, with either f/1.8 or f/1.4 maximum apertures – three or four stops better than the telephoto end of your standard zoom. Four stops is enough to lift your shutter speed from a hopeless 1/8sec to a capable 1/125sec.

Of course there are problems with shooting with such massive apertures. Lens quality is not at

Above: Shooting from the audience you face the challenge of getting close to the stage, as well as having to work with harsh lighting conditions and no flash.

its best here, with contrast levels and sharpness (particularly at the edges) taking a downward turn. It may not matter if you are after gritty, moody images, but do bear in mind that by stopping down a little you can improve image quality a great deal. There is even a school of thought that says one of the reasons for owning an f/1.4 lens in the first place is so you can shoot at f/2.8 without being wide open and losing quality.

You don't have much depth of field at large apertures, either, making focusing something of a challenge, especially if your subject is moving around. Continuous AF can help, but only if your camera is up to the job. With slower AF systems a lock-and-shoot approach works better, but do review your pictures often: it may be that you need to close down a bit to get a little more depth of field, and you can compensate for this by increasing ISO sensitivity further.

How fast?

The performance of digital cameras at high ISO sensitivities has increased significantly over the last few years, as image processors and noise reduction algorithms have got better. Noise is the

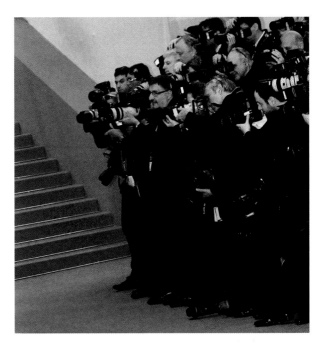

main problem with working at high ISO values. As the signal from the sensor is amplified, so the inherent noise in the electronic circuitry is amplified, too. Some cameras cope better with high ISO performance than others, with professional sports and action DSLRs from Canon and Nikon turning in excellent results up to ISO6,400 and providing emergency settings up to ISO102,000.

Do tests with your own camera to establish a level at which you are are happy with image quality. Shooting in black and white hides a multitude of sins, as does adding a bit of film-like grain at the post-processing stage.

Painting with light

Photographers tend to either love flash or hate it. But those who hate it are often remembering bad experiences, no doubt caused by using flash on-camera, with their DSLRs set to automatic. Take control of flash and you can use it creatively to give you effects that cannot be achieved in any other way.

One of the most creative ways to use flash is to paint with light. This is a technique that involves locking open the camera's shutter on a bulb (or long) exposure while you wander around the frame, manually triggering the flash at parts of the landscape. It's tremendous fun and can produce fantastic results, especially as the long exposure normally captures ambient light from the night sky, too. If your flash gun came with a set of coloured filters, try using these as you paint, swapping them around for different parts of the scene.

You'll need to set the flashgun to manual mode, and regulate its power output so you get a good exposure for the aperture you are using. This is another case of trial and error, so try a few test shots and keep reviewing the results on the camera's viewscreen, using the histogram

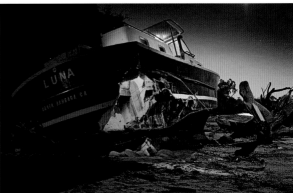

Above: This shot was taken just before dawn on Butterfly Beach in Montecito, California, after a bad storm. Exposed at 30sec, it was a mad dash to light up all the desired spots with coloured flashguns in time.

and clipping warnings to ensure you haven't got any blown highlights from over-exposure.

Architecture is an ideal subject for this approach to flash photography, and if you can find a set of derelict ruins to photograph then even better. Move around them, finding nooks and crannies and even firing your flash from inside the structure if this is accessible. You can use other sources of light, too – LED flashlights make great patterns as you trail them though the air.

SHOOTING A LIVE MUSIC EVENT

Gigs and concerts must be one of the most enjoyable subjects to shoot for any photographer, where getting close to the action lets you capture the thrill of the performance.

Everyone likes a gig, be it music, comedy or theatre, and such passionate performances are great opportunities for some people-photography. The environment is often challenging, with low-light, high-contrast conditions making it tricky to get the right exposure. Long shutter speeds can cause blur, and large apertures restrict depth of field. But persevere – the results can be worth it.

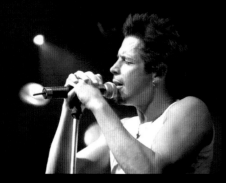

Above: *For this shot of Audioslave's Chris Connell, exposure was set by spot metering from his face. Nikon D3, 70–200mm f/2.8, 1/250sec at f/5.6, ISO1,600*

Use a fast aperture lens, and don't be afraid to open up and shoot close to wide open if you have to. What type of lens you need depends on where you position yourself relative to the action. With music it's often possible to get close up to the stage and shoot with a standard or wide-angle lens. With other subjects, such as theatre or jazz, you might be expected to shoot from further back with a telephoto lens.

Stages are lit in order to make a dramatic impression for the audience, but the high contrast levels can make things difficult for photographers. Your camera's metering systems are likely to get confused by a brightly lit performer against a dark black background. A way to ensure you are exposing for the right part of the scene is to use your camera's spot meter (see page 79) to take a reading from the performer's face and lock this in using AE-lock or manual exposure mode (see page 78). Light levels can change all the time, so do ensure that you keep checking the reading is still valid.

Ideally, you'll need to get an aperture/exposure combination that lets you create at least some depth of field and freeze the movement of your subject (unless you are going for some creative blur). Do this by raising the ISO sensitivity of your camera until you can get what you want. Lighting levels are often better at larger venues, and get worse the smaller the gig gets. Emerging artists playing in pubs and bars are notoriously difficult to shoot for this reason, but this kind of gig can let you practise your music photography without travelling miles from home or struggling to get a press pass.

It could be argued that what matters most to a gig photographer is access. Without it you are stuck shooting from the audience, and you may not even be allowed to take your camera with you. Permission to shoot photographs from the event organizers can provide you with access to the press pit at the front of the stage, where 'three songs, no flash' are the usual house rules.

ESSENTIAL KIT

• DSLR camera
• Preferably a wide-aperture lens
• Large capacity memory card

TIPS & TRICKS

• Try shooting in black and white for a more moody feel and to cover up any noise from increased ISO sensitivity.

• Engage continuous shooting mode, and resist the urge to review images on your screen all the time – you might miss the action.

• Use a big memory card, and take a spare. You don't want to run out of memory space during the performance.

Right: To capture some sense of background in this scene of Swan Lake, multi-zone metering was used.
Nikon D3, 70–200mm f/2.8, 1/250sec at f/3.5, ISO1,600

Below: This shot benefitted from very soft and even lighting at a Kylie Minogue concert in Milan, Italy.
Nikon D3 with 70–200mm f/2.8, 1/125sec at f/5.6, ISO1,600

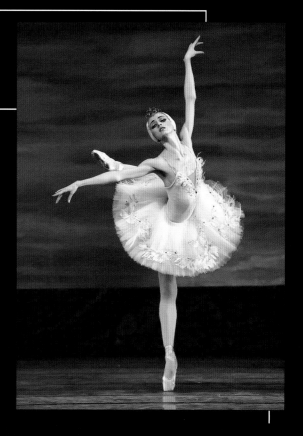

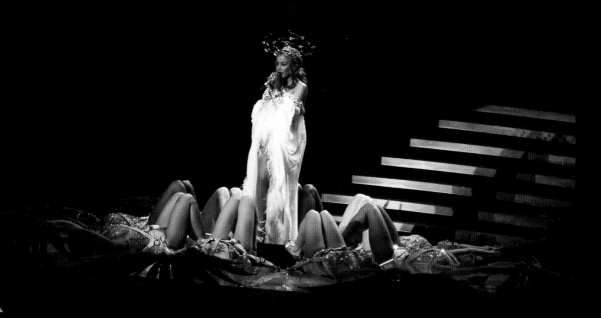

FOCUS ON
SHOOTING LIVE EVENTS
KAREN MCBRIDE LIVE PHOTOGRAPHER

Karen McBride began her career in photography shooting her school's sports' day, despite having no prior experience. She trained as a lithographic printer, but got back into photography after borrowing (and breaking!) a friend's camera. She now works for record labels, bands, models and recording studios.

Three words that describe you?
Good-looking, talkative, thoughtful.

important in case one area dries up – you'll then have a portfolio to fall back on in other areas.

Have you always worked digitally or did you start on film?
I started in film, but no-one will pay developing costs any more these days. I'm still glad that I did start in film, though, as I feel I still shoot with it mentally.

'You need to be honest and truthful to yourself, hard-working and believe in your skills.'

How did you get started?
I was always into art. I worked with a graphic designer who was into black and white photography and I was drawn to what he was doing. We used to go out after work and take pictures of derelict buildings. I swapped my then very primitive computer for an enlarger, then took night classes in photography to learn how to do everything properly. I'm still learning.

How do you succeed in your field?
It's really competitive out there; you need to be honest and truthful to yourself, hard-working and believe in your skills, because if you don't you have no right to expect others to.

The hardest part of your job?
Sending invoices and then chasing them up. It might sound silly, but getting paid for something you love takes some getting used to.

Do you work exclusively in this field?
I like to keep my options open. I think being skilled in other areas of photography is really

As U2 is inextricably linked with Anton Corbijn, is there a particular band/scene you think shaped your work?
I think if I were to be put into a 'scene' it would be new Manchester music like The Ting Tings.

How much of your work is commissioned and how much self-generated?
My commissioned work comes through a lot of self-promotion... so really it's self-generated.

What type of cameras do you shoot with? Does it depend on the location?
I tend to keep my kit quite minimal and stick to the same thing – my Nikon 70–200mm f/2.8 is donkeys' years old and has ingrained Glastonbury mud baked into the lens hood and sellotape holding the Nikon label back onto the body of the lens. It's my friend. I use a Nikon 50mm f/1.4 for my portraits and I love that too; it has great depth of field characteristics. Currently I use a Nikon D3. I've had it a while now and am still learning where everything is. I like technology but love the picture-taking more.

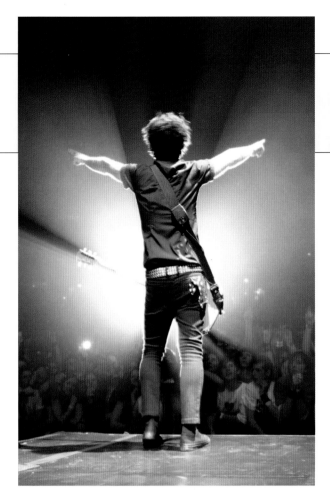

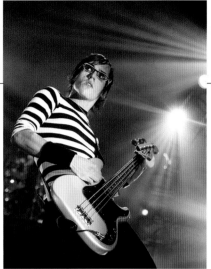

Above: As well as new Manchester music, Karen has also shot the band My Chemical Romance many times.

Left: A classic rock pose and one of Karen McBride's personal favourite images – a shot from a recent Green Day tour.

Below: Although Karen is well known for her music photography, she believes it's important to be able to shoot more than one type of genre.

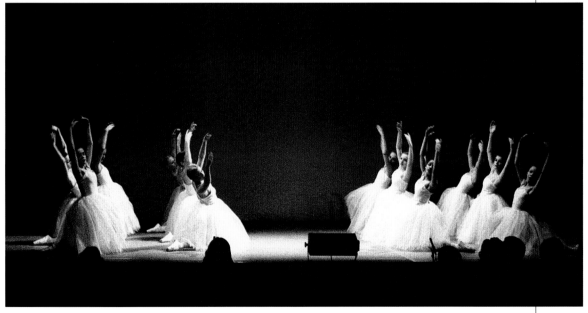

ASSIGNMENT
SHOOTING FIREWORKS ON A TRIPOD

Fireworks are great fun to shoot. Find a good vantage point and settle down with your tripod and DSLR to watch the display.

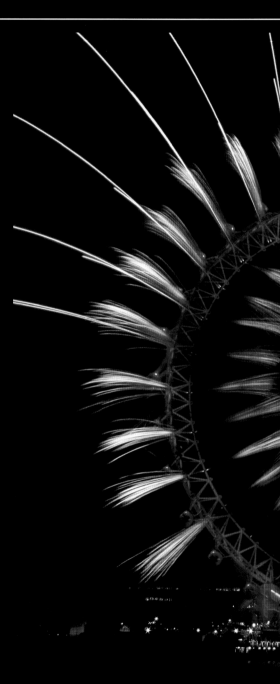

The urban night-time landscape transforms itself, becoming more magical than usual, and even more photogenic. Fireworks always look great, but photograph them in the context of a night-time landscape and they make a picture amazing.

Fireworks are great fun to photograph, and once you have practised your technique it's a pretty simple process, too. You'll need to use long shutter speeds to capture the movement of a few bursts through the frame, and it's best to do this with the camera's B setting (see page 214) so you can time the start and end of the exposure with the fireworks themselves. The difference between a 5sec and 8sec exposure is only just over half a stop, so don't worry if each shot varies in exposure time slightly. An aperture of f/8–11 should be fine, with a low ISO to maintain image quality. Obviously a tripod is mandatory, and a remote release is always a good idea when working with the B shutter-speed setting.

When you compose the shot, anticipate where the fireworks are going to be and leave space. It's hard to predict, so be prepared to alter your composition quickly when the display starts and you get a better idea of what is going on. Depending on the conditions, you may find you get the best shots at the beginning of the display. As the fireworks continue, noticeable levels of smoke build up in the sky which can spoil the view.

Right: A long exposure of 1sec allowed the whole explosion to be captured during this fireworks display on the River Thames in London.
Pentax K-7 with 18–55mm f/3.5–5.6, 1sec at f/4, ISO100

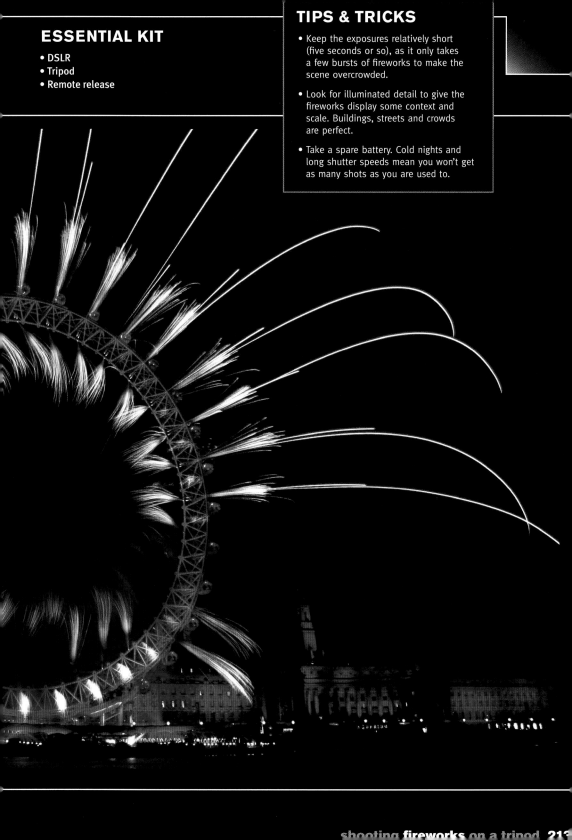

ESSENTIAL KIT

- DSLR
- Tripod
- Remote release

TIPS & TRICKS

- Keep the exposures relatively short (five seconds or so), as it only takes a few bursts of fireworks to make the scene overcrowded.

- Look for illuminated detail to give the fireworks display some context and scale. Buildings, streets and crowds are perfect.

- Take a spare battery. Cold nights and long shutter speeds mean you won't get as many shots as you are used to.

Astrophotography

You may never have thought about photographing the night sky before, but if you ever find yourself in a location with little light pollution on a clear, moon-free night, it's something you will really enjoy trying.

Although we don't notice it on the timescale of everyday movement, the motion of the stars through the night sky is enough to be captured on camera when shooting long exposures. Such images – often called star trails – are spectacular to look at and more easy to shoot than you might think.

Obviously this is a very low light situation, but just how low is a matter of guesswork. You can't meter for a night sky as the levels of available light are too small, meaning a trial and error approach is the best option. Start with a mid-range aperture of f/8 and try an exposure time of five minutes if your camera allows. To do this you will need to use your camera's bulb facility, marked as a 'B' setting on the shutter speed scale. The B setting allows you to keep the shutter open for as long as you keep your finger on the shutter release, although in practice this is likely to be a remote release to avoid camera shake.

All digital cameras have a limit on the length of exposure that can be achieved with a bulb exposure. Shorter limits of 30 seconds are common in entry-level cameras, and mean that you will need to take multiple frames and combine them afterwards in Photoshop to get the proper effect. Higher-spec DSLRs can handle bulb exposure of an hour or more, but there are a few technical issues to be wary of.

Just because you are shooting at lower ISO settings doesn't mean you are exempt from noise problems; this also comes from long exposures, manifesting itself in 'hot' or 'stuck' pixels that shine as bright red, blue or green. Thankfully this noise is easier to get rid of because it is more predictable. Most cameras have a long exposure noise-reduction for exposures longer than a predetermined limit, usually about half a second. A second exposure is recorded after the main shot, but with the shutter closed so all the camera sees is black. This is used as a reference map of the noises located, and is subtracted from the shot.

This process can take time when shooting star trails, because the noise reduction frame has to

Multi-exposure star trails

Your DSLR may not support bulb exposures of more than 30 seconds, but that doesn't mean you can't capture stunning star trails. Work with what you've got and shoot multiple 30sec exposures that you can splice together afterwards with image-editing software.

The best way of doing this is to set a 30sec shutter speed in manual exposure mode and engage continuous shooting mode. Set your camera up on its tripod pointing in the right direction, and depress the shutter button on the cable release to start the first exposure. While this is happening, lock the shutter release button down – this is how you would record a bulb exposure of a few hours. Now you can sit down with a cup of coffee and listen to your camera fire every 30 seconds.

It's important that you turn off the long exposure noise-reduction feature when doing this, otherwise you will get a 30 second gap between frames while noise reduction takes place, resulting in dotted-line star trails.

Import the frames into Photoshop and assemble them all in one document as separate layers (see pages 344–347). Change the blending mode of the layers to 'Lighten' (see page 356) and the tiny trails captured in each frame will blend into one.

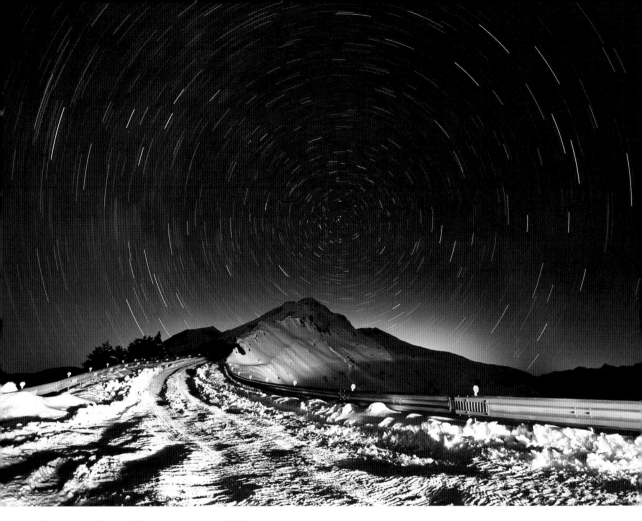

be recorded over the same amount of time as the main shot. So if you use a one hour exposure time to record the star trail, there will be a one hour period of noise reduction after this where the camera can't be used for anything else.

The second technical challenge is battery life: a long exposure could deplete it by well over half. For this reason it's handy to be able to charge or power your camera from your car's battery – there are accessories available that enable this.

Composition and conditions

A long exposure will pick up much more stellar detail than you can make out with the naked eye. If you want to emphasize the rotating of the earth and capture the circular movement of the stars that results, start by pointing your camera at one of the pole stars – Polaris in the northern hemisphere; Sigma Octanis in the southern. A star chart is a useful accessory when working in this field!

Above: With a 24mm lens and the largest available aperture of f/3.5, this shot was exposed for about three hours using Polaris, the fixed northern hemisphere pole star, as a focal point.

You may want to fill the frame with stars using a telephoto lens, or include some foreground detail in the frame for reference. If the latter, you can light up the foreground detail with a burst of flash, or by shining a torch or lantern around.

Successful stellar photography is not possible without the right conditions. Obviously you will need clear skies with no cloud, but also keep an eye on the phases of the moon. A full moon will swamp the sky with light and make it impossible to use an exposure of more than about five minutes. The best star trails are captured away from the light pollution of cities, on clear nights when there is little or no moonlight.

Black and white

We've come a long way from the blurred black and white images of early photography. Now we can shoot in high definition colour, seeing the results instantly and even capturing in 3D. So why do we still insist on going back to basics and shooting pictures in black and white?

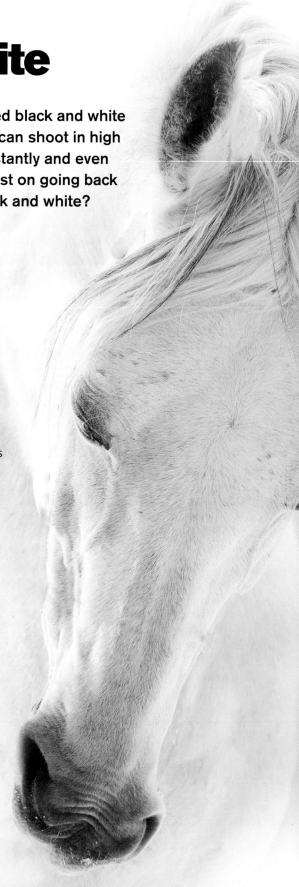

In some areas of photography, less is most definitely more. By shooting in black and white, it's as though we are removing the distraction of colour, freeing our minds to concentrate instead on shapes, lines, tones and texture. As a general rule, anything in photography that forces the viewer to use their imagination is a recipe for success, and shooting in black and white certainly does this.

Subjects that favour the mono approach include fine-art studies of flowers or nudes; architecture, where shapes and lines are more important than anything else; and reportage, where a more gritty look and feel can be given to a shot. Portraiture also sometimes benefits when the look you are going for is a fairly minimalist one.

Shooting in black and white

Almost all digital cameras have a black and white mode, which records pictures without colour, although it has to be said this is not the best way of producing monochrome photographs. Far more control can be wielded if colour shots are recorded as normal and then converted to black and white afterwards on a computer. This doesn't mean that the black and white mode on your camera is not useful, though. What it can do is let you see the world in monochrome, either by taking preview pictures in this mode, or by composing with live view. If you can shoot JPEG and raw files at the same time (all raw-shooting cameras can do this) then you'll find the JPEGs are captured in black and white while the raw files are saved in colour, allowing you to make the transformation to

Right: This white horse has been over-exposed for a high-key effect, and a large f/2.8 aperture used to restrict depth of field and blur the background.

monochrome yourself afterwards. If you are only shooting JPEG, then remember to reset to colour shooting mode before you capture the final frame.

There are a great many ways to convert an image to black and white using software such as Adobe Photoshop, and we'll cover this in chapter four (see pages 268–273).

Printing in black and white

If you think mono photos look good on screen, then you'll be blown away by a good monochrome print. It's worth taking the trouble, as there is a lot of variation between inkjet printers and high street labs.

If you get a third party lab to do your printing for you, then go and talk to them about black and white. They may have some hints and tips for you on how best to prepare the images for output. If you are printing at home and black and white is important to you, then you should choose a desktop inkjet printer that contains grey cartridges as well as the standard cyan, magenta, yellow and black. This lets the printer lay down delicate gradations between black and white without using the colour cartridges, which can look less natural.

Right, from top to bottom: A Montana landscape taken first in colour, then in black and white mode, and at the bottom with a red filter, giving the sky a much more dramatic texture.

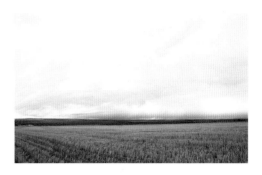

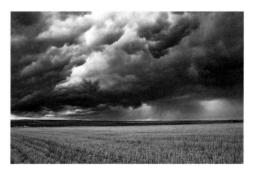

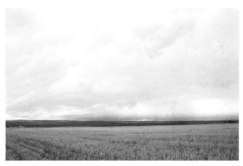

Filters in black and white photography

It may sound odd at first, but coloured filters are very useful in black and white photography. In a situation where two objects of contrasting colours can appear to be the same shade of grey in black and white, using the right coloured filters can lighten one object and darken another. This avoids a scene looking 'flat' in monochrome, and gives a picture more contrast.

Shooting monochrome through a blue filter means that blue objects will render as a lighter shade of grey, while the opposite colour, red, will appear darker. Similarly, green and blue filters lighten their own colours, and darken reds and oranges.

The most common situation where coloured filters are used in monochrome photography is when trying to separate grey clouds from pale blue skies. Both are rendered as the same shade of grey in black and white, so landscape photographers tend to use a red or orange filter to darken the blue of the sky; the grey clouds are unaffected. This enhances cloud detail and produces far more dramatic shots.

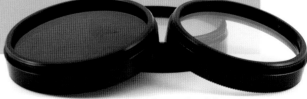

ASSIGNMENT
BLACK AND WHITE
STILL-LIFE PROJECT

You can find still-life pictures everywhere. Look for contrasts by comparing everyday objects with their surroundings, and emphasize the tension between tones and textures by shooting the whole thing in black and white.

We've seen that converting a photograph to black and white allows us to concentrate on lines, form and texture free from the distraction of colour. A good use of this technique is to bring together contrasting shapes and textures in the same image, exploiting the tension between different objects and materials. You can find such combinations while you are out and about – at the beach or in the park – or create them in your own home studio from household objects.

Bull's-eye compositions work well here (see page 60), positioning the object in the middle of the frame while using a contrasting texture or tone in the background. If you are having trouble visualizing what the scene will look like in black and white, try using your camera in 'live view' mode with black and white mode engaged, switching back to colour for the final shot. Or look through a strong coloured filter, which will give you an idea of what things look like when they are all the same hue.

Alternatively, try positioning objects of similar shape but different texture next to each other, exploiting any symmetry you can find. Again, you'll want to photograph the still life face-on, perhaps with a tripod to keep the camera positioned carefully over the set-up and eliminate vibrations.

You may be able to produce these images in pairs or more, in which case try and use the same or similar methods of black and white conversion. You'll want each image to look as similar as possible to the others.

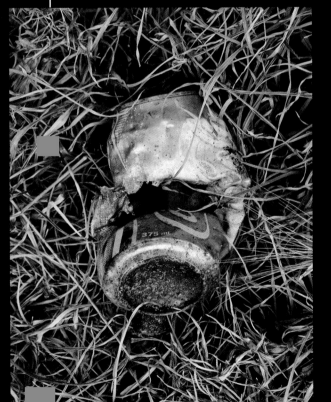

Left: The black and white treatment and central positioning emphasize the contrast between the textures and tones of the grass and rusting drinks can in this 'found' shot. Nikon D700 with 24–120mm f/3.5–5.6 lens, 1/125sec at f/8, ISO100

ESSENTIAL KIT

- Camera and standard lens
- Close-up attachments
- Tripod
- Computer and software for black and white conversion

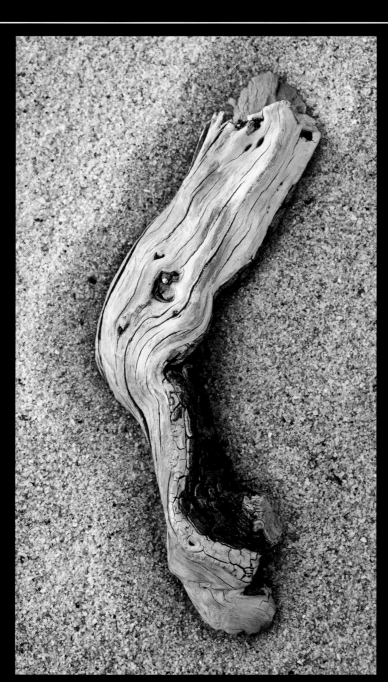

TIPS & TRICKS

There are a number of good subjects for this treatment:

- Stones on sand
- Wood on sand
- Metal on a velvet-like material
- Clothing laid out on stone or metal
- Different metals on each other

Left: Beaches yield many still-life shots. Smooth driftwood against grains of sand makes for a great image.
Nikon D700 with 24–120mm f/4–5.6 lens, 1/125sec at f/11, ISO100

Fine-art photography

People have been arguing about what constitutes art for centuries, but take comfort from the fact that if anyone is ever debating one of your fine-art pictures in this way, you have probably got it right.

Of all the approaches to photography we've encountered in this chapter, fine art is perhaps the most most difficult to define. For photography to be classified as fine art it doesn't have to feature a specific subject matter – in fact, many of the types of photography seen in other chapters could equally be talked about here in terms of fine art. The dictionary defines fine art imagery as a 'visual art whose products are to be appreciated for their imaginative, aesthetic or intellectual content' – in other words, photography that we like, or are intrigued, to look at.

Image quality is key in fine-art photography. Excepting those instances when you are deliberately making use of poor image quality for creative purposes (i.e. using a mobile phone or toy camera), you should always be aiming to maximize quality both when you capture it, and afterwards. Use your best equipment and work at low ISO sensitivities, on a tripod if need be.

You'll also need to present your fine art in a way that people can appreciate it. This usually means printing your images, and the high-quality ethos should apply here, too. Printing at home means you can stay in charge of the picture-making process from start to finish, although commercial photographic printers are often able to produce prints at much larger sizes. Sympathetic mounting and framing is the icing on the cake, and can enhance a good image even further.

Right: Fine-art subjects are only limited by your imagination. Any subject is permissible – as long as it's shot with imagination and in high quality.

Fine art and the natural world

Many of the pictures that find their way onto our walls have their origins in nature. Beauty in the natural world resonates with us on a fundamental level, so we connect with landscapes and seascapes, still-life pictures of flowers, and patterns in wood, stone and sand.

Landscapes are popular fine-art images because they are usually packed with detail, so there is always something to come back to – details you see, but have never noticed before. By varying your composition (see pages 58–61) you can decide whether you want to make an instant impact with a picture that might fatigue quickly, or produce a 'slow burn' that may not impress at first, but that people will grow to love over time. Neither approach is right; they are just different.

Continuing the nature theme, flowers tend to be a popular subject for fine art, especially when tackled in the form of a still life back at home or in the studio. The subjects can be home-grown or bought from a shop, though in either case make sure to choose the best specimens you can.

Explain to a florist that you are intending to use flowers for photography and they will help you look for good examples with plenty of colour and no damage to petals.

Flowers can be shot in several different ways. Face-on from above is popular for roses, gerberas and the like, producing a colourful, two-dimensional image. Lilies, on the other hand, are classically photographed from the side, allowing their graceful shapes to sweep across the frame. Whatever you are shooting, though, using soft window light is the perfect approach to lighting. Position your set-up and subject so the window is lighting it from the side, and use reflectors to even out contrast if you need to (see page 27).

When you are out and about, try to pay attention to the small details that are often missed, as these, too, can make stunning fine-art images if shot in the right way. Rocks in the sand, the texture of wood or a leaf back-lit by sunshine. When captured on camera and turned into a large, high-quality inkjet print, such details have the power to impress. In fact, still-life photography and fine art go hand-in-hand, perhaps because still life offers the photographer so much control over how the item looks. Almost anything can be photographed in a fine-art style – the only limit is your imagination. Old boxes of junk in the garage or attic throw up items that are just begging to be photographed under soft daylight, in black and white and with shallow depth of field.

Commercial use

There is money to be made from good fine-art photography. Most obviously you can sell prints of your work, although don't expect to land a six-week exhibition at a top gallery to begin with. Think about approaching coffee shops and restaurants that exhibit local artists' work, and keep the price down to an affordable level. You can also sell greetings cards, especially around Christmas time, Valentine's day, etc. Approach local craft shops about this, who will be able to advise you on pricing, too.

ASSIGNMENT
REFLECTIONS

The next time you are by a river or lake, pay attention to the patterns and shapes made by the reflections in the water. It's an alternative way to photograph architecture that also works well as fine-art imagery.

Reflections are good subject matter for fine-art photography because they cross that fine line between reality and surrealism. Realistic images of buildings reflected in rivers, lakes or canals are simple to spot and shoot, but for a more abstract approach to fine art, try to isolate the patterns and shapes in the swirling water.

For a reflections shot to work well, a combination of the right sunlight, architecture and water/wind conditions must all come together, so it's worth making a note of good locations and paying them a repeat visit every now and again. That said, there is plenty of camera and Photoshop technique that can help.

Conditions

It's fairly obvious that the body of water should lie between you and the object you are shooting, but it's also worth thinking about where you want the sun to be. For a clean, sharp reflection you want the building causing the reflection to be bathed in sunlight, and the water itself to be in shadow, so it's as dark as possible. Dark water won't register in the final shot as much as water lit up by the sun, and remember it's not the water you are photographing, but the reflection in it. Times of the day (and year) when the sun is low in the sky tend to produce these conditions, and it may take a couple of visits to a location to establish when the right time is.

The sun is not the only meteorological condition you need to think about; the direction and strength of the wind dictates the state of the surface of the water. Totally flat water produces a more accurate reflection, though ripples and swirls create the hectic random patterns we are after. Also, try to move about so you are shooting into a clean patch of water. Although floating crisp packets and drinks cans can be removed afterwards in Photoshop, it's better to avoid them in the first place.

Shooting the pictures

Any camera will work well for this assignment, but a DSLR gives you more control over exposure and focus, and lets you shoot in raw for more versatility in post-production. A telephoto lens is a good choice, unless you are close to the water. This will let you isolate patterns in-camera, rather than having to crop the frame afterwards. When exposing for a reflection, use your camera's spot metering to take a reading from the pattern itself, and not the water. Similarly, when focusing make sure it's the pattern that is sharp, not the water's surface. Engage continuous shooting and capture frames quickly as you see good patterns emerge.

Post-production

After opening up the pictures in your editing software, increase the contrast so the water's surface becomes nearly black, and the patterns in it pop with colour. Play with saturation, vibrance and clarity adjustments, too, until you are happy with the result. The Crop tool comes in handy for fine-tuning the final composition.

Right: Completely calm, still water would have produced a more realistic shot, but without the interest.
Nikon D700, 24–120mm f/4 lens, 1/125sec at f/8, ISO200

ESSENTIAL KIT

- DSLR or compact camera
- Telephoto lens
- Editing software, such as
  Adobe Photoshop Elements

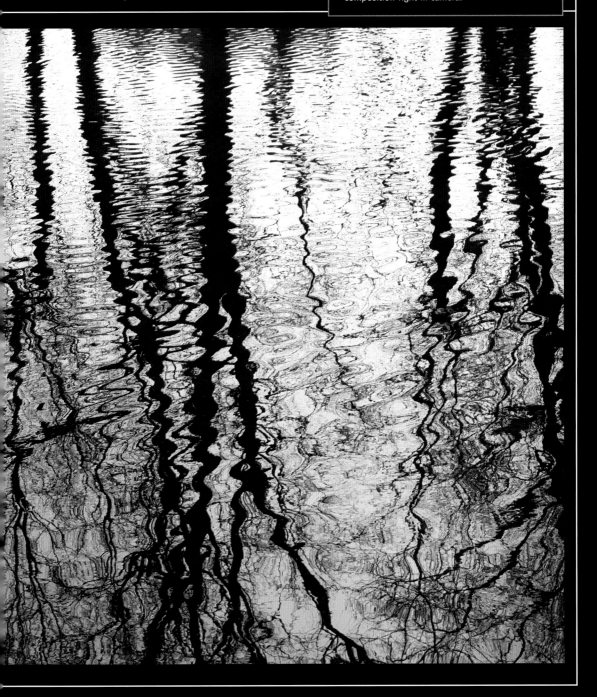

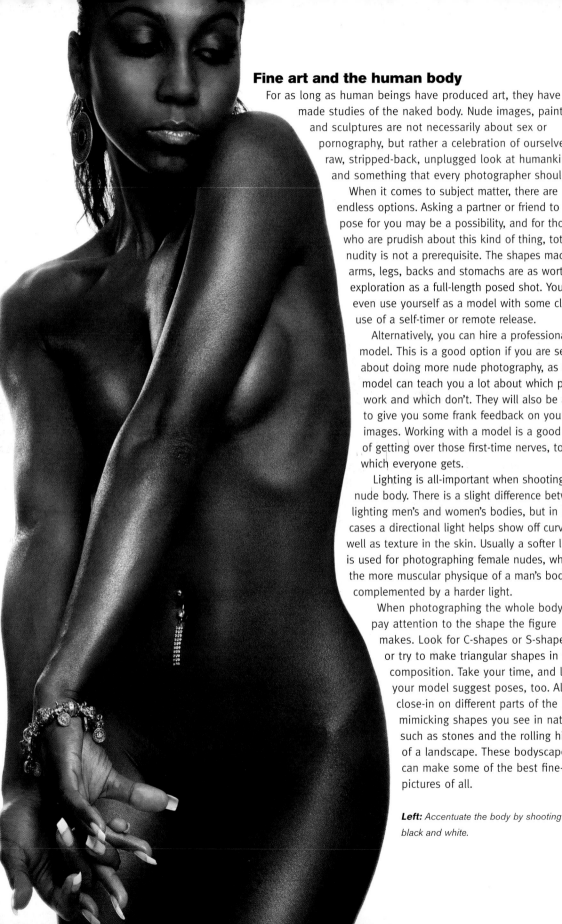

Fine art and the human body

For as long as human beings have produced art, they have made studies of the naked body. Nude images, paintings and sculptures are not necessarily about sex or pornography, but rather a celebration of ourselves. A raw, stripped-back, unplugged look at humankind, and something that every photographer should try.

When it comes to subject matter, there are endless options. Asking a partner or friend to pose for you may be a possibility, and for those who are prudish about this kind of thing, total nudity is not a prerequisite. The shapes made by arms, legs, backs and stomachs are as worthy of exploration as a full-length posed shot. You can even use yourself as a model with some clever use of a self-timer or remote release.

Alternatively, you can hire a professional model. This is a good option if you are serious about doing more nude photography, as a model can teach you a lot about which poses work and which don't. They will also be able to give you some frank feedback on your images. Working with a model is a good way of getting over those first-time nerves, too, which everyone gets.

Lighting is all-important when shooting the nude body. There is a slight difference between lighting men's and women's bodies, but in both cases a directional light helps show off curves as well as texture in the skin. Usually a softer light is used for photographing female nudes, while the more muscular physique of a man's body is complemented by a harder light.

When photographing the whole body, pay attention to the shape the figure makes. Look for C-shapes or S-shapes, or try to make triangular shapes in your composition. Take your time, and let your model suggest poses, too. Also close-in on different parts of the body, mimicking shapes you see in nature such as stones and the rolling hills of a landscape. These bodyscapes can make some of the best fine-art pictures of all.

Left: Accentuate the body by shooting in black and white.

Abstract versus reality

There is a certain freedom to fine-art photography: you can shoot what you like. And when you develop a certain style, which can include the subject matter you go for, you'll find that the pictures start coming more and more easily. The conventional subjects that have entertained fine-art photographers for years (bowls of fruit, flowers, landscapes, etc.) are great, but it's very hard to put your own stamp on them and make them something individual to your photographic style. Much better to seek out a more esoteric subject – something obscure in which you can create something beautiful, interesting or funny, where this isn't usually expected.

Abstract approaches to everyday subjects provide this subject matter in spades. Visit a scrapyard (not somewhere that people usually associate with great beauty) and have a look at the patterns in the rusting metal and rotting wood that is lying around. Explore this with a macro lens and look for patterns, filling the frame with texture. Do the same at the seaside with rocks, sand and seaweed, or even objects you see in the gutter as you are walking along the street. A lost glove dropped in the street and frozen by an overnight frost, for example.

The point is this: fine art is everywhere. And the ability to turn the ordinary into the extraordinary lies purely in your creative imagination. The skills that you'll learn in this book, and from other sources such as magazines and conversations with other photographers, will only expand on this. Fine-art photography is something that will grow with you as you mature as a photographer.

Themes: shooting a portfolio

A series of pictures always creates a bolder impression than a group of individual shots. It might be three images or a dozen, but a portfolio of fine-art shots means you have more options to frame and hang prints together, exhibit them in a show, and sell them to people wanting pairs of images for a room, for example. The tricky bit is coming up with the theme in the first place.

At its most simple level, this can be explorations of

Top tips for bodyscapes

1. Soften the light by using a net curtain in front of a window. This can also make a stunning background, too: take a spot exposure reading form your model's skin and let the net curtains over-expose and glow.
2. As well as shooting from your model's own level, try photographing them from above or below. Be bold, and experiment.
3. Keep it simple – less is more with fine-art nude photography. Elegant lines and shapes won't have the same effect if there are other factors competing for attention.
4. Monochrome works very well for this type of photography. If you do shoot in colour, desaturate it slightly to prevent the colours distracting from the shape and form in the picture.

similar subjects using the same photographic style. Different types of lily, for instance, photographed in the same black and white style. Or waves crashing on a beach – each one is guaranteed to be different from the last. You can also play with the theme more loosely than this, shooting very different images that share a cryptic theme. Don't be afraid of being quite surreal in your approach; humour is just as popular in fine art as beauty is.

Below: Look for landscapes in the human form. These bodyscapes imitate natural shapes, such as rolling countryside and hills.

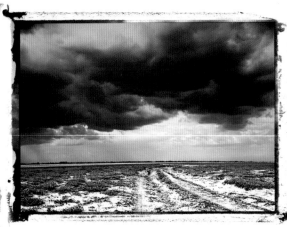

Above: When you're ready to print your fine-art image, complement it with a well-chosen border.

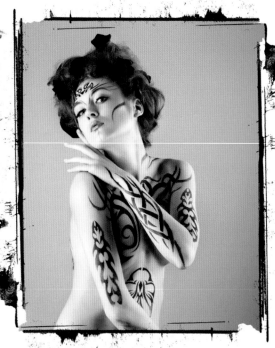

Above: A painted frame can add another dimension to the picture, if the subject lends itself to it.

Outputting and presentation

Even the best fine-art image is nothing unless it is outputted properly at the end of the photographic workflow process. Usually this means printing the image, but there are some things that need to be considered before this happens when we are thinking about how best to present an image.

An often-neglected part of any photograph is its border. The edges of the frame define where the picture ends and our imagination starts, so it's important to define where this is. Often a photograph does this itself by way of its composition and structure, but sometimes a black keyline around the edges of the frame help define where things begin and end. There are more stylish alternatives, too: simulated film rebates that hark back to the days of darkroom printing are very popular, as are hand-drawn edges or painted effects – we'll look at how to put these together in chapter four (see pages 248–249). Do keep things simple, and be careful not to overdo it. A border should be subtle and support the image, not compete with it.

Framing, mounting and matting follows a similar philosophy. Mounting a print on board helps give it rigidity, while a matte (a cardboard border) on the front helps to separate it from the frame. Plain white or cream mattes work best, and you can either cut these yourself with a specialist bevelled cutting tool, or get them produced at your local framing shop.

In photography, thin, simple frames are often the right choice. Black is popular, but also consider aluminium, wood and white-painted materials, too. While pre-made frames are more affordable, you'll get a much better result from a bespoke framer, who can make something of exactly the right size and give you advice on what approach works best.

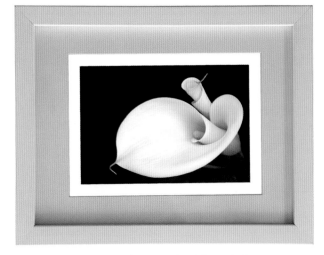

Above: A matte (cardboard border) sets the image apart from the frame, giving it breathing space.

Choice of printing material

When producing fine-art prints, the choice of printing media is dictated as much by the subject matter as by how the print is going to be viewed. Glossy papers accentuate detail, and give an impression of greater sharpness that is very good for images containing architecture or urban landscapes. On the downside, glossy papers reflect everything, so care must be taken when hanging them to avoid the reflections of windows and electric lights. Matt paper, on the other hand, is great for black and white images containing form, lines and texture: nudes and soft still-life images, for instance. There are many materials in between these extremes – usually referred to as semi-gloss, lustre, stipple, etc. – that provide the best of both worlds. Also look for papers that have a baryta base. This is the same material used in older, traditional, fibre-based darkroom papers, and has a luxurious feel. Most of this applies to those printing at home on a photo-quality inkjet printer. High-street printers or commercial photo labs will not offer the same range, although they may stock some speciality media.

Canvas printing is also very popular these days, and this can be done on the high street, internet or at home. External companies do tend to charge handsomely for wrap-around canvas blocks, which don't have a frame as such, but are instead stretched over a wooden lattice, with the image often carrying on around the sides, top and bottom. You can produce the same items at home for a great deal less on an inkjet printer, although you'll need a large-format machine to get decent sized blocks, and fitting the canvas to the frame is not an easy job.

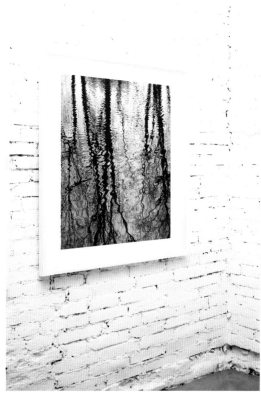

Above: A simple, stylish frame with generous space to show off your printed photograph is almost always preferable to more fussy frames.

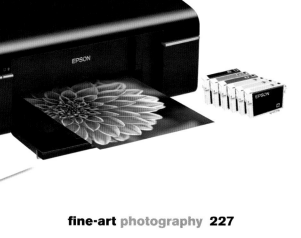

Right: A good inkjet printer can often not only print thicker photographic paper, but also thin canvas or photographic canvas sheets that are available from a number of suppliers.

ASSIGNMENT
ABSTRACT PATTERNS

Walk around any location and you will spot patterns that make great abstract photographs – it's just a case of looking hard enough.

Scrapyards are full of rusty metal, beaches are strewn with rocks in the sand, forests have bark, leaves and wood, while even the humble sidestreet is rich in details, textures and shapes.

The trick with abstract photography is to stop thinking about your subject as it is and instead start exploring its lines and patterns. When photographing a rusty car bonnet, for instance, all you are interested in is the rust and the contrast this makes with the remaining paint. Consider the shape of the light coming onto the surface, too; shadows are an equally valid subject.

There is so much freedom in this type of photography that you may find yourself struggling to produce anything that works. But remember the basics of composition we have already looked at. Can you put anything on a compositional third and use leading lines to guide the eye to this spot? If you can then this is a great start, and you'll soon find the compositions start to flow.

If you are photographing outside then, to a certain extent, you have to use the lighting conditions that are available to you. That's not to say, though, that you can't shape and mould the conditions a little using light modifiers such as reflectors, diffusers or even some off-camera flash. Light coming in from the side (often called relief lighting) will emphasize texture more by casting tiny shadows off the rough surface.

Finding fine art
What one person throws away, a photographer can find and turn into a stunning fine-art image. The late Bob Carlos Clarke was a prime example of a photographer who took this approach, finding objects at low tide on his regular walks on the bank of the River Thames in London. Clarke would bring old cutlery, knives, even underwear back to his studio and photograph it in monochrome against a number of different backgrounds. The results were huge, handprinted photographs that sell for thousands today.

You can develop a similar project of your own, either photographing objects in situ, where they lie, or bringing them back to shoot in your home studio. Daylight is a great light source for this type of work, using reflectors to even-out lighting where needed. Relief lighting will help emphasize texture. The opposite can be said of front-on lighting, which tends to produce flat, low-contrast results. Of course, intermediate positions produce effects between these two extremes, giving you fine control over how the subject looks to the camera.

Picking different backgrounds is almost as much fun as finding the subjects themselves. If you are shooting your found object on location then you won't have much choice about what your subject is resting on, but if you are working in your own home then it's worth keeping a collection of materials for just this use. Old paving slabs, floor tiles or roof slates are perfect for the job, as are sheets of wood and scratched-up metal. You can either go for a background that doesn't distract from the subject too much, or pick one that contrasts with it completely.

Try to shoot from above the subject and background, positioning your camera directly above it. You can do this easily if your tripod has a removable centre column that can then be repositioned horizontally. If your tripod cannot do this, you can position the whole thing horizontally on a chair or table over the subject, with the apparatus weighed down with some hefty books.

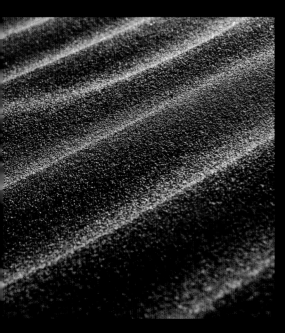

Left: *At the beach, look for ripples left in the sand by the retreating tide. Wait for the more directional, late-afternoon light for best contrast.*
Nikon D3, 50mm f/1.4 lens, 1/60sec at f/2.8, ISO400

Below: *The centre of a sunflower has a wonderfully regular pattern. Try shooting it head-on, contrasting it with the petals. Sunflower seedheads also make great subjects.*
Fujifilm FinePix S5 Pro with 105mm f/2.8 macro lens, 1/60sec at f/11, ISO200

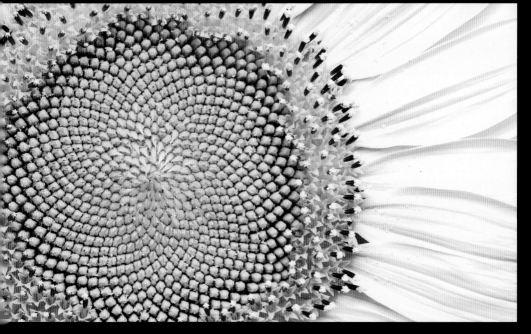

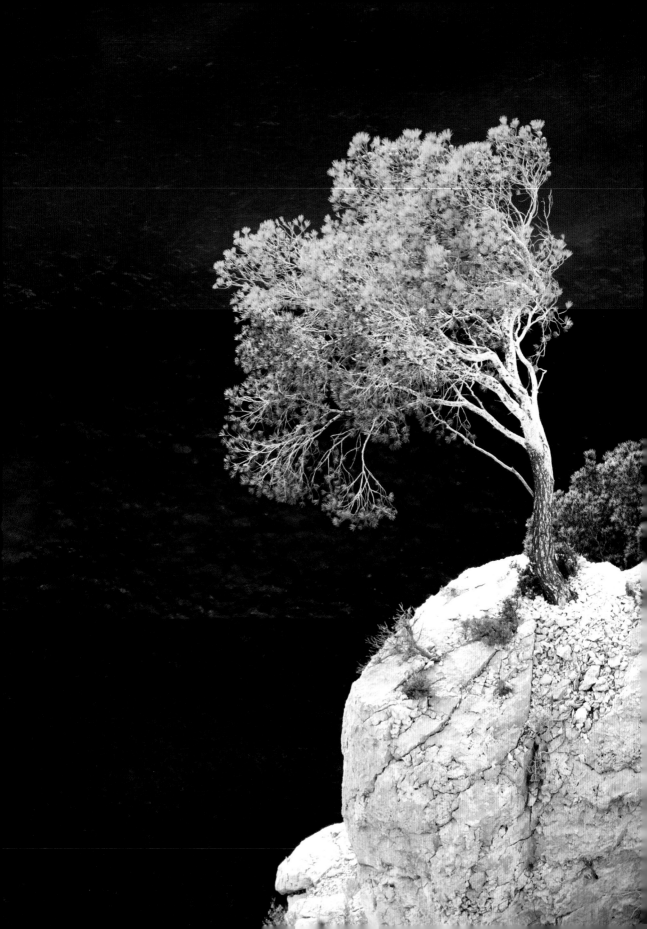

the digital
darkroom

When it comes to good photography, only half of the picture-making process happens in your camera. The next steps, which occur on your computer, are every bit as creative and demand just as much imagination, skill and hard work. In this chapter we'll look at how to get your pictures off the camera and onto your computer, where they can be edited into great images.

From **emulsion** to **data**

In the days of film, photographers used to have to spend hours in a darkened room breathing noxious chemicals if they wanted to influence their pictures after shooting. Thankfully, these days it's much easier.

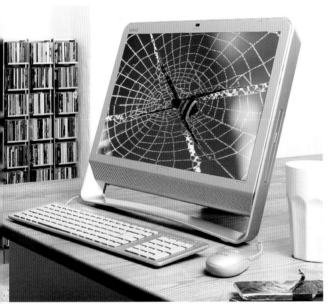

Above: Your desktop computer, combined with image software such as Adobe Photoshop, will let you take your photography to the next level.

For the pioneer photographers of the preceding centuries, capturing the picture in-camera was only the start of the photographic process. Processing film and printing negatives in a wet-chemical darkroom was where the second half of the creative process happened. Photographers could change contrast and colour balance, as well as selectively lighten ('dodge') or darken ('burn') prints by letting less or more light onto the light-sensitive paper they used.

These days, with digital technology, we can do all this and much, much more in the comfort of our home office. Tone, contrast and colour adjustments are a matter of a few simple mouse clicks. With some practise you'll learn how to merge images together, erase objects from a scene and produce prints of amazing quality. You'll also be able to email pictures around the world and make a website of your art, archiving it for years to come. All you need is a computer and some imaging software.

Whereas a few years ago buying a computer for digital imaging meant beefing up basic models with extra processor power, memory and other options, the relentless march of technology now means that most home computers have enough power for basic digital photography editing. You should still buy as much memory (RAM) as you can afford, though, and plenty of storage in the form of a large hard disk.

Transferring files

The first stage in digital photography editing is to transfer your image files from the camera's memory card to your computer so they can be worked on. This is as easy as connecting your camera to your computer using the USB cable that came with it. Turn the camera on and the memory card will mount on your computer desktop the same as any other disk would. You can browse this disk and copy files from it in the same way you'd navigate around a memory key or CD/DVD disk, although some camera manufacturers also supply software that does this for you.

Right: A card reader should be one of the first accessories you buy. It will allow you to transfer photos to your computer simply by slotting in the camera's memory card.

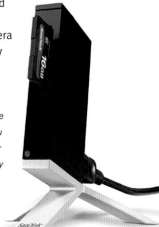

Backing up your files

Copying your image files across to your PC or Mac is great, but once the original card has been wiped, the only copy of the images is on your computer's hard disk, and we all know what happens to hard disks eventually.

When hard disks crash and die, all the data on them is usually lost, including all your photography and hard work. For this reason it is essential to keep a back-up of your hard disk, so that you can recover data if things go wrong. An external drive that connects to your PC via a USB or FireWire connection is the best bet. They are affordable, offer plenty of space and are quick to use. What's more, you can take them away and keep them somewhere else – a wise move just in case you are burgled. A back-up is no good at all if it gets stolen along with the original.

Right: *An external hard drive plugs into your computer via a USB or FireWire connection and is a good way of adding extra storage space for image files.*

Plugging your camera into your computer directly does have some disadvantages, though. The camera's battery must always be charged, and using it in disk mode drains battery charge very quickly indeed. Furthermore, the data transfer rate is slow, meaning you'll wait a long time for your images to arrive on your computer. You'll soon get fed up of waiting, and when you do you'll need to go and buy a card reader

A card reader stays attached to your computer (again usually via a USB connection) and has various slots into which you put a memory card containing your images. A reader doesn't need a battery to power it, and the speed of transfer is much faster. Many card readers have different sizes and shapes of card slot, so they can take the different types of memory card on the market. You'll see devices advertising compatability with 10–12 different memory card types, such as Compact Flash (CF), Secure Digital (SD), Multimedia Card (MCC), SD-HC, SD-XC, Sony memory sticks and xD cards. Even the mini and micro memory cards found in mobile phones are accommodated. A card reader is genuinely one of the most useful accessories you can buy for your digital darkroom.

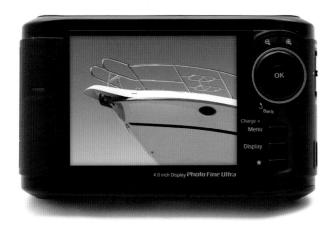

Left: *A portable storage device combines a hard drive with a card reader and a high resolution viewscreen so you can back-up and review images on location. The perfect accessory for the travelling photographer.*

Introducing **Photoshop**

One piece of software is synonymous with digital imaging. Adobe Photoshop is an application used by everyone from enthusiast photographers through to professionals, along with retouchers and even scientists. And it will likely be the backbone of your digital workflow, too.

t's the granddaddy of digital photography software. Adobe Photoshop was released for the first time back in 1990 and has been the industry standard for photographers, illustrators and retouchers for much of this time. It's a behemoth of an application that has more features than you will ever need and costs more than most cameras do. Fortunately for the amateur photographer, Adobe released Photoshop Elements in the late 1990s – a cut-down, easier to use version of the software with a more affordable price tag. Since then we have also seen Adobe Lightroom, an application that offers limited editing and output functions alongside very powerful indexing and cataloguing features and the ability to edit raw files non-destructively (see page 238).

It's these three applications that we will concentrate on in this chapter. This is not to say there are not alternatives out there, but the vast majority of photographers do tend to use one (or more) of these Adobe products, and chances are you will have also started to use them.

Photoshop and Photoshop Elements

Both variants of Adobe Photoshop (the full application and 'Elements') allow photographers to make both global changes (i.e. those that affect every part of the image) and localized adjustments (pixel-by-pixel editing) that are painted on with brushes. A huge variety of image formats can be opened, including the JPEG, TIFF and raw images shot by the average digital camera.

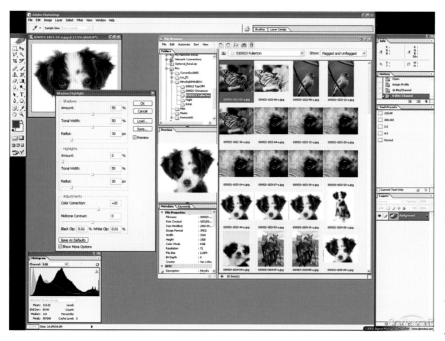

Left: Adobe Photoshop is the industry-standard image-editing application for photographers. This powerful software will let you make global tone and colour changes as well as edit an image pixel-by-pixel. You are only limited by your imagination.

In much the same way, images can be saved back out to any format you can think of after editing, although one extra option is available: the psd ('Photoshop document') file is the only file format that saves every layer, channel, path, selection and adjustment in your image, and as such it's worth saving your work in this format both when it's in progress and when it's complete.

Photoshop alternatives

In spite of Adobe's dominance of the digital photography market, there are alternative applications from different manufacturers. For those that dare to be different, there are a few options to consider, including:

Corel Paint Shop Pro (www.corel.com)
Roxio PhotoSuite (www.roxio.com)
Ulead PhotoImpact (www.ulead.com)
GIMP (www.gimp.org)
Picassa (www.google.com/picassa)

Plug-ins

Photoshop's awesome creative power is further expandable by the inclusion of plug-ins. Other software manufacturers can write smaller applications that run through Photoshop, Elements and Lightroom, rather than standing on their own. Some plug-ins perform very simple, but valuable, operations, while others are more complicated and offer a whole raft of adjustable features. Some offer brand new functionality; others simply provide a more simple route to otherwise complicated tasks.

It's worth searching out plug-ins on the internet, as most are distributed this way. Some are free, but most attract a fee for their use, often giving users a 30 day evaluation period.

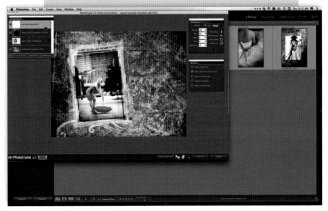

Right: Extra functionality can be added to Photoshop, Photoshop Elements and Lightroom using plug-ins from third-party manufacturers. Some are free, while others cost money. Effects range from simple sharpening and grain functions to sophisticated colour conversions and special effects.

Staying organized with Adobe Bridge

Packaged with every edition of Photoshop is Adobe Bridge, a file browser that allows images to be keyworded, labelled and even ranked according to how much you like them. While it doesn't have the powerful cataloguing features that Lightroom boasts, it is perfect for viewing thumbnail and preview images on the fly and searching through thousands of images according to keywords. Photoshop Elements also has these features, in a very full-featured file browser.

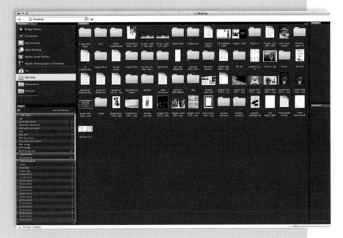

The Photoshop **interface**

The Photoshop interface can be somewhat intimidating when you first see it, but after a few uses you'll be navigating around the various menus, palettes and tools as if you'd known them all your life.

By default, your image will open up in the main window that occupies most of the screen. Down the left-hand side you'll find the toolbox (see right). Clicking on a tool changes the function of the mouse pointer – you'll find things such as Selection tools that enable you to work on only part of the image, and Cloning and Healing brushes that copy pixels from one place and brush them in somewhere else.

At the top there is an Options bar that displays the parameters for the tool currently active in the toolbox. Click on a different tool and the Options bar will change accordingly. On the right-hand side you'll find the various palettes that let you fine-tune how the application works. Here you'll find palettes containing different brush sizes and shapes, different colours, text options, image layers and even the 'undo' history. In fact, there are so many palettes that it isn't feasible to have them all showing at once. Some can be hidden, and others closed or made to float over the image area. At any time you can recall a palette by finding it in the main Window menu.

The secret to working in Photoshop quickly is to use as many keyboard shortcuts as you can. You don't need to remember them all, just the most useful ones. For instance, the square brackets keys] and [increase and decrease brush size, while the + and - keys alter the current zoom level. Here is a run-down of the tools found in the toolbox, along with the shortcut key for each one. Note that some toolbox spots contain more than one tool. You can access the others by clicking on the spot and holding down the mouse button, or holding down shift when you press the shortcut key.

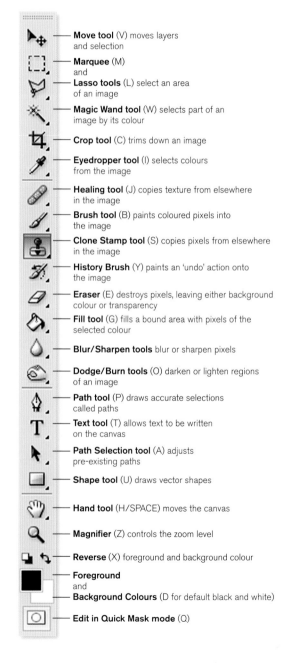

Move tool (V) moves layers and selection

Marquee (M) and

Lasso tools (L) select an area of an image

Magic Wand tool (W) selects part of an image by its colour

Crop tool (C) trims down an image

Eyedropper tool (I) selects colours from the image

Healing tool (J) copies texture from elsewhere in the image

Brush tool (B) paints coloured pixels into the image

Clone Stamp tool (S) copies pixels from elsewhere in the image

History Brush (Y) paints an 'undo' action onto the image

Eraser (E) destroys pixels, leaving either background colour or transparency

Fill tool (G) fills a bound area with pixels of the selected colour

Blur/Sharpen tools blur or sharpen pixels

Dodge/Burn tools (O) darken or lighten regions of an image

Path tool (P) draws accurate selections called paths

Text tool (T) allows text to be written on the canvas

Path Selection tool (A) adjusts pre-existing paths

Shape tool (U) draws vector shapes

Hand tool (H/SPACE) moves the canvas

Magnifier (Z) controls the zoom level

Reverse (X) foreground and background colour

Foreground and

Background Colours (D for default black and white)

Edit in Quick Mask mode (Q)

The Photoshop palettes

You'll use some of the numerous palettes in Photoshop more than others, depending on the way you work and what you are trying to do. Thankfully you can show and hide palettes and float them into different parts of the screen to save on space. If they were all open at the same time there wouldn't be much space left for your image! Here are some of the frequently used palettes you'll see in Photoshop and Photoshop Elements.

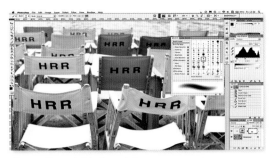

Above: *Keep visible the palettes you use most.*

Colour palette

Select colours here from a 'gradient ramp' or dial in RGB values for known colours.

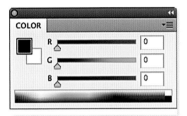

Layers

Create and edit composite images by layering pictures on top of each other (see page 344).

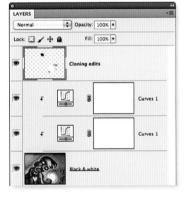

Paths

Very accurate selections that can be edited and adjusted. Useful for cutting out elements in a photograph.

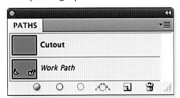

Adjustment layers

Apply common image adjustments as layers that sit on top of the image, which can be edited and masked off (see page 354).

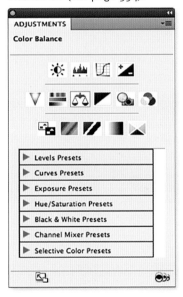

History

Step back through your work and undo individual edits. You can also create history 'snapshots' that remember the image in a certain state.

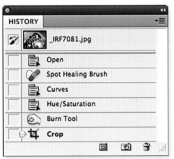

Editing **raw files**

Raw files represent the modern equivalent of a digital negative – a file containing every bit of data captured by the camera. Using them for digital editing in Photoshop opens the door to improved quality and more flexible ways of working.

Raw files are superior to JPEG files in terms of picture quality, containing more 'shades' of red, green and blue. They also offer more control during the editing stage, as they contain all of the information captured by the camera, including data which isn't currently shown but

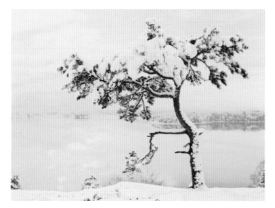

Above: An uncorrected raw file showing incorrect white balance and a lack of contrast – typical for such a file straight from the camera.

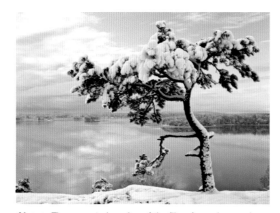

Above: The corrected version of the file, after colour and tone correction in the Adobe Camera Raw plug-in.

can be used for editing. JPEGs have had much of this information thrown away by the camera's processor during their creation.

On the other hand, JPEGs are smaller than raw files, making them easier to store and transfer. They also look much better straight out of the camera, whereas raw files require lots of attention before they look anywhere near decent.

Raw files require special software to process them into image files like JPEGs, and this is usually supplied on the disk that came with your camera. Additionally, Adobe has created a plug-in that opens raw files directly into Photoshop, allowing a great deal of global editing in the process. Called Adobe Camera Raw (ACR), this is fast becoming the gold standard for raw processing among enthusiast photographers.

No two raw files are the same. The format outputted by a Canon EOS 600D is not the same as that from a Pentax K-x, for instance, reflecting the difference between the construction of the two cameras. With more and more new camera releases, so more and more new raw file formats are generated, meaning all raw software, ACR included, needs to be updated (see www.adobe.com/adobecameraraw). While Adobe Camera Raw seems to be fairly back-compatible with older versions of Photoshop Elements, it is only compatible with the current version of Photoshop. This is a problem for those photographers who have just bought a new camera and are expecting to open their raw files into Photoshop through ACR. A full upgrade of the main application may be required, at considerable cost.

There are many controls in ACR, and generally speaking you should start at the top and work your way down. Let's have a look at the interface and see what each one does.

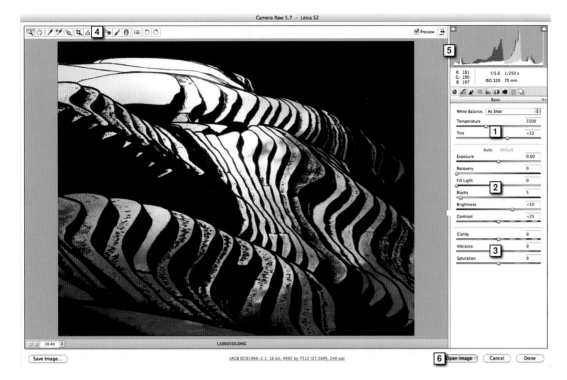

1. White balance controls

Set the colour temperature of the photograph with one of the presets, or manually with the Temperature and Tint sliders.

2. Basic exposure adjustments

Working from the top downwards: the Exposure slider controls overall brightness in the same way you'd control exposure in camera; the Recovery and Fill Light sliders aim to put detail back into any highlights and shadow areas that are too light or dark to show detail; the Brightness slider controls image brightness like Exposure does, but doesn't increase highlights to the point of saturation; and Contrast makes dark tones darker and light tones lighter.

3. Refinements to colour and contrast

Saturation increases or decreases the amount of colour in the image; Vibrance does the same but preserves skin tones and doesn't overcook already strong colours; and Clarity adds local contrast, which enhances contrast where the picture has texture but not in areas of continuous tone.

4. Selecting and editing controls

Left to right: Magnify tool zooms in on the image; Hand tool to move around the image; White Balance tool sets the image's white balance when clicked on an area of neutral tone; Colour Sampler tool drops marker points that monitor colour values in real time; Targeted Adjustment tool adjusts hue, saturation and curves in an image according to where you click; Crop tool crops the image to a new shape; Straighten tool levels the image relative to a line drawn over something that is supposed to be vertical or horizontal; Spot-Removal tool removes spots in your picture due to dirt on the camera's sensor; Anti-Red-Eye tool eliminates the red-eye caused by direct flash; adjustment brush and graduate fill for localized editing.

5. Image view area and histogram

The main window shows the image, while the histogram panel shows the distribution of tones through the image (see pages 80–81).

6. Open/save options

The 'Open' button opens the image directly into the Photoshop application; clicking 'done' exits the ACR plug-in without opening the image, but your changes are remembered; 'cancel' exits without remembering changes. Hold down alt/option on your keyboard and the cancel changes to a reset, which resets all options to their defaults without exiting. 'Save…' saves raw files without opening them in Photoshop first.

editing raw files 239

Adobe **Lightroom**

If you thought Photoshop was your only image-editing option, think again. Lightroom works as both stand-alone software and in harness with Photoshop to expand your repertoire of post-production skills.

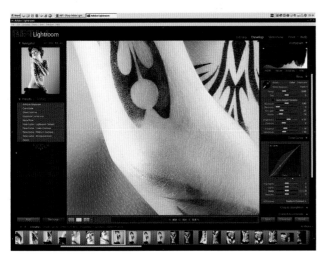

Above: *Adobe Lightroom software combines the organizational capabilities of an image catalogue with the creative power of a non-destructive raw converter.*

Adobe Lightroom is a different animal to Photoshop. It provides many global editing functions and a handful of localized brush-on editing tools, but the real advantage of the application lies in the way that it applies the edits to your pictures. Let's say that you increase the brightness of an image, then tweak its contrast and turn it black and white. These changes are stored in a database and applied to the image when you view, print or export it; the original file is always untouched. This way edits can be removed or changed at any time, without undoing everything else that has been done to the image since.

This so-called non-destructive approach to image editing works with JPEG and raw files alike, and could be a very powerful tool in your digital workflow.

Editing images is only half of what Lightroom can do, however. It also has very powerful cataloguing and indexing features, that help keep track of your pictures so you can find them quickly and easily. The application can take care of the task of importing pictures, storing them in any location on your hard disk, just as you would if you were copying files over manually. While it copies them, it also adds them to its main database so you can view, edit and adjust them. In this database, keywords can also be stored along with each picture (portrait, studio, daylight, male...) so you can search through thousands of images for a single topic. You can also rank pictures from one to five stars according to how good you think they are, and assign each one a custom label. Great for those times when you have hundreds of image files to go through to find the best couple of dozen frames.

Alternatives to Lightroom

Adobe is not the only manufacturer to have taken this approach to editing. At virtually the same time as Adobe released Lightroom, Apple released Aperture – a database-driven cataloguing and editing application. Sound familiar?

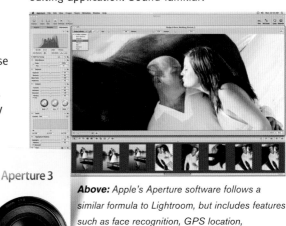

Above: *Apple's Aperture software follows a similar formula to Lightroom, but includes features such as face recognition, GPS location, photobook production and enhanced slideshows.*

Although there are many similarities between the two applications, there also many differences. Aperture also offers integrated photobook design (see page 394), slicker slideshows and the ability to tag your photos with GPS data. It even boasts face recognition abilities that identify who is in your pictures, and uses this information to sync with social networking sites such as Facebook. Aperture's interface is also a bit more user-friendly, although all this functionality seems to slow the application down somewhat compared to Lightroom. Aperture is also only available for the Apple Mac computer platform; Lightroom is available for both Mac and PC.

Non-destructive image editing can also be carried out in Photoshop, though not to the same degree. Adjustment layers (see page 354) and Smart filters (see page 362) can be used to ensure that pixels are not irreversibly changed during editing, and the original image can always be recovered.

Right: Graphics tablets offer more precision than a mouse – useful for when meticulous attention to detail is needed.

Involving Photoshop

Lightroom doesn't pretend to be a one-stop shop that provides all your picture-editing needs. In fact, integration with Photoshop (and Photoshop Elements) is so good that you'll be able to flip between the two applications pretty seamlessly by selecting Photo › Edit in › Edit in Photoshop.

At the end of the editing process, Lightroom can export files in all of the most popular formats, either to your hard drive or straight to DVD. It can also publish them to social networking websites, create proofing websites, email pictures and produce prints and contact sheets.

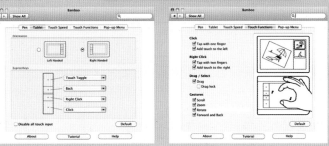

Graphics tablets

Using brushes to adjust only parts of a picture is a powerful way of editing your photography, but a steady hand is needed when working in detailed areas with small brushes. Only a certain level of dexterity can be achieved with a mouse or a trackpad. For a more accurate way of working, a graphics tablet is the way forward.

A graphics tablet is a sensitive surface that is linked to your computer in the same way as a mouse, via a USB cable or wireless connection. An electronic pen, or 'stylus', is used to draw on the tablet, giving the user an unparalleled level of accuracy. Various sizes are available; it's best to go for something not too small and not too big. An A5-size tablet is perfect for most needs.

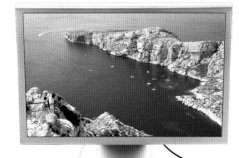

Above: Most graphics tablets are fully adjustable for left- or right-handed use, scroll speed and pen-pressure sensitivity.

ASSIGNMENT
CUSTOMIZING YOUR PHOTOSHOP WORKSPACE

Photoshop is a very powerful application, but the weight of its many features has made it rather complicated to use for the beginner. Anything you can do to make the interface easier to navigate has got to be a good thing – starting with customizing the screen layout.

Although the first version of Photoshop had just two palettes, the current version has dozens. These can be moved around the screen, minimized, docked or hidden. Some palettes are naturally grouped together according to their function, eg. the navigator, information and histogram windows are grouped to save clutter. But what if this doesn't suit the way you work? No problem, just drag one of the individual palettes out of the group; it will form a new group of its own. You are starting to build your own, custom Photoshop user interface.

Keyboard shortcuts
Photoshop's keyboard shortcuts can also be customized. You can change existing shortcuts,

or even make your own for commands that are lacking. For instance, it's annoying there isn't a shortcut to rotate the canvas by 90 degrees; you have to choose Image > Image Rotation > 90° CCW (or 90° CW) instead. To set up a custom shortcut for this, simply:
- Choose Edit > Keyboard Shortcuts to bring up the keyboard shortcuts and menus dialogue box.
- Find the command to be assigned the shortcut and click it once (rotate CCW is under the Image > Image Rotation section, mirroring the hierarchy of the menus).
- Click in the space for a keyboard shortcut and type the shortcut you want to use. Photoshop will tell you if this is already in use.

Remembering positions
Once you have created the ideal working space in Photoshop, memorize the positions of your palettes so they can be recalled at any time. Do this by choosing Windows > Workspace > Save Workspace... and entering a name for your layout ('Retouching' or 'Editing', for instance). This name now appears at the bottom of the Windows > Workspace menu and can be used at any time to reset the position of the palettes and windows.

Also useful is Photoshop's 'tool presets' feature. Tool presets are popular combinations of settings that can be recalled from a drop-down menu in the top-left corner of the options bar. For example, if you regularly crop to a specific size, enter this as a preset to save you having to enter the information manually each time.

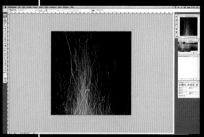

Left: The Photoshop workspace with free-floating palettes positioned around the screen according to preference.

Left: The same image in the same application but with the palettes docked for a more uncomplicated view.

ESSENTIAL KIT

- A computer – Mac or PC
- Adobe Photoshop or Photoshop Elements

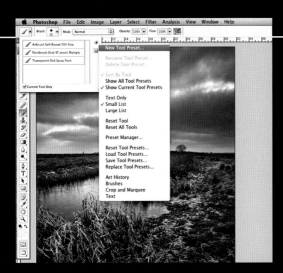

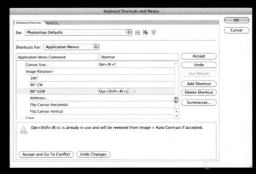

Above: Tool presets recall pre-determined settings for most of Photoshop's tools, saving time when working quickly.

Above: You can create and edit keyboard shortcuts for the various menu commands.

Below: Saving a workspace layout for instant recall from the Window menu. You can save different layouts for different tasks, too – retouching, picture viewing, text, etc.

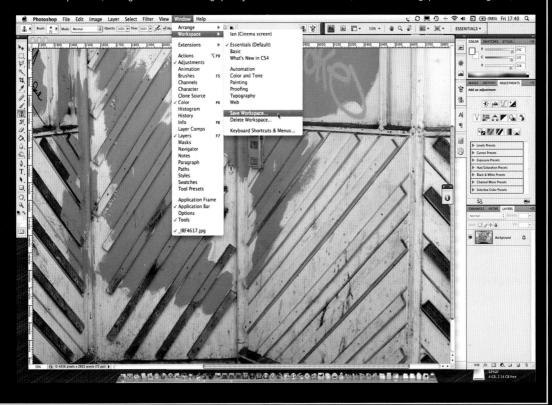

Exposure and histograms

The histogram occurs everywhere in digital photography, and understanding how it relates to applications such as Photoshop can really pay dividends when editing.

We've already seen how a histogram display on the back of your camera can tell you whether you have correctly exposed a scene or not (see pages 80–81), but histograms are also useful in post-production, too. All image editing software displays a histogram of some kind, which is not only useful for gauging exposure but also for making corrections.

But first let's recap what a histogram is and why it is useful. Put simply, a histogram graph shows how brightness levels are distributed in a photograph. The brightness of a certain pixel is plotted on the horizontal axis and given a number from zero (pure black) to 255 (pure white), with intermediate values in between. The number of pixels of a certain shade is indicated by the height of the column in the graph. For a correctly

exposed photograph of an average scene, you'd expect to see some pure black and a little pure white and an even distribution of information between these two.

Digital images consist of three colour channels: red, green and blue. The histogram we look at most of the time is for a composite RGB channel, but it's also possible to view the individual red-, green- and blue-channel histograms in most applications, or even overlay these on top of the RGB display. Looking at individual colour histograms can tell you about the presence of a colour cast (if one channel is out of line with the others) or if an area that is too bright (a 'blown highlight') is being caused by one oversaturated colour.

In Adobe Photoshop you can view a histogram in a dedicated palette that can be floated over the

Highlight and shadow warnings

Information running off the ends of a histogram's horizontal axis is a sign that we have lost detail in shadows that are too dark, or highlights that are too bright (or 'blown'), but the histogram is not the only warning device available to alert you to this issue. When processing a raw image in Adobe Camera Raw, or when editing in Lightroom, highlight and shadow warnings tell you if a region has lost detail by colouring it red or blue, respectively. You can turn this on momentarily by hovering your mouse pointer over the highlight or shadow warning triangles in the top corners of the histogram. Clicking them toggles the warning on and off, so you can make adjustments to correct the problem (see pages 246–247).

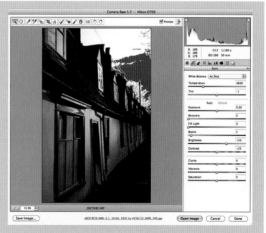

Above: Highlight and shadow warnings show when light or dark areas are about to go out of range and lose detail.

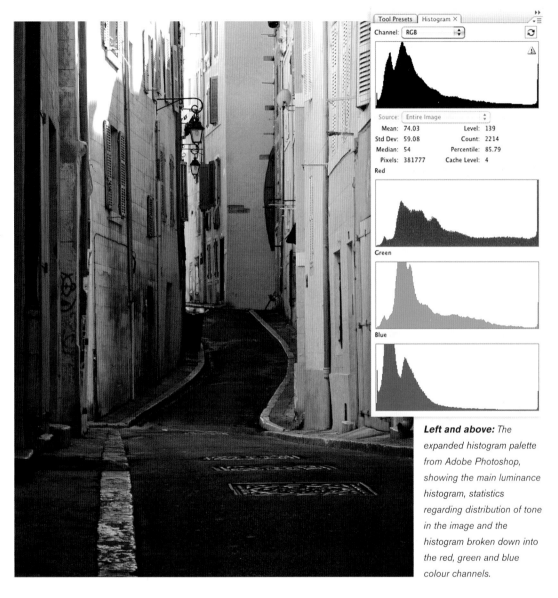

Tool Presets | Histogram ×

Channel: RGB

Source: Entire Image

Mean:	74.03	Level:	139
Std Dev:	59.08	Count:	2214
Median:	54	Percentile:	85.79
Pixels:	381777	Cache Level:	4

Red

Green

Blue

Left and above: *The expanded histogram palette from Adobe Photoshop, showing the main luminance histogram, statistics regarding distribution of tone in the image and the histogram broken down into the red, green and blue colour channels.*

image or docked to the side. You can make this active, if it's not already, by choosing Window › Histogram. Used in combination with the info palette, the histogram can tell you a great deal about your image. The info palette can be shown by choosing Window › Info or hitting F8, and it shows the red, green and blue values, between zero and 255, for any pixel over which you hover with the mouse pointer. What's more, you can drop a marker point down on the image with the Colour Sampler tool (which occupies the same spot in the toolbox as the Eyedropper; click and

hold to access it), and the RGB values at this point will be updated in real time as you make adjustments to the image.

You'll see the histogram crop up in many other places. In the Adobe Camera Raw plug-in it sits in the top right-hand corner and is crucial for getting the most from your raw files. In Lightroom it occupies a similar position, but is interactive. If you click and drag horizontally in the part of the histogram where you want to change the image, those parts of the image will change in brightness, while the others will stay the same.

Levels

So the histogram can tell us about exposure and the distribution of brightness within a picture, but wouldn't it be great if we could then redistribute those pixels to fix exposure problems? Well, that's more or less exactly what a levels adjustment does.

Editing a picture using levels is the most popular way of tweaking exposure. It's simple to perform and powerful enough for most situations. You'll find it in lots of photographic software, too, including cataloguing and scanning applications.

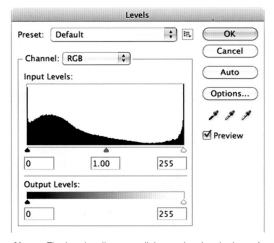

Above: *The Levels adjustment dialogue showing the image's histogram. The three markers underneath can be moved around to redefine where the histogram starts and ends, as well as its midpoint. The image adjusts its tone accordingly.*

In Adobe Photoshop the levels command is found in the Image › Adjustments menu. The levels dialogue box shows a large histogram of the whole image (or a selection of it, see page 398). The end points and the midpoint of the histogram are redefinable by clicking on and dragging the triangular markers on the x-axis. For instance, moving the black-point marker at the left-hand edge inwards defines which pixels are classified as black, i.e. have a brightness value of 0. Bring it in by five pixels and those shades that were previously very dark, of brightness value five or less, will now be jet black. The effect on the picture will be to darken it slightly, especially in the shadow areas.

Similarly, bringing in the white-point marker slightly refines shades that were previously just very bright as pure white. This brightens the picture, especially in the highlight areas. Bring in both the white and black points slightly and you'll be making the light tones lighter and the dark tones darker – which is a textbook definition of increasing contrast in a photograph.

It's not possible to move the black and white points the other way, past the 0 and 255 values to

Five editing tips using Levels

- Use the alt/option key to reveal which pixels are being changed by the levels adjustment.
- If you make a mistake, hold down alt/option to change the 'cancel' to a 'reset', which will take you back to the start without dismissing the dialogue box.
- Turn the preview on and off to see the effect of the change you have made on the image.
- Save a levels preset to apply to other images – a real timesaver when working on a series of images that all require the same adjustment. Choose 'Save Preset' from the palette menu next to the colour channel drop-down menu.
- Experiment with the pre-installed levels recipes in the preset drop-down menu. They may not be perfect for what you want, but they will be close.

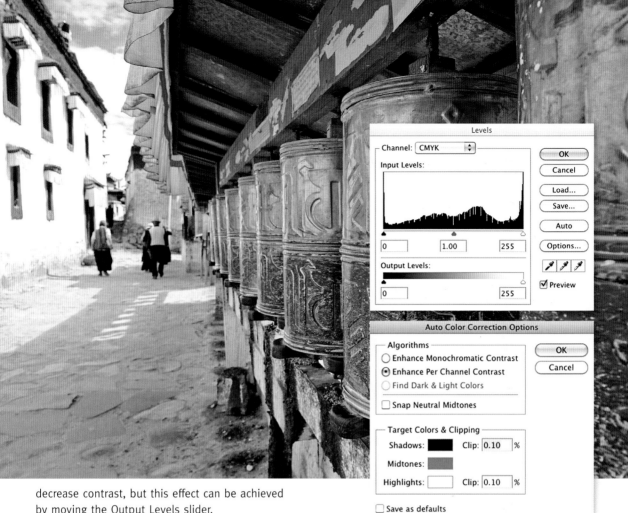

Levels

Channel: CMYK

Input Levels:

| 0 | 1.00 | 255 |

Output Levels:

| 0 | | 255 |

OK
Cancel
Load...
Save...
Auto
Options...

☑ Preview

Auto Color Correction Options

Algorithms
○ Enhance Monochromatic Contrast
◉ Enhance Per Channel Contrast
○ Find Dark & Light Colors

☐ Snap Neutral Midtones

Target Colors & Clipping

Shadows:		Clip: 0.10	%
Midtones:			
Highlights:		Clip: 0.10	%

☐ Save as defaults

OK
Cancel

decrease contrast, but this effect can be achieved by moving the Output Levels slider.

The middle marker point in the levels dialogue changes the brightness of midtones in the picture, and is perhaps the most useful for minor changes to brightness when you don't want to alter the very bright and very dark tones. In reality, though, all three points should be adjusted together for a good result.

Above: Clicking the Auto button in the levels dialogue box (or selecting Image > Auto Tone) adjusts the black and white points automatically so they meet at the beginning and end of the histogram. By default this change is applied to each colour channel separately which can result in a colour shift, as seen below.

Levels eyedroppers

The Eyedropper tools can be used to set the white, black and grey points by clicking on parts of the image that you want to be pure white, pure black, and mid-grey, respectively. Because this type of adjustment operates on each colour channel individually, it can cause a colour shift, so make sure you click tones that are of a neutral colour.

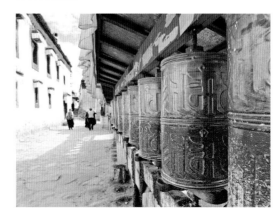

ASSIGNMENT
CREATING BORDERS FOR YOUR IMAGES

A border for your photo is a great finishing touch. A simple black line around an image can help keep the eye focused on your composition, and stop it straying off the edges.

The edges of a photograph are very important. They define where the picture stops and where the user must start to use their imagination. Sometimes a photograph naturally has edges, or its boundaries don't need to be well defined, but at other times adding a border to an image can really help to define the frame, and hence help your composition.

Whether to add a border or not, and which type of border works best, is largely dictated by how the picture will be seen. A photograph with a dark background doesn't need any help in defining where the frame ends when viewed on white paper or on a white wall, but on a webpage with a black background, it does. In this case a white line around the edge of the frame will help. Similarly, a high-key image (one comprising light tones) can benefit from a black border when printed on white paper.

Putting a border around an image like this is simply a matter of a few keystrokes in Photoshop. The secret to making it work visually is to keep things simple – a few pixels to stop the eye running off the edge of the frame is all that's needed.

Step 1. Open the image you want to frame into Photoshop or Elements and choose Select > Select All to make a selection of the whole canvas.

Step 2. Choose Edit > Stroke... and select the colour and width of the line. The thickness will depend on the pixel dimensions of the image, but try two to five pixels to start with.

Step 3. Unfortunately there is no preview function in the stroke dialogue, so you'll have to click OK to see the effect. If it looks wrong, choose Edit > Undo and try again.

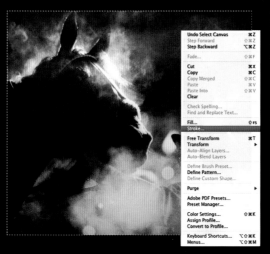

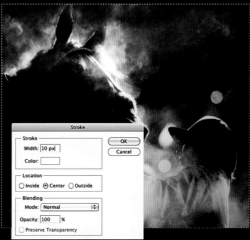

- For a multi-stroke border, apply a thick stroke first (say 20 pixels wide) then a thinner one (ten pixels) in a different colour.

- Always save a version of the picture without a border, in case you need to present it in a different way later on.

ESSENTIAL KIT

- A computer – Mac or PC
- Adobe Photoshop or Photoshop Elements

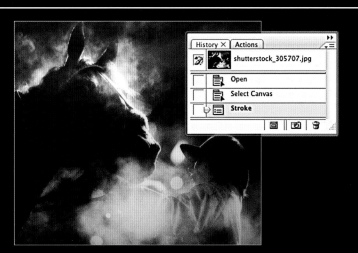

Below: *A white border around this image helps to define its limits and prevents the eye from wandering off the edge.*

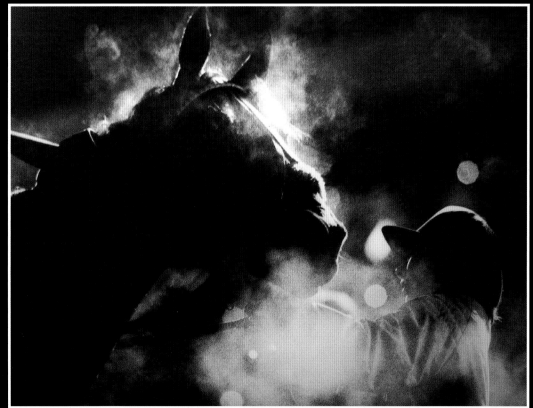

Highlights and shadows

If you've ever shot film images before, you may notice a difference in the way digital capture behaves towards the very bright and very dark parts of a photograph – the highlights and shadows.

t's easier to lose detail in highlights and shadows through under- or over-exposure, which is why you should take care to get your exposures as accurate as possible in-camera and review your work with the in-camera histogram.

To some degree this problem can be tackled at the editing stage by attempting to rescue highlight and shadow detail by reducing or increasing the brightness in these areas, although conventional 8-bit JPEGs don't respond so well to this treatment as raw files, or 16-bit images opened in Photoshop from raw files. This is because raw files and 16-bit images contain many more brightness levels, some that are outside the range of what is seen on-screen. In fact, it's these levels that are pulled back into the visible range when we attempt to rescue blown highlights and featureless shadows.

Shadow/highlight control

Photoshop has a dedicated adjustment tool for rescuing detail in shadows and highlights. The Highlight/Shadow command works out what is a highlight and what is a shadow by looking at surrounding pixels in each region of the image, and applies an adjustment to either darken bright

highlights or lighten dark shadows. Choose Image › Adjustments › Shadows/Highlights, and you will be presented with a dialogue containing a shadows control and a highlights control. By default, the shadows slider is set to 50 per cent, which is usually too much, so reset this to zero before continuing. In fact, small, subtle changes are really the way forward here. Don't make massive changes in one go or the image may not look very natural.

As with most Photoshop dialogue boxes, you can hold down alt/option to change the cancel button into a reset in case you get lost, and there are 'Load...' and 'Save...' buttons for creating presets. You'll notice a 'More Options...' tick box that transforms the dialogue box in to a more detailed (but confusing) layout.

In this state you can control exactly what Photoshop classes as a shadow or highlight with the two tonal width sliders, while the radius slider dictates how far around each pixel Photoshop will look to establish whether the region is a highlight or a shadow. Set this to roughly the same size (in pixels) as the subjects of interest in the photograph, and experiment for a good result. The midtone contrast aims to boost or reduce contrast in just the midtones of the image.

Rescuing highlights and shadows in Adobe Camera Raw

In Photoshop, Photoshop Elements and Lightroom it is far easier to rescue blown highlights and featureless shadows using a raw file. The ACR plug-in offers dedicated tools called recovery and fill-in that tackle highlights and shadows respectively, and the results are far more effective than can be achieved with a JPEG file.

Keep an eye on the histogram as you make the adjustments and you should start to see information come back in from outside the graph's range. Also turn on the highlight and shadow clipping warnings (see page 244) by clicking on the triangles in the top left and top right of the histogram screen, or activate them momentarily by holding down alt/option when you move the sliders.

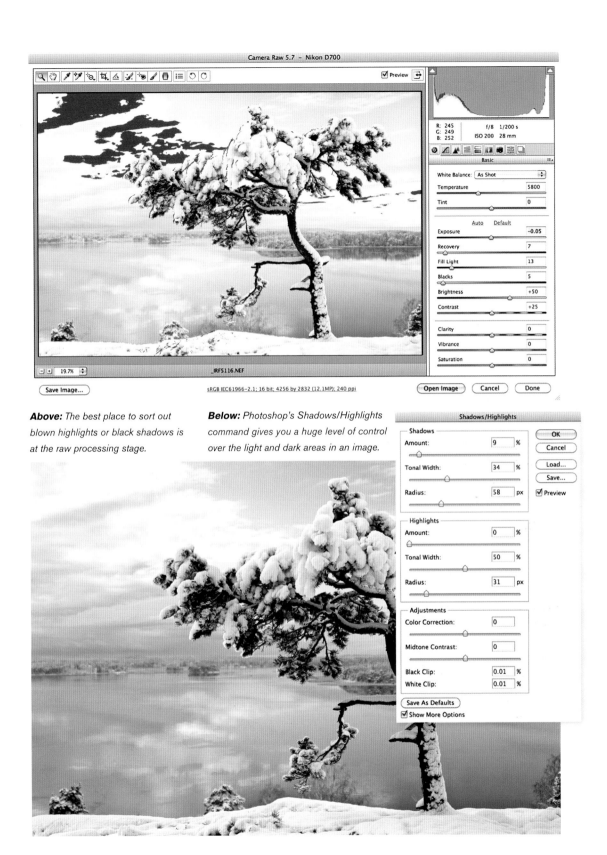

Above: *The best place to sort out blown highlights or black shadows is at the raw processing stage.*

Below: *Photoshop's Shadows/Highlights command gives you a huge level of control over the light and dark areas in an image.*

Dodging and **burning**

As well as lightening and darkening a photograph globally, it's also useful to be able to do this selectively in just one or two places – a practice referred to by photographers as dodging and burning.

The ability to change the exposure of an image is all very well, but what about when we want to darken or lighten just part of the scene, and leave the rest untouched? There are a few ways of doing this, but perhaps the easiest in Photoshop or Elements is to use the Dodge and Burn tools.

These somewhat cryptically named tools get their monikers from traditional darkroom practices involving the projection of film images onto light-sensitive paper. A photographer would give more (burning) or less (dodging) light to specific areas of the print to lighten or darken it. This usually involved shading areas of the paper with odd-shaped pieces of card, or even their hands. Thankfully, the modern-day equivalent is much easier, and more reproducible.

The Dodge and Burn tools occupy the same spot in the Photoshop toolbox. Click and hold on one to change to the other. Once activated, the mouse pointer changes to a brush and you can then paint on the areas where you want the print to be darker or lighter. You can change both the size and hardness of the brush you use from the brushes palette (Window › Brushes) or with the] and [keys for size and the } and { keys for hardness. You'll find a medium-sized, soft-edged brush works best for most dodging and burning tasks.

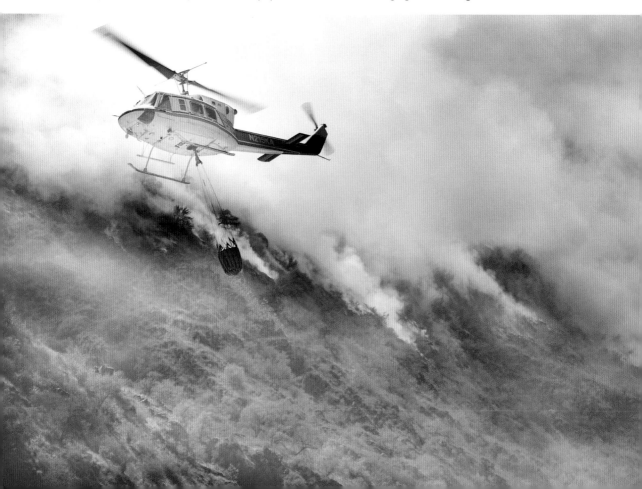

The strength of the burn or dodge can be controlled with a slider in the Options bar at the top of the screen. Rather than using a high strength, it's best to throttle this control back to between four and ten per cent and work over areas steadily with the same brush until you get the desired result. A graphics tablet is really useful for this type of work.

The Dodge and Burn tools often work better on monochrome images, in line with their traditional darkroom heritage, perhaps. Don't be afraid of going to town on skies in black and white landscapes to really bring out the dark and moody feel in them.

Dodging and burning in Lightroom and Adobe Camera Raw

Pixel-by-pixel editing of raw files in Lightroom or ACR is not as easy as it is for an image opened in Photoshop. That said, there are tools that perform dodging and burning very well. The adjustment brush applies an ordinary raw-file adjustment only to those parts of the image that you brush with

it. The size, softness and opacity of the brush can be adjusted with the on-screen controls, and the added bonus of working this way is that the nature of the adjustment itself can be adjusted afterwards, too. Just revisit the sliders and make your adjustments.

Setting around -0.5 on the Exposure scale and about -1 with the Brightness slider works well when burning, while some +0.5 exposure and +1 brightness is a good recipe for dodging. You can always come back and change these amounts later on.

Below left: The original image is slightly over-exposed in some areas (underneath the helicopter) and under-exposed in others.

Below: The over-exposed areas can be darkened using the Burn tool, with a large, soft-edged brush. The Exposure slider is set to a low value – around 15 per cent – to give lots of control over how much the image is darkened.

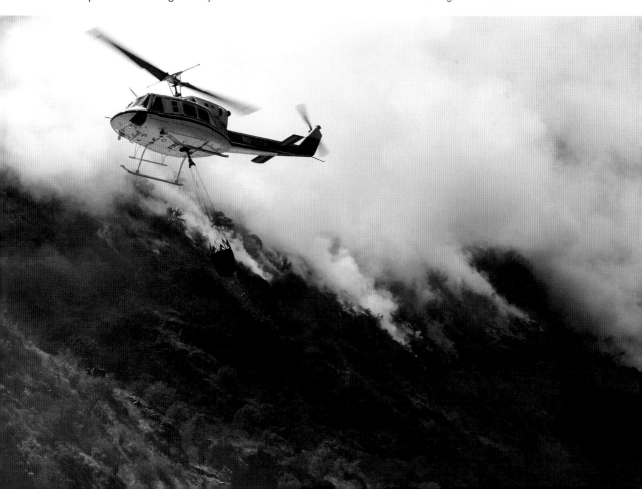

Removing **colour casts**

The different colours given off by different light sources are normally dealt with quite nicely by white balance, although there are also times when this needs some help during post-production editing.

olour casts can arise for all manner of reasons. Different light sources give off slightly different colours (or temperatures) of light, and reflective surfaces can colour light, too. Even your camera's auto white balance, which is supposed to correct for such problems, can get things wrong and give you a nasty coloured cast to get rid of. You may also want to add a colour cast intentionally, in order to evoke a certain mood in your photography.

There are multiple ways of handling colour casts in Photoshop, Elements and Lightroom, from purpose-designed tools, through to the use of more general adjustments such as levels. A good place to start is with the Colour Balance adjustment (Image › Adjustments › Color Balance...), which contains three principal sliders that offset red, green and blue against their complementary opposites cyan, magenta and yellow. With these controls it's possible to remove or create any colour cast, and by selecting one of the three tone balance ratio buttons we can even decide whether the adjustment applies to the image's shadows' midtones or highlights. Sliding controls around like this is a slightly hit-and-miss affair, and when you are relying on your screen to

Left: The Colour Balance tool is a simple but effective way of correcting (or introducing) colour casts.

Colours and their opposites

An understanding of how colours work together is important when eliminating (or indeed introducing) colour casts. The image shown here, known as a colour wheel, shows the relationship between the primary colours of red, green and blue and their complementary opposites cyan, magenta, and yellow. Adding one colour is the same as taking away its complementary opposite, i.e. adding cyan to an image has the same effect as taking away red. Likewise, adding yellow is the same as

taking away blue, and adding magenta is equivalent to taking away green. The Colour Balance dialogue box is arranged in exactly this fashion, with three sliders controlling how much cyan–red, green–magenta and yellow–blue is added or taken away. We'll also come across other instances where the colour wheel is useful in thinking about relationships between different hues.

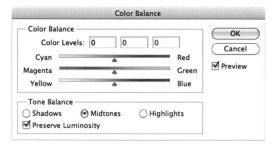

Left: The colour wheel describes the relationship between the colours red, green and blue and their opposites yellow, magenta and cyan.

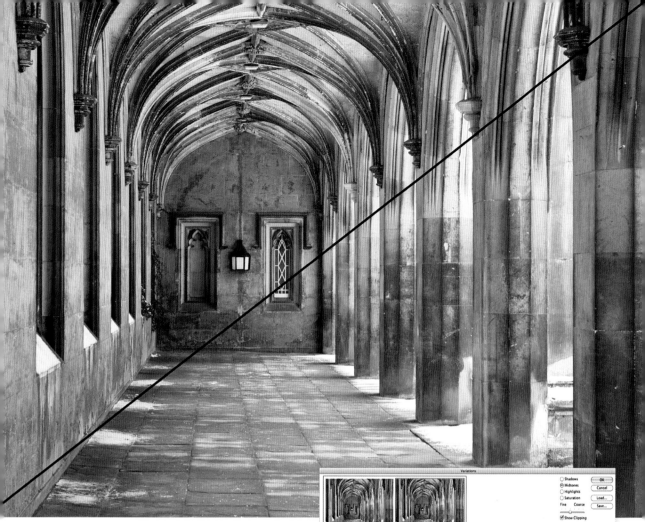

show you if you have a neutral result or not, you need to be pretty sure your screen is calibrated well enough to give you an accurate outcome.

If you don't get on with the Colour Balance tool, try a Variations adjustment instead (Image › Adjustments › Variations). The changes that are made work in a very similar way, although the interface gives you more of an idea of what to do in the first place. Six preview images surround a thumbnail of the current state of the image, with each one showing what would be achieved by adding a bit more red, cyan, green, magenta, yellow or blue. Again you can select which aspect of the image you want to change (highlights, midtones, shadows) and the degree by which each click will change the image, from fine to coarse. When ticked, the Show Clipping option will indicate when a change blows a highlight or leaves a shadow without detail.

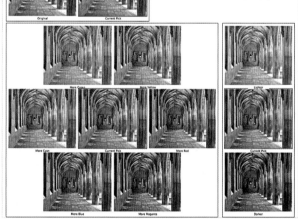

Above: Photoshop's Variations tool is a good way of adjusting colour balance when you don't quite know which direction to move in. Thumbnail previews show the effect of applying colour balance adjustments to the three colour channels. The adjustment can be directed towards to the highlights, shadows or midtones.

ASSIGNMENT
GIVING YOUR PICTURES A CROSS-PROCESSED LOOK

Recreate a classic retro look from the days of film photography using Photoshop and some basic levels adjustments.

In the days of film processing, those who shot colour could choose between colour print film and colour transparency film, often also called slide film. Print film produced negatives that were printed and transparency film produced positive images that could be projected, as well as printed and scanned. These two types of film require different chemistries to process them, but getting the processing wrong can produce interesting, if somewhat unpredictable, results. This is a practice known as cross-processing, which still works nicely when recreated digitally, giving your snaps a special vintage feel.

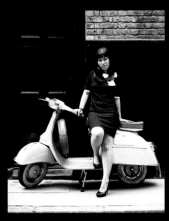

Above: *The cross-processed look is great for 1960s-style fashion images.*

Cross-processing print film through transparency-film chemistry, or indeed transparency film through print-film chemistry, produces images that have wild colour casts, high contrast and often blown highlights. It sounds awful, but for some subject matters the look works well. Fashion photography in the 1990s used cross-processing to tremendous effect, combining its wild treatment of colour with boldly coloured clothing and locations, but it works equally with something less stylized.

Done the traditional way, the effect can be rather unpredictable and inconsistent, with different combinations of films, processing labs and temperatures all contributing to the appearance of the pictures. Thankfully, today we can reproduce the cross-processing effect with a few clever Photoshop adjustments, making the whole thing a lot easier.

The secret to the cross-processing look is to adjust Levels in each colour channel, and not just in the composite RGB channel. Moving just the middle levels slider in each colour channel will give the image a colour cast, but also moving the white and black sliders will affect contrast, too. It takes some experimentation to come up with cross-processing recipes that work well, but try to follow the general rule of increasing contrast in two of the colour channels and lower contrast in the third.

Step 1. Open your original image into Photoshop and bring up the levels adjustment by choosing Image > Adjust > Levels.

Step 2. Select the red colour channel from the channel drop-down menu and bring in the white and black markers to increase the contrast.

Step 3. Do the same in the green channel, bringing the two end-point markers further in towards the middle by about 20–25 places.

Step 4. In the blue channel, lower the contrast by moving the output sliders in towards the middle. Also, darken the midtones by moving the centre point to the right.

Step 5. Make any necessary changes to the overall brightness of the image by making adjustments to the main RGB channel.

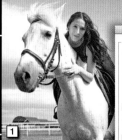

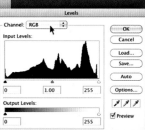

1

ESSENTIAL KIT

- PC or Mac computer
- Adobe Photoshop software

2

TIPS & TRICKS

- When you have a recipe that works well, save it for future use by choosing Save As... from the pop-up menu next to the channel menu.

- Cross-processing suits images containing strong colours. For the best results, shoot with increased saturation or boost saturation in Photoshop before starting.

- When adjusting levels for the overall image in the final step, don't be afraid of blowing some highlights for an authentic look.

3

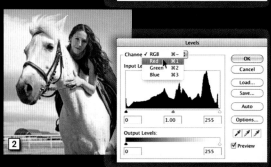

4

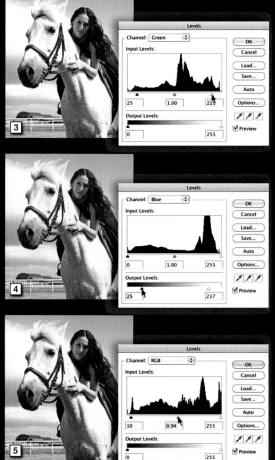

5

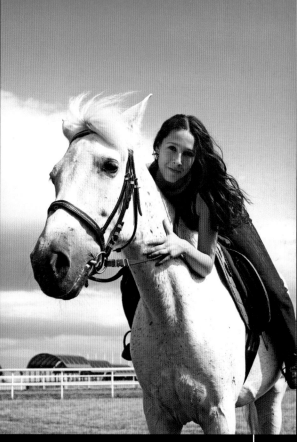

Above: *Five adjustments with Levels is all that's needed to create a retro colour cross-processed look.*

Colour saturation

How we treat colour in digital photography is crucial. We've already seen how colour casts can be introduced or cancelled out by using the correct white balance, or with tools such as Photoshop's Color Balance, Variations or Levels, but the strength and intensity of colour is important, too – a quality we call colour saturation.

The tools used for controlling saturation in Photoshop, Elements and Lightroom are all very similar. In Photoshop, access the Hue/Saturation adjustment by choosing Image > Adjustments > Hue/Saturation, which

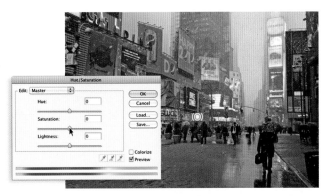

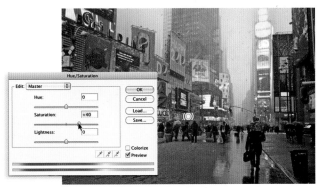

Above: Increasing Saturation boosts the boldness of colours throughout an image. This is done here in Adobe Photoshop with the application's Hue/Saturation adjustment.

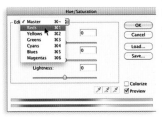

Left: To adjust single colours, select them from the drop-down menu.

will present you with a dialogue box containing three sliders: Hue, Saturation and Lightness. Saturation governs how strongly colours appear in a photograph, while Hue changes the identity of the colours themselves. You can make changes to the whole image by editing the master channel, or select a colour channel from the drop-down menu to be more specific. And to really fine-tune your selection, the Colour Eyedropper tools in the bottom right of the dialogue can be used to select a colour specifically from the image just by clicking on it. The sliders on the colour scales at the bottom determine how widely that selection applies.

In the example shown here, we have boosted the saturation of just the green colours in this picture by choosing 'Greens' from the drop-down menu and then refining the selection further by clicking a green part of the photograph with the Colour Eyedropper. Note that other shades can be added or subtracted to broaden or narrow the selection with the other two eyedroppers. The Saturation slider has then been dragged to the right to boost the green colours.

Adjusting hue

The Hue slider physically changes the colours in the photograph, mapping them onto new values. The transformation taking place is shown by the two graduated colour bars at the bottom of the dialogue box. The upper one indicates the colour as it is now in the image; the lower bar shows the colour it will become after the transformation. You can move the two bars relative to each other with the Hue slider, which will change the colours in the photograph according to their alignment.

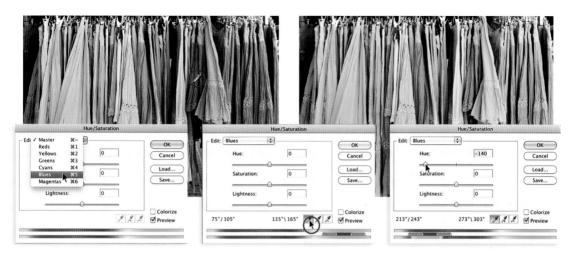

Above: To change the colour of only the purple objects in this picture, select a colour channel from the Edit drop-down menu and refine this by using the Eyedropper to choose a colour shade from a part of the image.

Adjusting the hue for an entire scene is of limited use, but combining a Hue adjustment with the Colour Eyedroppers is a great way to change selected colours to shades that work better. In the example above, the purple colours have been changed to green. The 'Magentas' option was chosen from the drop-down menu and the selection refined by clicking on the purples in the image. Moving the Hue slider to the right transformed the purples to greens: note the alignment of the two colour gradient bars.

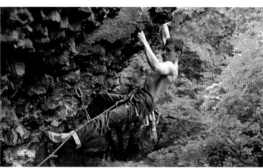

Vibrance and saturation

Recent software has incorporated another type of colour saturation tool, often called Vibrance. In Photoshop, Elements and Lightroom, Vibrance boosts colours just as the Hue/Saturation tool does, but it protects skin tones, which don't respond well to colour boosts. It also works harder on weak colours, and less on saturated ones. In Photoshop you can access the Vibrance tool under Image › Adjustments › Vibrance.

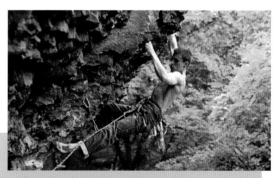

Right: Boosting the colours in this shot has given an unnatural look to the skin tones (middle). The Vibrance tool has boosted colours more subtly while leaving skin tones virtually untouched (below).

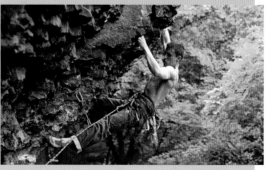

ASSIGNMENT
CHANGING EYE COLOUR

By combining the ability to select parts of a photograph with Photoshop's powerful adjustment features, we can transform some components while leaving others untouched.

A good example of this is in changing eye colour in a portrait. This is done quite simply by selecting the iris and pupil and applying a Hue/Saturation adjustment to just this area. Be sure to tidy up the selection, and pick an eye colour that suits your subject and isn't too over the top. Use all three controls in the Hue/Saturation dialogue box to ensure a natural-looking result.

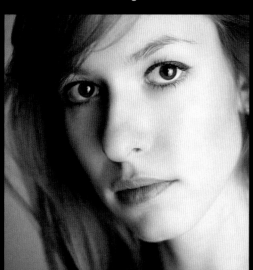

Above: *The original picture before editing, in which the subject has dark brown eyes.*

Step 1. Open the picture into Photoshop or Photoshop Elements and select the elliptical Marquee tool.

Step 2. Draw an ellipse around the first pupil, holding down the alt key as you drag, so that the shape is drawn from the centre outwards.

Step 3. Do the same for the other eye, but hold down the shift key as you do so. This adds the new selection to the existing one, instead of replacing it.

Step 4. Enter Quick Mask mode by hitting the 'Q' key and zoom in on each eye. With a small, soft-edged brush, tidy up your selection so it only includes the irises and pupils.

Step 5. Exit Quick Mask mode ('Q' key) and apply the Hue/Saturation layer. Move the Hue slider to change colour, and refine this with the saturation and lightness controls.

Step 6. When you have a natural-looking result, hit OK and zoom back out, pressing the ctrl/⌘ and 'D' keys to get rid of the selection.

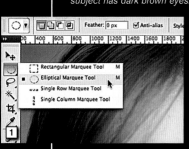

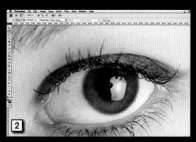

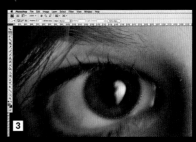

ESSENTIAL KIT

- PC or Mac computer
- Adobe Photoshop or Photoshop Elements

- Try creating the selection from scratch with the Quick Mask tool.
- You may want to apply other adjustments while the selection is active, such as a contrast enhancement via levels.

- A graphics tablet helps with fiddly detail work in quick mask mode.
- Choose an eye colour that suits your subject's complexion and hair colour.

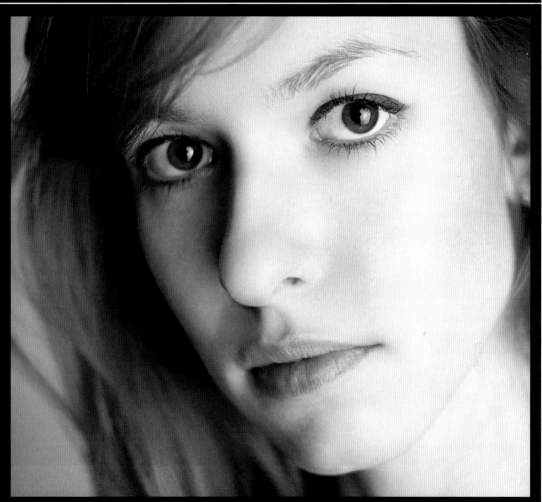

Above: *Photoshop's Quick Mask lets us apply a Hue/Saturation adjustment to just the iris, changing its colour from brown to green.*

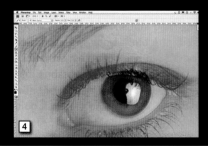

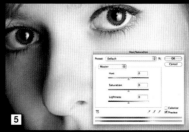

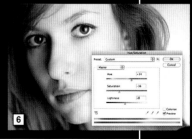

Making **selections**

So far, all of the adjustments we've made have applied to the whole image, but much of the power of digital editing lies in being able to affect just parts of a scene.

common (and easy) way of doing this is to make a selection before you apply the adjustment, which will then only apply to the area inside the selection. There are many ways to make a selection, and we'll look at some of the more elaborate ones later on in chapter five, but for now let's see what the Lasso and Marquee tools can do. The difference between these two tools (which can both be found at the top of the toolbox) is that the Marquee family draw enclosed shapes of regular sizes, while the Lasso tools can be used to draw around irregularly shaped objects. There are different

types of Marquee and Lasso in Photoshop's toolbox – click and hold on one of them to access the others.

The most useful Marquee shapes are the oval and rectangle, which become circle and square if the shift key is held down while they are being drawn out. The Marquee operates in a freehand mode, which draws in any direction you wish, as well as a polygonal mode for straight lines and a Magnetic Lasso that attempts to stick to high-contrast edges. This latter Lasso is great for selecting objects without their background when applying specific adjustments, or for cutting and pasting into another image.

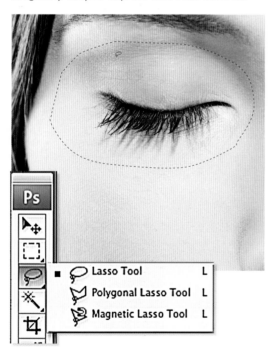

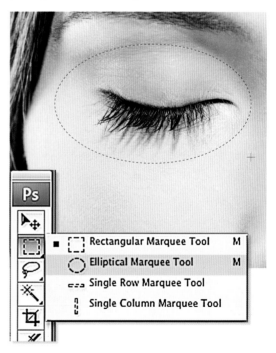

Above: *Use the Lasso tools to select irregular shapes. Clicking on the point where you started the selection closes it again.*

Above: *Marquee selections come in various forms, and are more suited to selecting areas of regular shapes.*

Modifying selections

Once it has been drawn, a selection can be modified before it is used. A number of commands can be found in Photoshop's Select › Modify menu. 'Border' turns the current selection into a border of a specified thickness, while 'Smooth' rounds off any sharp edges. 'Expand' and 'Contract' do exactly what you'd expect, growing and shrinking the selection by the required number of pixels. But it is 'Feather' that is by far the most useful modification to make.

Simply selecting an area of the image and applying a selection to it is seldom a recipe for a natural-looking result. The hard edge of the selection means the transition between the edited and unedited parts of the picture is too abrupt. Feathering the selection before using it softens this hard edge and gives a more natural result.

You'll see feathering options elsewhere in Photoshop, such as in the options bar when the Lasso tool is selected. This is very useful for automatically applying some feathering at the time the selection is made.

Below: These rusted, crushed cars have all been given a different colour by individually selecting each one with the Lasso tool, feathering the selection by five pixels and then applying a Hue/Saturation adjustment to the selected area, dragging the Hue slider to change colours.

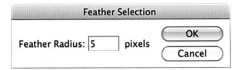

Quick mask

The are many other ways of applying a selection, but one of the most elegant has to be the Quick Mask. Once a selection has been drawn the conventional way, with the Lasso or Marquee tools, engaging Quick Mask mode lets you view this in terms of a red mask, with the parts that are not selected appearing as a pinky-red coloured mask. The nice touch is that you can paint and edit this mask with any of Photoshop's basic tools, such as the Paintbrush, Eraser, or even the Dodge and Burn brushes. When you exit Quick Mask mode, the familiar dotted line of the selection will return, incorporating any changes you made while painting.

Painting with a soft brush or with semi-transparency is also supported, with the semi-transparent areas being selected as feathered regions.

You can access Quick Mask mode in Photoshop by choosing Select › Edit in Quick Mask mode, clicking the shortcut at the bottom of the toolbox or simply by hitting 'Q' on the keyboard. It really is one of the most useful tools there is.

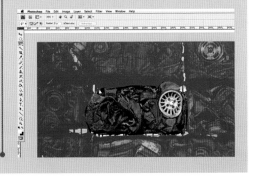

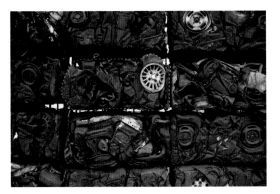

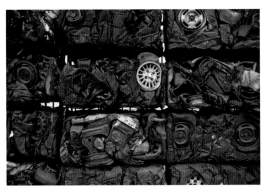

Cropping and straightening

There is no rule that says you have to stick with the size and shape of the frame your camera gives you. Cropping allows you to use any size of canvas you like.

Almost every digital imaging package has a Crop tool, and most work in the same way: draw a box around the part of the image you want to keep, then hit the return key to crop down to that new size. Obviously you throw away some pixels when doing this, so you'll not be able to print the new image at the same size as the old one, and you may notice some drop in image quality if you look very closely.

After dragging the crop rectangle out over your image, there is the opportunity to alter its position by dragging it about, change its size using the grab handles at the corners and sides, and rotate it. Rotating the crop frame is done by positioning the mouse pointer over one of the resize handles, then moving it outwards slightly, away from the frame by a small amount. You'll notice the mouse pointer change from a resize icon to a rotational one, and when you click and drag, the frame will rotate around its centre.

Aspect ratios

It's often useful to constrain the Crop tool to a specific aspect ratio, which may correspond to a size of picture frame, or a placeholder on a website. You can do this in Photoshop by entering values in the width and height boxes in the Options bar at the top of the screen. Keep the dimensions in physical units rather than pixels (cm, inches – it doesn't matter which, as this is only a ratio), and avoid putting anything in the resolution box as this will resize the picture at the same time as cropping it.

Alternatively there are a couple of quick shortcuts for maintaining aspect ratios: use the Crop tool with the shift key held down and the frame will automatically be drawn out square (i.e. a 1:1 ratio). Adjust an existing crop with the shift key held down and it will maintain its current aspect ratio while you adjust it.

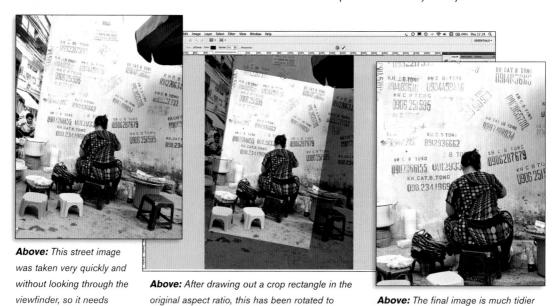

Above: This street image was taken very quickly and without looking through the viewfinder, so it needs levelling out and cropping.

Above: After drawing out a crop rectangle in the original aspect ratio, this has been rotated to compensate for the shooting angle.

Above: The final image is much tidier and better composed.

Rotating the image

There are lots of ways to rotate an image in Photoshop. At the most basic level you can rotate the image through steps of 90 degrees by choosing Image > Image Rotation > 90° CW (or indeed 90° CCW), which is very useful for reorienting pictures shot with the camera held vertically. For more subtle adjustments you can select the whole canvas (Select > Select All) and then use an Edit > Transform > Rotate command to rotate it with the mouse pointer (below).

If you know the angle you want to rotate the canvas by, choose Image > Rotation > Arbitary... and enter the value. If you don't know the value, but there is an edge in the scene that should be straight or vertical, you can use a great shortcut. Draw along the known straight edge with the Ruler tool (you'll find this on the same spot in the toolbox as the Eyedropper). Now choose Image > Rotation > Arbitary... and the correct value will already be there for you.

Free transformation

Rotation is just one of a number of transformations that Photoshop can do. Delve into the Edit > Transform menu and 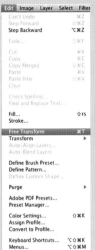 you'll find Scale Skew Warp and Perspective, to mention but a couple. The most useful is the Free Transform command, which combines many of the transformations into one. You can apply a free transform to any selection or layer and use the handles to rotate and scale, as well as skew and make perspective transformations. Hit return to commit the changes.

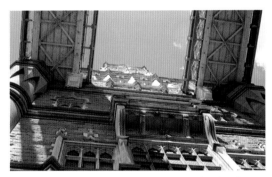

Above: The angles in this image are awkward, rather than deliberate, and need straightening for a better composition.

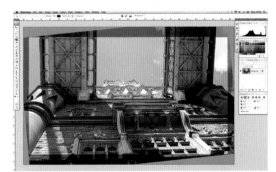

Above: Rotate the image manually until the angles are as desired. Once you have rotated the image, you will need to re-crop it with the Crop tool (right).

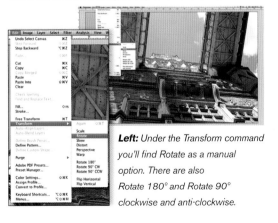

Left: Under the Transform command you'll find Rotate as a manual option. There are also Rotate 180° and Rotate 90° clockwise and anti-clockwise.

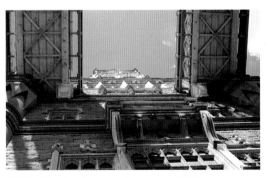

Above: The straightened and re-cropped image.

History in Photoshop

The history palette is so much more than a conventional undo tool. Used correctly, it also offers amazing possibilities for creative image editing.

Anyone used to using a home computer is familiar with the concept of the undo command. It's a kind of get-out-of-jail-free card that enables you to reverse the last action you performed. In Photoshop, the official undo command (Edit › Undo or ctrl/⌘–Z) only remembers one step, which may seem restrictive, but fear not: the history function can remember many more. Look in the history palette (Window › History) and you'll see them.

Undoing a recent command is as easy as clicking on the previous history state – Photoshop will jump back to this point, undoing anything you may have done along the way. By default Photoshop remembers 20 history states, although you can change this number in the application's preferences. Do be aware, though, that increasing the number of history states remembered will increase the amount of memory your computer will need. It's not advisable to stray from the default 20 states unless you have good reason, and your PC or Mac is fitted with lots of RAM.

Snapshots and new documents

There is nothing more irritating than spending time editing an image, only to find you can't step back in history to where you want to because you've gone way beyond the 20 remembered history states. It isn't practical to ask Photoshop to remember 100 states, for example, but you can use History Snapshots to ensure that one specific state is always remembered, even when you save the document.

Creating a snapshot is best done at an important moment during editing, just before you are going to begin experimenting with a tool that you are unsure will work. Click the Snapshot button at the bottom of the History palette to do this; you'll see the snapshot appear at the top of the palette just below the initial state of the image, which is always remembered. To step back to this snapshot state, simply click on it.

Next to the Snapshot button is another control that creates an entirely new document from the current history state. This is a useful approach if you intend to go off in a completely new direction with your editing, but also want to persist with the original effort, too, perhaps comparing the effectiveness of two similar methods.

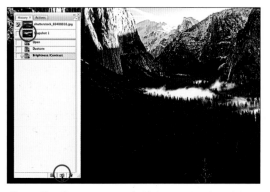

Above: *Creating a new snapshot lets you return to a state regardless of how many edits you have done since then.*

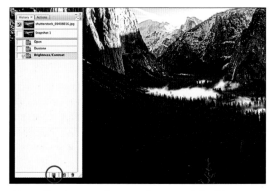

Above: *Create a new document from an existing history state and you can try out a different editing approach.*

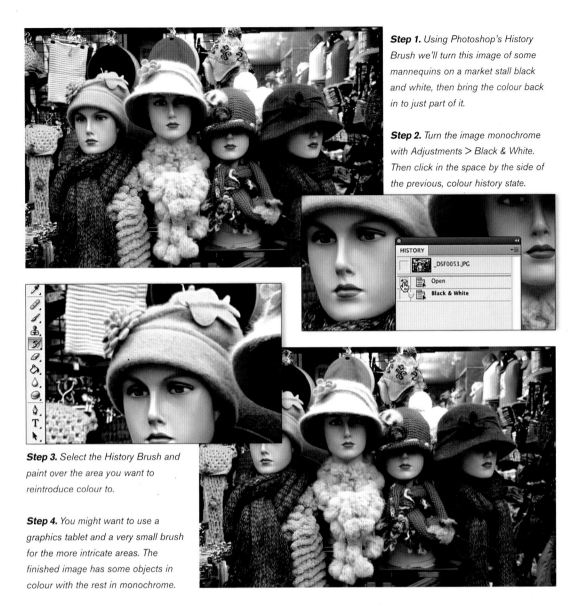

Step 1. *Using Photoshop's History Brush we'll turn this image of some mannequins on a market stall black and white, then bring the colour back in to just part of it.*

Step 2. *Turn the image monochrome with Adjustments > Black & White. Then click in the space by the side of the previous, colour history state.*

Step 3. *Select the History Brush and paint over the area you want to reintroduce colour to.*

Step 4. *You might want to use a graphics tablet and a very small brush for the more intricate areas. The finished image has some objects in colour with the rest in monochrome.*

History brush

The History Brush is what makes Photoshop's history palette more than just a glorified Undo tool. With it, you can apply an Undo action to just parts of the image, painting it on as you would do any other brush. The state that is painted on can be one in the past, or a current state that has just been undone. Choosing which is a simple matter of clicking in the small box to the left of the desired state, which sets the source for the History Brush. You can then select the History Brush tool from the toolbox and paint away on your image.

The uses for this technology are really only limited by your own imagination. Using the History Brush enables you to selectively apply any adjustment, filter or transformation to just part of the picture. For instance, if you want to send all of a photograph into black and white except for one object, simply choose Image > Adjustments > Black & White to remove the colour, then click in the small square next to the previous history state. The History Brush will now paint in the previous coloured state, allowing you to render some parts of the scene in colour and some in monochrome.

Black and white

Converting pictures to black and white in Photoshop is a much better way of shooting monochrome images than simply creating them in-camera. You'll have more control, and get better results.

Back in chapter three, we looked briefly at black and white photography, exploring its universal popularity even in today's technicoloured age. Although it's possible to shoot black and white images on your digital camera, that is not necessarily the best route for producing stunning monochrome photos. The conversion from colour to monochrome in-camera is crude, giving you little or no control and usually a very mediocre result. A much better route is to shoot a colour image and convert it to black and white in Photoshop, or similar software.

There are many ways to convert a picture to black and white, and each one gives a slightly different effect. One-click options include going from RGB colour mode to greyscale colour mode (Image > Mode > Grayscale), or desaturating the image by choosing Image > Adjustments > Desaturate. This is a step up from shooting in-camera mono, but it still doesn't give you much control over how colours are translated into black and white.

Left: Black and white images have a timeless quality about them that works well for fine-art style purposes.

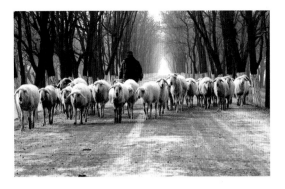

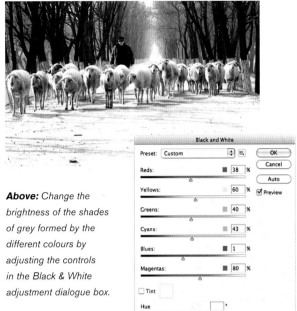

Much better is the dedicated black and white adjustment built in to Photoshop and Elements. This not only converts the image to mono, but also lets you select the brightness of the shades of grey for the various colours in the image. For example, a scene featuring a red house against a blue sky containing grey clouds may well translate into monochrome poorly, with all three colours coming out as the same shade of grey. By adjusting the red and blue sliders in the black and white adjustment dialogue, the red can be lightened and the blue darkened, so that all the colours are distinct and visible and the image has some contrast.

This is the same effect that using coloured filters has on in-camera black and white, except with the advantage that you can decide which effect to apply after you have taken the shot. You'll notice that several presets are available in the drop-down menu that appears at the top of the dialogue box, which simulate the effect of on-camera filters. These are excellent starting points for your own adjustments, and you can make your own by selecting 'Save As...' from the small palette menu next to the preset menu.

Above: *Change the brightness of the shades of grey formed by the different colours by adjusting the controls in the Black & White adjustment dialogue box.*

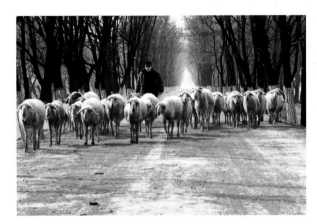

Black and white in Lightroom

Being non-destructive, black and white conversions in Lightroom are even more powerful than those in Photoshop. It's easy to combine the black and white conversion with other adjustments such as contrast, vignetting and noise, and then still come back to the black and white controls and make further changes.

Access monochrome mode by entering the develop module and clicking on the black and white label in the basic palette. This will send the image black and white, and allow you to use the other controls to fine-tune the image, including using coloured filters. A number of black and white options are pre-installed and ready for you in the presets palette on the left-hand side of the screen.

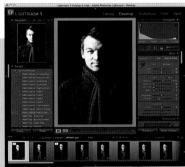

Above: *Adobe Lightroom gives fantastic control over black and white conversion.*

CREATING A BLACK AND WHITE STILL LIFE

Shoot this classic black and white still life and follow in the footsteps of some very famous photographers, who have all captured the beauty of nature in monochrome.

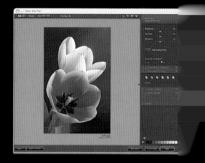

A classic subject for still-life photographers has always been flowers. It might seem strange to choose to photograph such a colourful subject in black and white, but by doing so you are showing people a familiar subject from a new perspective. When shooting subjects such as this, lighting should be soft, yet directional. Window light is perfect for the job, as long as you avoid direct sunlight. Setting up the camera so the window is at 90 degrees is a good start, and you can always use a reflector (see page 27) to reduce excessive contrast.

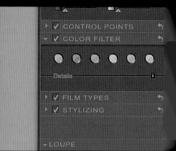

The background should be plain and clutter-free so as not to distract from the flower. You'll need to get in close, but your standard zoom is fine for this. Digital compacts should also be able to turn in a decent performance. If you shoot in raw, it's worth setting your camera to black and white shooting mode. This way you'll see in black and white on the camera's viewscreen, but capture in colour so you have a decent file to convert afterwards.

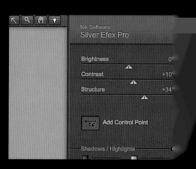

After shooting, transfer the files to your computer and open the images one by one into Photoshop or Elements. For each image, convert to monochrome with the Image › Adjustments › Black & White command, and tweak the result for contrast with a levels adjustment (Image › Adjustments › Levels). If shooting against a black background, use the black-point Eyedropper to ensure this is a proper black. Likewise with a white backdrop and the white Eyedropper.

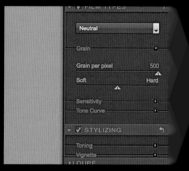

ESSENTIAL KIT

- PC or Mac computer
- Adobe Photoshop or Photoshop Elements

TIPS & TRICKS

- Inject some local contrast into the picture with controls such as Clarity or Structure. Each application uses a different term.

- Add some grain for an old fashioned film-like look. In Photoshop use Filters > Noise > Add Noise, enabling the monochrome and gaussian options.

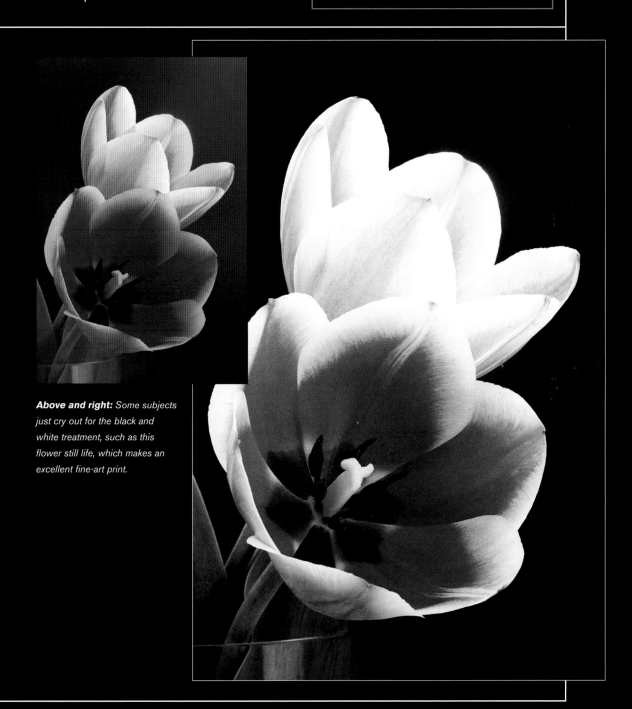

Above and right: Some subjects just cry out for the black and white treatment, such as this flower still life, which makes an excellent fine-art print.

Enhancing **black** and **white**

After making the conversion to black and white, there are still lots of tweaks and changes that can be made to an image, using the same tools that are useful in colour photography.

Perhaps the most useful of these are the tools that affect contrast. Black and white photography is very effective when shot in low-contrast conditions, such as on a cloudy day, and processed up to give a high-contrast result.

One of the best adjustments for doing this is levels (Image > Adjustment > Levels). Move in the black slider to darken the dark tones and the white slider to lighten the light tones, using the middle grey slider to correct for any overall changes in brightness. You can be more aggressive with this than you would be with a colour image, as black and white images can handle more blown highlights and featureless shadows. It all adds to the mood!

The Dodge and Burn tools are also very good for making more localized changes. Again, don't be frightened to use them more forcefully than you

Below left and right: Some black and white conversions can leave the picture looking a bit flat (left) so don't be afraid to boost contrast with a curves or levels adjustment (right).

might have done in the colour world, especially on broody skies full of textured cloud.

After a conversion to monochrome in Photoshop Elements, the image below has had its contrast increased with a Levels adjustment, and the edges of the frame have been darkened with the Burn tool. A small amount of grain has been added, too.

Plug-ins and black and white

It is with such fastidiousness that photographers make the transformation from colour to black and white, that a whole mini-industry has sprung up offering Photoshop plug-ins that tackle the job in various ways. Some make the process easier, while others try to mimic the printing process of a traditional wet-chemistry darkroom and deliver the best quality conversion possible.

Plug-ins are accessed through Photoshop's Filters menu, although most are also available for Elements and Lightroom, and some for PaintShop Pro and Apple's Aperture software. Prices of plug-ins vary from the affordable to the extortionate,

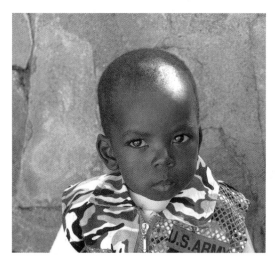

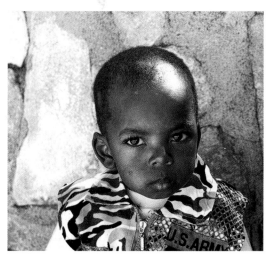

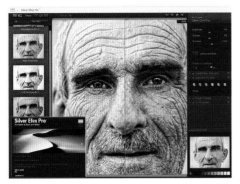

Above: Plug-ins such as Nik Software's Silver Efex Pro make creative black and white easy.

roughly in line with the features they offer. Most offer the ability to simulate coloured filters, but this functionality is offered in Photoshop, too, so you should be looking at more features than this if you are considering investing.

Many black and white conversion plug-ins emulate the effect of different traditional black and white films, papers and processing techniques. For instance, Silver Efex Pro from Nik Software (www.niksoftware.com) has preset options for many favourite traditional films, from names such as Kodak, Agfa and Fuji that simulate the films' colour response, contrast and even grain. More affordable is BW Workflow Pro (www.fredmiranda.com/DBWpro), which offers duotone functionality for tinted and toned prints, as well as the ability to simulate infrared-style black and white photography.

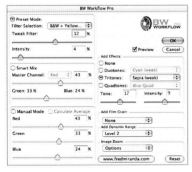

Above: BW Workflow Pro operates on traditional darkroom principles.

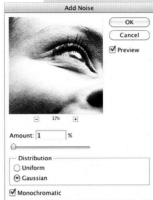

Above: Photoshop's 'Add Noise' filter.

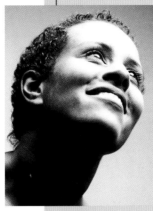

Above: Some grain or noise can really add to the look and feel of a black and white photograph.

Above: Lightroom's 'Add Noise' filter.

Grain, not noise

Although we go to great lengths as photographers to eliminate digital noise from our images, adding some grain to a black and white picture can actually enhance its mood. Grain is different from noise, resembling more closely the fine structure of traditional film. Although many black and white plug-ins add grain to varying extents, you can also do this in Adobe Photoshop and Elements with the 'Add Noise...' filter, which is to be found in the Filter › Noise submenu.

There is not much to using the Add Noise filter, although for the most grain-like result you should tick the gaussian and monochromatic options. Explore how much noise looks good by dragging the Amount slider around. You should actually only need a small amount: between two and five per cent.

In Lightroom you can now add grain as part of the editing process. You'll find a grain palette in the Develop module that has three sliders, offering much more control. In addition to the Amount control, which dictates how much grain there will be, the Size and Roughness sliders govern the size and sharpness of each grain particle.

Toning and tinting

Monochrome doesn't always have to mean black and white; any two colours will do. Greys are just lighter shades of black, so we can pick any dark colour for the basis of a monochrome image. This is the basis of tinting and toning.

The difference between tinting and toning is often overlooked, but is an important one. Substituting a colour for white in a black and white picture is known as tinting, while toning refers to the practice of using a colour instead of black. In some traditional chemical darkroom terminologies, tinting refers to the colouring of the paper (the white bit) and toning to colouring of the silver (the black bit).

There are lots of ways to apply a colour to a black and white picture, but one of the simplest is the tint option built into the Black and White adjustment tool in Photoshop and Photoshop Elements. Simply tick the tint box and choose the colour either by dragging the Hue bar around or clicking the coloured box. The default saturation setting is always a bit strong; less is more when it comes to adding colour, so try a value of between three and eight per cent.

Duotone images

Duotone technology has its roots in the printing industry, where it is used to create high quality reproductions of images on paper. Photoshop has a duotone colour mode that can be used to good effect when creating black and white images. The idea is to replace one or both of the black and white colours, and introduce a colour tint or tone by using 'inks' of a different hue. Conventional photography applications tend to work better if you replace the white colour, but you can experiment with more avant-garde effects by changing the black, too.

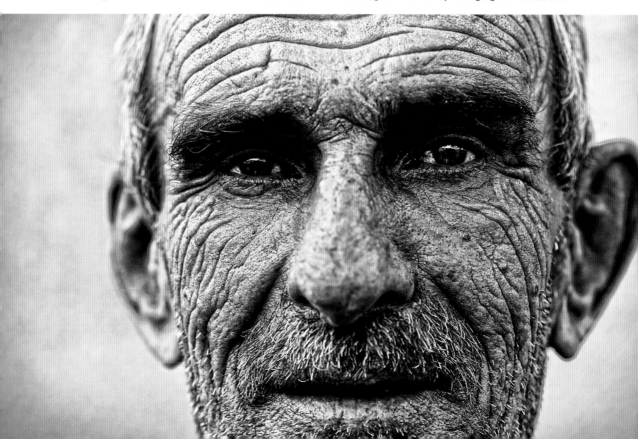

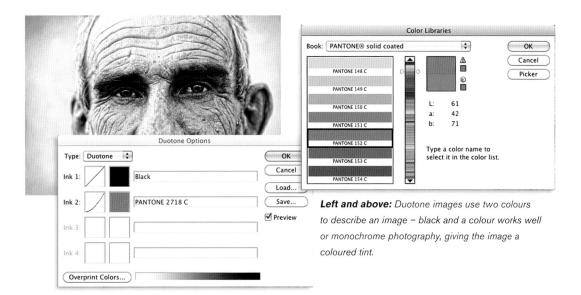

Left and above: Duotone images use two colours to describe an image − black and a colour works well or monochrome photography, giving the image a coloured tint.

To access duotone settings in Photoshop, first turn your image to greyscale (Image > Mode > Grayscale) and thus discard all colour information from it. Now you can switch over to duotone mode (Image > Mode > Duotone) and you will be presented with a dialogue box containing two colour swatches: black and white. Click on each and you'll be able to select alternative colours and give the image tint and tone. You'll see the effect preview in real time.

A range of presets is available from the drop-down menu at the top of the screen, including tritone and quadtone settings. As their names suggest, these have three and four colour shades respectively and are great for creating very subtle tonal variations in a colour tint or tone.

Bringing back some colour

Once an image has been converted to monochrome, it's possible to fade out the effect to let some of the colour return. This is something typically done with layers, and we'll look more at this way of working in chapter five (see page 344). But the effect can still be created with the little-known fade command.

Convert an image to black and white using any of the methods we've looked at here. Image Adjustments > Black & White... is the best. When you've made the adjustments and clicked OK, look in the Edit menu and you'll see an option to fade the last command (eg. Fade > Black & White). Use this slider to let the original colour image back in to an extent that looks good. This is a great way of creating that muted colour look, and looks good combined with a boost in contrast.

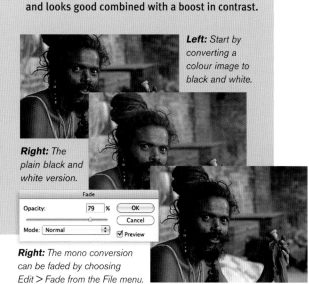

Left: Start by converting a colour image to black and white.

Right: The plain black and white version.

Right: The mono conversion can be faded by choosing Edit > Fade from the File menu.

Opposite: Black and white images with lots of texture, contrast and detail lend themselves to toning very well.

ASSIGNMENT
SPLIT TONING

Once you've mastered basic toning and tinting, how about trying split toning? This is the practice of tinting highlights one colour and shadow areas another.

Toning and tinting can really enhance the mood of a black and white photograph, and give a quite normal-looking mono print a subtle lift. Warming up an image is done with yellow, red or orange tones, while tinting with blue or cyan results in a steely, cold look. But there is another way of adding colour to a monochrome picture. So-called split toning of a photograph involves tinting the highlights with one colour and the shadow areas with another. In the traditional chemical darkroom this is a fairly complicated affair, but for the Photoshop user it's as simple as a few adjustments with the Colour Balance tool.

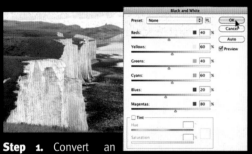

Step 1. Convert an image to black and white. Any method other than Image > Mode > Grayscale is fine, although it's good to get in to the habit of using the Black and White adjustment (Image > Adjustments > Black & White).

Step 2. Select Image > Adjustments > Color Balance and click the Highlights ratio button to specify the parts of the image we are going to change first. Apply the tint by moving the sliders around to get the colour you want.

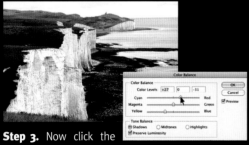

Step 3. Now click the Shadows ratio button to flip over the darker areas of the picture. Again, apply a colour by moving the sliders around. Getting the right combination of highlight and shadow colour may take some experimentation.

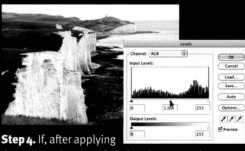

Step 4. If, after applying the split toning, you feel the picture needs more or less contrast, or needs brightening or darkening, apply a levels adjustment (Image > Adjustments > Levels) to do this.

ESSENTIAL KIT

- PC or Mac computer
- Adobe Photoshop or Photoshop Elements

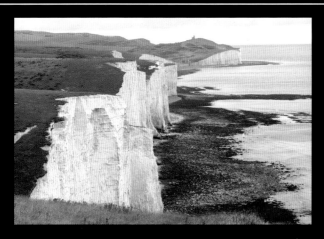

TIPS & TRICKS

- Pick a picture that has plenty of contrast. You'll need light shades and dark shades to tone differently.

- Experiment with different colour combinations. Blue and yellow work well, as do blue and green, and brown and purple.

Left and below: Images have to have some contrast in order for split toning to work; dark areas and light areas are both needed in order to get both tones working well.

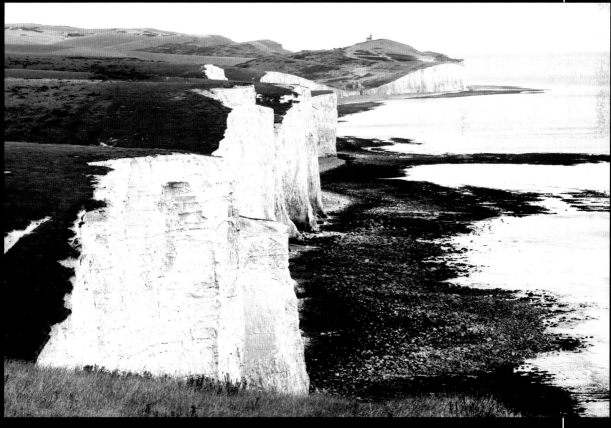

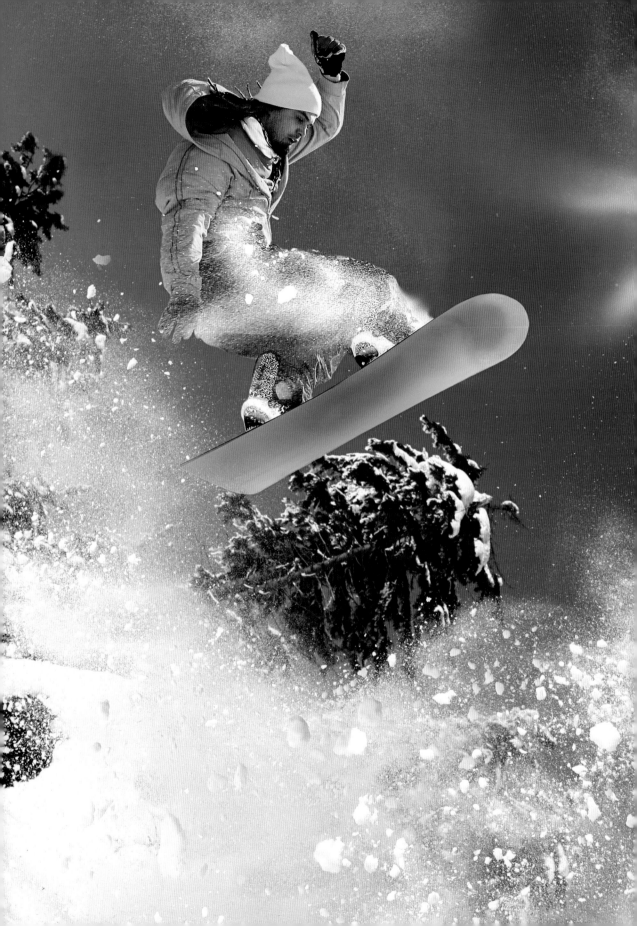

advanced
darkroom
techniques

We've seen how images can be stored, edited and fine-tuned using your home computer and some imaging software – now let's look at how to take this to the next level and perform advanced editing and manipulation. We can either edit images to be as realistic as possible, or heavily edit them to achieve hyper-realistic photographs of scenes that are impossible to capture normally.

Working with **raw files**

When deciding whether to shoot JPEG or raw files, we have to consider the trade-off between convenience and image quality that results. So let's look at raw files in more detail and explore what they can do for you.

We've already established that raw files can offer more control in the digital darkroom and deliver better image quality (see page 238). We have also learned that special software is required to read raw files and convert them to files that can be printed or opened, or imported into Photoshop. But what can we achieve with a raw file that we can't with a smaller, more convenient JPEG file?

Dynamic range

A raw file contains many more brightness levels than a JPEG file, meaning detail lost in bright highlights and dark shadows is still present and may be recovered. We have already learned that, in a JPEG file, solid black is represented by a numerical value of zero and bright white by the number 255. Imagine for a moment that a raw file contains extra values outside of this range, at less than 0 and more than 255. Even though these shades are not visible when we are editing and viewing pictures, they can be reassigned and brought into the viewable range with a few basic adjustments in raw-processing software.

For example, if areas in a bright sky are devoid of detail thanks to blown or clipped highlights, these areas can often be recovered by using the Exposure or Recovery sliders in your raw-processing software. Similarly, you can add detail back to black shadows with the Exposure, Fill Light or Blacks controls.

Although you can use highlight and shadow adjustments in Photoshop on JPEG files, you can't add new information to areas where this has been lost. In a raw file this information is still present, you just can't see it until it's recovered with the tools available to you in Adobe Camera Raw (ACR).

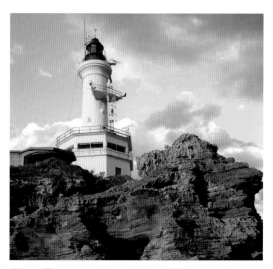

Above: *The compression applied to JPEG images often causes banding in areas containing more subtle colour gradients like a blue sky.*

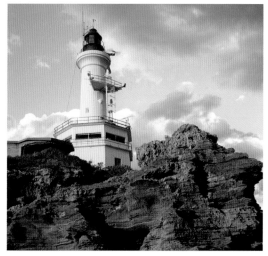

Above: *No banding is seen in the same image captured as a raw file, which is less compressed and contains a lot more data.*

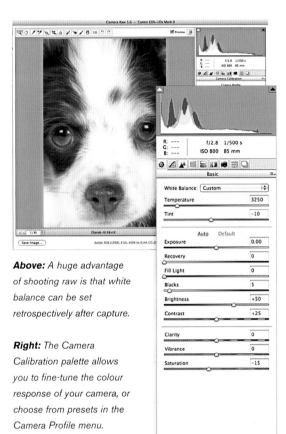

Above: *A huge advantage of shooting raw is that white balance can be set retrospectively after capture.*

Right: *The Camera Calibration palette allows you to fine-tune the colour response of your camera, or choose from presets in the Camera Profile menu.*

White balance

The same luxury that lets us adjust dynamic range also lets us set white balance after shooting. Having many more levels in each of the red, green and blue colour channels allows us to move the black, white and mid-points in each to adjust colour balance without losing any information or image quality.

Freed from the struggle of getting white balance right in-camera, there are all manner of methods available to let you set it in ACR or similar software. The easiest is to adjust white balance manually until it looks right – assuming your computer's screen is also colour neutral (see pages 292–293). This is done with two white balance sliders: Colour Temperature varies between blue and yellow; Colour Tint between magenta and green. These are the only controls you need to ensure your image is colour neutral under just about any light source.

It's good to have somewhere to start, though, and the preset options built into your raw-processing application provide this. Select one closest to the conditions you were shooting in (or 'As Shot' for the white balance your camera picked automatically) and fine-tune this with the Colour and Tint sliders. Having something in the frame that you know is colour neutral helps enormously to get this right. In fact it opens up the most powerful white balance tool of all.

In ACR, the white balance tool is found in the toolbar at the top of the screen and resembles the eyedroppers seen in the Levels adjustment. Use it to click on the colour-neutral object in the scene and ACR will set the white balance accordingly, using this as a reference. Commonly used colour-neutral references include stone buildings or roads, or painted white surfaces. You can even include your own neutral reference if one isn't there already.

Camera calibration

Most of the tools you will use for everyday raw-file editing are housed in the first tab in Adobe Camera Raw, and it's rarely you'll feel the need to delve deeper and explore the others. That said, it's worth looking at the Camera Calibration tab, and in particular the Camera Profile settings.

These settings dictate how colour is handled in your raw file, and go some way to addressing the criticism that JPEGs often have better colour impact than their raw file equivalents. You'll see an 'Adobe Standard' option in the Camera Profile, which is the default option, and also some extra settings such as Landscape, Portrait, Neutral and Vivid. Exactly which other settings you see may depend on the camera you own.

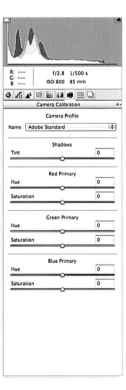

Optimizing raw files

Getting the most from a raw file involves making adjustments in just the right way. It's best to follow a simple routine when processing images in Adobe Camera Raw, using the controls in the same order each time. That said, this doesn't mean you can't nip back and make changes – the non-destructive nature of raw-file editing means you can come back to the file at any time and make adjustments to the data that came off your camera.

Let's break down the editing process into four stages: tone, colour, composition and final touches. We'll use this portrait of two clowns as our example. Being the very first frame of the shoot, it's very under-exposed, as the lighting and camera settings weren't quite right. But the expressions on the subjects' faces are very good, and were not reproduced as well in the rest of the shoot. Can raw processing rescue the image?

Tone control

As a rule of thumb, work your way down the sliders from top to bottom. To brighten the image we'll use the Exposure slider first, dragging it to the right. Use your judgement, aided by the histogram, to get the image looking about right. Pushing the Exposure adjustment too far will clip the highlights (you can use the highlight warning – or hold down alt – to see if this is happening), but don't feel you have to stop adjusting exposure if this happens. Just move on to the next slider, Recovery, and use this to bring back detail lost in bright highlights. Don't worry about so-called specular highlights, either – the sparkling reflections off water or metal. These are meant to be bright and you don't need to rescue them.

Next, look at the Blacks slider. This has +5 applied by default and can be increased to define how many pixels in the image are defined as black. In this case it's been taken down to -3 to

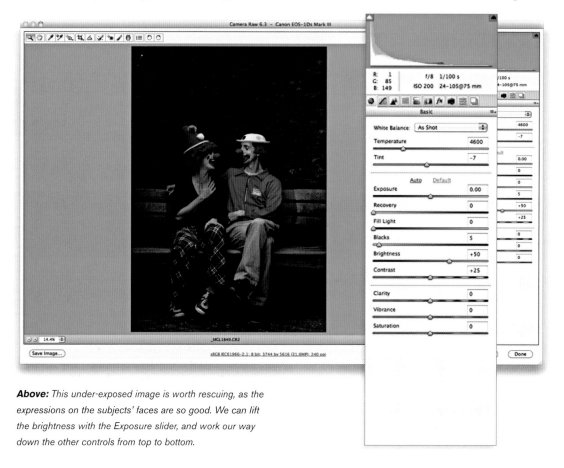

Above: *This under-exposed image is worth rescuing, as the expressions on the subjects' faces are so good. We can lift the brightness with the Exposure slider, and work our way down the other controls from top to bottom.*

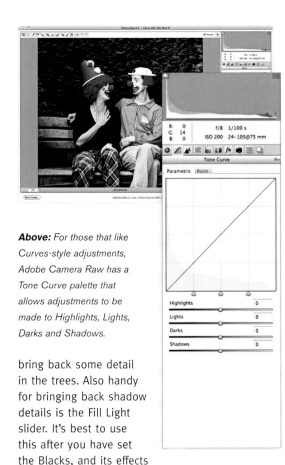

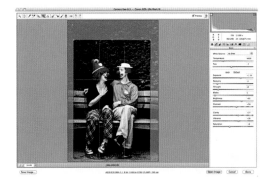

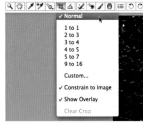

bring back some detail in the trees. Also handy for bringing back shadow details is the Fill Light slider. It's best to use this after you have set the Blacks, and its effects are not always as pronounced. Whether you will have to use this adjustment depends on the picture. Here, +10 has been applied to lighten the shadows in the background a little more.

The Brightness slider should always be set after the Exposure, Blacks and Recovery sliders have been used. This adjusts mid-tones without spoiling the highlights and shadows we have just got right – behaving a little like the mid-point slider in a Levels adjustment. By doing the above we have already set the image's contrast, but if this needs a fine-tune at the end of the tonal adjustments then the Contrast slider is the perfect tool for the job.

Colour control

The first aspect of colour that needs sorting is white balance. In this case (as in most cases, in fact) the camera's auto setting has done very well, but clicking with the white balance tool on a neutral area can make subtle improvements. The increases in contrast and exposure have made the reds stand out too much. We can take these down a notch with the Saturation control, and then restore colour to other parts of the picture by increasing Vibrance to compensate. Saturation affects all colours equally, but Vibrance boosts those that are muted in preference to those that are already strong, and also leaves skin tones alone so they don't become overcooked.

Composition

Tweaking composition is sometimes done more easily in Adobe Camera Raw than it is in Photoshop itself. The Crop tool works much the same as it does in the main Photoshop application, but with the added advantage of having the facility to revisit the crop at any time and make changes. Also useful is the dedicated Straighten tool. Use this to draw a straight line along something in the picture that is supposed to be horizontal or vertical and the crop will automatically rotate to make this so. It's a great rescue technique for landscapes where you haven't quite got the horizon straight, or a portrait photograph where you want the subject's eyes to be dead-level.

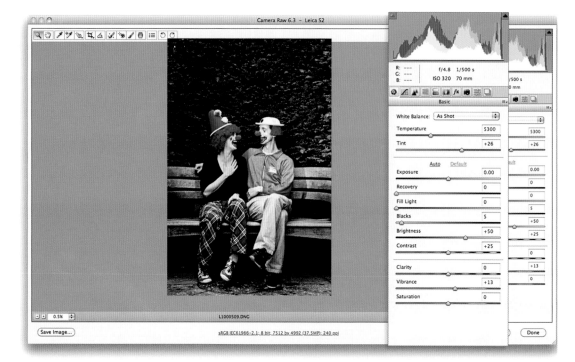

Final touches

Before clicking 'Open' to bring the file into Photoshop, there are a couple of other controls that can enhance the picture's appearance. Virtually all images can benefit from some application of the Clarity slider, which gives contrast a boost at the local level – a property that film photographers used to call acutance. Don't go crazy here, but do try to use a little clarity to boost texture in detailed areas.

Working in a similar way to this are the Sharpness controls, which you'll find in the Detail tab. Sharpening also boosts local contrast but on

Above: Final touches to any raw file processing include Clarity (a local contrast adjustment) as well as Vibrance and Saturation, which control colour intensity.

a much smaller scale, enhancing the difference between light and dark along edges, which gives the image the look of being sharper. As we'll see on pages 306–309, all digital images need digital sharpening to some extent, but opinions differ as to whether this should be done at the end of the workflow or the beginning. Applying the default level of sharpening as you open the file into Photoshop certainly doesn't hurt, though.

XMP files

The settings you make in Adobe Camera Raw or Lightroom are not saved into the raw file – this is actually never touched – but they are saved separately so that when you return to edit the file for a second or third time, the previous development settings are remembered. Raw-file development settings are saved in one of two ways: in a database or cache inside the application, or as so-called sidecar files that have the same name as the image file, only with the file extension XMP.

XMP stands for extensible metadata platform, and was developed by Adobe for this purpose. The advantage of saving settings as an xmp file is that if you transfer your files to another computer, then the development settings and metadata will still be available, as long as the xmp files are copied along with the image files.

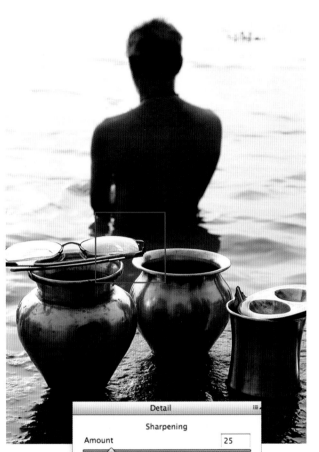

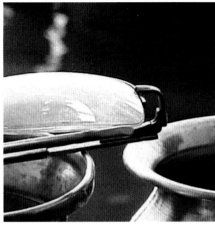

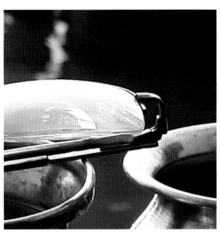

Above: *Adobe Camera Raw features a powerful noise-reduction function that reduces unsightly artefacts caused by high ISO shooting (above top) to a much cleaner and crisper image (above).*

Finally, you may want to consider applying some noise reduction to the image if it was shot at high ISO sensitivity and has a speckled or noisy appearance as a result. Noise reduction in the latest version of ACR is the best that has been around for a long time, and works very well to improve the appearance of photographs shot at high ISO in low light. Use the Colour slider to remove any coloured, mottled noise, and the Luminance slider to combat the monochrome speckles. It's important to judge the effect of these controls at 100 per cent zoom level. Use the drop-down menu in the bottom left-hand corner to view the image this way.

Lens corrections

A more recent development in raw processing is the inclusion of lens profiles in software. These add-ons can be used to correct electronically for optical problems with lenses, such as pincushion or barrel distortion, chromatic aberrations (also known as coloured fringing) and light fall-off towards the edges of the frame.

In earlier versions of Photoshop and Photoshop Elements it was possible to correct for these factors manually, with sliders governing the amount of correction applied. This is a very time-consuming and inaccurate process, however. In Photoshop CS5 and Lightroom 3, automatic lens correction is applied, with the software detecting which lens was used from the information in the file's metadata (see page 400). If data for this lens is available, ACR applies it to the image automatically, and the effect can be surprisingly pronounced.

Camera and lens manufacturers supply Adobe with the profiles, and the list of those lenses that are supported is growing all the time. Having such electronic control is no substitute for a really well engineered, good-quality lens, but it can make a good lump of glass even better and improve your pictures considerably.

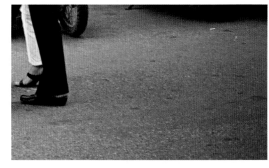

Above: *Light fall-off darkens the frame towards its edges.*

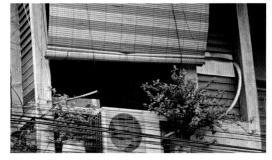

Above: *Barrel distortion bends straight lines at the edges.*

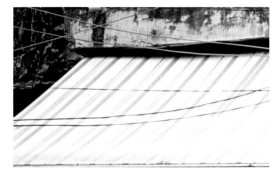

Above: *Chromatic aberrations manifest as coloured fringing.*

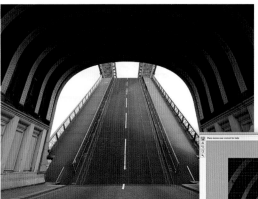

Right: *The Photoshop Lens Correction filter is designed to fix common flaws such as barrel distortion, lens vignettes or chromatic aberration. It can be run automatically, or you can create your own lens profiles for your camera, which is a great utility.*

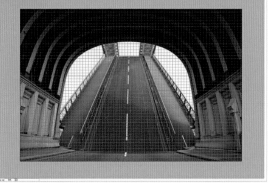

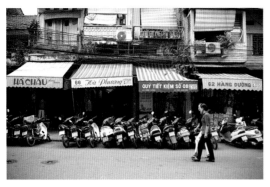

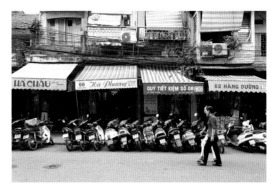

Above: *Using a cheap lens often means many problems with image quality, some of which can be fixed with the Lens Correction feature in Adobe Camera Raw.*

Left: *The same image after digital lens correction in Adobe Camera Raw. Distortion, chromatic aberration and fall-off have all been corrected to a more than acceptable level.*

Raw or JPEG? What to shoot and when

Shooting raw

For	Against
Improved image quality	Large file sizes mean bigger memory cards and hard disks
More flexible white balance	Need to process before you can edit, share, etc.
Non-destructive	Need for up-to-date software
More dynamic range	

Shooting JPEG

For	Against
Convenient	Compression means a loss of image quality in areas of continuous tone
Small file sizes mean easy storage	Limited dynamic range
Ready straight from the camera	Limited control over white balance and sharpening – once it's set, it's set
Often look better than raw files before any editing	

ASSIGNMENT
SETTING WHITE BALANCE RETROSPECTIVELY

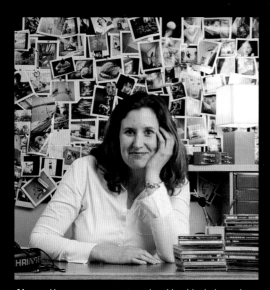

Above: *Your camera may struggle with white balance in situations where there is more than one source of lighting.*

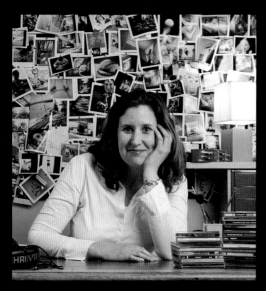

Above: *After setting white balance with a grey card, colours and skin tones are more natural.*

Setting the white balance retrospectively is a much more accurate way of making sure you get your colours right, especially when it comes to skin tones.

One of the benefits of shooting in raw is the ability to set white balance accurately after shooting the image. This is never more useful than when shooting portraits, where an accurate white balance ensures natural skin tones.

White balance can be set for the whole shoot by including a neutral target – such as a grey card or sheet of white paper – in the first frame, and using this as a reference at the raw-processing stage. Other frames shot under identical lighting conditions can then be synchronized with the reference frame, ensuring they are colour accurate.

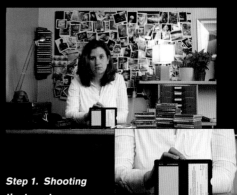

Step 1. Shooting the target
In the first frame of your shoot, ask your subject to hold a neutral target. Once this frame is captured, you can get rid of the target until you change lighting conditions, and shoot the rest of the frames.

TIPS & TRICKS

- You can use a commercially available grey card or colour checker as your neutral target, or simply a piece of white paper if you are on a budget.

- If you know you want to apply the measured white balance to other images that are not open in ACR, save the settings by choosing 'Save Settings...' from the palette menu. You can recall them later with 'Load Settings...', or the 'Previous Conversion' command.

- If the lighting changes, so may the colour temperature. Therefore always shoot a new white-balance target frame when changing your lighting set-up.

ESSENTIAL KIT

- Adobe Photoshop, Elements or Lightroom
- PC or Mac computer
- DSLR or compact camera with raw capability
- Neutral target

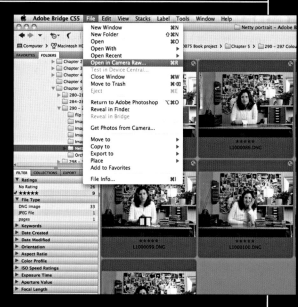

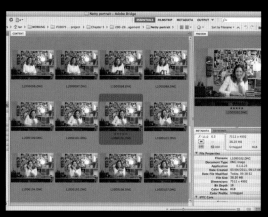

Step 2. Looking at the raw files

After completing the shoot, transfer all the raw files to your computer. When deciding which files to keep or discard, also include the reference frame in your final edit.

Step 3. Opening the files

Open all the files in Adobe Camera Raw, whether by selecting them and dragging them into Photoshop, or by selecting them all in Adobe Bridge and choosing File > Open In Adobe Camera Raw.

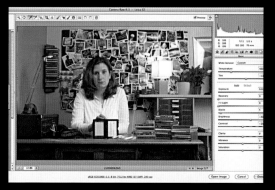

Step 4. Setting white balance

Find the reference frame and choose the white balance tool from the top-right corner of the screen. Use this to click the neutral grey target (zoom in if you have to) and you should see the white balance change.

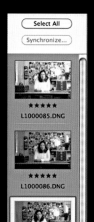

Step 5. Synchronizing all frames

Apply this white balance to the other frames by clicking 'Select All' and 'Synchronize'. You can then either open all the files into Photoshop for editing or click 'Done' which dismisses the ACR dialogue but remembers the white balance changes. Now you can open each file individually as normal.

Colour management

How do we know that the colours we see when we are editing our photographs are the same as other people will see when they look at them on screen or as prints? The answer is, we can't. But a colour calibrated workflow can help get as close as possible.

Each device in the digital photography chain deals with colour slightly differently, be it a camera, computer display, printer or projector. Colour management technology forces all of these links in the chain to show colour in the same way, or as near to identical as can be achieved.

If we photograph a bowl of fruit containing a green apple, a yellow lemon and a few red strawberries, the shades of green, yellow and red may differ between real life, what is captured by the camera, what is shown on screen and what is outputted at the end of the digital workflow. Colour management gives each of these devices a profile, which changes each colour in the image slightly so it mimics the photograph's appearance elsewhere in the workflow.

At the start of the colour management chain is the capturing device: usually a camera, but sometimes also a scanner. Cameras have profiles built in to their programming that identify how each sees colour – and the differences between how different makes and models of camera do this can be huge. Fortunately you will never have to encounter the camera's colour profile, as each image is given a working colour profile when it is written to a card as a JPEG file, or converted from a raw file on a computer.

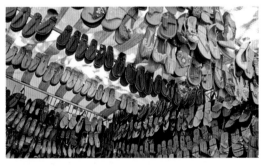
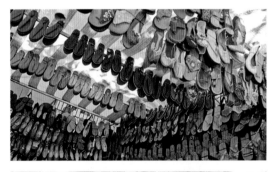
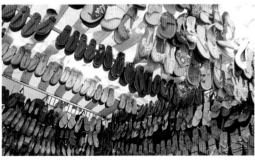
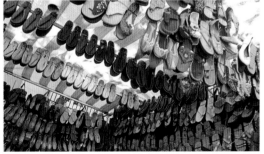

Above: How do you know whether your images look the same on your screen as on other people's screens? Or on paper?

Or in print in a publication? This is where colour management offers a route to more consistent digital images.

A working profile is the colour space in which you will edit pictures on your computer. Two are in common usage: Adobe RGB 1998 and sRGB. You can often set a digital camera to save JPEG files in one of these two profiles, and there are many arguments over which of these provides the best results. These days, however, sRGB has emerged as something of a standard, providing a wide gamut of colours compatible with all manner of devices, from screens and websites to printers and high-street minilabs.

Screen colour profiles

To ensure that the screens we are using to view the image are reproducing the colours of the working space correctly, these are also given a colour profile. This takes each pixel of the image and applies an adjustment to it, so that what we see is the same as exists at every other step along the way. Creating a colour profile for your screen is a vital part of colour management, and is fairly easy to do. In fact, if you adopt just one change from these pages on colour management, creating an accurate screen profile should be it.

A screen profile can be created in a number of ways. The most affordable is to use the software that comes with your operating system or imaging software. Apple users will find an application for doing this in the Displays control panel (under the Colour tab, click Calibrate), while those using Microsoft Windows should look to the Adobe Gamma application that is installed along with Photoshop or Elements.

These applications fine-tune the brightness, white point and colour reproduction of your display, based on your responses to various questions. A profile is produced based on this process that fine-tunes colours in your photography to then see them at the correct brightness and white balance, and with accurate colour reproduction.

Though convenient, calibrating a screen this way is inherently subjective. A screen calibration device can be used for a more objective approach. Such pieces of hardware are relatively inexpensive and work by looking at coloured squares produced on screen by specialist software. Some devices even measure the ambient light in your working surroundings and also take this into account.

Converting from raw into colour spaces

Raw files do not have a colour space attached to them; this is defined at the point where JPEG files are created. This can be in your camera, if you have set it to shoot JPEG files, or in your raw-processing software, if you are shooting raw. With Adobe Camera Raw, the colour space into which your file will be opened is defined in a dialogue accessed through the link at the bottom of the screen. Click this and you can select the colour space from the drop-down menu.

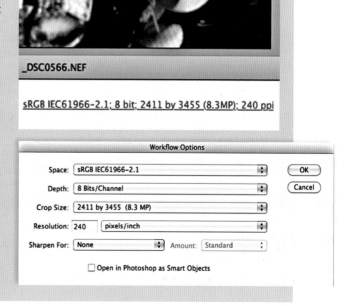

Above right: *ACR shows you the working colour space it will generate at the bottom of the screen. Click it to change this (and other) workflow options.*

Right: *From the Workflow Options box, choose the working colour space from the Space menu.*

Calibrating your screen

An accurately calibrated screen is the foundation of colour management, upon which we can build a completely colour-consistent digital workflow.

By calibrating your computer's screen you can ensure that the colours you see are as near to identical as possible to other people also using calibrated screens. Carrying out such a calibration also means you can be more confident that the colours you are seeing on screen are those that the camera shot and that exist in real life.

Every monitor's make up is different – all of them with their own unique fingerprint. With increasing age, the performance deteriorates due to the LCD cells wearing out. As a result, the colours look different on each monitor but regular calibrating normally helps. Thankfully, calibrating your screen is very easy, thanks to the prevalence of affordable screen calibration devices designed specifically with amateur digital photographers in mind.

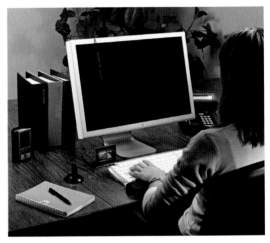

Above: *A screen calibration device will ensure that your screen is calibrated to show the same colours as others using the same equipment.*

Configuring colour settings in Photoshop

There are many ways that Photoshop can handle colour, and these are governed by the application's Color Settings dialogue box (found at the bottom of the Edit menu). Part of colour management is about workflow, and it is here that we can ensure that each picture is treated identically on arrival in Photoshop.

Ignore the CMYK options (this is useful only in the pre-press industry) and set the default RGB working space to sRGB. Also set the RGB colour management policy to 'Convert to Working RGB'. This will ensure that any pictures imported into Photoshop that do not have sRGB as their working colour space are converted into this state.

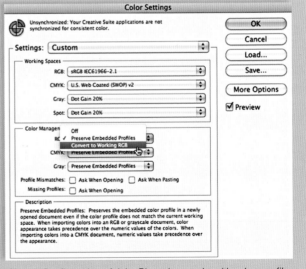

Above: *Configure how Adobe Photoshop works with colour profiles and display prompts in the Color Settings dialogue box.*

Calibrate your screen with a Huey

One of the most popular of these devices is the Huey from X-Rite. It's inexpensive, easy to use, and has useful extra features, such as the ability to calibrate a dual monitor set-up and monitor ambient lighting conditions. Let's have a look how the Huey can be used to calibrate a typical LCD screen in a few easy steps.

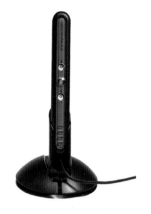

Step 1. Install the software on your computer by following its step-by-step instructions upon launch.

Step 2. Plug in the calibration device and launch the software.

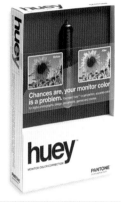

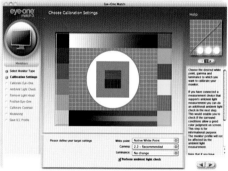

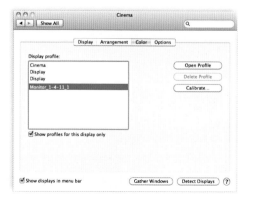

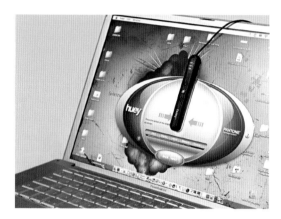

Step 3. The software will guide you through what to do next – put the calibrator on the screen and follow the on-screen instructions.

Step 4. At the end of the calibration process your display should look slightly different, as it will now be using the new profile.

Step 5. The X-Rite software can remind you when next to calibrate your screen. You should do this at least once a month.

Other screen calibration devices

The i1 is made by the same company that makes the Huey, but offers more accurate colour calibration for screens.

Datacolor, another manufacturer in this market, know a great deal about colour management. Their Spyder calibration device has been on the market for a number of years. In its latest update it offers accurate profiling of dual screen set-ups and easy to use software.

Output **colour profiles**

The last link in the colour management chain is to look at the colour profile of the image-displaying device. This could be as specific as the inkjet printer being used to make a hard copy, or as general as the internet, where everyone can have a different set-up on their computer screens.

We've seen that assigning colour profiles to the cameras and displays in our workflow, as well as to the image itself in the form of a working colour space, gives us consistency of colour as we edit. Similarly, at the end of the workflow, profiles are used to ensure that this consistency is carried over into the photograph that others will see, ensuring they have the same viewing experience.

Colour on the web
Much of your photography may be viewed online, or at least on-screen, making colour consistency for your audience difficult to achieve. People sitting at different computers in different rooms (in different countries!) may have very different screens to you, not to mention lighting conditions. How on earth can we take this into account?

Well, you can only do so much. With your online audience all potentially using different displays, we need a common colour profile that is device-independent and that everyone can access. Fortunately we already have this – it's the working colour space in which you edited the image. The sRGB colour space has become the default for online images – in fact, it's the only one that most web browsers support.

Beyond this, however, your viewers have to take some responsibility. They will only see the same colours as you in an sRGB-profile image if they have also calibrated their display, using software

Right: Photoshop and Photoshop Elements' 'Save for Web' command ensures files are saved correctly for the internet. File size, file naming and, of course, colour profiles are all taken care of, with images being converted to the sRGB colour space.

or a screen calibration device. Some websites even make this statement, adding a greyscale bar to help users set the brightness and contrast correctly.

Printing with colour consistency
For many photographers, achieving the same colours in a final print as are displayed on-screen is the holy grail of colour management, but getting this right is quite a challenge. For a start, the way that the two types of image are created is fundamentally different: on-screen images are seen thanks to emitted light from a bright light source; a print is seen using reflected light, that bounces off the surface. This difference is significant enough to make exact colour matching impossible.

However, we can get near enough by making sure our screens are calibrated, using a good working space while editing, and using a print profile when outputting the image to the printer. Like a camera's profile and a screen's profile, a print profile is just another set of figures that describes how another piece of hardware produces numerous standards of colours. When we translate an image into a print profile, we translate its colours so they output as closely as possible to what we see on-screen.

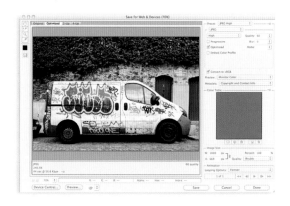

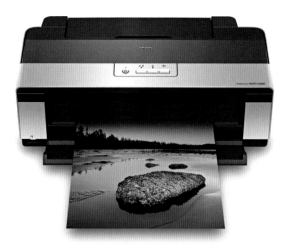

Right: Making prints with colours that match those seen on screen is a tough technical challenge, but is worth it for those wanting the ultimate in print quality.

Set your printer driver to auto colour mode and all of this is taken care of for you behind the scenes, but we can take charge of the profile that is used for more accurate results. We need specific and different print profiles for individual printers as well as different papers, third-party inks (if used) and even different print settings. To measure these profiles yourself you'll need a print profile spectrophotometer, a lot of paper and ink and the patience of a saint, but paper manufacturers often supply profiles that are fine-tuned to their products. You can either download them from their website, or print a target consisting of various square coloured patches and return this to the paper manufacturer (or a third-party service) and have someone else do the hard work of making a print profile for you.

Always remember when you are using a print profile manually to turn off the auto colour settings. If you forget this, the image will be translated twice, and the colours and tones will be far from accurate compared to your screen.

Where should I put colour profiles?

If you are using printer colour profiles that you have made yourself, or that have been supplied by a third party, such as a paper manufacturer, you'll need to put these in the right directory on your computer in order for them to work correctly with your software. This location differs from computer to computer, depending on how old it is and what type of operating system you are using.

For Windows 7, Vista and XP
Copy profiles into the directory \windows\ system32\spool\drivers\color. You can use the colour control panel applet to copy to this location for you, or in Windows XP, right-click the file icon and select Install Profile.

Windows 2000 or NT
Copy profiles into the directory \winnt\ system32\spool\drivers\color.

Right: A selection of ICC colour profiles installed on an Apple Mac running the OS X operating system.

Apple Mac OS X
Storing colour profiles in the directory /Library/ ColorSync/Profiles allows all users of the computer to access them. If you don't have administrator privileges, try /Users/[username]/Library/ ColorSync/Profiles. Anything stored here will only be visible to that user.

CAMERA CALIBRATION WITH AN X-RITE COLOUR PASSPORT

Calibrating your camera for colour used to be a terribly complicated business, but a new breed of affordable colour targets is making the process much easier.

It can be argued that, if you want a colour-accurate digital workflow, then you need to start at the beginning of the image-making process and create a colour profile for your camera. Most of the time this is probably overkill, but if you need to produce colours that are as true to life as possible, then shooting in raw and using a custom-made colour profile is the way forward.

This used to be a very difficult thing to do, but a new breed of easy-to-use camera calibration products are making the whole process a lot more simple. One such product is the ColorChecker Passport from X-Rite. This affordable solution comes in two parts: a robust colour calibration chart comprising a number of standardized coloured squares in a tough plastic case, and some very clever software that finds the calibration chart in any picture and uses the known standards to produce a colour profile specifically for the camera lens and lighting in use.

The software comes in two forms: a stand-alone application and a plug-in for Adobe's Lightroom raw-processing software. To use the stand-alone application you'll need to be producing DNG raw files; use Adobe's DNG converter to convert your camera's raw files to this format (www.adobe.com/dng). The Lightroom plug-in works with all raw files supported by Adobe Camera Raw.

After installing the X-Rite software, the ColorChecker is easy to use. Let's see how it helps achieve more accurate colours in this still-life photograph of an orchid, using the Adobe Lightroom plug-in.

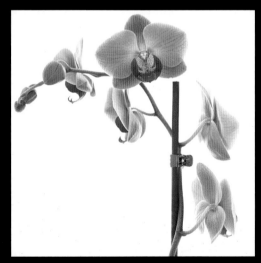

Above: *In this unprocessed image, colours appear too bleached and light.*

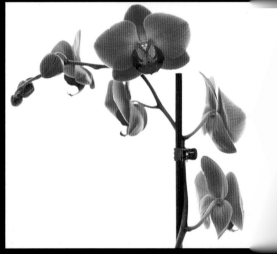

Above: *Colours in the image processed with the ColorChecker Passport profile are more true to life.*

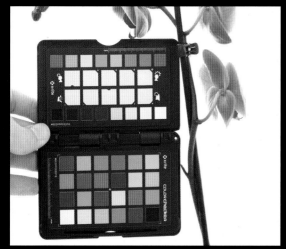

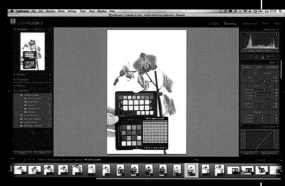

Step 1. *The image of the orchid isn't bad, but the colour of the petals isn't very true to life (they are more purple than pink). The stems are not green in real life either – they are brown. Shooting a frame with the ColorChecker Passport card in the shot will let us create a colour profile for the camera being used that should help to achieve better results.*

Step 2. *In Adobe Lightroom, choose the frame containing the colour target and set the white balance by clicking on one of the grey colour-neutral squares in the colour checker target. You should see an instant improvement already, with the colours shifting to appear more true to life.*

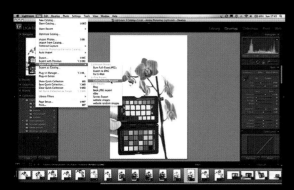

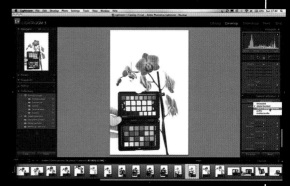

Step 3. *For even more colour accuracy select File > Export With Preset > ColorChecker Passport. Behind the scenes, Lightroom will export the image to the ColorChecker software, which will create a new camera colour profile based on the standards in the target.*

Step 4. *When this is complete you'll be instructed to quit and restart Lightroom so the software can read the new profile. Once this is complete you'll find the new profile listed in the Profile menu in the application's Camera Calibration tab.*

Correcting with **curves**

Curves might look complicated on first inspection, but they are simply levels adjustments taken to the next stage. Master them, and you'll never look back.

The Levels tool provides us with a powerful and intuitive way to adjust the tones in an image. We can use a levels adjustment to selectively boost shadows, highlights or mid-tones, and even make these corrections in individual colour channels to fix or introduce colour casts in an image. But what if instead of just three points on the x-axis you could adjust the tones anywhere in the image? This is the basic premise of the curves adjustment.

How curves work

Bring up the curves dialogue by choosing Image > Adjustments > Curves. You'll see a graph with a greyscale on both the x and y axes, and a straight diagonal line going through the middle of it. The greyscale on the bottom of the graph represents the tones in the image as they are at the moment, while the greyscale on the left-hand y-axis represents the tones that will be in the image after the adjustment has been made.

Pick any brightness level on the x-axis and move up in a straight line until you hit the diagonal line. Now change direction and move out to the y-axis. The brightness level you hit should be the same, because the line is straight and no adjustments have been made yet. But by changing the shape of the line into a curve we can change the point of impact on the y-axis, and hence the tone of the image at exactly this point.

For instance, pushing up the curve at the top right-hand end makes the light tones in a photograph even lighter, while leaving the other areas untouched. Conversely, pulling the curve

1. Output tones
Brightness levels in the photograph after the curves adjustment has been made.

2. Input tones
Brightness levels already in the photograph before the curves adjustment is applied.

3. Channel menu
Select the colour channel to be changed by the adjustment.

4. Eyedroppers
Choose bright, dark or midpoints by clicking on the image.

5. Options
Here you can save presets for future use as well as load already saved curve settings and default curves.

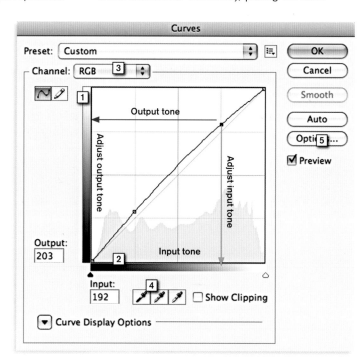

Curves in Lightroom

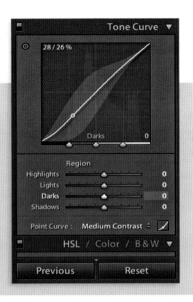

Adobe Lightroom provides a Tone Curve adjustment in the Develop module, but the number of points you can actually adjust is limited to four: Shadows, Darks, Lights and Highlights. You can also take a slider-based approach to this adjustment, adjusting the same four settings with the controls below the curve, or click on parts of the image with the target tool. Lightroom will adjust the tone curve point closest to that part of the image.

Right: A curves adjustment is available in Adobe Lightroom, too, but it is less precise than the tool in the main Photoshop application, with only four adjustment points available.

downwards in this region makes them darker. The same applies at the lower left-hand end of the scale, where darker tones are defined. In fact, by pushing up the highlights end of the curve, while also pulling down the shadow end, you will boost contrast in a picture. Raising or lowering the middle of the curve slightly will affect the mid-tones.

You don't have to make massive curves adjustments to achieve the right effect – in fact, over-correcting an image using curves will cause problems. It is much better to use small movements, and be aware that general shapes cause certain effects.

As with many other adjustments in Photoshop and Elements, you can create presets of your favourite settings, and indeed Adobe have provided some to get you started in the Preset drop-down menu.

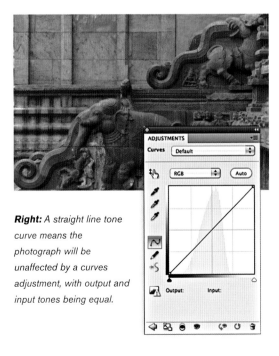

Right: A straight line tone curve means the photograph will be unaffected by a curves adjustment, with output and input tones being equal.

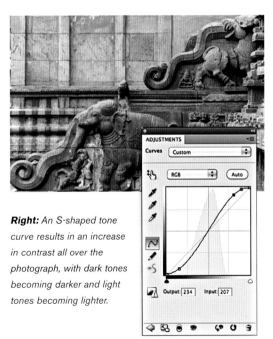

Right: An S-shaped tone curve results in an increase in contrast all over the photograph, with dark tones becoming darker and light tones becoming lighter.

Curves recipes

More important than thinking about exactly which tonal value is mapped onto which during a curves adjustment is the general shape of the curve being used. Such shapes are characteristic of the effect that they apply to a photograph, and knowing which shape does what can save you a lot of time when editing for brightness and tones.

For instance, an S-shaped curve increases contrast, since it makes tones at the dark end of the scale darker, while those at the light end become lighter. Unsurprisingly, an inverted S-shape curve has the opposite effect, lowering contrast throughout a picture

While it's useful to know a handful of such shapes off by heart, you can also save some as presets in the Curves dialogue. Do this by clicking the small palette menu symbol next to the Preset drop-down menu and giving each a memorable name. Adobe has already provided some for you to be getting on with.

Let's have a look at some commonly used recipes involving different curve shapes and see what effect they have on a photograph.

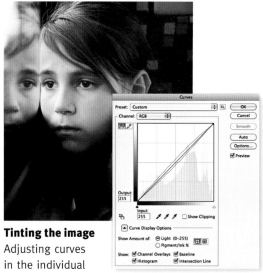

Tinting the image
Adjusting curves in the individual colour channels introduces or neutralizes a colour cast, according to the same principles as apply to Levels (see pages 246–247) and Colour Balance (see page 254). Depending on what part of the curve you adjust, the colour tint applies more to the shadows, mid-tones or highlights and works the same when applied to duotones.

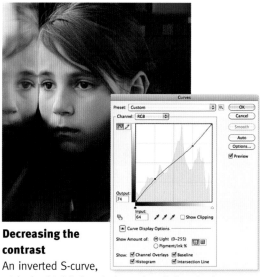

Increasing the contrast
An subtle S-shaped curve, with the highlights brightened and the shadows darkened, increases the general contrast in the image. You should also, of course, try out some of the contrast presets supplied under the Preset drop-down menu. Again, these can be modified manually.

Decreasing the contrast
An inverted S-curve, with the highlights darkened and the shadows brightened, decreases contrast in the image. This can sometimes be helpful when you want to rescue dark parts in an image that have lost a lot of detail due to the wrong conversion from raw, or wrong exposure or ISO setting.

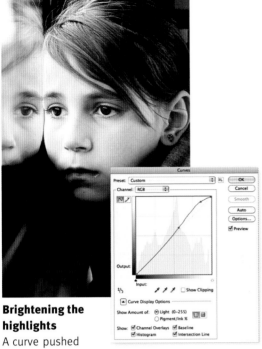

Brightening the highlights

A curve pushed up at the right-hand end boosts light tones while keeping shadows as they are.

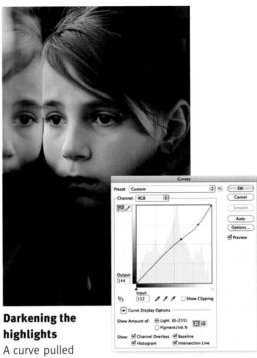

Darkening the highlights

A curve pulled down at the right-hand end darkens light tones while keeping shadows as they are.

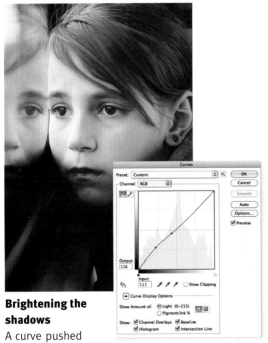

Brightening the shadows

A curve pushed up at the left-hand end lightens dark areas while preserving highlights.

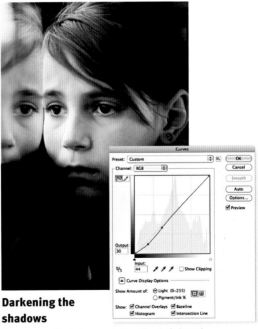

Darkening the shadows

A curve pulled down at the the left-hand end darkens shadow areas while leaving highlights unchanged.

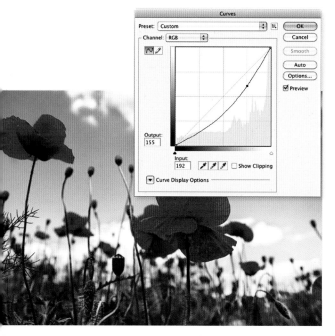

Adjusting curves by clicking on the image

If you don't know what part of the image corresponds to what point on the curve, you can define and adjust points on the curve simply by clicking on, or hovering over, the image. When you bring up the Curves dialogue, the pointer changes to an eyedropper by default. Click anywhere on the image and a point will appear on the curve corresponding to that brightness level. By ctrl+alt/⌘+alt-clicking you can add the point at this position, so you make adjustments by dragging it around with your mouse or hitting the cursor arrow keys. A similar action is brought about with

Left and below: Exactly the right point on the tone curve to lighten the blue sky was found by ⌘+alt-clicking (ctrl+alt-clicking) on the sky. This placed a corresponding point on the curve that could be adjusted by eye until the right shade of blue was found.

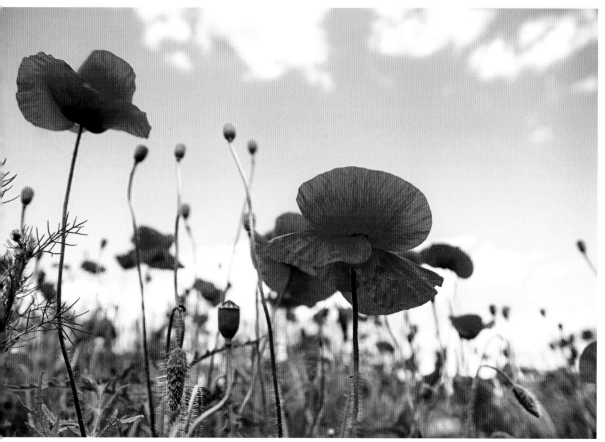

the tool that looks like a finger with an up–down arrow next to it. Click this and you can click on the image to define a curve adjustment point while also dragging up and down to adjust the curve – great when working quickly.

Also present along the bottom edge of the histogram display are three eyedroppers. These operate in the same way as in the levels adjustment dialogue box, defining the lightest and darkest points in each colour channel, or the composite RGB channel, as well as the mid-grey neutral value. Be aware that by default these operate individually in all three channels, and so can cause a colour shift if you click anything other than a colour-neutral part of the picture.
Also present is the 'Show Clipping' option, which shows parts of the picture that will be pushed out of range (blown highlights or clipped shadows) by the adjustment. The same thing can be activated momentarily when using the eyedroppers by holding down the alt key.

Histograms and the levels adjustment

Even though curves has been in Photoshop since version one, it still gets updates from time to time. A few Photoshop versions ago, a histogram was added to the background of the graph display, which can be very useful if you don't quite know where you want to adjust the curve. Put very simply, adjusting the curve in a part of the histogram where there is lots of pixel data will

have more effect on the photograph than adjusting in an area where there is little or no data.

Contrast is dictated by the gradient of a curve, and you can enhance contrast selectively by altering the gradient in one section of the tonal range only. The histogram is useful in this situation as it lets you see where the changes you are making will lie. Are they matching the mid-tones properly? Or a collection of bright tones coinciding with an area in the picture?

Below and bottom left: Pay attention to the histogram in the Curves dialogue box; it's telling you where to adjust the curve. Making a change where there is no histogram data will not result in a change, whereas adjusting the curve's gradient where there are most pixels will have a huge effect.

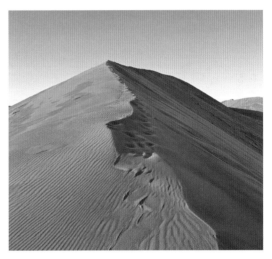

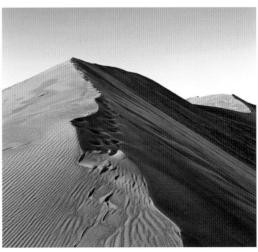

DIGITAL LITH PRINTING

Some old-fashioned darkroom techniques have a lingering appeal, even in this modern digital age. The lith print is a notoriously difficult thing to get right traditionally, but much easier when recreated in Adobe Photoshop.

Lith printing is an old black and white photographic printing technique used in traditional wet-chemical darkrooms. By over-exposing the print and using weak, diluted chemicals, it is possible to produce a very grainy, high-contrast image with characteristically deep shadows and soft, bright highlights. Lith printing is a very difficult thing to do well, as well as being very unpredictable, but in the digital darkroom things are completely different, as here we have a lot more control over the outcome. Photoshop makes the effect easier to achieve and completely reproducible.

You will soon get a feel for which images are right for this sort of treatment. To simulate a lith print in Photoshop, we have to break down the image into its highlights and shadows and then treat each area individually, and differently. Once we have done that, we will be able to combine them again to achieve the final result.

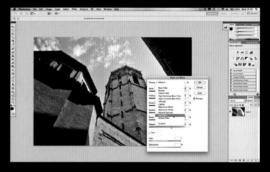

Step 1. *In Photoshop, convert your image to monochrome by choosing Image > Adjust > Black & White... We've used a preset here to darken the sky slightly.*

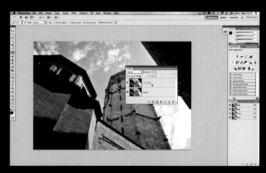

Step 2. *Rename the background layer by double-clicking it and typing in the new name 'Shadows'. Duplicate this and call the new layer 'Highlights'.*

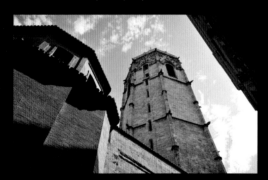

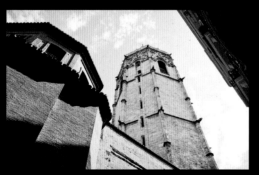

ESSENTIAL KIT

- PC or Mac
- Adobe Photoshop

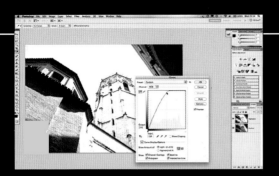

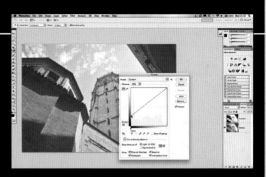

Step 3. *With the Highlights layer active, choose Image >
Adjustments > Curves and push up the top of the curve so
the highlights burn out and become bright white. You'll see
this happen live if you have the Preview box ticked.*

Step 4. *Switch off the Highlights layer by clicking the eye
icon next to it. Select the Shadows layer and apply another
curves adjustment, raising the left end of the curve to give the
image less shadow contrast.*

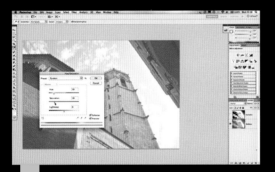

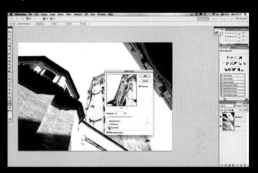

Step 5. *With the Shadows layer still active, apply a sepia
tone by choosing Image > Adjustments > Hue/Saturation.
Tick the 'Colorize' box and choose a yellow colour.*

Step 6. *Click on the eye icon to show the Highlights layer.
Add noise by choosing Filter > Noise > Add Noise... Apply
Unsharp Mask with a larger radius – five or six pixels.*

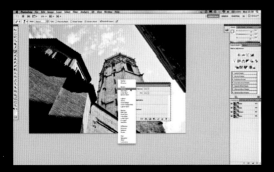

TIPS & TRICKS

- The same effect can be achieved with levels if
  you don't want to mess about with curves.

- Use curves adjustment layers for a non-
  destructive approach.

- This effect suits subjects that are low in contrast
  and light in tone to start with.

- Try saving an action of the steps and apply it to
  different images to see how the approach works
  for different tonal ranges.

- This can be a great way to lift a black and white
  conversion that is looking a bit flat.

Step 7. *Finally, merge the two layers by changing the
blending mode to Multiply. Apply a final curves adjustment
if the overall brightness needs a tweak.*

Sharpening

Sharpening is an important part of photography, whether in-camera or in Photoshop, and is something every photographer needs to be aware of.

Owing to the way they are captured, all digital images need sharpening at some point in the workflow. In front of your camera's sensor a piece of glass called a low-pass filter removes artefacts such as coloured fringing and moire effects (swirls seen in detailed materials such as fabric), but this has the side effect of softening the image slightly. To overcome this, electronic sharpening algorithms are used to give the appearance of increased sharpness. This can happen in-camera as part of the process by which JPEG files are made, or afterwards in your imaging software if you shoot raw.

What is sharpness?

To understand how digital sharpening works, it's helpful to ask ourselves what sharpness is. The term can actually be broken down into two terms: resolution and acutance.

Resolution is the amount of detail that can be captured in a photograph. This is governed by the number of pixels on the camera's chip and the resolving power of the lens in use. Although digital photographers generally think of pixels when they hear the word 'resolution', the quality of your lens is equally as important. A 100-megapixel camera cannot resolve any more detail than what is projected onto it by the lens being used.

Acutance is best defined as the change in brightness that occurs across an edge. The higher the contrast across an edge, the more the edge will stand out and the sharper it will seem. More edge-contrast gives a more abrupt change from light to dark, and the appearance of increased sharpness.

Below: Of the two components of sharpness, resolution determines how many leaves and branches we can see on these trees; acutance governs how sharp they look.

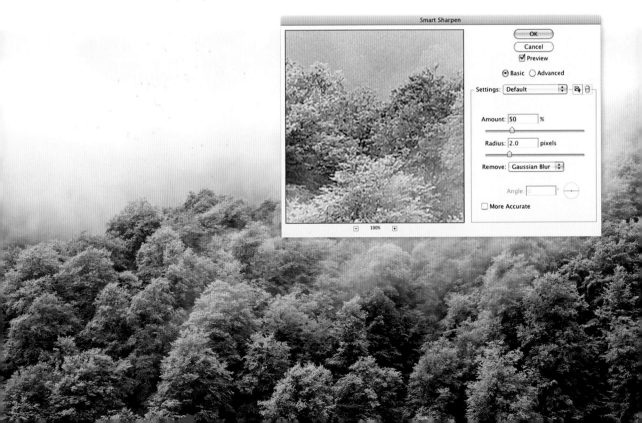

It is acutance, and not resolution, that is enhanced in digital sharpening processes. It's important to keep this in mind: applying digital sharpening cannot increase the level of detail you capture, only its appearance.

Unsharp Mask

The most common form of digital sharpening is confusingly called Unsharp Mask – a technique that inherits its name from a traditional wet-chemical darkroom printing technique. This is the algorithm that has been used by digital cameras, scanners and imaging software for years, and it works well in most cases.

In most imaging software, including Photoshop and Elements, Unsharp Mask (USM) has three controls: Amount, Radius and Threshold. These all perform different functions, but it's important to use them together to get the right result.

Amount

Once the USM filter finds an edge in a picture, the Amount control defines how much contrast is enhanced from one side of the edge to the other. A good starting point is 100 per cent, and you can't do too much damage by varying this value between 50 and 150 per cent.

Radius

The Radius control defines how far either side of an edge the sharpening effect should extend. The higher the value, the more pixels are affected and the more pronounced the sharpening effect. The correct radius value depends on the picture's output resolution. An edge in a small 600 x 600 pixel photo for the web has fewer pixels than a 3,000 x 3,000 pixel image for print. As a rule of thumb, a good radius value can be determined by taking the output resolution and dividing it by 200. For a print at 300ppi, the correct radius is around 1.5; for a screen resolution image at 96ppi about 0.5 is right. Using a radius that is too high results in artefacts and poor image quality.

Threshold

We only want sharpening to apply to areas in a picture where there is edge detail, and sometimes there is more subtle detail that we don't want sharpened. The Threshold slider can be used to tell the USM filter to not sharpen edges unless they already have a certain level of acutance. A value of zero means the filter will sharpen everything. A value of ten means that if the pixels across an edge are less than ten brightness levels apart, they will be left alone – good for getting USM to leave alone areas of continuous tone, like smooth blue skies.

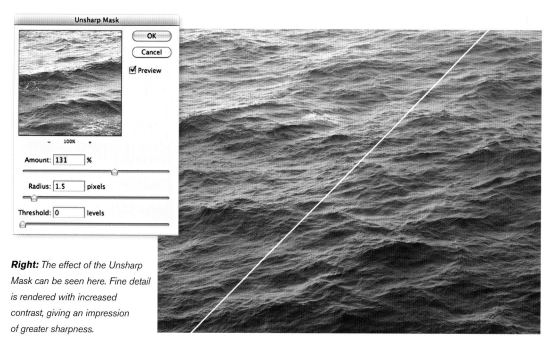

Right: *The effect of the Unsharp Mask can be seen here. Fine detail is rendered with increased contrast, giving an impression of greater sharpness.*

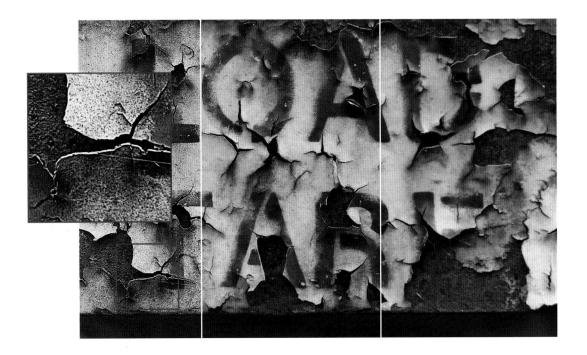

Too much sharpness

Although at first it sounds strange, it is possible to over-sharpen a photograph. Over-the-top application of the USM filter, particularly the Radius control, leads to ugly halos around objects. This is a very common fault in the work of novice photographers, and cannot be undone once it's been applied.

To be sure you are applying the right amount of sharpening, save an unsharpened version that you can sharpen before you print or save for the web. These two forms of output require different radius values when performing sharpening.

Always apply sharpening while viewing the image at 100 per cent, so you can see any halos forming, and don't be afraid of not applying any sharpening at all: not all pictures need it, especially JPEGs straight from the camera.

Smart sharpness

Despite the ubiquitous nature of USM in imaging software and hardware, a refinement to this filter exists in the form of the Smart Sharpen filter in

Right: Photoshop's Smart Sharpen filter gives more control over which areas are sharpened and enables photographers to control artefacts such as dark or bright halos.

Above: The region on the left has been oversharpened and shows unsightly halos around high-contrast edges. The central region is normally sharpened and the right-hand region is not sharpened, and lacks some punch and bite.

Photoshop (Filters > Sharpen > Smart Sharpen...) and the Enhance Sharpness function in Photoshop Elements (Enhance > Adjust Sharpness...). These offer increased performance over the basic USM by offering a choice of the type of blur algorithm that is used in the sharpening process. Choosing 'Lens Blur' from the drop-down menu forces the filter to concentrate on those parts of a picture that need

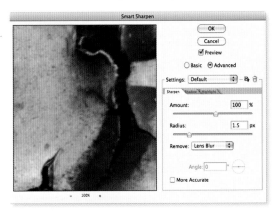

sharpening – namely the edges – and leave areas of continuous tone alone. In theory, this means skin tones and blue skies will not be sharpened, whereas hair and tree details will be.

Choosing 'Gaussian Blur' from the 'Remove' drop-down menu forces the filter to act in the same way as USM. Finally there is a 'Motion Blur' option, which tries to reduce camera shake. This rarely works well, though it's worth trying if you've got a small amount of blur spoiling a photograph.

A few extra options are available for combatting artefacts. These are accessed by clicking the Advanced Radius button, which causes two tabs called Shadow and Highlight to appear. Under these tabs you'll find controls for minimizing halos. These take on a white or black appearance depending on where they are in the image, hence the need for the two approaches.

The Shadow and Highlight controls work in the same way: the Tonal Width and Radius sliders determine what is classed as an artefact, with the former specifying the range of tones considered and the latter the distance (in pixels) over which artefacts are searched for. Once artefacts are found, the Amount slider specifies the amount by which the halos are reduced. Using these controls means more aggressive sharpening can be applied, when required, and the artefacts brought back into line.

Alternative approaches to sharpening

There are some tips and tricks that can be used to apply sharpening in different ways than the usual USM and Smart Sharpen filters. Some are useful when the traditional techniques are just not working on a photograph.

LAB channel sharpening
Flip over from RGB to LAB colour mode (Image > Mode > Lab Color). The LAB colour mode describes the image in terms of a lightness channel (L) and two colour channels (A and B), instead of three colour channels (R, G and B). Applying sharpening to just the Lightness channel avoids the presence of coloured artefacts. Make sure the channels palette is showing (Window > Channels) and click on just the Lightness channel. The image will turn black and white. Apply sharpening to this in the usual way with USM or Smart Sharpen, then flip back to RGB for the rest of the editing.

Sharpening with a low-pass layer
To take control of the sharpening process completely, duplicate the layer in which the image is currently sitting by choosing Layer > Duplicate Layer... and apply the High Pass filter to this new layer (Filters > High Pass...). Experiment with the radius value, which has the same effect as the radius in USM. Start with a value of 1.5. Click OK to apply the filter then change the blending mode of the new high-pass filter to Overlay (you'll find the blending mode drop-down menu in the Layers palette). If the effect is too strong, you can fade it with the Opacity slider (also in the Layers palette).

Below: Sharpening just the lightness channel in LAB mode decreases the number of coloured artefacts introduced by the sharpening process.

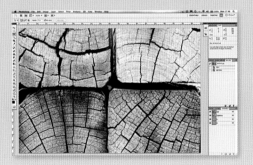
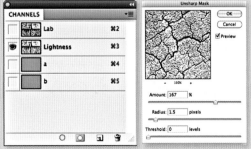

Resizing images

You'll often encounter the need to resize images based on how you are going to use them. This might be to make them smaller for websites or email, or larger for printing on a larger scale.

Resizing images is not the most glamorous post-production skill you will ever learn, but it is one of the most important. There are many instances when you will need to output images at a specific size, for example when uploading to websites that have a maximum pixel or file size. You might even need to increase the size of a photograph, too, and know when to stop when doing this so as not to spoil image quality.

The most commonly used method of resizing images in Photoshop is the application's Image › Image Resize command. In this dialogue you can change the trade-off between physical size (cm, inches, etc.) and resolution (pixels per cm, pixels per inch, etc.), as well as change the actual pixel count of the images. To do the latter you'll need to

make sure the Resample Image box is ticked. This will enable you to enter new pixel dimensions into the width and height boxes. You can also change these units to a percentage, which can be easier to understand when resizing an image relatively.

So, for example, if a website is asking for images no larger than 1,000 pixels along the longest edge, enter 1,000 in the width or height box (depending on the orientation of the image) and click OK. Your image will resize and you'll see the new physical file size in megabytes in the bottom left of the window.

The method by which Photoshop changes image size can be changed from the drop-down menu in the Image Resize dialogue. Choose 'Bicubic Sharper' when making a file smaller in order to retain as much image quality as possible.

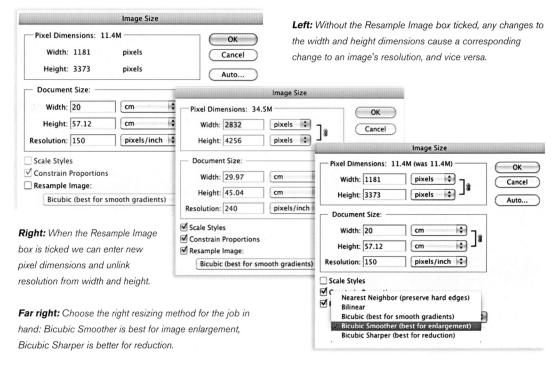

Left: Without the Resample Image box ticked, any changes to the width and height dimensions cause a corresponding change to an image's resolution, and vice versa.

Right: *When the Resample Image box is ticked we can enter new pixel dimensions and unlink resolution from width and height.*

Far right: *Choose the right resizing method for the job in hand: Bicubic Smoother is best for image enlargement, Bicubic Sharper is better for reduction.*

Right: One of Photoshop's hidden secrets: the Image
Processor enables you to resize multiple files in one go as a
batch process, renaming them along the way if needed.

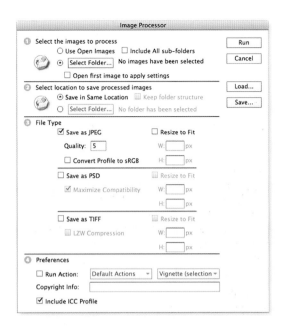

Interpolation and increasing file size

As well as decreasing an image's size, you can
also increase it, boosting the pixel count. Simply
type a larger value into the width and height
boxes in the Image Resize dialogue box, and
select 'Bicubic Smoother' for the best results.

Before you get too excited about increasing
the size of images in this way, it's important
to point out that you can't get the quality of a
20-megapixel camera from a 10-megapixel camera
by doing this. Just because the number of pixels
in the image is greater does not mean that there
will be a corresponding increase in resolution.
Images are increased in size by a process called
interpolation, which involves inserting artificial
pixels that have been made up by Photoshop
based on neighbouring pixels. Interpolation is
useful for increasing an image's file size by up to
50 per cent, but print at sizes any greater than
this and you'll start to see image quality problems.

Automating the process

Imagine for a moment that you have 20 or
so images to resize to precise dimensions,
perhaps for upload to a website. It's a big job
going in and changing each one by hand, and
there is always the possibility that you might
key in a wrong number and make a mistake.
What you need here is Photoshop's Image
Processor. You'll find this under File > Scripts
> Image Processor; the interface is pretty
straightforward to get your head around.
Go through sections one to four, specifying
where your images are, where they will end
up, what you want to happen to them and any
preferences you may have. Click OK and the
image processor will go through all the
images for you while you put your feet up.

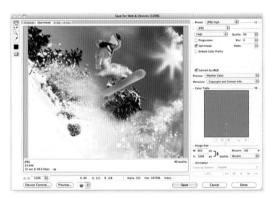

Above: The Save for Web dialogue allows you to choose pixel
dimensions or specify a physical file size.

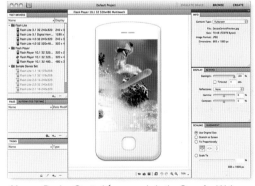

Above: Device Central (accessed via the Save for Web
function) makes saving for devices like smart phones easier.

ASSIGNMENT
SHARPENING IN PORTRAITS

Sometimes we only want to sharpen the features that matter, and leave the others alone. Let's see how it can be done using Photoshop's History Brush.

In portraiture, we often don't want to sharpen all of the features in an image, but rather only those that matter. For instance, your subject's eyes are often the main focus of the picture, and these can look better with a bit of sharpening. On the other hand, sharpening does not do skin any favours, enhancing wrinkles and pores.

A way around this is to apply sharpening selectively to only part of the picture. There are a couple of ways of doing this, and here we'll look at how to use the History Brush and Unsharp Mask filter to sharpen only parts of the picture. You could also use multiple layers and layer masking techniques, which we'll look at in more detail on pages 350–351.

Below: *The original image is already nice and clear, but we want to bring out the characteristic detail a little.*

Below: *We have selectively sharpened eyes and hair, but not the skin, which we want to keep very smooth.*

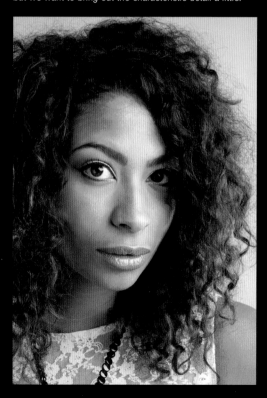

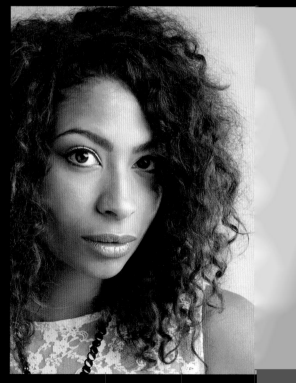

TIPS & TRICKS

- It can be quicker to undo the sharpening effect by stepping back in history, then reapply the effect to the areas where it's needed. Do this by selecting the sharpened history states as the brush's source.

- Use a small, soft-edged brush for the smaller details. You can also reduce the opacity of the History Brush using the Opacity slider in the Info bar to apply reduced strength sharpening where you want to keep it softer.

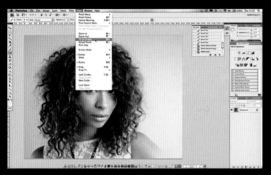

Step 1. Open the image you want to work on into Photoshop or Photoshop Elements and zoom it up to fill the screen.

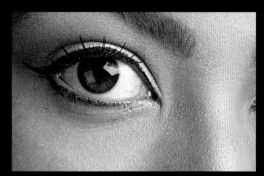

Step 4. The effect is good, but is not very flattering. We can selectively undo this with the History Brush tool.

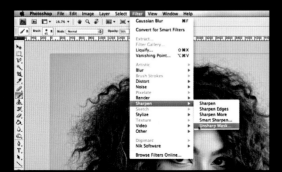

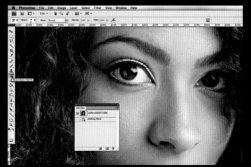

Cloning and healing

The Clone tool is one of the most useful Photoshop tools there is for the digital retoucher, allowing us to copy pixels from one part of an image to another. Along with its counterpart, the Healing Brush, this lets us move objects around the frame, or even remove them altogether.

The basic premise of the Clone Stamp tool is a simple one: it copies pixels from one place to another. Set a source location in a photograph and you can paint pixels from it over the top of details elsewhere. With clever selection of the source area, you'll soon find you can eliminate unwanted details so convincingly that no one will ever know they were there.

For instance, let's imagine you get back home after a hard day shooting and notice a plastic bag in the foreground of one of your shots. Or an electricity cable or aircraft vapour trail in the sky. Don't despair: the Clone Stamp tool lets you copy some grass or sky over the top of the offending item, hiding it from view in just a few mouse clicks.

The Clone Stamp is pretty easy to use, too. First, alt-click on the image to define where you are going to clone pixels from – this is the source point. Now paint normally and you'll notice that what you are painting is the image from under the source point, which moves about to match what you are painting. All the usual brush features apply – opacity, brush size, edge hardness, etc. – and these can be adjusted from the Brush palette, the Options bar at the top of the screen or through the ever-useful keyboard shortcuts] and [for size, and shift-] and shift-[for edge hardness. A graphics tablet is really handy here for detailed work, and pressure sensitive tablets can be programmed to change size, opacity or hardness in response to pressure.

Below: This is a good image to try and clone out something undesirable. Cloning is most successful where the background is plain or a little textured, but without distinctive patterns.

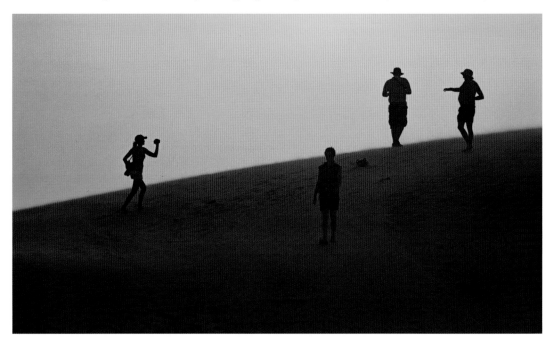

Choosing sources

Successful cloning depends on good selection of the source location. Look for somewhere of the same brightness and colour, as well as the same texture and pattern. In the Options bar you'll notice a tick box marked 'Aligned'. With this checked, the source location will move to follow the Clone Stamp tool itself while painting, and also remember its location when you lift off the mouse button momentarily. With this box un-ticked, the source location resets to the point it was first defined every time you lift your finger off the mouse.

The Clone Source palette (Window › Clone Source) contains even more options, specifically the ability to store four different source locations at one time. This means you don't have to lose one source point when you sample another area of the picture. Below this are options to manually set the offset distance between the source and painting cursors, and perhaps more usefully, the scale with which the material will be cloned. You can even choose to rotate the pixels through an angle.

Below: Cloning sky and sand from one part of the image to another has left us with just one person instead of four.

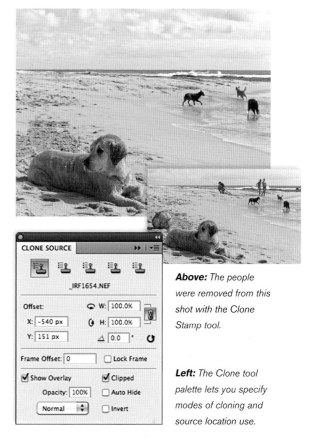

Above: The people were removed from this shot with the Clone Stamp tool.

Left: The Clone tool palette lets you specify modes of cloning and source location use.

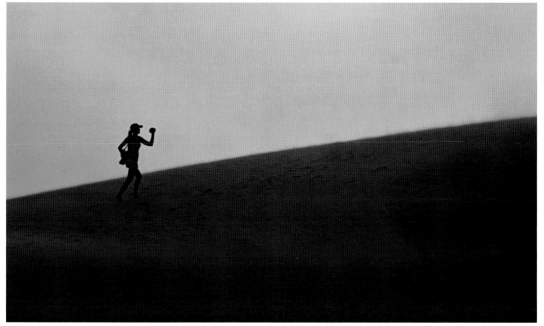

Healing and patching

We've seen that the success of a cloning operation often relies on the quality of the source material being copied, but what do you do if there just isn't the right type of area to clone from? This is where the Healing Brush comes in – an evolution of the Clone Stamp tool that looks at the source destination differently, separating the texture, colour and luminance (brightness) information. When this is painted into a new location, the texture from the source destination is merged with the colour and luminosity of the new location, making it much easier to get a seamless result. A small area outside the region that is painted is also used by Photoshop or Elements in the calculation, which is why you might notice some smudging when getting close to contrasting regions. Best stay away from these and tidy it up afterwards with the conventional Brush tool.

The Healing tool really is a revelation when it comes to airbrushing-out unwanted detail. The technology can be applied to lighting stands or the background edges in studio shots, unwanted objects or people in landscapes and architectural photos – even reflections and shadows in still-life pictures. Plus, of course, fashion and beauty work where spots, pimples and wrinkles can all be cloned and healed away to leave flawless skin.

The Patch tool does a similar job, although the method of applying it is slightly different. Intended to help with large areas, the Patch tool lets you draw a selection around the object (you can do this with the Patch tool itself, or with any of the Lasso or Marquee tools) and then drag that selection to another part of the picture where you want to sample texture from. Again, only texture is copied, and is merged with the colour and brightness at the destination.

Below left: There is lots going on in this busy scene, which is a good practice image for our healing and patching skills.
Below: Some of the tourists have now been removed using the Healing Brush and patch tools, a good approach in images where the manual Clone Stamp might prove difficult.

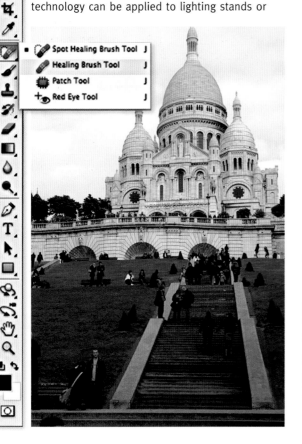

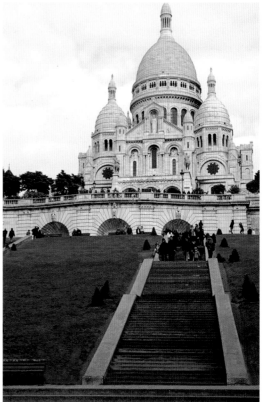

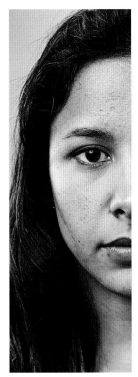
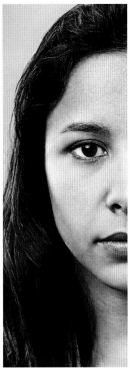

Above: *The Spot Healing Brush is perfect for eliminating spots, pimples and freckles, and smoothing skin to eliminate wrinkles and skin texture. You may also have to use the Clone Stamp and Healing Brush tools to get the perfect result, but the Spot Healing Brush can save a lot of time.*

The Spot Healing Brush

Like the normal Healing Brush, the Spot Healing Brush is a texture replacement tool that attempts to replace texture in one area with that from another, while leaving colour and brightness alone. Where the Healing Brush (and indeed the Clone Stamp tool) need us to tell them where to take this new texture from, the Spot Healing Brush makes its own mind up. Click on a problem area and the tool looks for texture from the areas immediately surrounding the painted area, and uses this as a source automatically. Most of the time it works very well, working very effectively on spots and blemishes – as the name implies. It isn't designed to tackle large problem areas, however, and these are best approached with the Clone Stamp, Healing Brush and patch tools.

There are a few parameters you can set in the Options bar at the top of the screen. Try changing the blending mode to 'Lighten' and Photoshop will only replace pixels that are darker than the normal skin tone, which most spots are. Also present are the 'Proximity Match' and 'Create Texture' modes. By default the brush works in Proximity Match mode, where it searches the surrounding edge of the painted area for texture. If this doesn't work, and gives you a bad result, flip over to Create Texture instead, which searches the entire painted region.

Lightroom ACR and healing

Cloning and healing technology is not just native to Photoshop, it is even built in to the raw converters in Adobe Camera Raw and Adobe Lightroom. In ACR, the spot removal tool allows you to draw circles around small objects that need to be removed, with Clone or Heal selectable as options from the drop-down menu on the right. In Lightroom the facilities are the same, and are available at the top of the Develop module.

Size the brush appropriately to cover the offending blemish, and click it once to apply the brush. The software will place a corresponding circle a small distance away where it will take texture from, in the case of healing, or copy from, if clone is selected.

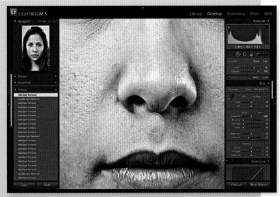

Above: *Healing and cloning works slightly differently in Lightroom. Click to drop a circle over the offending blemish; a second circle will move to the side, which defines the source location where information is copied from.*

Tricky situations and advanced techniques

You'll find yourself cloning and healing in all areas of your digital workflow, but there are some situations where using these tools is harder than others. But with some experience, and these hints and tips, you'll find your way out of most sticky situations.

Smudging when using the Healing tool

Get too close to another object when working with the Healing Brush, and you'll notice it smudge into the area being edited. This is because the Healing Brush uses some information from around the edges of the painted area when it is working out what colour and luminosity to use. To fix the issue, draw a selection around the area being edited with the Marquee tool, blocking off the object causing the problem. Feather this by two pixels and use the Healing tool as you would normally. The selection will stop the brush smudging.

Avoiding repeating patterns

It's common to see repeating patterns in areas that have been painted on with multiple cloning operations. This can be avoided by frequently reselecting (alt-clicking) the source area.

Work at high magnification

When carrying out detailed cloning work, view the image at high magnification so you can see what you are doing properly. Don't be afraid of zooming up beyond 100 per cent. The image will appear blocky, as you are viewing pixels bigger than they actually are, but you can keep zooming out to check the cloning is looking good on a more normal scale.

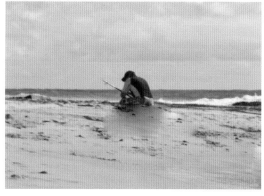

Above: When using the Healing tool, it's common to see smudges when working near high-contrast edges.

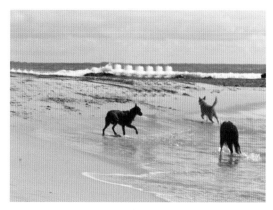

Above: Avoid repeating patterns in cloned areas by continuing to sample from new locations.

Below: Work precisely and slowly, viewing the image at high magnification for the most accuracy.

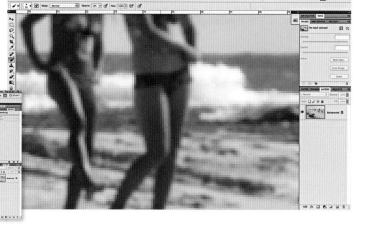

Using cloning and healing together

Often it's not a case of working out which of these tools is best for a certain job – they are complementary and can be used together. For instance, where the Healing Brush will struggle to cover a large area, you can use the Clone Stamp tool to cover things as best you can, then smooth out the differences with the Healing Brush or Patch tool afterwards.

Moving objects, not just covering them up

The Clone tool is not just for removing objects – it can move them, too. For instance you might want a person present in the foreground of an architectural shot but not quite in the place they were shot. Choose the person as a clone source and paint them in somewhere else, then delete them from the original location by cloning background over the top.

Clone overlay options

By default the source detail is shown underneath the Clone Stamp and Healing Brush tools, clipped to the size of the brush you are using. In the Clone Source palette you can change the opacity of this so you can see some of the original image through the overlay, giving you more accuracy when placing the cursor. Additionally you can have the whole image showing as a preview by unticking the 'Clipped' box, although you'll want to reduce the opacity a little, too, so you can see where you are painting.

Cloning and healing in perspective

When dramatic perspective is involved, cloning can become complicated. Using a part of the foreground to replace something in the background, or vice versa, is difficult to get right, as details can change in size drastically as the replacement pixels are brushed on. To overcome these issues, Photoshop includes a tool for cloning and healing in planes of perspective. Access it through Filters › Vanishing Point...

The Vanishing Point interface comprises a full-size image-editing window with a column of tools down the left-hand side. The first thing to do is to use the 'Create Plane' tool to define the perspective plane in which we want to work. Select this and draw a trapezium over the part of the image you will be editing. Next, choose the Clone Stamp tool and choose a source location as you would normally, by alt-clicking. There are brush options at the top of the screen, and you can tick a box to turn the Clone Stamp into a Healing Brush. When you are finished, click OK to confirm your edit and return to Photoshop.

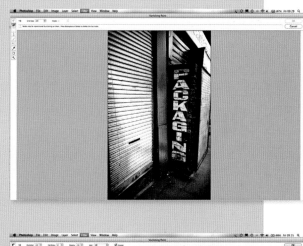

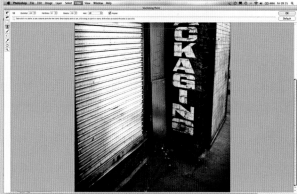

Right above and below: Photoshop's Vanishing Point filter is very helpful when it comes to cloning and healing in planes of perspective.

ASSIGNMENT
RESTORING AN OLD PHOTOGRAPH

Restoring an old photograph to its former glory is a good use for your cloning and healing skills, and a excellent way of keeping old memories alive.

We have all got a box of old family photographs somewhere. Often the charm of these ordinary snaps has come about slowly over the years, with changing styles and fashions reminding us of how everyday scenes have changed. But the passage of time can also damage such precious memories, with prints fading or turning strange colours. Tears and creases are also common, as are dust and dirt on a print's surface. Fortunately almost all of these issues are fixable with some digital photography – in particular, judicious use of the Clone Stamp and Healing Brush tools in Photoshop.

The first stage is to make a really good scan of the print. Do this in colour mode to collect as much information as possible, and select a high enough scanning resolution to make a good size print at the end of the process, say 10 x 8 inches. Once your scan is complete, open this into Photoshop or Elements and have a good look at it. Does it need straightening? If so, make this the first thing you do, either with Elements' Straighten tool or, in Photoshop, using a transformation (Edit > Free Transform).

Many old prints have picked up some kind of colour cast over the years, which you can eliminate by using a black and white conversion. The standard Adobe conversion will do fine (in Photoshop, Image > Adjustments > Black & White). Don't be afraid to use the various colour sliders to ensure that the image has the right brightness and contrast.

Right: The crease where this picture was folded can be removed with Photoshop's Clone Stamp and Healing Brush.

Healing the damage

Any damage to the surface of the print – be that dirt, dust, creases or even tears – can be removed with careful use of the Clone Stamp, Healing Brush and Patch tools. 'Careful' means working slowly and precisely, with a graphics tablet if necessary, and at 100 per cent magnification. Work your way around the image methodically, adopting a spiral pattern if necessary, working in from the edges to the centre. If you are using the Clone Stamp or Healing Brush tools, choose undamaged areas of similar tone and pattern to copy over the damaged areas. The Spot Healing Brush (either in its basic form or with the Content Aware option switched on) will attempt to second-guess what should be under the damage – often with varying degrees of success.

For a finishing touch, add a new border to replace the no doubt dog-eared, scruffy-looking one that currently exists. The best way of doing this is to use the Crop tool to get a good, clean finish, then expand the canvas size slightly (Image > Canvas Size...) and add a simple keyline border with Edit > Stroke (see pages 248–249).

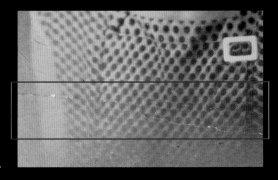

TIPS & TRICKS

• The more time you take with the cloning and Healing Brush, the better the end result will be. Using a small brush many times instead of a large one a few times is better.

• Be methodical when cloning and healing. Work your way around the print in a spiral, starting at the outside and ending in the middle, so you can be sure you have covered everywhere.

• Many cloning and healing steps can quickly fill up all the history space available (20 states by default). Make use of the history snapshot tool to remember key states you might want to undo back to (see page 266).

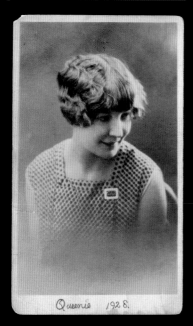

Above: *This picture suffers from a yellow cast and some fading, as well as dirt marks and a crease across the middle.*

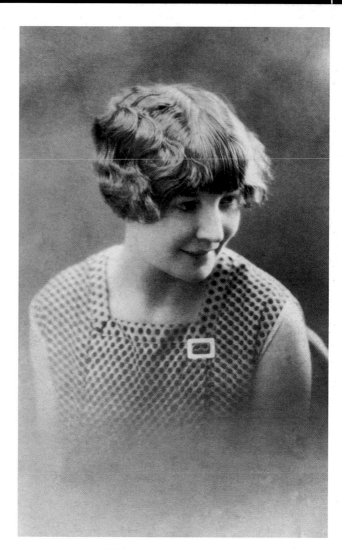

Above: *The dust and dirt marks have been removed with the Clone Stamp and Healing Brush tools, and the colour cast and fade problems fixed with a levels adjustment.*

Content-aware Healing

A revolutionary addition to the Spot Healing Brush is the Content Aware option. Where the normal Spot Healing Brush looks only around the edges of the painted area for destination texture, switching to Content Aware mode tells it to analyze the whole picture. Just paint over the offending item and Photoshop will work out what is likely to be the best replacement for it and put this in instead. You could almost be forgiven for thinking that black magic is at work, the results are so good.

Content-aware Healing is most effective with very detailed backgrounds. Such situations require careful work with conventional Cloning and Healing tools that can take hours to perfect. It's always worth trying a content-aware approach to speed things up.

The technology also applies when filling in areas, acting much like the Patch tool. Draw around the object to be removed and select Edit › Fill, or use the keyboard shortcut shift-delete. Make sure 'Content Aware' is selected in the drop-down menu and click OK. Photoshop will fill the area with its best guess at what should be there.

Removing the people from this landscape scene would normally be a lengthy process with the Clone Stamp and Healing Brush tools. The complicated background means careful selection of the right portions of the image must be made in order for the editing to appear convincing. It's definitely worth trying the content-aware technology built in to the Spot Healing Brush and Fill tools to see if it can do the job any faster.

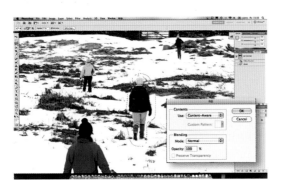

Step 1. *Removing the first person from the scene is a simple matter of selecting them with the Lasso tool, feathering the selection and hitting shift-delete to fill the selected area with content-aware pixels.*

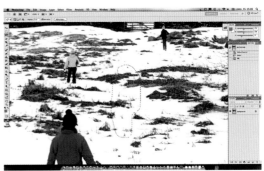

Step 2. *The content-aware fill has made a great job of removing the person from this landscape, using texture from elsewhere in the scene. Let's move on to the next one, removing her in a similar way.*

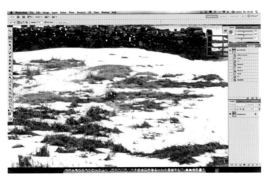

Step 3. *Not quite such a good result, but not bad. A black smudge is left behind, but this can be removed by applying the Spot Healing Brush again. If you are still struggling, see if a conventional Clone Stamp edit can help tidy things up.*

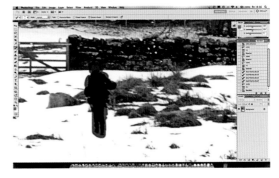

Step 4. *The final person to be removed is taken out with the Spot Healing Brush, with content aware enabled. Even though her head overlaps with the brick wall, the background is replaced perfectly.*

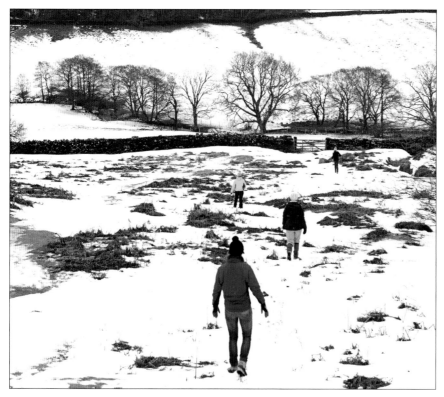

Left: Cloning and healing in a very detailed scene like this landscape requires careful selection of source areas, which can be very time consuming. The Spot Healing Brush's Content Aware option can really speed things up.

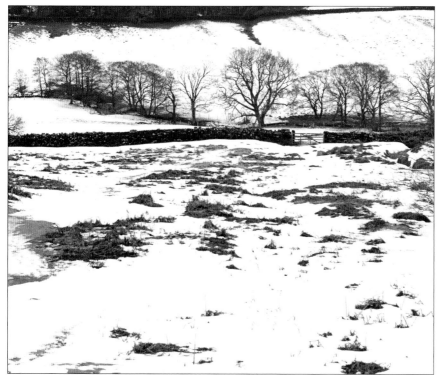

Left: With the Content Aware option switched on, the Spot Healing Brush analyzes the whole frame for suitable source pixels, using them to remove these walkers from the foreground almost automatically.

CREATING A DUST PROFILE FOR YOUR CAMERA

The Healing tools built in to Adobe Camera Raw and Lightroom are great for getting rid of dust spots on your camera's sensor. Let's see how to save time by automatically spotting dust marks in every image you take.

The spot-removal tools in Photoshop and Lightroom's raw converters are excellent at getting rid of the black smudges caused by dust and dirt on your camera's sensor. In an ideal world this should be cleaned off with specialist sensor-cleaning tools, but this isn't always possible in the field. Instead, let's look at how to get rid of the dirt spots digitally with the spot removal tool in Adobe Camera Raw. It's a quick enough job to do, although for a 20-image shoot the work soon becomes tedious. Thankfully, a neat trick with ACR's synchronize tool means you only have to find the dust spots once. Let's see how it's done.

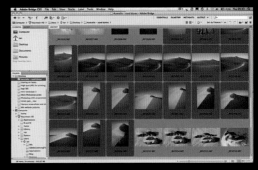

Step 1. You can load all your dust-ridden images into Adobe Camera Raw at once either by dragging them all into the main Photoshop application, or by browsing for them in Bridge and choosing File > Open in Camera Raw.

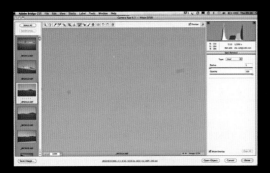

Step 2. Pick one of the images and examine it at high magnification so you can see all the sensor dust-marks. Whenever you find one, click on it with the spot removal tool, which will heal it by copying texture from the surrounding area. You'll see two circles: one over the blemish and the other over the area being copied. You can move and resize both if you don't get this right first time.

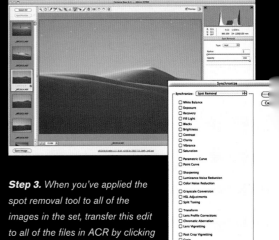

Step 3. When you've applied the spot removal tool to all of the images in the set, transfer this edit to all of the files in ACR by clicking Select All in the side bar, followed by Synchronize. Tick just the spot removal option.

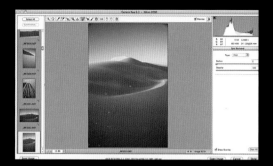

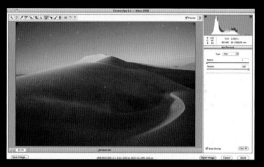

Step 4. *Dust marks are located at the same place in each frame, meaning the spot removal edits are always in the right location for all the images. Give each frame a quick glance to make sure the healing edit has worked properly, and move the spot removal circles if necessary.*

Step 5. *You can open all the images into Photoshop by clicking Select All and Open, but if you have lots of files you probably don't want to do that. Instead, click Done. This will dismiss ACR but the edits will be remembered next time you open a file.*

Dust profiles in Adobe Lightroom

You can perform the same trick in Adobe Lightroom, although the process is slightly different. Again, pick one image, go to the Develop module, and go through this thoroughly to remove the dust marks with the spot removal tool. With this done, select all the images in the series and click the Synchronize button in the bottom right of the screen. Tick the Spot Removal option in the Copy Settings box and click OK to apply it to all the frames.

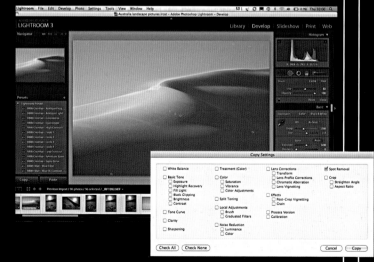

Panoramic photography

The long, thin, panoramic format has been popular with photographers, cinematographers and artists for decades, and it can do wonders for your images, too.

The panoramic format is a popular way in which to view the world, perhaps because it mimics so closely the view we see with our own eyes, which is considerably wider than it is tall. Landscape photographers in particular appreciate the panoramic format, which lets them achieve a wide angle of view without having worry about having to fill a massive expanse of foreground with something.

In the past, specialist film cameras were used to shoot the world in panoramic format, capturing a wide angle horizontally and a not-so-wide angle vertically in order to produce negatives or transparencies in the ratio 17:6. Nowadays, with digital photography, there are two ways of creating the same kind of result: cropping or stitching.

Below: An urban landscape like this panoramic image, made by stitching together four separately shot frames.

Cropping for panoramic

The most simple way of producing a panoramic photograph is to crop off the top and bottom of the frame to leave a long, thin strip. The width of the image is defined by the angle of view of the lens in use, and the exact frame shape can be determined in Photoshop (or equivalent) when cropping.

While easy to do, the cropping method also has disadvantages: there is no greater angle of view than can be achieved in a normal photograph, and image quality also suffers. In the cropping process you will effectively be throwing away resolution, so what might have been a 12-megapixel image to begin with becomes a 6- or 7-megapixel image when cropped to panoramic. This restricts the print size you can make from such a file, and limits the amount of detail that can be captured. A better way to produce panoramic images is to photograph each part of the scene separately and stitch each one together using specialist imaging software.

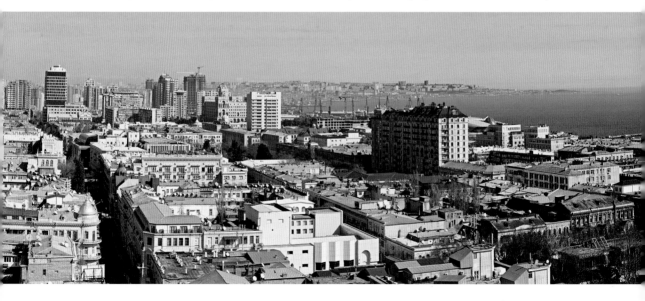

Stitching for panoramic

The concept of stitching is a simple one: sweep left to right over the scene, shooting images as you go. Afterwards these frames are opened up in Photoshop, Elements or one of the many specialist panoramic imaging applications available, where they can be seamlessly merged together to create one long, thin picture.

Where cropping a picture to make a panorama lowers pixel counts, stitching frames together results in a much higher-resolution final image, often up to the equivalent of a 50 megapixel shot or greater. This means we can print such images at large sizes and they are packed with detail. On the other hand, such pixel counts mean large file sizes, so you'll need a lot of RAM and disk space to work with the images and store them.

Many advances in stitching have been made in recent years, most of which enable excellent results to be generated very easily. The splicing process itself is hugely complicated, but thanks to the super-smart software now available to photographers, much of the technical difficulty is taken care of automatically behind the scenes. That said, there are many shooting techniques that can both make life easier and produce better results.

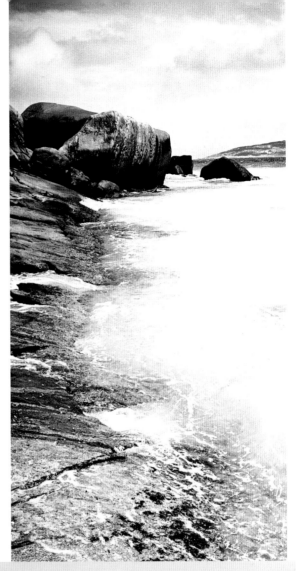

Right: *Panoramic images don't always have to be horizontal. Think about cropping them vertically, too.*

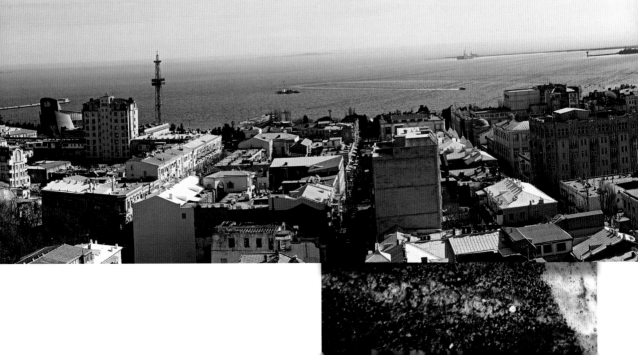

ASSIGNMENT
SHOOTING A STITCHED PANORAMIC LANDSCAPE

Next time you see a sweeping view, consider taking not just one picture, but a series, splicing together the frames to produce a stunning panoramic image.

The panoramic format is great for shooting landscapes. The best way to approach them is to shoot multiple frames while swinging the camera left to right (or right to left). These frames can then be merged together in Photoshop or Elements with the application's Photomerge command.

The quality of the final panorama is influenced hugely by technique at the shooting stage, and there are a few golden rules that should always be followed. The first is to always use a tripod. This will enable you to pan the camera smoothly and in a straight line, and also keep the camera level. Not doing this will result in mismatching frames, and curving horizons as opposed to flat, straight ones.

Additionally, always use the camera turned vertically to make the most of your camera's resolution. There are more pixels along the long edge of the frame than the short edge, so it makes sense to use this as the height of the final panorama. The width will be defined by the angle you rotate through.

With each frame being shot separately, it is very important to stop your camera picking different settings when the camera is moved. This applies particularly to exposure: if this shifts in value from frame to frame then the final stitched picture will vary in brightness across the frame in distinct bands. Much better to lock in a exposure value using manual mode, picking an average value that is good for the whole scene and using a small aperture to look after depth of field (see pages 84–87) if necessary. Also set your camera to prevent automatic white balance and focusing.

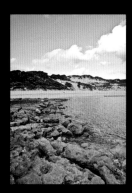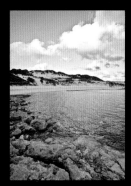

Overlap each frame by 25–30 per cent, keeping your eye on a landmark in the frame as you rotate the camera as a point of reference. The stitching software needs common portions in each image to be able to merge them together.

The merging process

Open the component images into Photoshop and select File > Automate > Photomerge... A dialogue will open asking you to specify a layout and the source files. Leave the layout set to auto and click the 'Add Open Files' button to use the images you have just opened. Click the OK button and Photoshop will stitch together the frames into one document.

The final document comprises multiple layers, and by switching each one on and off you can see how Photoshop has merged each frame. It's worth saving this layered image then flattening it (Layers > Flatten) and saving a copy you can work on. Zoom in and inspect the scene at 100 per cent magnification, using the Clone Stamp and Healing Brush to correct for any stitching errors.

ESSENTIAL KIT

- DSLR or compact camera with standard or telephoto lens
- Tripod
- Adobe Photoshop or Elements or specialist software

- When determining an average exposure for the scene, swing the camera as you will when shooting and look how the brightness varies. You want to pick a value that gives no more than two stops variation over the frame.

- A hotshoe-mounted spirit level will help you get the camera level. You can buy one from your local camera dealer.

- Try not to take too long to capture the frames, in order to avoid the light changing and the clouds moving.

Below (left to right): *The individual frames were shot upright with the camera in manual exposure and focus modes to ensure continuity. Afterwards, the sequence was stitched together with Photoshop's Photomerge (bottom).*

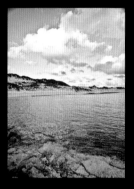
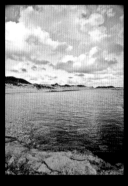
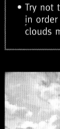
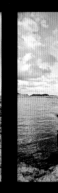

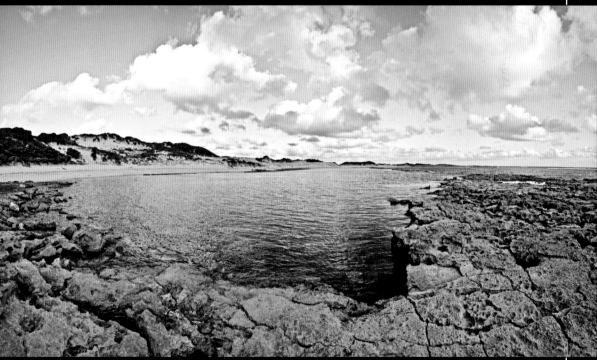

360-degree panoramic stitching

Once you've stitched together a few panoramic landscapes, you'll most likely have caught the bug and want to try more adventurous things. There is no real limit for the width of a stitched panoramic – except for when you have turned in a complete circle and arrive back at the beginning. In fact, shooting a complete 360-degree set of images is a great way of capturing your environment. Just make sure you move out of the way of the camera as you swing round!

When stitching together a complete 360-degree circle of images, you can choose which frame is the middle of the picture, and hence which are the ends. It's a nice trick to choose a composition where the same object appears on the left- and right-hand side of the picture, proving you have turned a full circle. You should notice that straight lines warp and bend as they come near to the camera and then get further away, and if a wide-angle lens is used you'll see crazy perspective effects in the foreground.

Dealing with the foreground

Including both near and far detail in a stitched panoramic image opens up new problems, compared with a simple three- or four-frame stitch of a far-off landscape, where everything is considered to be at a distance of infinity. When rotating the camera on a normal tripod, or when handheld, some of that movement is not just turning the camera but moving it side-to-side, too. Any movement of the camera like this results in frames not overlapping perfectly, causing misalignment in the stitching process – something known in the trade as parallax error.

The secret to eliminating parallax error in panoramic photography is to rotate the camera around a point known as the NPP, or no-parallax point (often incorrectly called the nodal point). The NPP is not only peculiar to an individual camera, but also specific lenses and zoom settings. Finding the NPP is pretty straightforward once you have had a few goes at it (see panel), but you will need a specialist panoramic tripod head in order to do this, and use the settings to take pictures. Panoramic

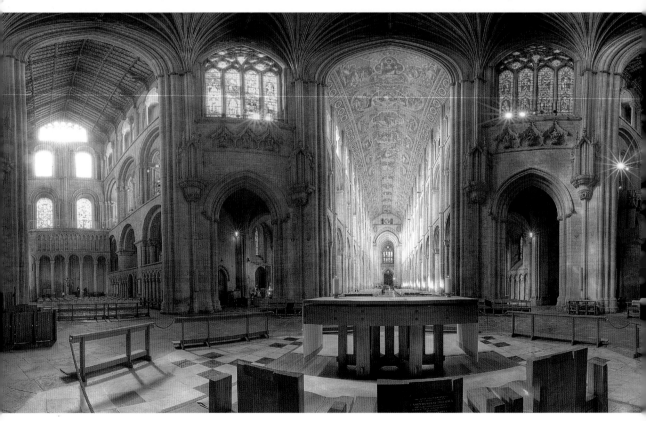

How to find a no-parallax point

Finding a no-parallax point uses methods that are similar to the reasons for needing to do this in the first place. With the camera mounted vertically on a tripod fitted with a specialist panoramic head, we need to position two objects, one near and one far, so they are aligned when viewed in the centre of the frame. Now swing the camera left and right so that the objects are positioned on the right and left of the frame. Are they still aligned with each other? If so you are rotating around the NPP and your images will be free of parallax error.

If not, move the camera backwards or forwards until you reach a point where this is the case. Make a note of the position (most panoramic heads have a numbered scale) so you'll be able to recall this lens-specific setting quickly when shooting in the field.

The near and far objects can be anything you like: two pencils viewed across a table; a window frame edge and a far-off tree; or two lighting stands in a studio. You can even do a quick emergency calibration in the field if you are using a new lens by picking objects in the scene.

heads have become more affordable in recent years, and are worth the investment if you think you are going to do a lot of panoramic shooting that includes foreground detail such as interiors, urban landscapes or gardens.

Below: *A 360-degree panoramic photograph of the interior of a church, shot with a 28mm lens. A panoramic tripod head was used to eliminate any parallax error caused by turning the camera.*

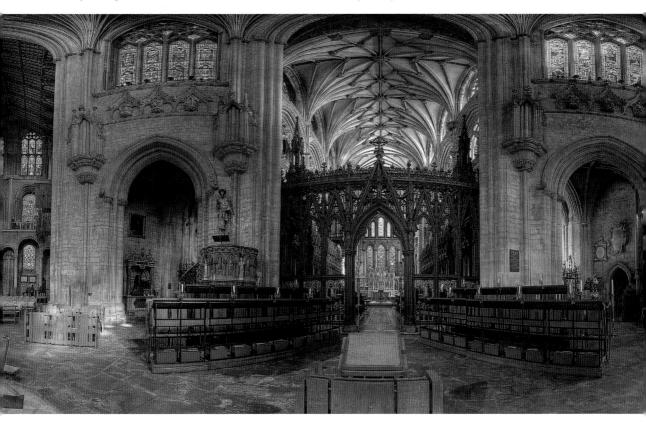

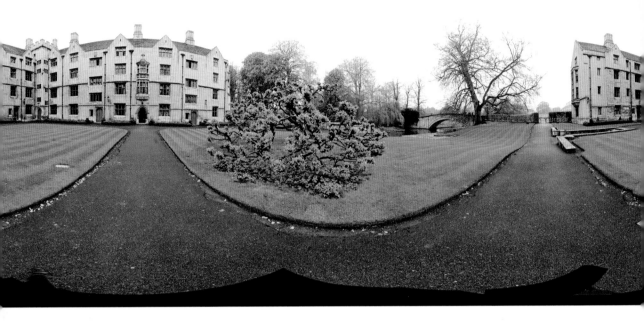

Complete spheres

For those wanting something really advanced to get their teeth into, the next logical step on from a complete 360-degree circle is the complete sphere. This involves total coverage of the space around the camera, looking up and down as well as left and right to capture each and every piece of information. When flattened out, these views can look amazing, and there are other uses for them, too, such as producing the type of virtual-reality tours that you see on websites and DVDs.

Most panoramic tripod heads offer the ability to look up and down as well as left and right. A view looking up is called a zenith, while that looking down is known as a nadir, and we'll need both of these to complete a sphere. The zenith is the easiest to shoot, just be careful to crouch down so you don't include yourself in the frame by mistake. The nadir is more difficult, as the tripod legs and bracket are in the way. For this reason, it's best to take two nadir shots 180 degrees apart and merge them to get rid of the tripod head and bracket in the frame. The Clone Stamp and Healing Brush tools can be used to get rid of the legs from the shot – for this reason, it's helpful to position the tripod on a plain surface that will be easy to clone.

Complete sphere stitching is harder for a computer to do than a full circle, or a few shots spanning 180 degrees. You'll need more advanced software: Photoshop Extended with its 3D capabilities, or specialist stitching software such as Autodesk Stitcher (www.autodesk.com) or PTgui (www.ptgui.com).

Above and top: A complete sphere panoramic photograph, wrapped in on itself to form a photosphere. The black areas at the bottom are where tripod legs have been cut out of the photo. They have been edited out with the content-aware Spot Healing Brush in Photoshop (see pages 322–323).

Photospheres

Up until now we have just flattened out our stitched panoramas onto a flat (virtual) surface to make conventional pictures for print or web. There is another way, however: with a complete sphere or complete circle we can wrap the panorama around in a circle, bringing the two ends together to form a kind of globe or sphere. Photoshop has a command designed for this very purpose. With your 360-degree image on screen, select Filter > Distort > Polar Co-ordinates. Make sure the 'Rectangular to Polar' option is selected, and hit OK.

Photoshop will wrap the image upwards in a circle so by default the sky will be at the centre. If you want the ground to be in the centre of the picture, choose Image > Image Rotation > 180° prior to applying the polar co-ordinates filter. Next, make the canvas square by choosing Select > All and Edit > Free Transform, then dragging in the left-hand resize handle.

Complete sphere images constructed with a zenith and nadir will look like a full sphere, while those that are just a full circle will show a pinch in the middle.

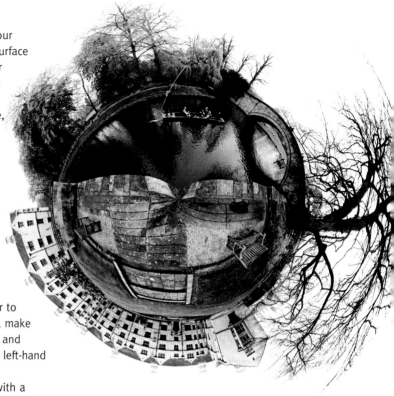

Above: This panoramic photosphere image features a pinch at the centre that occurs because the very bottom of the scene was not photographed.

Stitching with fisheye lenses

If you are lucky enough to own a full-frame fisheye lens – that is, one so wide that it has a 180-degree angle of view – then it is possible to produce a complete sphere panorama from just two images. Shoot the first looking one way, then the other after rotating the tripod through 180 degrees.

Although more simple than messing about with nadirs and zeniths, this approach can sometimes produce inferior results, as image quality at the edge of the fisheye frame will not be up to much. With this in mind you might as well shoot three frames: you'll get more overlap and it's not much more work. Bear in mind that you'll need specialist software that can correct the extreme distortion of these lenses.

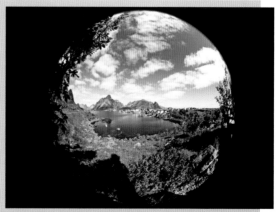

Above: A full-frame fisheye lens sees 180 degrees in all directions, taking in the edges of the lens itself and giving this most unusual view of the world.

ASSIGNMENT
BREAKING THE RULES

Sometimes it pays to break the rules and experiment with techniques that are unorthodox. Not doing things quite perfectly can often give you a more creative result than going by the book.

Panoramic photography is full of rules: get plenty of overlap between frames, set exposure manually, keep the camera level. The list goes on. But all of these are designed to give us the most perfect, real-world result. What about bending (or breaking) some of these rules to get something more creative?

On the level
You may have noticed by now that if you don't level the camera properly before shooting your panorama frames, the horizon in the finished image will not be straight. In fact it will undulate annoyingly across the frame. But if you really exaggerate the angle of the camera so it is more than just not quite level, the effect can look pretty good. Pick a scene where the horizon is really prominent and try to coincide detail in the foreground with areas where the camera is pointing downwards. You'll need plenty of depth of field (see pages 84–87) to get good front-to-back sharpness.

Below: By angling the camera on a panoramic tripod head, the horizon has developed a distinctly curvy shape. The photographer's shadow is also included, as is the same dog twice.

Mismatched overlap
Before digital photography came along, stitching and panoramic photography looked very different. While it was possible to get a convincing and exact overlap between two or three frames, the multi-frame wide-angle affairs we can produce nowadays were just not possible. But that didn't stop some notable artists from shooting multiple frames of their subject, stitching them together to form montages.

The most notable of these is the British artist David Hockney, whose large-scale montages often featured hundreds of small prints painstakingly arranged to form a picture. Precision overlap was not the aim of the game. Deliberate misalignment, rotation and even duplication gave Hockney's images something special that had never been seen before on such a scale.

You can try this, too, either by assembling and aligning each frame as a new layer in Photoshop, or by doing things the old-fashioned way, making a set of prints and laying them out on a large piece of mounting board or background paper. It's a great project. Be as haphazard and abstract as you like and experiment. You don't have to use glue and commit your creation to permanency; when you are happy with an arrangement, photograph it as a whole with your camera and start again.

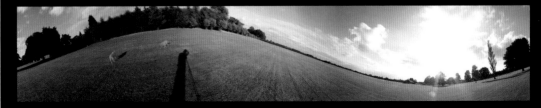

ESSENTIAL KIT

- Digital SLR or compact camera
- Tripod with panoramic head
- Desktop printer or online printing service

TIPS & TRICKS

- Try moving an object or a person between frames, so they appear in the panorama more than once.

- Use a long lens to produce your joiners, zooming in on detail and covering the area with pictures.

Above: These 14 frames were shot on an Apple iPhone, then imported into Photoshop and overlapped on individual layers to form this montage.

High dynamic range

The human eye is much more sensitive than the average digital camera, but with high dynamic range technology we can capture images that are far more lifelike, and in some cases take us into the world of fantasy.

We've seen plenty of instances so far where successfully recording extremes of light and dark with a camera can be very difficult. Often the photographer is forced to choose between exposing for the shadows and having the highlights go too bright, or the other way around, exposing for the highlights and ending up with black, featureless shadows.

The brightness range that can be captured on camera is known as dynamic range, and unfortunately that which can be seen by the average DSLR or compact camera is not a patch on what the human eye can see. In a standard JPEG image we can expect to resolve detail in highlights and shadows when they are 5–6 stops apart. The human eye can resolve 20+ stops of dynamic range, which is why we are often disappointed when we photograph a landscape that looks great in reality, but on camera fails to impress, with washed-out skies or dark, dull foregrounds.

We've already seen some ways of evening out such excessive contrast, compressing a wide range of brightnesses in the smaller dynamic range of the humble JPEG. Grad ND filters are a popular way of doing this in the field (see page 25), with the slightly darkened portion of the filter being

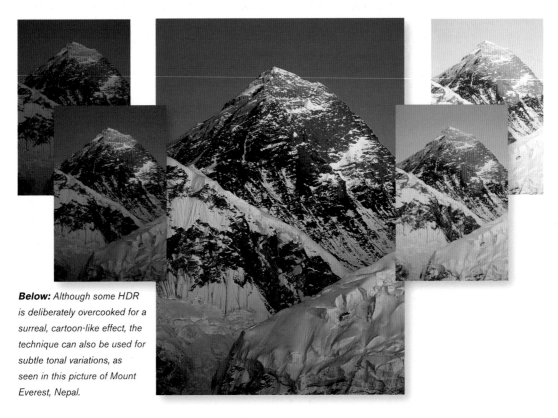

Below: *Although some HDR is deliberately overcooked for a surreal, cartoon-like effect, the technique can also be used for subtle tonal variations, as seen in this picture of Mount Everest, Nepal.*

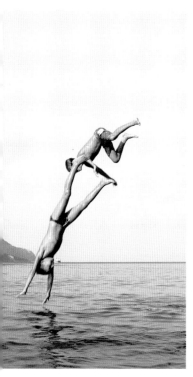 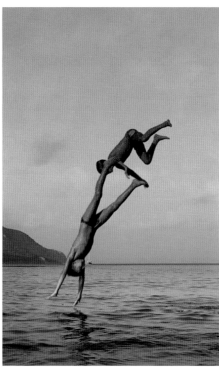 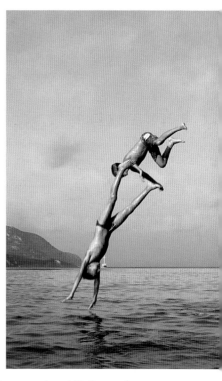

positioned over the brighter parts of the scene. There are even digital equivalents of the grad ND in Adobe Camera Raw and Lightroom. But no matter whether they are real or virtual, grad filters suffer from the same problem: what happens when the transition between light and dark is more complicated than the flat, straight line of the horizon?

Positioning a grad filter across any other shape is a compromise, as you'll end up darkening something that doesn't need it, or not darkening something else that does. Thankfully, digital post-processing has brought us another solution: high dynamic range imaging.

The new answer to excess contrast

Instead of trying to suppress brightness in selected parts of the frame, high dynamic range (HDR) imaging relies on the photographer capturing all of the information in the scene by shooting multiple frames from the same angle but at different exposures. These are then brought into a computer where a composite is made containing all of the brightness information from all of the frames. Finally, in a process

Above, left to right: Where a graduated ND filter won't do, HDR can often be very successful. In the unfiltered image (left) the sky is burned out, but using a grad ND to calm this down (centre) also darkens the two jumping boys. HDR (right) avoids the problem, bringing detail back to the sky while leaving the subjects bright and clear.

called tone mapping, this high dynamic range is compressed into a much smaller one that we can view on conventional screens and then print on conventional paper.

The uses for HDR are many and varied. As well as being popular with landscape photographers, the technology also works well for those shooting architecture or interiors, where it enables detail in all parts of the room to be captured. The tone-mapping process can often have the side effect of boosting local contrast, too, so detail really stands out and colours can become bold and super-saturated. This has lead to a dichotomy in HDR, with some photographers deliberately overcooking the technique to produce almost comic book-like effects, while other deplore this approach and go for a more natural look and feel.

Shooting your first HDR image

The HDR process begins with capturing the scene in-camera. The idea is to record all of the information in the scene, both in the deepest shadows and the brightest highlights, so we'll need to shoot multiple exposures at different exposure settings. Typically, three frames is the minimum for HDR work: one correctly exposed, one two stops over-exposed, and another two stops under-exposed. If the brightness range is even greater than this, consider widening the exposure range by shooting an extra two frames at +4 and -4 stops relative to the correctly exposed frame.

When shooting the component frames, it is very important to keep the camera still and ensure there is no subject movement between shots. A tripod is mandatory. The process can be made considerably easier by finding the autobracketing feature on your camera, which automatically adjusts the exposure by a set amount (two stops, for example) as you shoot consecutive frames.

If the camera's continuous shooting mode is also used, then the whole process can be over in less than a second, minimizing the chances of something moving in the frame.

Merging the files and tone mapping

You can use Adobe Photoshop to produce HDR images, and the functionality is also available in Elements under the guise of the Photomerge Exposure command. That said, specialist software still produces the best results. Look at Photomatix (www.hdrsoft.com), the granddaddy of HDR applications, and HDR Efex Pro from Nik Software (www.niksoftware.com).

In Adobe Photoshop CS5 the HDR functionality has been given a makeover, and no doubt other Adobe products will inherit the technology, too. Let's see how an HDR image is created from three separately shot frames.

Below: Shoot three different exposures and merge them with HDR to get extra shadow and highlight detail.

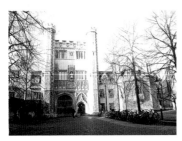 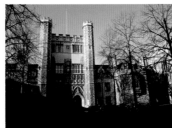 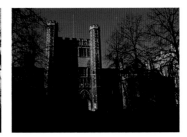

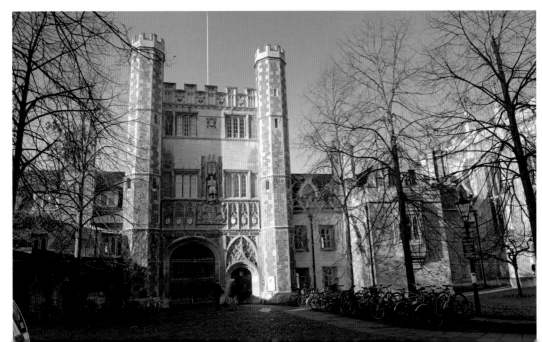

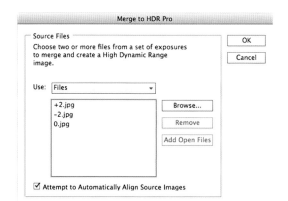

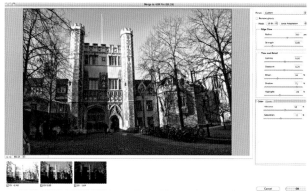

Step 1. *In Photoshop, choose Automate > Merge to HDR Pro. In the resulting dialogue box click 'Browse...', navigate to the component images on your hard drive and select them. Tick the 'Align Images' box and click OK.*

Step 2. *The 'Merge to HDR Pro' dialogue opens with a preview of the main image, thumbnails at the bottom and controls at the side. The preview will look pretty flat to begin with. Let's use the controls to inject some life.*

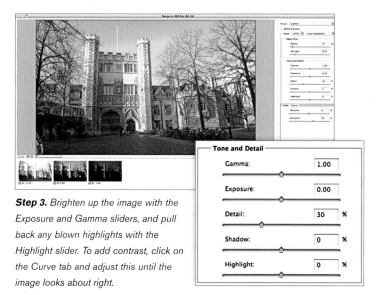

Step 3. *Brighten up the image with the Exposure and Gamma sliders, and pull back any blown highlights with the Highlight slider. To add contrast, click on the Curve tab and adjust this until the image looks about right.*

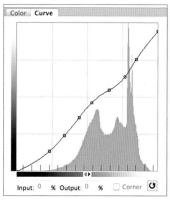

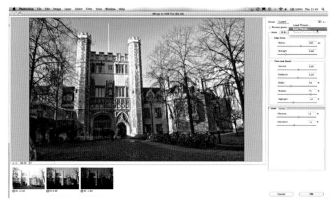

Step 4. *This might take some work, so be sure to save the setting you've just used as a preset. This way you'll be able to recall the setting if you want to give the merge process another go. Click OK and the finished HDR will open in Photoshop for further editing.*

HDR from a single file

Creating an HDR image from three bracketed shots may produce good quality results, but there is one obvious problem: the three component shots have to be taken at different times. If there is any movement between the frames then you will see 'ghosts' (semi-transparent objects) in the final picture. No matter how fast your continuous shooting speed, there are some situations (seaside and urban landscapes, for instance) that will always present the problem.

One solution is to turn to the raw file for help. The average raw file contains much more dynamic range than a JPEG file – up to 12 stops, versus just five stops for the JPEG. Using the controls in Adobe Camera Raw we can process three different JPEG files of varying brightnesses from a single raw file, at -2, 0 and +2 on the Exposure slider scale. These can then be imported into your favourite HDR application as normal, and a tone-mapped image produced from the other end.

The results from this HDR method are not as good quality as those obtained by merging three separately shot images, however. There is not as much dynamic range, and noise is more of a problem. In fact it is worth keeping the ISO setting on your camera right down as low as you can for this very reason.

Nevertheless, this is a good way of applying HDR to subjects that would be near impossible to tackle with the bracketed-exposures approach.

Below: Whether generated from a single raw file or three separately shot exposures, HDR is perfect for interiors.

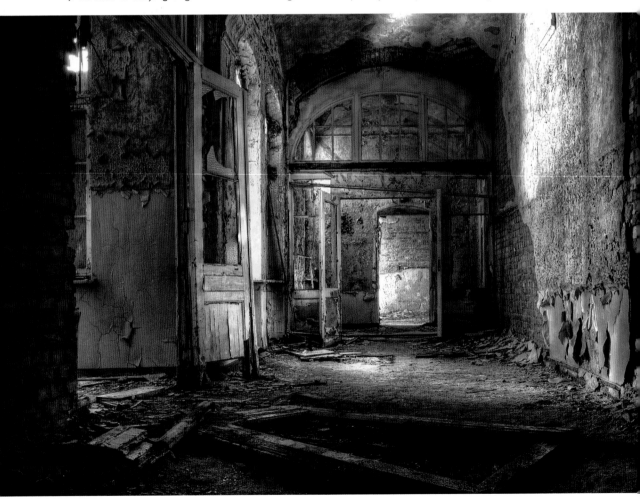

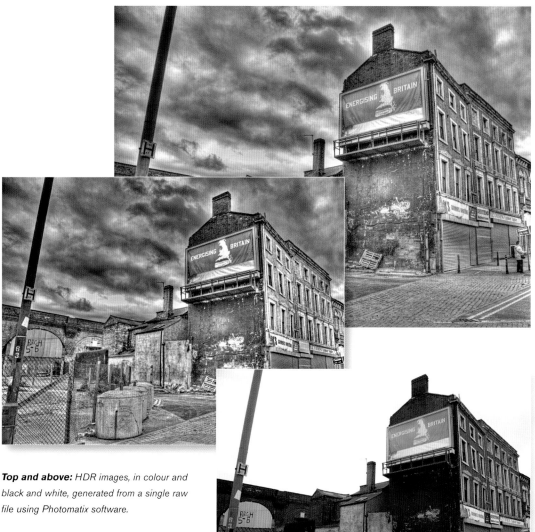

Top and above: HDR images, in colour and black and white, generated from a single raw file using Photomatix software.

Right: The raw file processed as a normal image, with much less dynamic range.

Black and white and HDR

As with most areas of photography, it's always worth trying something in black and white. In fact, it turns out that HDR works very well indeed in this medium, especially in scenes where detail and local contrast are important.

There are two approaches to producing a monochromatic HDR. Firstly you can use the colour controls in Photomatix or Photoshop's 'Merge to HDR Pro' to take the colour out of the image at the merging stage. Alternatively you can process the image in colour as normal, then use the controls available to you in Photoshop or Elements to convert to black and white. Which of these two methods you choose will depend largely on personal preference, though it can be argued that you have more control over the monochrome conversion when doing it afterwards in Photoshop.

ASSIGNMENT
USING HDR TO SHOOT ARCHITECTURE

Sometimes no one, single exposure value is right for a situation. But shooting at three different exposures and combining the results is a powerful tool, especially in architectural photography.

One of the problems faced when photographing architecture is getting the right exposure to capture detail in every part of the scene. Exposing for the darkest parts of the scene (shadows and foreground) means that the brighter parts (the sky, and buildings in bright light) often over-expose to the point of becoming devoid of detail – what's known in the trade as a blown highlight. Similarly, if you expose for the lightest part of the scene, then the darkest areas will be too under-exposed to show any detail.

The problem can be resolved by picking a midway exposure that allows both the highlights and the shadows to record properly. You can do this by exposing for a part of the scene that is of average brightness, or relying on your evaluative metering system to get this right most of the time. But there are instances when the extremes of light and dark – what photographers call the 'dynamic range' of a scene – are simply too far apart to be captured together using just one exposure value.

In these circumstances, it may not be possible to record all of the detail in an image with just one exposure, but it is with three. So-called high dynamic range (HDR) imaging involves capturing multiple frames of the same scene – shot from exactly the same point, but with different exposures. Usually one frame is captured with the f/stop and shutter speed indicated by the camera's metering, then at two stops over this value and two stops below.

The resulting image files are then imported into specialist imaging software, which takes information from all three shots and compresses the tonal range down so we can see it as one image – a process known as tone mapping. It's a great technique for shooting architecture and urban landscapes.

You don't have to have particularly advanced equipment to shoot HDR images. Any camera (even a compact) will suffice, so long as you can apply exposure compensation to force it to over-expose and under-expose, or shoot in manual exposure mode. A tripod is mandatory, too, so that the position of the camera doesn't move between frames. With this in mind, this technique does not work well if objects are moving in the scene – such as people, or cars. The movement of the clouds in the sky can be negated by shooting the frames as quickly as possible.

When it comes to specialist HDR software, Photomatix is excellent, and well worth a look (www.hdrsoft.com). Newer versions of Adobe Photoshop and Photoshop Elements also have this functionality built into them, though, so if you own versions CS4 or 9 respectively then you already have all the software you need.

When tone mapping your image (see page 337) you can opt to keep things realistic and lifelike or ramp up the effect for a hyper-real look. Either way can work, although the over-the-top approach is now starting to look a little hackneyed (though undeniably good fun, too).

ESSENTIAL KIT

- DSLR or compact with exposure compensation or manual exposure mode
- Tripod and remote release
- HDR software

TIPS & TRICKS

- Make sure the camera stays in exactly the same place when you shoot the frames.

- Make life easier by combining your camera's auto exposure bracketing (which varies the exposure for you shot-by-shot) with continuous shooting mode.

- Shooting two stops either side of the correct exposure should be fine for most situations, but don't be afraid to increase this in very high-contrast situations.

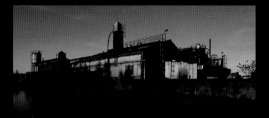

Top to bottom: Taking the over-the-top approach to HDR has given this architectural landscape strong colours and punchy details. The three exposures, all using an aperture of f/5.6 and shutter speeds of 1/60sec, 1/250sec and 1/1,000sec at ISO200, combine for a vivid end result.

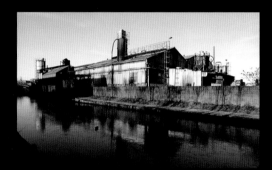

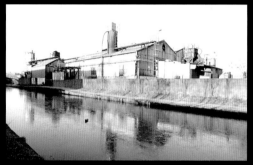

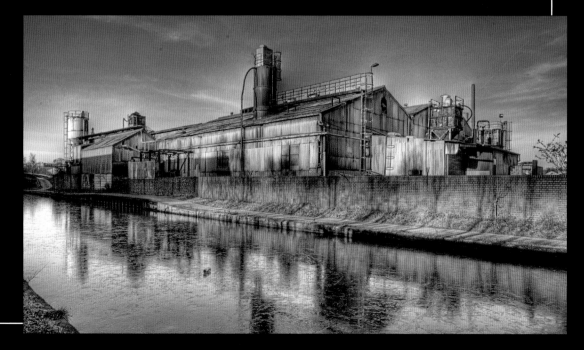

Layers

Working with layers opens up hundreds of new editing options, from the ability to superimpose multiple images to the application of non-destructive adjustments. Once you've mastered layers, you'll never look back.

The ability to create images that comprise multiple layers opens up new creative opportunities, as well as ways of working more efficiently. The concept is a simple one and is exactly the same as having images drawn on multiple sheets of paper stacked on top of each other. By default, we see the image on the top sheet of paper, but we can see all or part of the image on the sheets below, too, by making holes in the top sheet or using semi-transparent paper, such as tracing paper.

So it is with the electronic virtual layers that make up an image in Photoshop. We can superimpose objects on top of each other (see below), and even make some images semi-transparent, to create exciting composites and fantasy creations. Such techniques are useful in more conventional photography, too, replacing a flat, featureless sky with something more dramatic, or combining two group shots so that everyone is looking at the camera at the same time. The possibilities are endless.

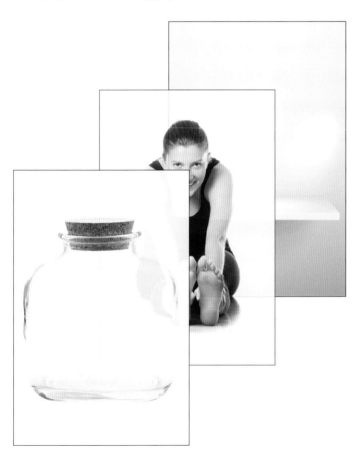

Right and left: *Think of layered images as being made from sheets of paper stacked on top of each other. Here three layers, each containing a different picture (bottle, person, shelf), have been blended together to form a composite image.*

Below: *The Photoshop Layers palette shows the extra adjustment layers and layer masks that were needed to make the image work.*

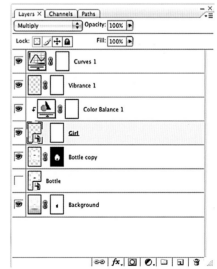

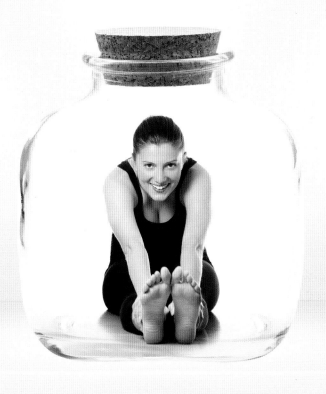

Photoshop and layers

In Photoshop and Elements, layers are shown, created and organized in the Layers palette (Window › Layers), while Photoshop's Layers menu also contains useful tools and commands. To create a new layer choose Layer › New Layer, or click the New Layer shortcut in the Layers palette. Each layer is shown as a new line in the Layers palette, with its name next to a thumbnail preview. The eye symbol next to this shows whether the layer is visible or not; click it once to turn the layer on and off.

The layer that is highlighted is known as the active layer, and is the one that all edits will apply to; you can change which layer is the active layer just by clicking on it. This means that brush work, as well as transformations and filters, will all be applied to the currently selected layer. Layers can be deleted by dragging them onto the small dustbin icon at the bottom of the palette, or

duplicated by dragging them onto the new layer icon. The order of individual layers can be changed in this palette simply by dragging them around.

To see how this works in practice, open an image into Photoshop, and choose the type tool from the toolbox on the left of the screen. Click anywhere on the image and you'll be able to type some text over the top of it. Format your text with whatever font and colour you like, then either click the tick symbol in the Options bar to confirm it or just choose any other tool. Look in the Layers palette and you'll notice the text has been added as a seperate layer that is sitting above the image.

The new text layer just has a 'T' as its thumbnail icon, although the layer's name will adopt the first few words of the added text by default. The original image stays in a layer called 'Background'. Click the eye symbol next to the text layer and you'll notice that it will disappear; click it again to bring it back. Select the Move tool from

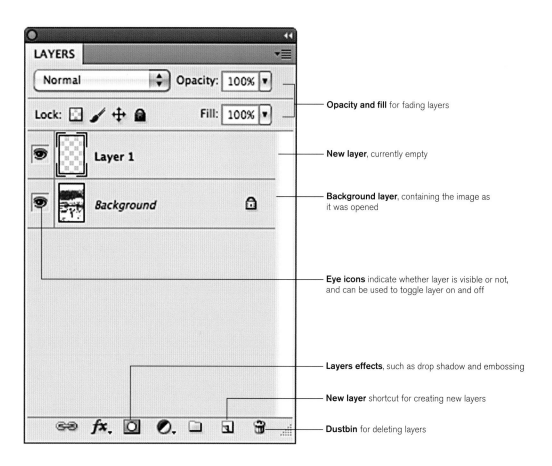

Opacity and fill for fading layers

New layer, currently empty

Background layer, containing the image as it was opened

Eye icons indicate whether layer is visible or not, and can be used to toggle layer on and off

Layers effects, such as drop shadow and embossing

New layer shortcut for creating new layers

Dustbin for deleting layers

the toolbox (top-most tool) and you'll be able to move the text layer around by dragging it. Lastly, choose Edit > Transform > Flip Horizontal; the text layer will flip while the background image layer doesn't. (To make other transformations you'll have to rasterize the text layer into conventional pixel-based layer with Layers > Rasterize > Type.)

The take-home message here is that commands and adjustments only apply to the layer (or layers) that you have selected, and that working in this way allows us to edit certain elements while leaving others alone.

London

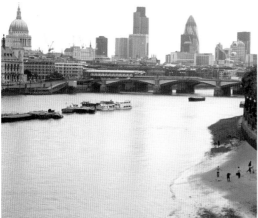

London
Summer 2008

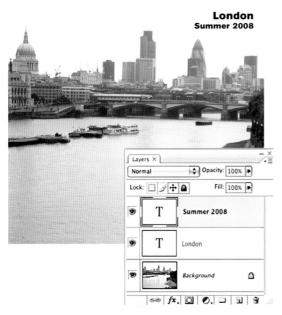

The background layer

Open a photograph into Photoshop or Elements and you'll notice that, by default, it goes into a layer called 'Background'. The name is in italics and there is a small padlock symbol next to it. This background layer is special, in that there are a few restrictions placed on it that limit what you can do.

- Background layers cannot be transparent, or contain any transparency.
- As such you cannot erase them, or any part of them.
- You can't delete them, either. Note that the dustbin is greyed out when the background layer is selected.
- Background layers can't be moved or transformed – this is where the lock symbol comes in.
- You can't reorder a background layer relative to other layers.

This might all seem a bit draconian, but the reason for these restrictions is a good one. Opening your image into a background layer protects it from accidental, permanent damage and encourages you to use other layers to apply edits in a non-destructive way.

You can convert a background layer to a normal layer very easily: alt-double-clicking the layer name instantly transforms it to a normal layer with none of the above restrictions. Renaming the layer (double-clicking the name) also has this effect, and you can select Layer > New > New Layer from 'Background...' if you want to do things the long way.

Left: Photoshop's type tool automatically adds a layer to an image to hold any text that is written on it. You'll see this as a new layer in the Layers palette, sitting on top of the background layer. Each new text entry is added as a separate layer, so ensure you select the correct layer (by clicking on it) if you need to edit the text at any point.

Cutting out

Once layers are stacked over each other, removing parts of them lets others beneath show through, allowing you to superimpose one picture on another.

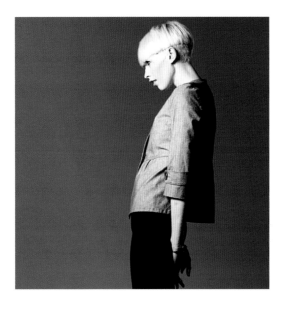 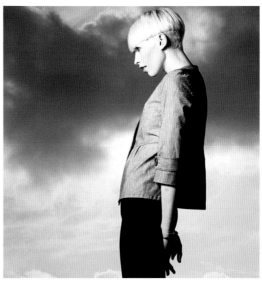

Above: *Cutting out the subject of this portrait from her plain grey background lets us substitute a more interesting one underneath.*

Below: *Of the many tools we could use to make the cut out, the Magic Wand works well here, sticking to high contrast edges automatically.*

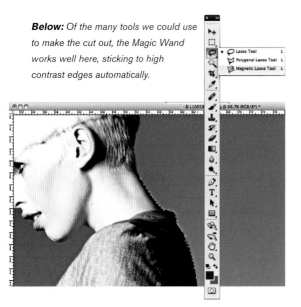

A multi-layered image is all very well, but unless we can see the layers beneath the uppermost one, then there isn't much point. One way of doing this is to produce transparent areas in the upper layers in order to allow pixels in the layers below to shine through. Going back to the analogy where layers are represented by sheets of paper on top of each other, this is rather like cutting holes in some sheets to let us see others below.

Transparency is allowed in all layers except the background layer (see page 347) and can be created in a number of ways. The easiest way is to use the Eraser tool to delete pixels, painting this on in exactly the same way as for a Paint Brush, Healing tool or any of the brush tools. The size, shape and hardness of the Eraser brush can be changed via the Brushes palette or the usual shortcuts (see page 236), and you'll notice that areas of transparency are represented by a white/grey checkerboard pattern. The pattern is there to show you that the area is transparent but there is nothing to see through the hole yet.

To create something underneath the top layer, you could create a new layer in the document (Layers > New > Layer... or click the shortcut in the Layers palette) and draw something. But we are interested in photography here, not illustration. To insert another photographic image as a new layer, first open it as a new document in its own window as usual. Then drag the background layer from the Layers palette of one document to the main window of the other. Alternatively you can copy one image into the clipboard (Select > All; Edit > Copy) and paste it into the other image's window (Edit > Paste). Re-order the layers, if necessary, by dragging them around in the Layers palette. Now you should see the new photograph peeping through the hole you made in the top layer.

Using selections

The eraser is not often used for creating transparency in layers because it is difficult to apply precisely, and accuracy when cutting out objects is vital if the end result is to look believable and realistic. Instead, let's try using a selection, which offers much more control. There are a number of different selection tools that can be useful when cutting out, but the basic principle is the same for all of them: make a selection on the topmost layer, feather it slightly to soften the edges and hit delete to remove content from the layer and create transparency. Drawing an outline around an object with the Lasso tool is a time-consuming process, but the longer you take over this, the better the end result will be.

That said, the Magnetic Lasso can save you a lot of time. This shares a location in the toolbox with the normal Lasso and is 'sticky' in that it tries to stick automatically to high-contrast edges. Just how high the contrast needs to be can be specified in the toolbar with the Distance and Contrast options. Trace around the object carefully, using a graphics tablet if more precision is required. Once you get back to where you started, you'll notice the selection close itself.

No selection is ever pixel perfect, but you can tidy things up by flipping over into Quick Mask

Auto selections

Other tools for selecting objects more quickly and automatically include the Magic Wand, which selects all pixels of similar colours (just how similar can be specified in the options bar), and the quick selection tool, which does the same thing but works by being painted over the object being selected. These techniques are far from perfect in terms of accuracy, but they do give you a quick starting point for further refinement with the Quick Mask tool.

mode (shortcut 'Q', see page 236) and using small brushstrokes to correct any mistakes. Exit Quick Mask mode when you are happy, then invert the selection (Select > Inverse) to ensure it is the background you will delete, not the subject. Feather the selection by two pixels using the box in the Options bar, or by choosing Select > Modify > Feather... and hit the delete key to remove the background and let the layer beneath shine through.

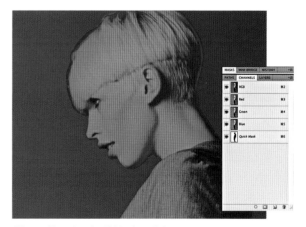

Above: Pressing the 'Q' keyboard shortcut accesses Photoshop's Quick Mask shortcut, which shows dotted-line selections as a semi-opaque red mask that can be edited with any of the application's brush and filter tools.

Masks and masking

The problem with using the Eraser tool or a select-and-delete approach to creating transparency in layers is that the editing is destructive – that is, it requires a permanent change to the pixels in the image.

The trouble with destructive editing is that, beyond the 20 or so states remembered by Photoshop's history, you cannot come back and change things if they are not quite right. The only option is to start again, but given the huge amounts of time required to cut out objects accurately with selections, this is not very practical.

Using layer masks instead of cutting out or erasing is a non-destructive way of introducing transparency to a layer. Instead of deleting pixels we don't want to see, we mask them off. The layer mask can be edited with nearly all of Photoshop's tools, and you can come back to it at any time during the editing process. If you realize you haven't quite got the transparency right in one of your layers, you can simply change it without starting anything from the beginning again.

Below: Using masks to add colour to a mono image.

Making masks

Apply a mask to a layer by selecting the layer to which you want it to belong and then clicking the 'New Layer Mask' shortcut in the Layers palette. Another thumbnail will appear for that layer, which represents the new layer mask. By default it will be white, meaning nothing is masked off, but painting some black on the image while this thumbnail is selected will mask off pixels, letting those beneath show through. Painting in a shade of grey instead of pure black makes the layer semi-transparent.

It's important to realize that you can paint and edit the mask as much as you want when it's selected in the Layers palette. Photoshop's interface doesn't make it very clear when the layer mask is selected, but if you look closely, the mask's thumbnail has four extra black-line corners around it when it's selected. Click on the image layer's own thumbnail to get back to a state where edits apply to the image and not the mask.

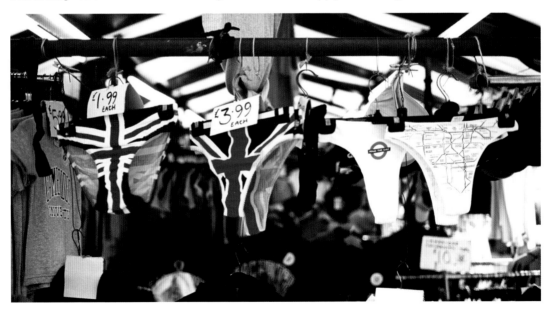

Masks and selections

There is a relationship between masks and ordinary selections. Right-clicking on a layer mask thumbnail icon and choosing 'Add Mask to Selection' causes the current mask to become a dotted-line selection. Conversely, if you make a selection with the Lasso or Marquee tools, or even with Quick Mask mode, you can convert this to a layer mask by clicking on the new layer mask shortcut with the selection active, or by choosing Layer > Layer Mask > Hide Selection (or Reveal Selection, depending on whether you want to start by hiding what is under the mask or by revealing).

Selective monochrome with layer masks

In chapter four we saw how to create an image that was part-colour and part-monochrome using the History Brush to selectively undo the 'convert to black and white' process (see page 267). A better way of achieving this effect is to use two layers, one colour and one black and white, and a layer mask to allow one to show through the other. Being non-destructive, this way of working will allow you to come back and alter what is colour or mono at any point in the editing process, whereas with the History Brush technique you have to decide what's what and stick to it.

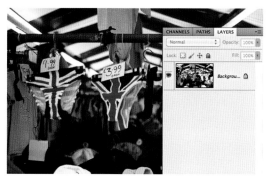

Step 1. *Open the image you wish to edit into Photoshop and duplicate the background layer by dragging it onto the 'New Layer' shortcut button. Call the new layer 'Black and White'.*

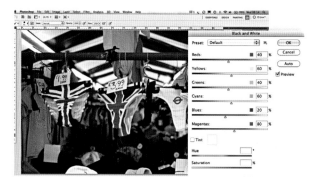

Step 2. *Convert the new layer to monochrome using your favourite technique. A plug-in was used here, but you could use Photoshop or Elements' black and white adjustment.*

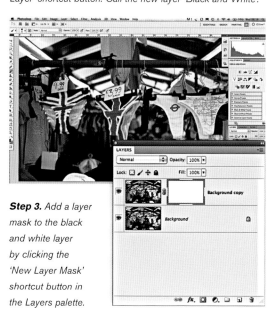

Step 3. *Add a layer mask to the black and white layer by clicking the 'New Layer Mask' shortcut button in the Layers palette.*

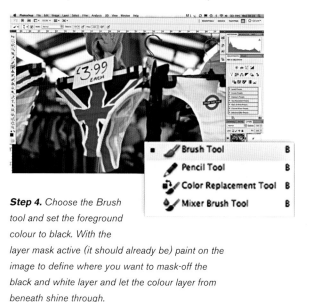

Step 4. *Choose the Brush tool and set the foreground colour to black. With the layer mask active (it should already be) paint on the image to define where you want to mask-off the black and white layer and let the colour layer from beneath shine through.*

REPLACING SKIES WITH LAYERS AND MASKS

Replace a washed-out sky with a well-exposed one to take your landscape photographs to another level.

I t's hard to capture detail in the sky and foreground of a photograph because of the difference in brightness between the two regions. We've already seen how in-camera filter techniques can even-out this extreme contrast, and we've see how high dynamic range imaging can help, too (see pages 336–337). But sometimes there isn't the time to think your photography through – a scene captured on the spur of the moment can often feature a sky that is a washed-out expanse of bright white.

If this sounds familiar then don't panic. You can replace the sky in a landscape image using layers, a layer mask, and a steady hand. The technique involves importing another (well-exposed) sky image and positioning this in a separate layer beneath the layer containing the landscape. A layer mask is then used to let the new sky layer show through part of the original image where the bright white sky sits. It's a simple procedure that will reinforce a lot about how layers and masks work in other situations.

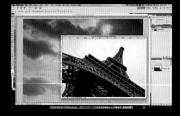

Step 1. *Open the photograph that needs its sky replacing, and the substitute sky image.*

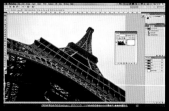

Step 2. *Change the background layer into a normal layer by alt-double-clicking it. Add a layer mask by clicking the shortcut button.*

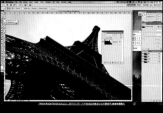

Step 3. *Apply the mask by using the Magic Wand to select all of the sky and hit delete to fill this area with black.*

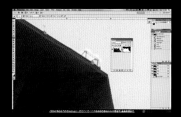

Step 4. *An automatic method never works perfectly, but because this is a mask we can tidy things up. Zoom in to 100 per cent and paint black ink for more mask, and white ink for less.*

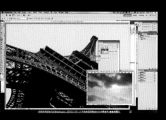

Step 5. *Bring in the new sky as a new layer, dragging it over from the Layers palette. Re-order the layers so the new sky is on the bottom.*

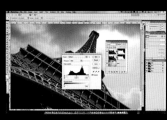

Step 6. *You can make levels adjustments to both of these layers to get their contrast, brightness and colour tone looking right.*

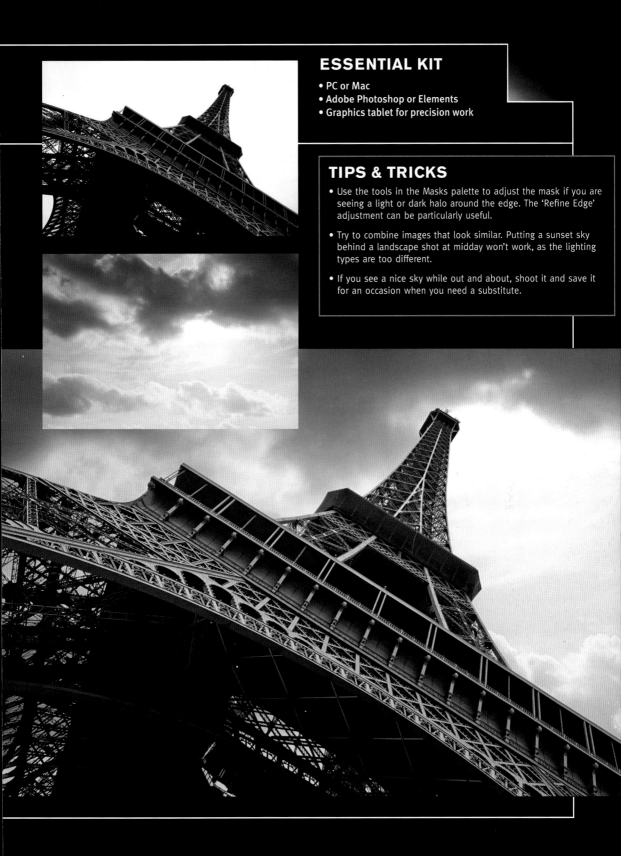

TIPS & TRICKS

- Use the tools in the Masks palette to adjust the mask if you are seeing a light or dark halo around the edge. The 'Refine Edge' adjustment can be particularly useful.

- Try to combine images that look similar. Putting a sunset sky behind a landscape shot at midday won't work, as the lighting types are too different.

- If you see a nice sky while out and about, shoot it and save it for an occasion when you need a substitute.

Adjustment layers

Sheets of editable pixels are not the only type of layer that Photoshop has to offer. The non-destructive principle extends as far as adjustments such as curves, levels and hue saturation, too.

n fact, adjustment layers offer the ability to apply nearly all of the common image adjustments used by digital photographers as separate layers that hover above the background image-holding layer, as opposed to affecting the image permanently.

The advantage of working in this way is that you can come back to an adjustment at any time and make changes to it without undoing anything else you have done since then. Let's take the hypothetical example of an image that we open into Photoshop and adjust for brightness with a levels correction. Afterwards, we crop it, do

some cloning and healing, boost the saturation of the sky and apply a border. What if we then wish we had made the levels adjustment slightly differently? We can step back in history, but by doing so we will have to undo the border, saturation, cloning and crop steps too. Not a very efficient way of working.

Now let's see how adjustment layers can help us do things differently. Applying an adjustment layer is really no more difficult than applying it directly. Instead of choosing Image › Adjustment › Levels for a levels adjustment, choose Layer › New Adjustment Layer › Levels, and the same dialogue you are

Shortcuts – click once
to apply an adjustment
layer instantly

Below: *Photoshop adjustment layers are chosen either from the Adjustments or the Layers palette. Each one is shown separately in the Layers palette along with a layer mask that is created automatically.*

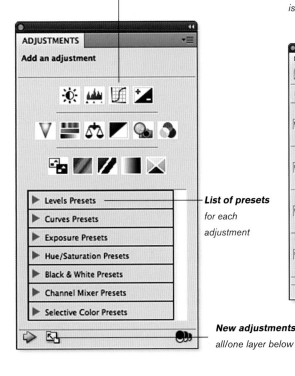

List of presets
for each
adjustment

New adjustments *affect*
all/one layer below

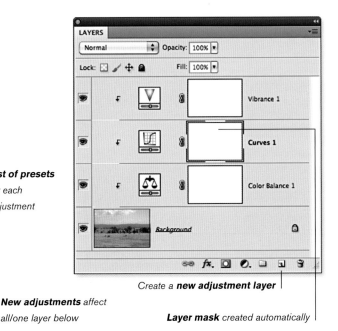

Create a **new adjustment layer**

Layer mask created automatically

354 **advanced darkroom** **techniques**

An adjustment layer

familiar with will appear in the Adjustments palette on the right of the screen. Make the necessary changes to the settings and the image will update in real time. You can now change these levels at any time, no matter what else you are doing, by visiting the Adjustments palette.

You can also apply adjustment layers by clicking on the shortcut in the Layers palette. The adjustment layer can apply to all of the layers below it, or just the one immediately below it, depending on whether the 'Clip to Layer' shortcut button is active or not in the Adjustments palette. Like normal layers, the opacity (intensity) of the effect may be decreased by throttling back the Opacity slider.

You'll notice that an adjustment layer has a layer mask appended to it by default, meaning that you can apply the adjustment selectively to only parts of the image by brushing on black or white paint with the Brush tool. This is also a non-destructive editing approach – the mask can be revisited at any time, just like the adjustment itself.

Below: Three adjustment layers have been applied to this image: a curves layer to brighten it, a colour balance layer to correct white balance, and a vibrance layer to boost saturation.

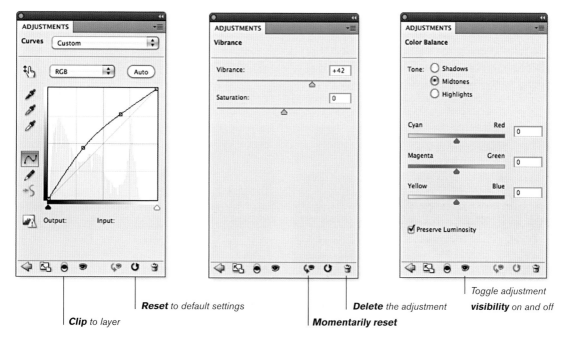

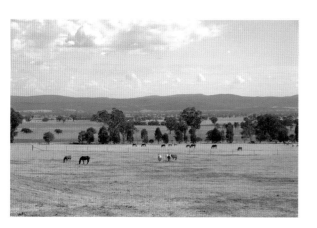

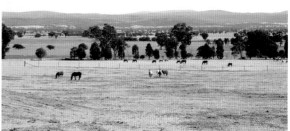

Clip *to layer*

Reset *to default settings*

Momentarily reset

Delete *the adjustment*

Toggle adjustment **visibility** *on and off*

Blending modes

The key to working with layered images is understanding how blending modes change the way the individual layers interact with each other.

Transparency isn't the only way we can show one layer through another – blending modes also govern how layers interact with each other. By default, a layer's blending mode is set to normal, meaning it obscures the layer underneath. But there are many other options available, all with different uses.

A layer's blending mode is changed using the drop-down menu in the Layers palette. Each layer has its own blending mode, so if you change it for one layer in a document, the others are not changed. Although Adobe defines precisely what each blending mode does (you can find an almost impenetrable description of each in the application's help files), you'll find yourself simply trying each one out to see which one fits. That said, there are a few blending mode recipes that are very useful indeed to the digital photographer.

Darken and Lighten
Changing the blending mode to Darken causes Photoshop to compare corresponding pixels in both layers and display the one that is darker. Conversely, the Lighten blending mode causes the lighter of the two pixels to be shown. This is useful when you have an object shot on a white or black background and you want to superimpose this on another image quickly. Choose Darken to remove a white background and Lighten to remove a black one.

Multiply and Screen
Like the Darken blending mode, Multiply makes the picture darker, but does so by multiplying together the pixel values in each layer. It's rather like holding up two old photographic slides sandwiched together. You'd see both images superimposed, but the result would be darker, as the light has to travel through both of them. The Screen blending mode does the exact opposite of this, dividing the two pixel values by each other and lightening the image.

Overlay and Soft Light
Overlay combines the Screen and Multiply blending modes, lightening light areas and darkening dark areas to give the impression of more contrast. Try duplicating a layer and changing the blending mode of the duplicate to Overlay. You'll notice the difference straightaway. If the colours are too harsh, change the duplicate layer to black and white. Soft Light is a less harsh form of Overlay, and you can also tone down the effect by reducing the opacity of the duplicated layer.

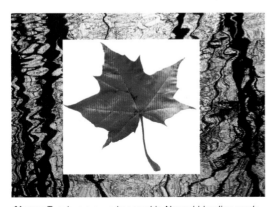

Above: *Two layers superimposed in Normal blending mode.*

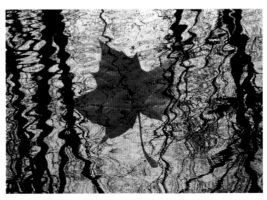

Above: *The layers overlaid with the Multiply blending mode.*

In detail: Photoshop blending modes

Each of Photoshop's blending modes does a different job of controlling how two corresponding pixels in separate layers interact with each other. In these definitions, the 'base colour' is the original colour in the bottom layer, the 'blend colour' is the colour being applied by the upper layer and the 'result colour' is the colour resulting from the blend.

Normal Default mode for each new layer. Only the blend colour displayed.

Dissolve Result colour is a random choice of the blend or base colours. Only affects layers of reduced transparency.

Darken Compares the base and blend colours and chooses the darkest of the two for each pixel.

Multiply Multiplies the base colour by the blend colour to make a new result colour for each pixel. Multiplying by black gives black; multiplying by white leaves it unchanged.

Color Burn Darkens the base colour according to the blend colour by increasing contrast.

Linear Burn Darkens the base colour according to the blend colour by decreasing brightness.

Lighten Compares the base and blend colours and chooses the lightest of the two for each pixel.

Screen Multiplies the reciprocal of the blend and base colours together – the result colour is always lighter.

Color Dodge Lightens the base colour according to the blend colour by decreasing contrast.

Linear Dodge Brightens the base colour according to the blend colour by increasing brightness.

Overlay Multiplies or screens the colours, depending on the base colour. Light areas are lightened; dark areas are darkened.

Soft Light Lightens or darkens the colours, depending on the blend colour. If the blend colour is lighter than 50 per cent grey, the image is lightened; if it is darker than 50 per cent grey, it is darkened.

Hard Light Multiplies or screens the colours, depending on the blend colour. If the blend colour is lighter than 50 per cent, the image is screened; if it is darker than 50 per cent, the image is multiplied.

Vivid Light Burns or dodges the colours by decreasing contrast, depending on the blend colour. If the blend colour is lighter than 50 per cent grey, the image is lightened. If it's darker than 50 per cent grey, it is darkened.

Linear Light Burns or dodges colours by increasing brightness, depending on the blend colour. If the blend colour is lighter than 50 per cent grey, the image is lightened by increasing the brightness. If the blend colour is darker than 50 per cent, the image is darkened by decreasing the brightness.

Pin Light Replaces colours depending on the blend colour. If the blend colour is lighter than 50 per cent grey, pixels darker than the blend colour are replaced. If the blend colour is darker than 50 per cent grey, pixels lighter than the blend colour are replaced.

Hard Mix Saturates each colour channel by adding the blend and base colours together.

Difference Compares the colour in each channel and subtracts the base from the blend or the blend from the base, depending on which has the greater brightness value.

Exclusion Similar in effect to the Difference blending mode, but lower in contrast.

Hue Creates a result colour with the hue of the blend colour and the luminance and saturation of the base colour – good for tinting and toning.

Saturation For each pixel, creates a result colour with the luminance and hue of the base colour, but the saturation of the blend colour.

Color For each pixel, creates a result colour with the luminance of the base colour and the hue and saturation of the blend colour.

Luminosity For each pixel, creates a result colour with the hue and saturation of the base colour and the luminance of the blend colour.

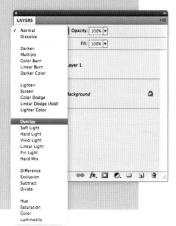

Retouching with layers

We've already seen how to clone and heal an image, but doing so fills your history and is hard to undo. Retouching with layers solves this problem.

We saw on pages 314–323 how to copy data from elsewhere in the image and use it to paint over the top of unwanted objects in order to disguise them. But the problem with cloning and healing is that it requires many separate clicks, each of which is recorded in Photoshop's history as a separate event. It doesn't take long before you run out of the 20 default history states and you can't go back and undo anything before you started cloning – you'll have to go back to the very beginning and start again. For this reason (and many more) it's a good idea to keep your healing and cloning edits separate from the main image by putting them on a different layer.

As well as being non-destructive, there are creative advantages to this, too: you can choose the blending mode of the edits, as well as the transparency of the cloning layer, and therefore how much (if anything) of the original detail you can see through the cloned material on top of it. You can use layer masks to edit the edits you've made, and in fact any of Photoshop's main editing tools can be used to modify the clones and heals separately to the main image.

Cloning in layers

Let's see how cloning and healing is used in layers on this cityscape image. It needs some work as the skyline is very messy, with cranes obscuring the view and a couple of clouds visible in the sky. This is all detail that can be hidden from view with cloned detail from elsewhere.

Left and below: The cranes on the skyline of this urban landscape were removed with the Clone Stamp and Healing Brush tools, with the edits being made on a new layer.

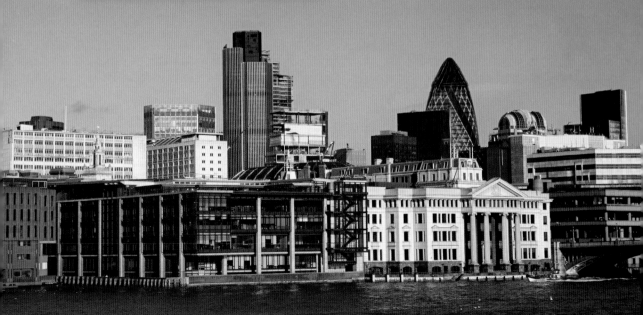

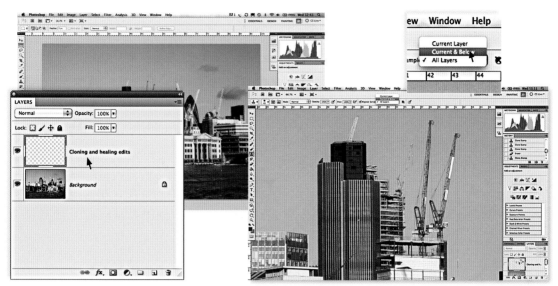

Step 1. Open the image into Photoshop or Photoshop Elements and create a new layer by clicking the shortcut in the Layers palette or by choosing Layer > New > Layer... Name it 'Cloning and healing' so you don't get confused.

Step 2. Find an area you want to work on with the Clone Stamp or Healing Brush and choose the appropriate tool. In the Options bar at the top of the screen, choose 'Current & Below' from the drop-down menu to tell Photoshop to sample from both layers.

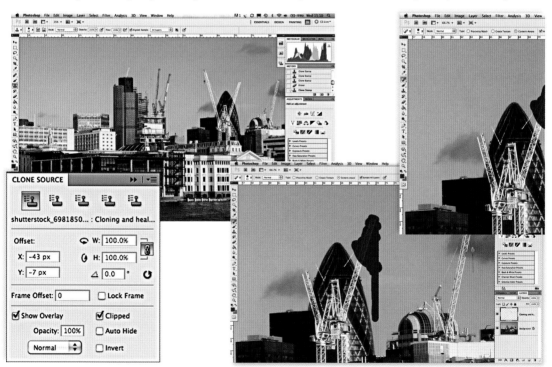

Step 3. Work away as normal, sampling from a source point by alt-clicking and painting over the offending dust, dirt, etc. You can use this approach with the Spot Healing Brush, too, by making sure the 'Sample All Layers' box is ticked.

Step 4. Notice that the cloning and healing edits are contained on one layer and the original image on another. Any adjustment layers placed above should apply to both layers below in order for the edits to remain convincing.

ADDING TEXTURES USING SMART OBJECTS AND BLENDING MODES

Give your photography a distressed look and feel by adding layers containing textures in Adobe Photoshop.

Adding texture to photographs, especially portraits, can transform the look of an image, making it feel more gritty and elemental. Such textures are available very cheaply from online image libraries, or you can go and shoot them yourself – look for scratched and weather-beaten metal sheeting, dirty paving slabs, old wood – anything that has a distressed look to it. Importing the texture into the picture being edited as a 'smart

object' offers some advantages over defining it as a normal layer. Shoot the textures in raw and you can use the creative power of Adobe Camera Raw (ACR) to modify white balance and tone to fit the main image perfectly. It's not something done easily the first time around, but opening the raw file as a smart object means you can revisit these settings once you've seen what the texture looks like in place, with the appropriate blending mode selected. Let's see how it's done.

Below: This simple portrait and a close-up shot of a paving slab were converted to smart objects before being blended together in the same image.

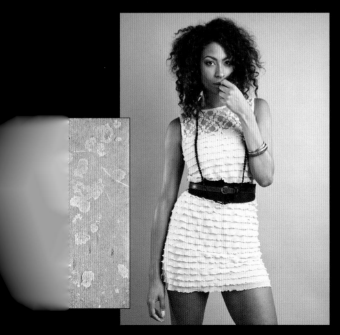

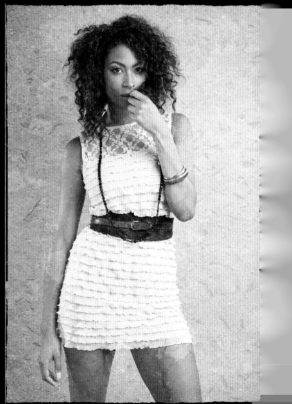

ESSENTIAL KIT

- Compact camera or DSLR to shoot portrait and texture files
- PC or Mac computer
- Adobe Photoshop software

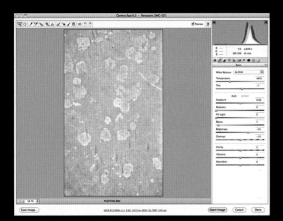

Step 1. Open the portrait into Photoshop, then open the raw file containing the texture image into ACR. Fine-tune the texture to suit the main image, for instance using the white balance controls to generate a warm cast. Hold down shift and click Open to bring the image into Photoshop as a smart object.

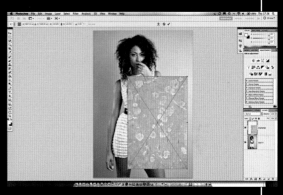

Step 2. Drag the smart object layer into the portrait image window and use a free transform (Edit > Free Transform) to resize it to cover the image completely. Now change the blending mode to Overlay or Soft Light using the drop-down menu in the Layers palette. You should see the image shine through the texture.

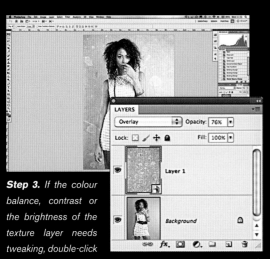

Step 3. If the colour balance, contrast or the brightness of the texture layer needs tweaking, double-click the small smart object icon in that layers icon in the Layers palette. This will return you to ACR where you can make the adjustments. You can also bring in more textures and layer these on top of each other to combine effects.

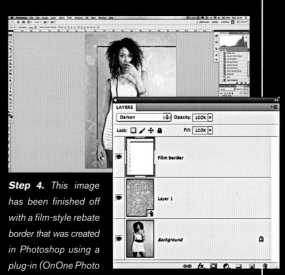

Step 4. This image has been finished off with a film-style rebate border that was created in Photoshop using a plug-in (OnOne Photo Frame). You can also buy these borders as stock images and even make your own by scanning old negatives or painted and drawn shapes.

Smart objects and layers

Take the principles of non-destructive editing a stage further by using Adobe Photoshop's re-editable smart layers to make adjustments to your images.

The editing principles that come with layers, layer masks and adjustment layers offer a new way of working in Photoshop. This non-destructive methodology is a more efficient, cleaner way of working, enabling you to revisit adjustments and edits without undoing everything your have done since then. But this is only the start of non-destructive editing in Photoshop. For still more advanced techniques, we can turn to smart layers and smart objects to enable us to apply and revisit raw processing settings and filter effects non-destructively throughout the editing process.

Smart objects

You can bring additional picture elements into an existing Photoshop document as new layers by dragging and dropping them between layers palettes or by using the copy and paste clipboard commands. At any time you can additionally change a normal layer into a smart object by right-clicking on it in the Layers palette and choosing 'Convert to Smart Object'. Smart objects have the important quality that you can resize and transform them as much as you like without losing any quality. This is not so with normal layers.

Try it for yourself: create a two-layered image in Photoshop by opening two image files and dragging one of the background layers into the other image's main window. Now resize layer one with the Free Transform command, decreasing the size of the layer so it's very small, and hit return to commit the change. The problem now comes if you change your mind and make the layer bigger again – try it with another free transform, returning layer one to its original size. The quality is not what it should be, since Photoshop threw away a lot of the original resolution in the first free transform. Smart layers get around this problem.

Go back and perform this exercise again, except this time change layer one into a smart layer before you resize it. You should find that you can resize,

i Smart filters

Smart filters follow a similar principle. When applying filter effects normally, the filter's parameters can only be adjusted once, and after you click OK the only way to adjust the options is to undo the effect (and everything you've done since) and reapply. With smart filters things are different.

Choose Filter > Convert for smart filters and you'll now be able to apply filter effects non-destructively, revisiting their settings at any time. Smart filter effects appear in the Layers palette and you can edit them any time by double-clicking on them.

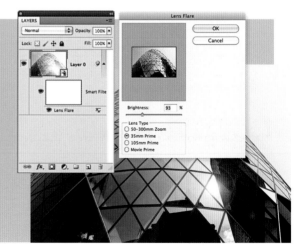

ACR and smart objects

Perhaps the ultimate use for this smart technology is Adobe Camera Raw's ability to open a raw image directly into Photoshop as a smart object. This means that, at any time, you can revisit ACR to make changes to the raw-processing settings, then carry on with the editing. You can do this as many times as you like, giving you phenomenal control over the tones, colours and detail in your image all the way through the editing process.

Just be aware that, as with all smart object work, file sizes can grow to be rather huge. For this reason, non-destructive editing works best on computers with a decent amount of RAM.

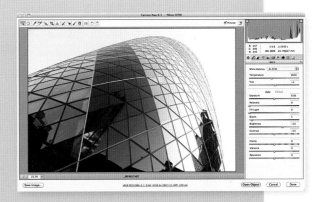

rotate, flip and skew the layer as much as you want, hit return, and still be able to revisit the layer with another free transform, with no loss of quality.

This is a great way of positioning and scaling objects when you are creating composite images. At some point you will have to convert smart objects back to ordinary layers in order to edit

them with other tools, such as the Healing Brush or Clone Stamp, but until then you can resize and adjust components in your composite to get things looking just right.

Below: *Repeated resizing of a normal layer (left) causes problems, while a smart object (right) keeps its image quality.*

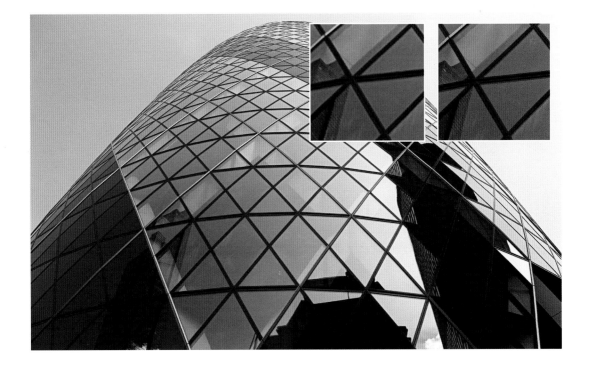

ASSIGNMENT
MINIATURE LANDSCAPES

The miniature landscape effect is making its way onto more DSLRs and compacts as an in-camera filter effect, but you can also apply it using Photoshop in a few minutes.

The rise of the miniature landscape effect has been rapid and huge. A few years ago, photographers started to shoot urban landscapes with perspective control lenses, blurring some parts of the scene in order to make it look like it's a model. This works because we are used to seeing limited depth of field and shallow focus when small objects are photographed up close with a macro lens, extension tube or supplementary close-up lens.

Not everyone has access to specialized perspective control lenses, although the effect can be simulated using Photoshop's blur filters and a depth map, drawn onto the scene as a Gradient Fill tool. Increasingly these days the effect can also be applied in-camera, too, although this gives less control than the post-production method, and limited quality.

Let's see how to apply the miniature landscape effect with Quick Mask and the lens blur filter.

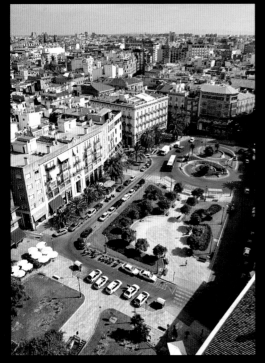

Above: *Before filter effect.*

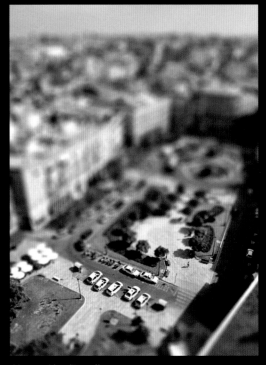

Above: *After filter effect.*

Quick Mask mode (see page 349). Select the Gradient Fill tool and the Reflected Gradient option from the top of the screen.

background colours. Draw a line from the point you want to be in focus to a point some distance away. You'll see a red band.

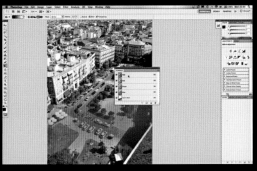

Step 3. *Bring up the Channels palette. The Quick Mask channel will be active, but click the RGB channel instead. The red band will stay visible.*

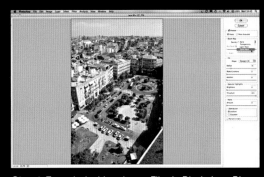

Step 4. *To apply the blur, choose Filter > Blur > Lens Blur… Under the depth map section, choose Quick Mask from the Source drop-down menu.*

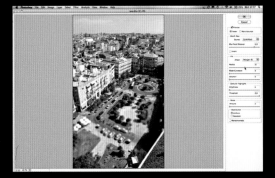

Step 5. *Increase the radius until you see the image blur, leaving the part you wanted to keep in-focus sharp. This gives the impression that the scene is small and model-like.*

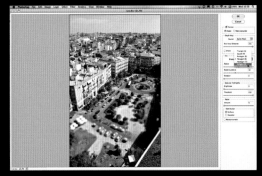

Step 6. *You can modify the quality of the blur with the other controls in the dialogue. Consider changing the iris shape to octagonal and increasing the blade curvature a little.*

Retouching portraits

There is something fascinating about retouching people in photographs. Maybe it's because the face is so personal, or perhaps we are just intrigued by the ability to correct our flaws and perfect our outward appearance.

Retouching in portraits, fashion images and advertising is more than commonplace in mainstream media these days. In fact it's hard to find a commercial picture that hasn't been under the brush in one way or another. Skin is smoothed, eyes are whitened and teeth straightened. Hair is trimmed, wrinkles are smoothed and bodies are sculpted. When taken to the extreme, digital retouching can leave some people looking like completely different people – and not necessarily in a good way.

At the more amateur end, though, retouching can also result in a portrait that really does your subject justice. Knowing that they will be given the airbrush treatment will give your sitter the confidence that the spot that erupted on their chin the day before the shoot won't be a problem, and a confident subject is a relaxed subject, which can only be a good thing.

How far you go in the retouching process isn't just limited by a sense of how real you want a portrait to be – it's also determined by how much time you can spend in front of the screen. Professional retouchers spend hours, if not days, perfecting their images, and they will be more efficient than most of us mere amateurs. But regardless of the skill you have with Photoshop, the same principle applies: the quality of the result you'll achieve is directly proportional to the time you can spend on it.

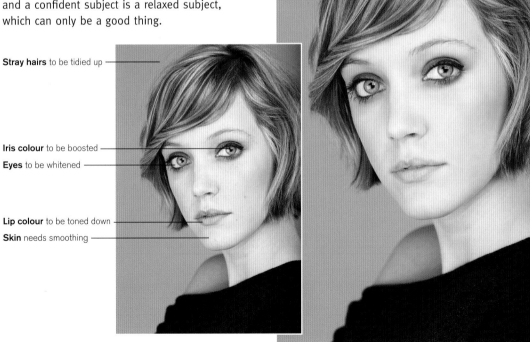

Stray hairs to be tidied up

Iris colour to be boosted

Eyes to be whitened

Lip colour to be toned down

Skin needs smoothing

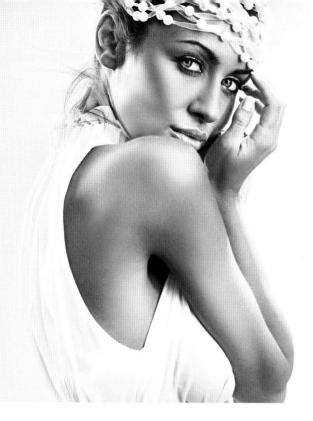

Getting specific

Anything goes when it comes to post-production, although there are some common elements that you will always find yourself working on. For example, skin is something that gets attention from retouchers all the time, with the Clone Stamp and Healing Brush being used to remove spots, pimples, moles and wrinkles. With some patience and the right filters, you can remove blotches, even-out tone and colour and even soften the texture of pores, although there is always a danger of going too far and creating a china-doll effect, which doesn't look good outside the pages of a glossy fashion magazine.

Eyes and teeth can be visited with the sponge tool, which selectively desaturates what it is painted over, removing any colour that shouldn't be there. You can brighten these areas slightly, too, although again be wary of going too far.

Most of the techniques we'll look at here for digital retouching are non-destructive because they make good use of layers and layer masks. This is an important approach to take, as it means you can revisit areas of the post-production edit that look over the top and tone them down without starting again from scratch.

The ethics of retouching

Every now and again retouching is pilloried as one of the evils of our modern age. It is claimed that excessive retouching of images in mainstream media gives young people a false impression of how they should look and can lead to eating disorders and body dysmorphia.

Getting rid of retouching won't solve these issues, but putting it in context might help. Historically, retouching has always taken place. Oil paintings of kings and queens often depicted them as larger and stronger, or more beautiful, than they were in real life. Even make-up, which has been used for centuries, is designed to make us look better than we really are.

Retouching is here to stay, but by spreading the word that virtually every celebrity picture you see in today's media has been tweaked in some way, perhaps we can begin to stop people comparing themselves to body shapes or faces that simply do not exist. And you would do well to keep the amount of retouching in your own pictures under control, too.

Skin **smoothing**

Smoothing skin is a popular part of post-production retouching. Ask your subject if they want you to smooth out any wrinkles or remove any spots, and the answer will always be 'yes'.

Retouching skin is what many portrait and fashion photographers are interested in learning. It's a great skill to have, and your subjects will thank you for being able to sort out any dermatological problems for them with some Photoshop work. When you are looking at those flawless beauty shots in fashion magazines, however, do please remember a couple of things. Firstly, flawless skin is not created entirely in Photoshop. Good photographic-quality make-up applied by a qualified make-up artist can often be half the job, as can good lighting technique. Get these right and your time in Photoshop will be drastically reduced.

Secondly, there is no digital shortcut to retouched skin. Some applications and plug-ins promise an automated route, but none do as good a job as a manual approach by hand. You'll get out of the process what you put in – so always take your time, and work slowly and carefully.

The Clone Stamp and Healing Brush are obviously very effective ways for clearing up obvious problems, like a spot, pimple or scar. Sample good skin from nearby and copy it over the top. The Healing Brush is usually better for this type of thing, but do also try its cousin the Spot Healing Brush, which can save some time and still provide a good result. Work at high magnification so you can see the effect and anticipate any problems. You may even want to keep your cloning and healing work separate on an additional layer.

With the obvious blemishes sorted out, you can either stop there or carry on to achieve that high-fashion look, which is a lot of fun for both you and your subject. To smooth skin to a porcelain-like finish, you can carry on blurring it with the Healing Brush, taking a long time to work your way over the surface piece by piece. Alternatively, you can take a shortcut using a blur filter. This will not give you quite the same quality of result, but it is much faster.

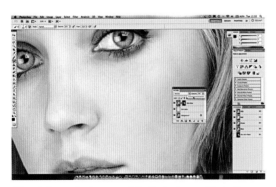

Step 1. *Open the image up into Photoshop or Photoshop Elements and create a new layer by selecting Layer > New Layer... or clicking the shortcut in the Layers palette. Call the new layers 'Skin Edits'.*

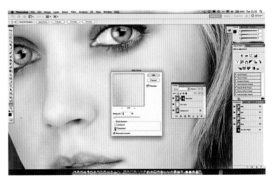

Step 2. *With the Clone Stamp and Healing Brush tools, go round the image and remove spots, pimples and wrinkles. Do this on the Skin Edit layer, making sure you have the 'Sample All Layers' option ticked.*

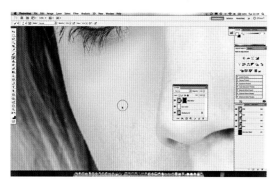

Step 3. *Select the Background and Skin Edits layers and use the keystroke shift–alt–ctrl–E (shift–alt–⌘–E on a Mac) to make a new layer from those below. Rename this one 'Skin Blur'.*

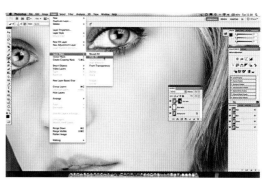

Step 4. *Choose Filter > Blur > Gaussian Blur and drag the Amount slider to around 20 or so to completely blur the image in the Skin Blur layer. Hit OK when you are happy.*

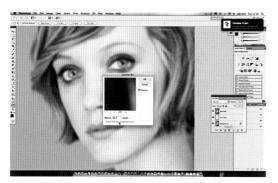

Step 5. *Add a layer mask (see pages 350–351) to the Skin Blur layer (Layer > Layer Mask > Hide All). Begin to paint the blur back in with the Brush tool, using white to do this and with the layer mask icon selected.*

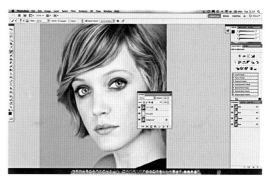

Step 6. *Paint the blur back in over areas of skin, using a very small, soft-edged brush when you get close to details such as eyelashes and lips. Take your time, and use a graphics tablet if possible.*

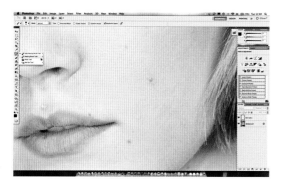

Step 7. *Apply some texture back to the Skin Blur layer (not the mask) by choosing Filter > Noise > Add Noise… 2–3 per cent should do, with the Monochromatic and Gaussian options selected.*

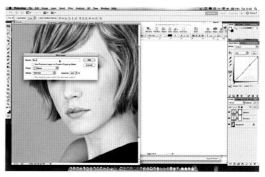

Step 8. *Now reduce the opacity of the Skin Blur layer with the slider in the Layers palette. The other layers will shine through from below, restoring some original texture. How much will depend on your own photo and the effect you want to create.*

The **details**

When it comes to retouching, the devil is in the detail. Eyes, teeth and hair can all be visited by the Photoshop toolbox, but just be careful to keep it real. Good retouching shouldn't look retouched.

Portrait and beauty retouching is about more than just skin. Attention to detail is what turns a good photograph into a stunning image. We must also look at the subject's eyes (are they sparkling and clear?), teeth (are they mark-free and white?) and hair (any strays or dark roots?). This might all sound a bit like hard work, but all of these problems can be tackled using tools we have already encountered in the preceding chapters. Lets see how it's done.

Eyes

It's said that the eyes are the windows to the soul, and they are certainly the focus of many portrait photographs. Common problems with eyes include the whites of the eyes containing red blood vessels, clumps of mascara on the ends of eyelashes and bags underneath the eyes from too many late nights.

The whites of the eyes can be refreshed by desaturating them of colour with the Sponge tool. This shares a spot in the toolbox with the Dodge and Burn tools, and can be set to desaturate any areas it is painted over. Use it with a small, soft-edged brush. Alternatively, for a non-destructive approach, you can use a Hue/Saturation adjustment layer (see pages 354–355), paired with a layer mask to limit the desaturation to those areas you want.

It's tempting to brighten the whites of the eyes with the Dodge tool or a Levels adjustment layer and a layer mask, but do be aware that overdoing this can leave you with unnatural looking results. The eyes should always continue to look moist, and over-brightening can spoil this. Better to apply brightening to the whole of the eye, iris and pupil included, and keep it very subtle.

If the blood vessels in your subject's eyes are very pronounced, then try eliminating some of them with the Healing Brush tool, sampling from areas of plain white and using a very small brush to paint with.

We saw on pages 260–261 how to selectively change the colour of a subject's eyes. Using the same principle, we can alter the intensity of their eye colour by adjusting the Saturation and Lightness sliders instead of the Hue control.

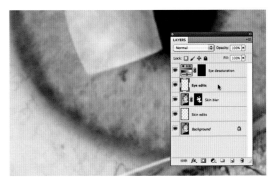

Above: *Any redness in the eyes can be desaturated with the Sponge tool or a Hue/Saturation adjustment layer.*

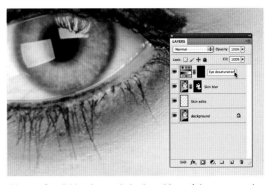

Above: *Small blood vessels in the whites of the eyes can be removed with the Clone Stamp tool.*

Teeth

Teeth are an altogether more simple affair. Using the Clone Stamp, Healing Brush and Spot Healing Brush tools, we can remove any spots, marks or lipstick that might be visible and reconstruct the edges to hide any chips. You can call on the Sponge tool to take any general colouration away from teeth, but don't be as heavy-handed as you were with the whites of the eyes. Drag the Intensity slider down a little, to around ten per cent, and work over the areas until you are happy. People are often self-conscious about their teeth and any problems with them, so be sensitive about this area and don't go too far.

Here we have tidied up a few marks on our subject's lips, using the Clone Stamp tool, a Curves adjustment layer and a layer mask. We've also slightly toned down their colour with a Hue/Saturation adjustment layer.

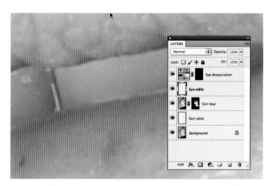

Above: *Marks on the teeth can be removed with the Clone Stamp or Healing Brush, or whitened with the Sponge tool.*

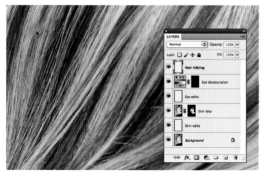

Above: *Stray hairs are a common problem. Again, they can be removed using the Clone Stamp tool on a new layer.*

Hair

Even a small amount of work on your subject's hair can make a big difference. In particular look out for stray single hairs that extend out from the sitter's head onto the background. Tidying these up with the Clone Stamp tool gives a picture a much cleaner look. Similarly, hairs protruding over the subject's eyes and face can be distracting. Remove them with the Spot Healing Brush with the Content Aware option selected. Keep these edits non-destructive by making them on a layer of their own (see page 358).

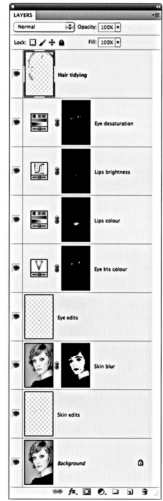

Left: *The final image has no fewer than nine individual layers in it. These are saved in a Photoshop PSD file for future editing, while a smaller JPEG file is saved for viewing, sharing and printing.*

ASSIGNMENT
SHOOTING A
BEAUTY MAKEOVER

A makeover is a great gift for a friend or relative, but it's even more personal if you can style, shoot and retouch it yourself, and finish it off with a framed print at the end.

The concept behind a makeover is simple: take someone who is not used to being treated like a celebrity or model, get their make-up and hair done, style them in some great clothes and shoot their picture as if they were going to appear in a top magazine. Unlike conventional portraiture, the idea is to get them looking as different to how they usually look as possible – as glamorous, sexy and dressed-up as you can.

How far you can take this will depend a great deal on how much access you have to clothes, props and studio space, as well as your prowess with a make-up brush. This might involve calling in favours and borrowing items of clothing. If make-up is not your thing, do you know anyone who can help?

When it comes to ideas for a shoot like this, there is nothing wrong with borrowing some inspiration from photographs you might have seen

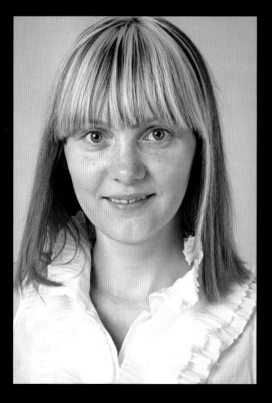
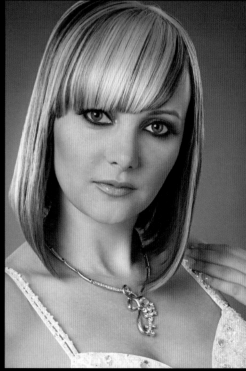

in the media or on the internet. Keep a scrapbook or tear sheet and ask your subject to do the same. Try to deconstruct the images and figure out how they were lit, composed and constructed. This way you'll be able to plan exactly how you are going to organize your makeover shoot.

Printing and presentation

No matter how good the photography, the gift of a makeover won't live up to its full potential unless it's printed well and looks good. If you have a good quality inkjet printer, consider getting some top quality fine-art paper and making the best print you can. Alternatively use an online print lab, who may even mount and frame the image for you. Affordable frames are available on the high street, and small touches like signing the mount and inscribing 'Happy Birthday' can make the gift more personal.

Left: A good make-up artist, some soft but directional studio lighting and a bit of Photoshop retouching can bring a spot of glamour to anyone's photograph.

Smoky eye make-up

One of the best ways to enhance your model's eyes is, of course, eye make-up, and one of the great classics is the smoky-eye look. This looks particularly good with formal outfits and settings and can vary in colour and tone. For example, grey tones work with almost every other colour, whereas plum tones need darker eyes – it all depends on the general feel you want to achieve. As a general rule, darker make-up works well with darker photographs, and lighter shades work better in daylight settings.

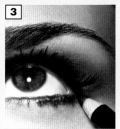
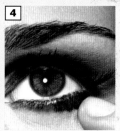

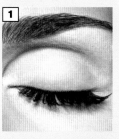
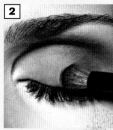

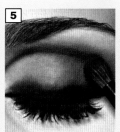
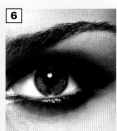

1. Blend foundation into your eyelid to act as a base, and finish with a touch of face powder.
2. Brush a smoky eyeshadow over the whole lid.
3. Apply eyeliner right around the lash line.
4. Smudge the eyeliner to soften the edge.
5. Add a darker shade next to the lash line, on top of the eyeliner, and smudge with your finger.
6. Add a final coat of mascara to finish.

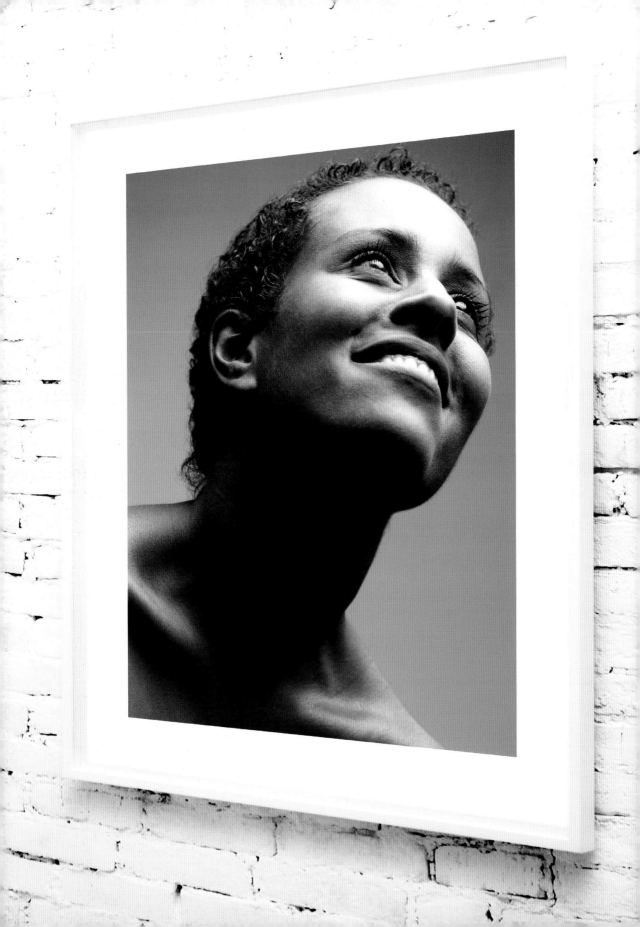

finishing
touches

You've shot photographs, edited them,
retouched them, and now you are (quite rightly)
happy with the results. So what are the next steps?
How do you get your images seen by the rest
of the world? Let's look at how to make prints,
websites, slideshows and even make
a bit of cash from your camera by
selling your pictures as stock.

Printing at home

The desktop inkjet printer has become the photographer's best friend, enabling photo-quality prints at various sizes to be created in the comfort of your own home.

Printing your photographs from home offers one huge advantage over other methods of printing – the ability to stay in control. Although getting a print perfect yourself can be a time-consuming and costly business, it is also very rewarding, and the only way to be sure you are going to end up with an image that looks as similar to what you see on screen as possible. And once the right settings are found, the process is completely reproducible, so you can make as many copies as you like, for sale, framing or as gifts for friends and family.

There are a number of important links in the home-printing chain: a good quality inkjet printer doesn't cost the earth these days and you'll need to think about choosing the right kind of paper, too, but something that sometimes gets overlooked is the software that we print with. The printer driver looks after communication between your computer and the printer. Setting this up properly each time you print is vital for getting good quality results.

Print software settings

While each manufacturer's printer driver interface will look slightly different, the options you are presented with for any given printer will be largely the same in all applications, from Microsoft Word or Excel through to photo-editing programmes such as Adobe Photoshop or Photoshop Elements. Some options need to be set according to the type of media you are using, and there is only one correct setting. Others change the type of print effect or performance you'll get from the printer, whether that's colour saturation or print speed and so on.

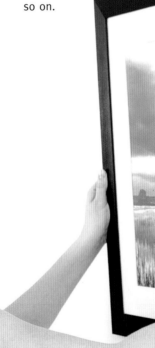

Right: There's nothing better than seeing one of your own pictures printed well and hanging on the wall.

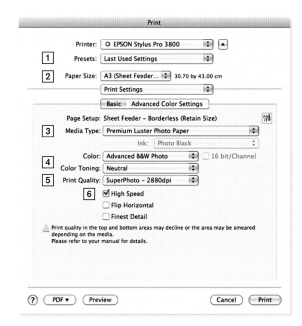

1. Presets *Collections of print settings for different, commonly used media types can be saved here.*

2. Paper size *This printer accepts paper from 6 x 4 inches up to 17 x 24 inches. More commonly, inkjet printers accept paper up to A4 or A3 in size.*

3. Media type *The most important setting to get right, this tells the printer what kind of paper you are using. Different paper types require different amounts of ink (to compensate for different absorption). Colour shifts may also occur between paper types, and this is compensated for by the printer driver.*

4. Colour and colour toning *Some printers contain shades of grey for enhanced black and white performance. These are activated by selecting black and white instead of colour. Colour tone settings give options for warm, neutral or cool mono prints.*

5. Print quality *The more dots of ink per square inch the printer can put down, the better the print quality will appear. On the other hand, more ink takes longer to put down, affecting print speed, and uses up more ink from the cartridges.*

6. High speed option *This tells the printer to deposit ink when moving left-to-right and right-to-left. When unticked, ink is only put down on the paper in one direction.*

Above: *The Print dialogue box for an Epson Stylus Pro 3800 inkjet printer, showing commonly used paper and colour settings.*

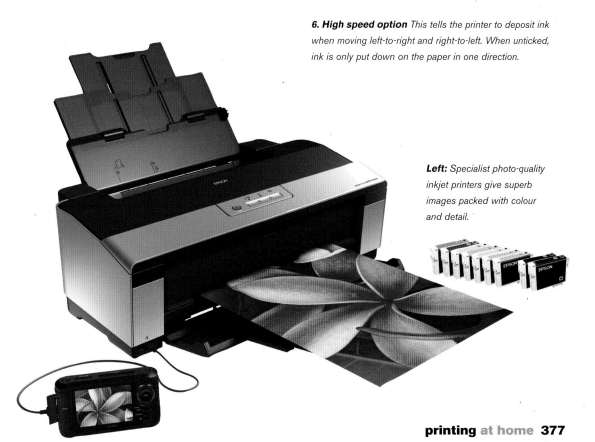

Left: *Specialist photo-quality inkjet printers give superb images packed with colour and detail.*

ASSIGNMENT
MAKING A GREETINGS CARD

Nothing gives a greetings card a personal touch like making it yourself, and being a photographer you have the perfect material to do the job.

Even in this age of social networking and email, getting an old-fashioned greetings card in the post is the best way of being wished happy birthday, happy anniversary or best wishes on whatever holiday season you are celebrating. You can take the easy option here and buy a card, or you can make one yourself using one of the many image applications that have this ability.

Adobe Photoshop Elements lets you design greetings cards using your own photography. Take advantage of Adobe's design elements (backgrounds, ornaments and type effects), or if you are pretty handy with Elements, design the whole thing from scratch. Alternatively you can download loads of free Photoshop templates for spoof magazine covers on websites like www.fakemagazinecover.com or www.fototrix.com.

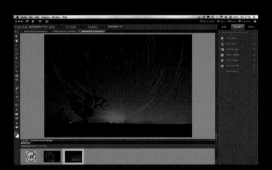

Step 1. Open a few images that you might want to use in your card's design. Next click on the Create tab on the far right, and choose 'Greetings Card' from the options below.

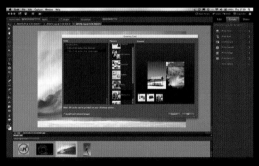

Step 2. The greetings card dialogue box will pop up, presenting you with a variety of options. Choose a design and an orientation (landscape or portrait).

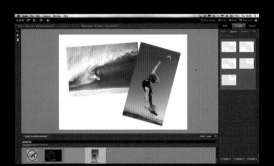

Step 3. Elements automatically flows in the images you have selected into the design. At this stage you can click on the Layouts tab, and double-click on alternative layouts.

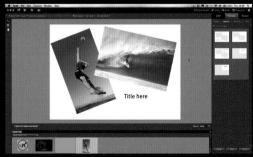

Step 4. Double-clicking on the images reveals resize/rotate handles with which you can reposition the images. A slider lets you zoom them in the frame.

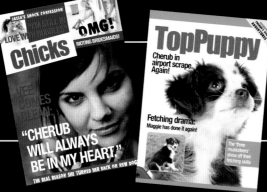

Above: *Photoshop templates for spoof magazine covers are easily downloadable and can be great fun!*

ESSENTIAL KIT

- PC or Mac
- Adobe Elements software
- Library of your own photography
- Inkjet printer

TIPS & TRICKS

- Look for graphic images when you are out and about that will make good motifs on your greetings cards. Try to find motifs that mean something to the recipient.

- You can buy blank cards pre-cut to exactly the right size that will go through your home printer, with envelopes included.

- Why not order a few dozen cards when you are coming up to a holiday period? Remember to leave plenty of time.

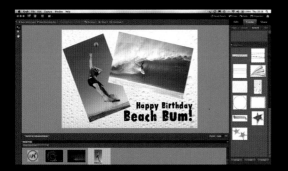

Step 5. *Edit and add text as well as ornaments, backgrounds or other effects from the Artwork tab. You can reorder, arrange and align using options at the top of the screen.*

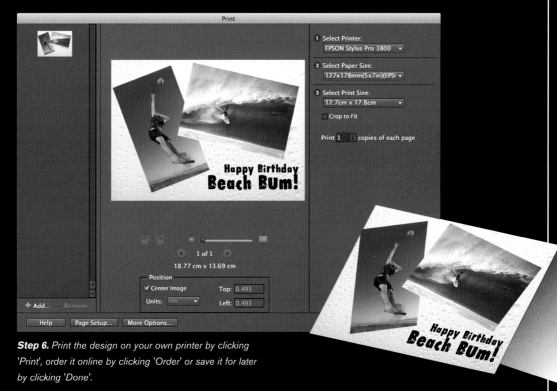

Step 6. *Print the design on your own printer by clicking 'Print', order it online by clicking 'Order' or save it for later by clicking 'Done'.*

Printing from Photoshop

The stage before the printer driver control screen is the print dialogue box, i.e. the box we see when we choose File › Print. This is the same in most applications, although Photoshop's version of the print dialogue is slightly more feature-packed than other applications. In Photoshop CS5, the print screen contains options governing the size of the printed image, where it is on the page, whether any printer's crop marks will be displayed and how colour management is handled. In older versions of Photoshop this screen is called 'Print with Preview...' but Adobe deemed it so useful they promoted it to the standard 'Print...' screen in CS3 onwards.

Adobe Photoshop Elements has a similar interface, though a little more friendly and without some of the high-end professional features. In the main screen you can select which printer you are printing to, as well as the paper size and the size and position of the image on that paper. Click 'More Options...' and you'll be able to flip the image (handy when printing t-shirt transfers), add borders and control colour management.

Below: *The print dialogue boxes in Adobe Photoshop (bottom) and Elements (below) give tremendous control over output.*

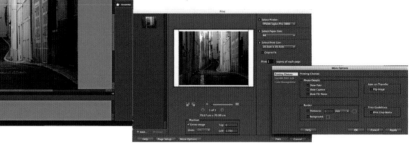

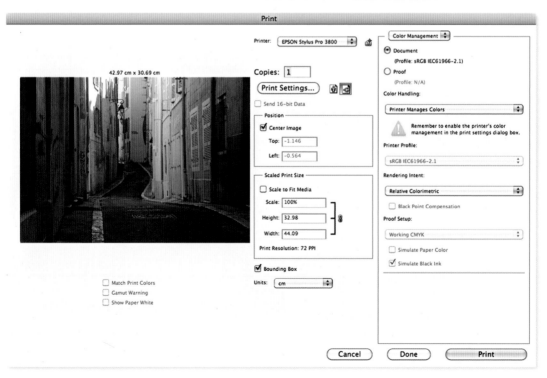

Contact sheets

Contact sheets get their name from a traditional darkroom technique where strips of negatives were laid down in contact with a sheet of photographic paper and exposed to light. The result was a grid of thumbnail images showing each frame taken on the roll. We can also produce this effect in Photoshop – great for showing people the results of a shoot, or keeping an index record of images to accompany back-ups.

In Photoshop you can either make a contact sheet from Bridge, or by choosing Automate › Contact Sheet from the main Photoshop application. In the Contact Sheet dialogue box, specify where the images are on your system (or just select them if you are in Bridge), how big the page size is, and choose how many images you want in each column or row. Click OK and wait patiently while Photoshop assembles each image as a thumbnail on the page, which you can then print, save or email once finished.

In Photoshop Elements the process is slightly easier – choose File › Contact Sheet II and follow the same instructions as above. Adobe Lightroom also has many contact sheet options in its Print module, and these can be customized to hold different numbers of images, sizes of thumbnails, etc.

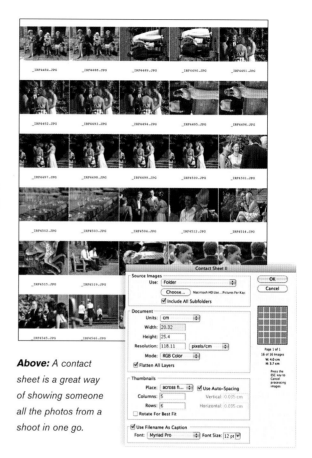

Above: *A contact sheet is a great way of showing someone all the photos from a shoot in one go.*

Resizing for print

Although the 'Print...' dialogue boxes in Photoshop and Elements allow you to resize an image at the printing stage, it is still worth having a go at doing this manually so you can appreciate what the print commands are doing behind the scenes. As with interpolating or shrinking images (see pages 310–311), choose Image › Image Size... In this box, untick the Resample Image box and enter the size at which you would like to print the image. The resolution will change accordingly, getting smaller as your print size gets bigger. You will start to notice a quality drop-off once the resolution falls below 200ppi, and you should avoid printing at all below 150ppi. If you need to print larger than the size at which this point occurs, you will either need to interpolate the image a little (but don't go mad with it) or, better still, shoot on a higher resolution camera.

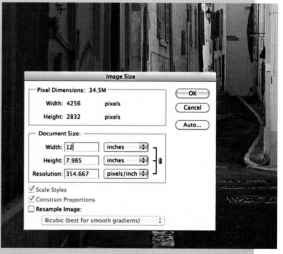

Above: *You can enter a physical print size in Photoshop's Print dialogue box.*

Printing on the high street

Every town has a print shop or photo lab where you can get prints made. This is a great resource to get to know well and use.

The humble photo-processing lab has gone through a metamorphosis over the last decade, as digital photography has come to the fore. While these businesses used to thrive on the number of rolls of film they could process and print in a week, they are now digital print houses where you can have your images outputted onto anything, from paper and t-shirts to canvas. High-street print shops accept virtually any digital storage medium you can think of, too. Take images in on a memory card, pen drive, CD/DVD or portable hard disk and they will be able to read them straight into the minilab processing machine where they'll be printed on real photographic paper in a flash. Some shops even accept pictures shot on your cellphone via Bluetooth – no plugging in required.

The downside of printing at a high-street photo lab is that you have to give up control over the printing process and trust the staff to get it right for you. This isn't the end of the world – if you

find a good print company, stick with it and get to know the people that work there. And if you are ever really disappointed with the results, tell the lab why and ask them to reprint it.

Some shops do offer you a degree of control through kiosks installed on the customer side of the counter. Here you can insert your memory card or CD/DVD and upload the pictures you want to print to the minilab yourself, where the operator will take over. Before they do, though, you'll be able to crop and rotate them, as well as pick the right print size and ratio and even apply (somewhat tacky) effects, though it is best to do the more adventurous stuff at home on your own computer.

The real advantage of a print shop is that it lets you have access to print sizes and materials that you would need a very expensive printer to create yourself at home. Depending on file size, they will be able to print at up to A1 or even A0 size, and on materials such as canvas and perspex, too. Mugs, keyrings, calendars, t-shirts, mousemats and

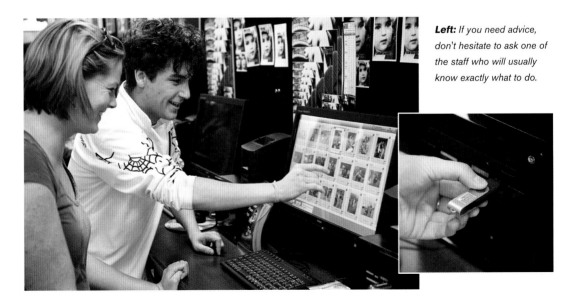

Left: If you need advice, don't hesitate to ask one of the staff who will usually know exactly what to do.

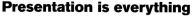

Right: You'd never be able to afford to run a printer like this at home (and where would you keep it?), but your local print shop may have one.

all manner of other things are all on offer here, and make great presents for friends and family.

It can also be useful to get your printing done on the high street when the quantity of prints you are making is high. It's more efficient to drop off a memory card containing 100 image files as you are doing your grocery shopping, coming back an hour later to 100 7 x 5 inch prints, than it is to attempt to print such a job at home. And it's cheaper too: many labs give bulk order discounts for 30, 50, 75 or 100 prints ordered at the same time.

Presentation is everything

It's not unusual to find a good selection of frames and mounts in a high street print shop, in sizes ranging from compact to enormous. It's a good place to shop for them, too, as you can try out different combinations while you wait for your

images to be printed, and ensure they go well with your photos – both in terms of size and style. Custom framing costs more than ready-made options, and takes longer, but you don't have to compromise on anything and can get the perfect presentation for your photography.

Below: Your local high-street print shop is a good place to find ready-made frames with pre-cut mounts, as well as bespoke framing using a variety of materials.

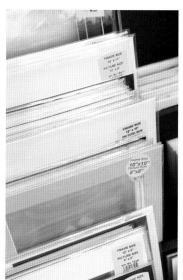
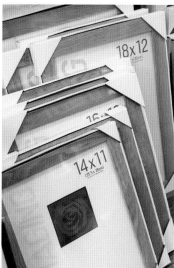
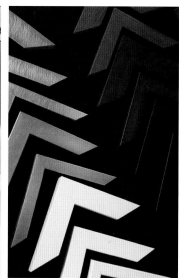

ASSIGNMENT
MAKING A PRINT PORTFOLIO

In the world of professional photography, your book, or print portfolio, is one of the principal marketing tools available for showing off your images.

Although there are many ways to show your images on the internet, on smart phones and on tablet computers and the like, the humble print book still takes some beating. Good quality photographic prints aren't seen so much these days, so the novelty of seeing 20 of your best pictures printed up to A3 size in a luxurious portfolio case is bound to make a good impression. You don't have to be trying to win over the art director of a top international fashion magazine, either; this is a good way of showing off your very best images to friends and family, too.

There are a number of portfolio case companies around, and you can pay wildly varying prices for them, too. At the budget end of the scale, try your local art shop who will undoubtedly stock the tough plastic cases beloved by art students. You can also buy clear plastic sleeves for your prints, which clip into the case's ringbinder system. It's a bit basic but can still look good, and the removable sleeves mean that you can reorder your pictures, or swap images in and out, very easily.

Stepping up a bit in terms of quality means you'll be looking at a bespoke print book from a specialist company. These can cost up to ten times the price of your basic student folio, often being hand-constructed from leather or some other luxury material. They do look the part, though, and show off your prints beautifully well.

When printing images for a portfolio, try to avoid glossy paper as this will reflect whatever is behind the person as they look at your images – usually the lights on the ceiling above them. Instead opt for a lustre or semi-matt paper that

will have more sharpness than a matt paper, but fewer reflections than a gloss paper. Use the best image quality you can – this is not a time for skimping. If your own inkjet printer isn't up to the job, consider a third-party printing company or specialist photographic lab. Also give some thought to the running order of the pictures in the book. It's best to avoid flitting between subjects and styles when you could group pictures together that have something in common.

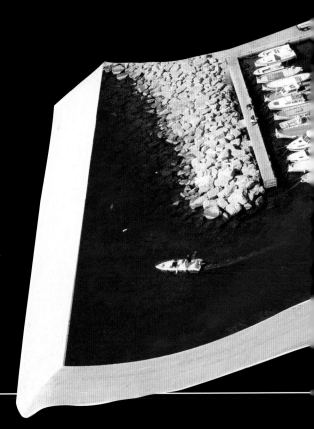

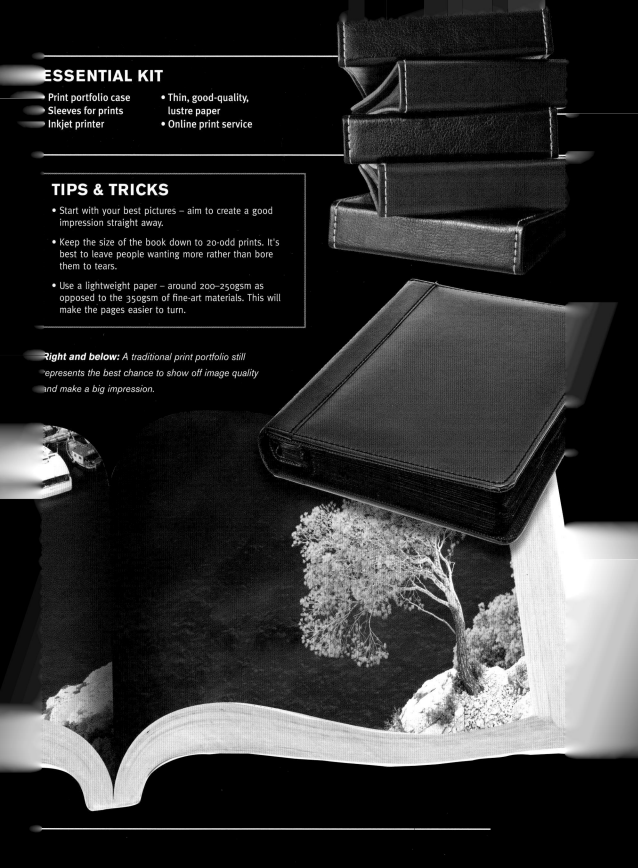

ESSENTIAL KIT

- Print portfolio case
- Sleeves for prints
- Inkjet printer
- Thin, good-quality, lustre paper
- Online print service

TIPS & TRICKS

- Start with your best pictures – aim to create a good impression straight away.

- Keep the size of the book down to 20-odd prints. It's best to leave people wanting more rather than bore them to tears.

- Use a lightweight paper – around 200–250gsm as opposed to the 350gsm of fine-art materials. This will make the pages easier to turn.

Right and below: A traditional print portfolio still represents the best chance to show off image quality and make a big impression.

Online print services

Most businesses have migrated to the web in some form or another, and photographic print processing is certainly no exception, with lots of online options to choose from.

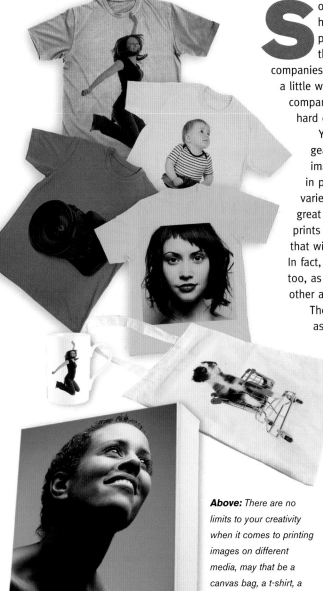

So far we've seen how to make your own prints at home using a photo-quality inkjet printer, or get them produced at a high-street photo lab or print shop, but there is a third way. There are lots of photo printing companies on the internet, too, and if you don't mind waiting a little while for the results to be posted back to you, these companies can be a great option when it comes to making hard copies of your images.

You'll find two types of online print producer: those geared around delivering medium to large quantities of images quickly and cheaply, and those who specialize in producing the best print quality they can on a wide variety of different media. The first of these options is great when you are producing a set of 6 x 4 or 7 x 5 prints for a friend or relative, or the kind of enlargement that will be displayed in the kitchen with fridge magnets. In fact, many of these companies also make fridge magnets too, as well as mugs, t-shirts, canvases and all manner of other accessories.

The principle is easy enough: prepare your images as normal using Photoshop, Elements, iPhoto or whatever software you prefer, then use the print company's online ordering tools to upload JPEG files over the internet. Often this is via a secure webpage, but some online printers have produced their own software that lives on your machine and makes the whole process a little more slick. Alternatively, some photo-editing applications – such as Photoshop Elements and Apple's iPhoto and Aperture – have print ordering built into them, which makes the process even easier.

The second type of online print business is the fine-art specialist, more interested in producing one enlargement of fantastic quality than 100 machine prints. Expect to be able to download colour profiles for their printers and choose from a selection of paper types and sizes.

Above: There are no limits to your creativity when it comes to printing images on different media, may that be a canvas bag, a t-shirt, a mug or a canvas of your favourite portrait.

Sharing prints online

You are not the only person who can order copies of your photographs online as prints. Some of the large internet print suppliers offer online album services so other people can order them, too.

This is a great way of sharing images with friends and family, who can browse for their favourite pictures and order as many copies as they like, in whatever size they want. Perfect for weddings, birthdays or any other celebration.

The biggest international online photo print companies include Photobox (www.photobox.com) and Snapfish (www.snapfish.com), who allow overseas ordering, too.

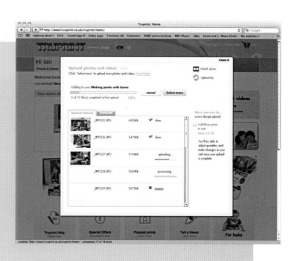

The online print ordering process in Adobe Photoshop Elements

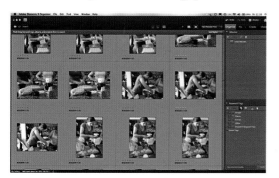

Step 1. Select the pictures you want to print in the application's organizer.

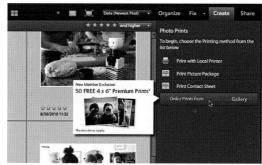

Step 2. Choose 'Create Prints' from the create module and select an online print company.

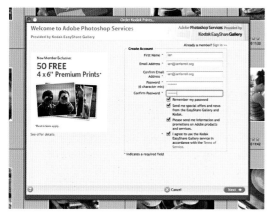

Step 3. Register with the print provider, giving them your name and address.

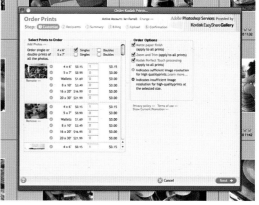

Step 4. Proceed through the upload instructions – you'll get your pictures in the post in a few days.

Your pictures on the **internet**

Getting your pictures on the internet is the key to sharing them with others – from your friends and family, to other photographers who can critique your pictures and give you new ideas for future shoots.

There are more ways to get your pictures on the internet than you can imagine, and even more are invented every day. Social networking sites such as Facebook let you put holiday snaps and party pictures up by simply dragging and dropping them, or uploading them via the site's interface. Caption them, sort them into albums and tag the people in them and you are done. But there are slightly more refined ways of showing your pictures to the cyber world.

Flickr is a social networking site that is actually built around photography. It's used by photographers wanting to show off their images in a more serious context, as well as party-going snappers sharing pictures with their mates. You can contribute to shared 'pools' containing similarly themed images from different photographers, and even set up groups of your own. Flickr allows people to comment on and rate your images, which is a good way of getting feedback on your technique and composition, as well as problem-solving when you are stuck.

If you want a way of putting your images quickly on the web without relying on a third-party company such as Flickr (or one of the many others out there), try using the web photo

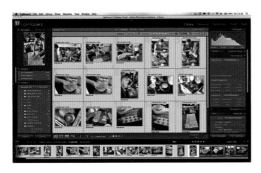

Step 1. Select the appropriate pictures in Lightroom (or the Bridge or Elements' file browser).

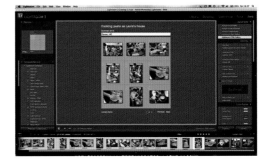

Step 2. In Lightroom, choose the web module and begin entering your personal information into the interface.

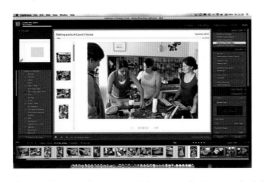

Step 3. You can choose one of the preset designs on the left or customize your own by changing the options on the right.

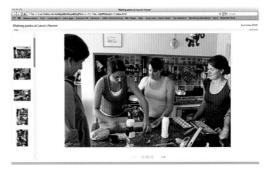

Step 4. Upload the finished site to your own webspace. You'll need to enter address, log-in and password details.

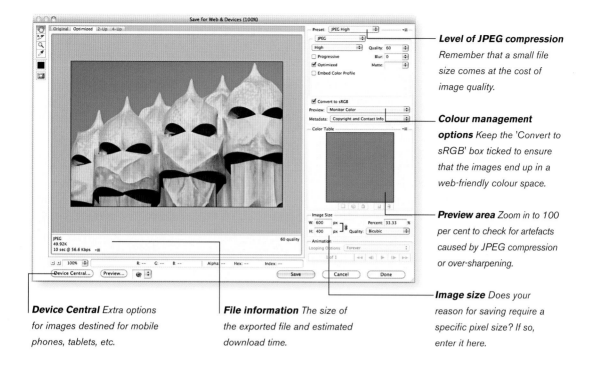

Level of JPEG compression *Remember that a small file size comes at the cost of image quality.*

Colour management options *Keep the 'Convert to sRGB' box ticked to ensure that the images end up in a web-friendly colour space.*

Preview area *Zoom in to 100 per cent to check for artefacts caused by JPEG compression or over-sharpening.*

Image size *Does your reason for saving require a specific pixel size? If so, enter it here.*

Device Central *Extra options for images destined for mobile phones, tablets, etc.*

File information *The size of the exported file and estimated download time.*

gallery features built into your editing software. These are excellent for letting people browse the results of a shoot at their leisure, or for showing people photos from your holiday or an event such as a wedding.

In Photoshop you'll find these under the File › Automate › Web Photo... command; in Elements you'll need the Online Album command in the Share tab. Adobe Lightroom also has a website facility located in a module all of its own, called Web, which you'll find in the top right-hand corner of the screen. There are lots of options to fill in, from the name and subheading of the site to your own personal details and contact information. You can also control the visual design of the site to a large degree, specifying the size and quantity of thumbnails as well as the colour scheme and typeface. There are so many options, in fact, it can be hard to know where to begin, which is is why it's great that Adobe has given plenty of preset designs to get you started. Some work with HTML – the original language of the web – while others are written in Flash, which offers more elaborate effects and designs, but with reduced compatibility for smart phones and older web browsers.

Saving images for the web

There are a number of routine conversions that need to be made in Photoshop, Elements or a similar retouching program every time we save an image for the web. We must choose JPEG as the file type and set the proper amount of compression (see page 42), as well as setting the colour profile of the file to sRGB if this is not already the case. The image may need resizing to a specific file size or set of pixel dimensions, and some photographers like to put custom metadata into the file as well, giving contact and copyright details (see page 401) or any other amount of relevant data like exposure time or location. Of course all of this is possible in Photoshop or Elements, but it soon becomes a bit of a bind when doing it all the time. Hence the 'Save for Web and Devices...' command in the file menu. Choose this and you'll be presented with numerous web-useful options, as well as a preview of your image. You can choose which of the three common web formats you want to save in (JPEG, GIF or PNG, although photographers usually always use JPEG) and tweak any options before you click the save button.

MAKING AN ONLINE PORTFOLIO SITE

An online portfolio is all about you and your photography – a window on the world that will let people see who you are, what you do with your camera and how well you do it.

If you are after something more serious, and more personalized, than a Flickr or Facebook page, then you might like to investigate having a dedicated website built around you and your photography. There are many companies on the internet who will design and build a site for you, often using templates to keep the price down to an affordable level, although unique, bespoke designs are also available at a premium.

When thinking about what you want from a website of your own, consider what pages you want to include and how these should relate to each other. Draw up a hierarchy, starting at the homepage, which people will see when they first visit the site, and progressing on to the next tier of pages such as information about you, contact details, what cameras you use and your picture galleries. Under this last tab you might have further subsections: portrait, landscape, fine art and so on.

This family tree of webpages is the first, and most important, part of the site design process. Even if it isn't you who will be doing the hardcore computer wizardry required to make the site operational, you can give such a diagram to your web designer, who will appreciate it greatly.

Working with a web designer is a collaboration. You can be involved in the look and feel of the site and give your input into what is working for you in terms of logo design and typography, etc. Also ask if a content management system can be incorporated to allow you to change the content of the website (text and pictures) without having to change the site's coding. Freely available content management systems such as Joomla and Wordpress are easy to set up and implement, and very easy to use when making changes to the site later on.

What's in a name?

Also important is picking the right name for your website – or to use the correct terminology, the right domain name. The domain name is the part of a web address that comes after the 'www' in your browser. The most obvious choice is your name, although unless you have a very unusual name, it is likely that yours is already taken. Don't

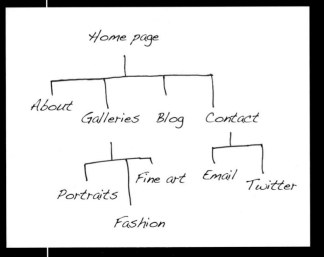

Left: At the beginning of the design process, map out your thoughts on paper. This will be the most important element you can give your web designer.

ESSENTIAL KIT

- ► PC or Mac
- ► Collection of related images

TIPS & TRICKS

- Split up your pictures into themed galleries to keep them consistent. Aim to have between 10–20 images in a single gallery.

- Stick with uncomplicated, simple designs that show off your photography and don't compete for attention.

- Be aware that Flash-based websites may look better, but are less compatible with older web browsers and some smart phones.

forget to try all of the domain endings, though, such as .net, .me and .co.uk, not just the ever-popular .com. You can also add 'photography' or 'photographer' to the end of your name to increase the likelihood of finding it available.

You can buy a name and rent space from an internet service provider. They will register the domain on your behalf, and bundle it with a web hosting package, if you wish, that provides space on a backed-up server somewhere as well as email addresses and FTP facilities for transferring large files.

Once you have a domain name of your own, you can use it for anything. The beautifully

designed website crafted by your web designer can live there, your email address can use it and your photoblog can live there, too – great if you are shooting a 365 project, for example (see page 169).

Below: A professionally designed portfolio site is the best way of showing your images to the world, as this example from Kate Hopewell-Smith shows.

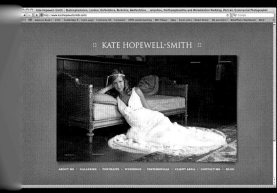
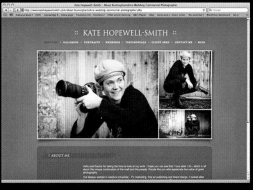
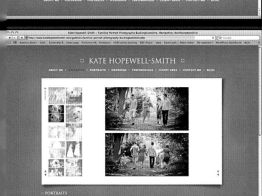
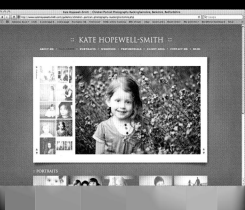

Creating **slideshows**

A great way to show photographs from a trip, party or day out is to create a slideshow. Tell the story of the day, set it to music and entertain your friends and family with it.

When we tell a story with our photographs, it's nice to able to tell that story back to those looking at the final, edited pictures. A great way of doing this is to compile a slideshow of images that can be played back on a computer, over the web or on a TV via a DVD player.

Slideshows work well for storytelling because you can control everything about them, from the running order of the pictures to the music that accompanies them. We can determine the length of time that each slide is on the screen, and the type of transition from one shot into the next. Panning and zooming movements can also be applied – sometimes known as the 'Ken Burns effect' after the American director of the same name who pioneered the technique.

Much like editing video footage, the time you leave each image on screen determines the look and feel of the story you are telling. Short durations with quick transitions give an air of urgency, especially when accompanied by fast-tempo music. On the other hand, leaving images up for a little longer, and complementing them with smooth fades and slower music, results in a more relaxed end result.

Slideshow software

Lots of software packages can produce slick-looking slideshows, although for once Photoshop and Elements aren't the pick of the bunch. These two applications produce PDF-based slideshows that will run on any computer, but they don't allow special effects, variable timing, music or title effects. For these it's time to turn to another package. Here are a few that do the job very well.

Apple iPhoto and Aperture

Although only available to owners of Apple computers, these two photo-editing applications

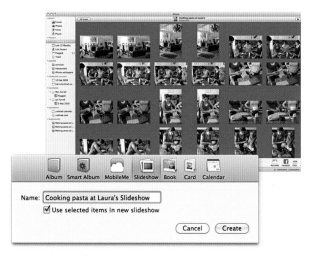

Step 1. *Sort the pictures in your image-editing application, in this case Apple's iPhoto, and create a new slideshow.*

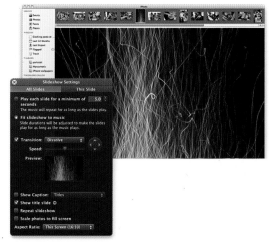

Step 2. *Set titles, transitions between slides and any special effects, reordering the images to tell a story.*

have accomplished slideshow modules. The timing of each slide can be set individually, along with the transition that will take it into the next one. Ken Burns effects can be included, too. You can also pick music from your entire iTunes library to accompany the slideshow, which can be outputted in a variety of resolutions. See www.apple.com for more information.

PicturesToExe

This PC-based application has been around for a number of years, and as such has become fully featured and popular, with a base of loyal fans. Start by exporting JPEG images of the slides, then import them into PicturesToExe. Here you can assemble them into the right order, give each a transition and add a soundtrack. The nice thing about this software is that the saved slideshow file is independent of the application itself, so you can give it to anyone with a PC (or now a Mac, too) and it will run as a self-contained slideshow file at great quality. See www.wnsoft.com for more information.

Adobe Lightroom

The all-in-one workflow package from Adobe has a much better slideshow package than its stablemates Photoshop and Elements. You can find the slideshow module on the top right of the screen, and while a number of options are available to you, it's not quite as user-friendly as other offerings. However, you can use any pictures already in your Lightroom database without creating special versions. The application will play slideshows by itself, or export them to PDF or a video format for playback on the internet or TV. See www.adobe.com/lightroom for more information.

FotoMagico

Another Mac-only application that allows you to take images from iPhoto, Aperture, Lightroom and Flickr, as well as those just hanging around on your hard disk. You can mix video and still images and add titles, transitions and music straight from iTunes. You can also use special effects to pan across long, thin panoramic images, instead of cropping them. See www.boinx.com for more information.

PhotoSnack

A different approach is PhotoSnack, a web-based slideshow creation tool that allows you to upload images and create slick-looking, Flash-based slideshows that can be sent across the internet. It's a great option for when you are travelling and want to send home something a bit more informative and fun than a postcard. See www.photosnack.com for more information.

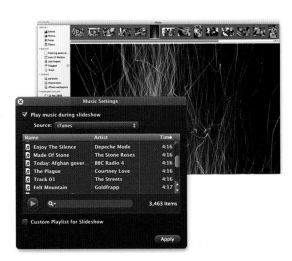

Step 3. *Choose a soundtrack, either using built-in music or your own iTunes music library*

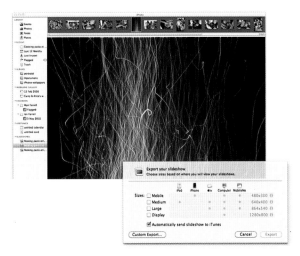

Step 4. *Export the slideshow in the right format for playback on TV, computer or internet sites such as YouTube.*

Printing **photobooks**

Photobooks are a great way of enjoying a printed collection of photographs from a trip, party or event. Combine pictures with text, graphics and even maps for a complete record of your trip.

One of the more exciting developments in photo printing in recent years has been the rise of the photobook: your images printed and bound into a real book, with a cover and a dustjacket. At last you can be published!

Photobooks are more the thing of internet printing companies rather than high-street shops, because they require quite a lot of input from you, the photographer. This is more fun than you might think though, and will be sure to bring out the inner graphic designer in you. Some image-editing software has the ability to design

Below: Write your own recipe book: Take pictures of your favourite dishes as and when you make them, write down the recipe and once you've accumulated a nice collection, get them formatted and printed with one of the many online providers like Snapfish or Photocreator – a great birthday or Christmas present for your loved ones.

photobooks built-in – Apple's Aperture and iPhoto are particularly good and feature some stunning designs. Other companies provide software with which you can design your book from the processed and edited pictures on your computer.

The concept is a simple one. At the beginning of the design process you need to decide what size and shape of book you are going for, what cover material will be used, and so on. There will be a minimum number of pages (usually around 20) that will be included with the basic price – you can add pages later for an extra cost per page. Once you have a series of empty pages in front of you it's time to fill them with your pictures, which is usually done by dragging and dropping thumbnails from a library. There will be a choice of page templates, from the simple and classic, with lots of white space, to the crazy, with all manner of cartoons, picture frames and text boxes on them. Obviously pick one that goes with the

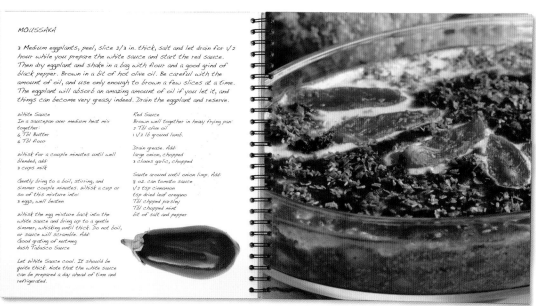

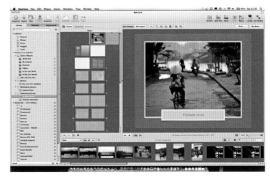

Right: Apple's Aperture software offers extremely powerful book creation tools, with a selection of pre-designed templates and the facility to create your own layouts, too.

project you are aiming for, and vary the pace of the book, too, by swapping between pages that contain just one image and those containing lots.

When you are ready to go, the pages are formatted and saved as PDF files (the standard file format of the printing industry) and uploaded to the printer's server. Here they'll be printed, trimmed, bound, packaged and sent back to you, all in a few days.

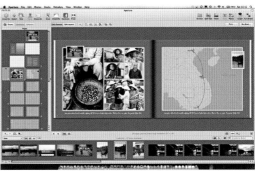

The quality of photobooks varies from company to company, but all are generally impressive. Just bear in mind that you get what you pay for, so if one product seems a bit more expensive than others, that might be because it features better quality paper, or a wrap-around dustjacket on the cover. Some software even allows you to include maps of the places you have been to on your travels, using GPS information from your camera (if available) to create a route and add place names.

The uses of photobooks are limited only by your imagination. They are a great way to assemble memories from your travels, the first year of a baby's life, pictures shot as a guest at a wedding (a book makes a great present), or even a compilation of retouched old prints from the family photo box.

Below: A photobook, like this one produced in Apple iPhoto, is a great way to tie together memories from a trip or holiday. Some designs even let you enter text from a diary or journal and include maps, as well.

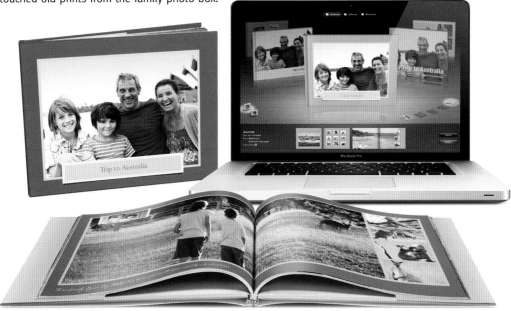

ASSIGNMENT
CREATING YOUR OWN COFFEE-TABLE ART BOOK

Photographic art books are always impressive, with their full-bleed printing and hardback covers. And now, with luxury photobook printing, there's no reason why you shouldn't have one of your own.

Assuming you have dabbled in some fine-art photography, you may be wondering what else you can do with the beautiful images you've shot, apart from putting them on the wall. For many fine-art photographers, the pinnacle of their achievements is the first time they publish a book of their work. You've probably seen them in your local bookstore: glossy, large-format affairs with hard covers and brilliant image quality. Purely an exercise in showing off – but then there is nothing wrong with that, if your photography is worth displaying.

Nowadays, with the quality of some of the photobooks on offer, you too can print your own book of fine-art images, and even sell it over the internet if you pick the right print company. Printers such as Blurb and Lulu differ from other photobook manufacturers because, as well as supplying a book for your library, they can also sell them via their online shop. This means that other people all around the world can buy your photography, in book form. While you shouldn't expect instant fame and fortune, with some viral marketing on social networking platforms, and the right price point, you could sell a few copies to fellow snappers.

Making it work

The secret to a good art book is not trying to cram too much in. Be sure that the pictures included are cohesive and relate to each other in some form. They might have been shot as part of a still-life or reportage assignment – or what better way to end your 365 project (see page

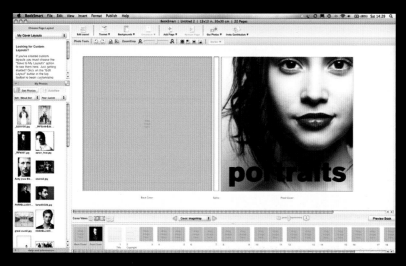

Left: Blurb's book creation software is free to download from www.blurb.com and features a raft of templates and design tools. Import your images to the library and place them on the page by dragging and dropping them.

TIPS & TRICKS

• Think about the flow of the book, in terms of pictures and design. Break up pages featuring just one image with others featuring two or three.

• Some book printers allow full-bleed images, i.e. those that run off the edges of the page for a borderless, high-impact look. Don't do this on every page, though.

• You could also order a sample copy and evaluate if your picture selection and page design works before you put it on sale.

• If you are handy with graphic-design software such as Adobe InDesign, you can use this to create your photobooks, too. Some companies even have templates for download.

169)? Look at a book from a famous photographer and you'll see how this works. It's not a random collection of the artist's favourite images, but rather a story of the idea that spawned the project in the first place.

Text is minimal in such books, but a preface or introduction of around 500 words is good idea. If you want to caption pictures, make sure you do it in a consistent style, both graphically (fonts and colours) and in terms of style (punctuation and grammar).

Lastly, have a think about the cover. This should have impact, making people want to pick up the book and open it. It might not be your best picture that does this, but rather one that creates instant impact – remember that symmetrical, bull's-eye compositions create more impact than other types of image (see page 60).

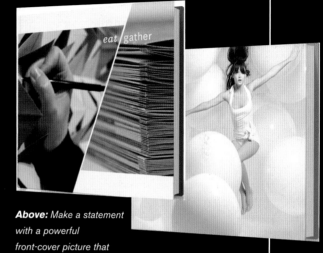

Above: *Make a statement with a powerful front-cover picture that will attract attention.*

Below: *Use full-bleed images to show them off, and only include those that you are sure will make an impression.*

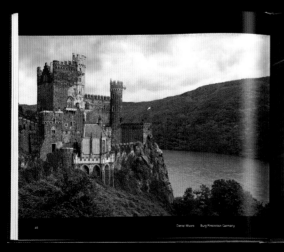
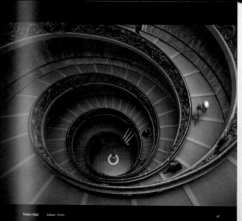

Your first **exhibition**

There are lots of places you can hold a photography exhibition, from cafés and shops to galleries. All will give you an appreciative audience, and may even let you sell a few fine-art prints, too.

For many photographers, the chance to see their images on the wall at an exhibition represents the ultimate achievement.

Your photography, brilliantly framed and displayed for an appreciative audience, who may be so appreciative they might even part with some money and buy a print. Who could ask for more?

In reality, staging an exhibition is hard work and requires investment, both in terms of time and money. While the end result is never going to make you a millionaire, it can be a brilliant marketing exercise if you are trying to become a professional

photographer, and it is a very rewarding experience. Success is really an exercise in attention to detail. Everything needs to be meticulously planned, from the venue to the type of paper the images will be printed on.

Picking a venue

It's unlikely that, for your first exhibition and as an unknown photographer, you will be able to just walk into a gallery off the street, show them your pictures and get a slot in their exhibition calendar. To begin with you'll need to consider other venues

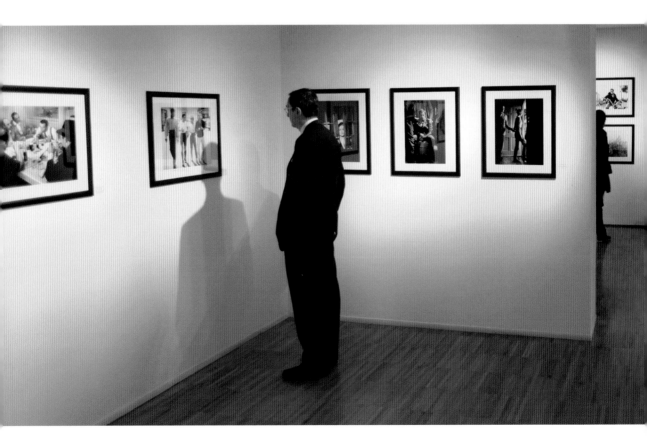

– cafés, restaurants, pubs and bookshops. These venues often have programmes featuring guest art on their walls, changing the artist every few weeks, which is a good deal for all involved. The venue in question gets free, regularly changing art on their walls, and you get an exhibition space for free and a chance to put your photography under the noses of a lot of people. And if you sell any, a café's commission will be a fraction of that changed by a gallery, too.

Alternatively, look into whether your area has an open studios scheme, where artists open up their homes or workplaces to the public as exhibition spaces for a few weekends of the year.

Printing and presentation

The presentation of your images in an exhibition has to be first rate; it's as simple as that. If you are printing them yourself, select a good quality semi-gloss or lustre fine-art paper, and don't forget to sign them on the front. You'll want to frame the images, and here a professional framer will do the best job, though it will cost more. Unfortunately this is an area where cutting corners shows in the quality of the end result, and can lead to missed sales that would otherwise have helped with the extra expense. If you use pre-made frames from a high street or online store, then do at least get the mattes that hold the pictures within the frames cut by hand so they are a perfect fit.

When picking the style of frame, remember the golden rule: keep it simple. People have come to see your picture, not the frame. Don't use anything over the top that will compete for attention with the image. If in doubt, go for a simple thin, black frame, with a white matte inside it.

Pricing and marketing

It's great if you can sell a few images from your show. Aside from the obvious advantages of having some extra cash in your pocket, nothing is more satisfying than knowing that someone liked your picture so much they parted with money to have a copy. Choosing the right price point is very important and depends not only on what you are selling but also to whom. Photographs might sell in galleries for more than they do in cafés and bars, but this is only a reflection on the type of people who go to these two very different venues, and what mood they are in. Someone may love your picture on the wall of a café, but if they only came in to grab a cappuccino, they are probably not going to be in the right frame of mind to buy a print for gallery prices.

In these smaller, more informal venues, prints aren't the only thing you can sell. Why not produce a series of postcards or greetings cards showing the same images as the main exhibition? Positioned at the counter, you might be able to sell quite a few over the course of the show.

It's usual for the venue to take a cut of anything you sell, but this is an area where cafés score highly. A professional gallery might take 50 per cent of the sale price, but cafés, bars and restaurants are less cut-throat and should only demand 10–20 per cent.

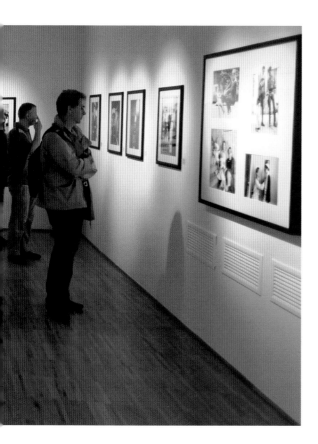

Left: Think carefully about framing and mounting – all the pictures should be presented using a consistent theme that complements your photographic style.

Protecting your images online

Who owns the pictures you take? You do, of course. But on the internet your pictures need protecting from those who might want to pass them off as their own, use them commercially or even sell them on.

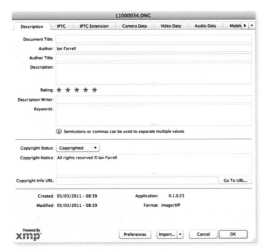

Above: *Entering copyright information in Photoshop, Elements or Lightroom. You don't need to do this all in one go; use a metadata template to apply to all the images in a set.*

If your images are online then they are at risk of being stolen and used without your consent. This might sound like an over-reaction, but unfortunately it's true. It is very straightforward to download and copy a picture from a website, which means that if your pictures are on the web, then they could also be in someone else's Powerpoint presentation, magazine, website, book or advert without you knowing – or receiving a penny in compensation.

So how can you prevent this from happening? Thankfully the law is on your side in matters like this – or more specifically, copyright law is. While the details of the legal rights afforded under such legislation vary from country to country, the crux of copyright is the same the world over: it protects your intellectual property (in this case your photographs) from being copied and used without your express permission. When you put an image on the internet – be it on your website

or on a social networking site – it can be said to be in the public domain, but this does not mean that you have no copyright protection. The copyright of a photograph automatically belongs to a photographer, and it stays with them until they give it up.

Nevertheless there are still an awful lot of copyright breaches every year, but you can protect yourself with a few clever tricks and common-sense measures.

Declare your ownership
Ignorance is no defence but if, when you catch someone using one of your pictures illegally, they claim to have not known who the picture belongs to, you might find it difficult to prove that they did. Your case is helped by your name being associated with the image file – more specifically in the metadata. Your image editing software can help you do this. If you use Photoshop's or Elements' 'Save for Web...' command, you'll notice you can input copyright infomation here, which will be embedded in the file's metadata header. Lightroom also has options for doing this, either on import or export, and some DSLRs even let you input this information in-camera, so that each picture taken is automatically tagged.

Keep it small
You can limit the usefulness of a picture by keeping its file size small. A certain number of pixels are needed for a photograph to be printed in a magazine or advertisement, and if they aren't there then your image can't be misused in this way. You can select what image resolution a website such as Flickr or Facebook will use when you upload your files. Remember, though, that there are plenty of on-screen ways for your images to be used, too – in web adverts, presentations and even in video clips.

Watermarking

You can declare a photograph to be yours by marking it more clearly than with just metadata. A watermark is a semi-transparent text mark that lies over the photograph itself. Your name will be visible on the image – making it unsuitable for use by anyone else – but because the text is slighty see-through, the details of the picture can still be seen.

Some software (Lightroom, Aperture) can add a watermark to images automatically on export, and plug-ins are available for Photoshop and Elements to equip them with this facility, too. Alternatively you can add a watermark yourself with a text layer and some tricks with blending modes and transparency.

Watermarking is sometimes seen as the last resort. It detracts from the image, and you should consider carefully whether the risks of someone stealing a photograph are really significant enough to warrant spoiling the effect of the image.

Do you have to put it on the internet?

Lastly, but obviously, ask yourself whether you have to put the image on the internet in the first place. The only cast-iron way to prevent internet theft is, unfortunately, not to put images up on the web to begin with. If it is a particularly sensitive or commercially valuable image, then this might be the route to take.

Watermarking your photos

Although there are automatic watermarking features in some applications, it's very easy to create watermarked images in Adobe Photoshop and Elements without resorting to additional software. If you follow these four simple steps shown below, and save your steps as an action in Photoshop, you will be able to automate this for a limitless amount of images.

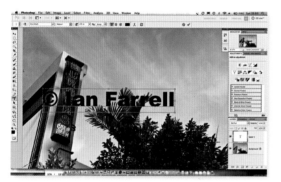

Step 1. *Open the image into Adobe Photoshop and select the Text tool. Click on the part of the image you want to watermark and type your name, preceded by a © (copyright) symbol.*

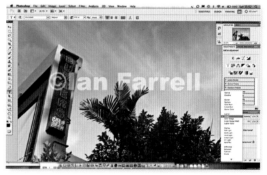

Step 2. *Format the text to the correct size and a mid-grey colour. You'll notice that this text is on a separate layer; change its blending mode to 'Screen' to complete the watermark.*

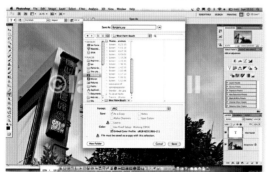

Step 3. *Keeping the watermark as a separate layer means you can switch it off to save a non-marked version. Saving a JPEG with the layer switched on means the watermark is saved, too.*

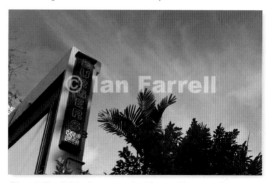

Step 4. *The finished, watermarked image. The text will be hard for anyone to remove, even with Photoshop's Cloning and Healing tools, but doesn't get in the way of the picture too much.*

Selling stock photography

Launching a career in professional photography is a major commitment that not everyone can undertake, but stock libraries are a way of generating some extra cash from your camera without jacking in the day job.

Image libraries sell photography to all manner of businesses, from advertising agencies and packaging companies through to magazine and book publishers. It's an industry worth billions around the world, and it can be accessed not only by professional photographers but by talented amateurs, too.

What makes stock photography so compatible with amateur photography is that the image library takes care of all of the marketing, sales and administration for you, enabling you to continue working in your day job and treating anything you get from photography as a second income. You can take pictures at weekends and on holidays, and only a small amount of extra time is needed

in your normal digital workflow to upload to the libraries' online shops, where they will be on sale to anyone in the world.

There are, of course, some provisos. Image libraries are happy to take submissions from amateur and semi-professional photographers, but that doesn't mean they will take any old rubbish. The stock photography market is a competitive one, and all libraries are keen to maintain the quality (both technical and artistic) of the images they offer for sale.

Below: A trip away presents a great opportunity for stock sales. Try to captures landscapes, people shots, street scenes and objects that capture the character of the place.

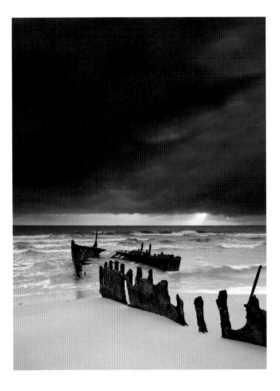

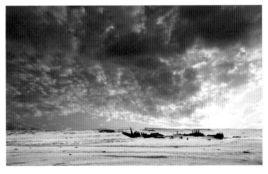

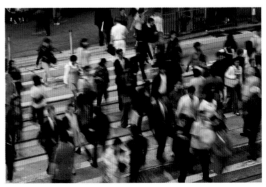

Types of stock photography

There are a few types of stock photography, and the way that libraries market and sell pictures also varies. At its most basic level, a stock photography sale can be split into one of two types: rights managed and royalty free. The first of these provides the best deal for a photographer but is expensive for the client. A rights-managed sale means that the library will sell a client a licence to use your photograph for a specific purpose. The amount they pay will vary according to what they want to do with it, for instance a picture used inside a magazine will command less money than one used on an advertising billboard. If the client wants to use it again, then they will have to pay for it again.

The opposite of this model is royalty free, where a client buys the image to use in any way they want at any time. Copyright stays with you as the photographer, though, and you can sell the picture again to as many people as you want. For the client, royalty free is cheaper and represents good value, but often the best quality photography is sold under the more expensive rights-managed model. Furthermore, rights-managed deals can also include exclusivity, where the client pays extra to ensure that no-one else will use the image for an agreed period. This is essential in advertising; no company would want a competitor using the same image in a rival ad campaign.

Whether you choose rights managed or royalty free will depend on the market you are trying to sell to, and the paperwork you have to support your images (see box, below). Royalty free is a better bet for those new to the stock photography game, thanks to its simpler way of working.

A more recent adaptation of royalty-free image sales is so-called microstock photography. Agencies specializing in this business model sell pictures for very little money (some of the big US-based libraries advertise pictures for a couple of dollars each), but aim to do so many times to make a decent profit.

Model release forms

In most countries there are rules regarding what you can and can't do commercially with someone's photograph. Take a picture of a stranger in the street and this picture can only be published editorially – that is, in a magazine, book or newspaper to support a story. It cannot be used in anything like an advertisement or in publicity material where the person would be seen to be endorsing a product or service, unless that person has given their permission for this to happen. This permission is given in the form of a model release form – a legal document, signed by the photographer and subject, that gives the photographer permission to use the images for any purpose.

This situation doesn't just apply to strangers on the street, but also to models who you pay to pose for you. For this reason it is always worth getting a model to sign such a release form at the end of the shoot. Most will do so without question as this is perfectly normal industry practice.

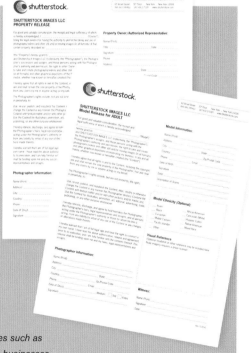

Right: *You can get model release forms online through agencies such as Shutterstock, or from stationers selling pre-written contracts for businesses.*

Finding and approaching a stock library

There are many image libraries out there, from huge, multi-subject libraries containing millions of pictures to smaller, specialist providers working in a specific field. For the amateur dipping their toe into stock photography for the fist time, one of the online microstock companies is a good bet – try iStock (www.istockphoto.com) or Shutterstock (www.shutterstock.com).

The first thing you should do after finding a library is to find and read their contributor guidelines thoroughly. And when you have done that, read them again. All libraries have some kind of quality-control process, and some require you to make a test submission to ensure that your image quality is up to the job. The likelihood of you getting through this test submission process first time is substantially improved if you know all of the technical specifications required. What is the minimum file size? Are JPEG files OK, or are larger TIFFs needed? Should images be left unsharpened? What about compression?

It's worth keeping this first test submission small, just submitting the minimum number of images. Once this is out of the way, it's in your interest to submit as many images as possible to the collection – the more you have in the library, the more sales you'll get and the faster your 'new camera' fund will increase.

Keywording and subject matter

Once your images are selected and uploaded, there is still work to be done. Each image needs to have a series of keywords associated with it. These are the terms that potential customers will be typing in when they search the library for pictures. If one or more of your keywords matches what they type, then your pictures will be presented in the search results. For this reason, the art of keywording is very important indeed.

Look at the image and try and think laterally as well as literally. What does the image contain? People, cars, places? What are the people doing? List activities, jobs and hobbies as specifically and generally as possible. What about feelings? Happiness, sadness, clean, busy, successful, cold – these are all examples of effective keywords that can sum up the mood of a photograph.

You will often be submitting images to a library that you have already taken, or that have been shot for another purpose, such as travel images from a holiday. You might also start to shoot pictures specifically for your stock collection, and when doing this some insider knowledge on what the customer wants can be really useful. Your library may do this for you; some publish blogs and newsletters detailing the subjects that are selling well at the moment, or if any areas in the library need a refresh. Additionally, you should keep an eye on the news for topics that you think may become magazine articles in the future. For example, those countries that have banned

Hints and tips for successful stock

- Pay close attention to popular culture, current trends and news topics, and shoot images accordingly.

- Shoot raw – libraries will thank you for the extra image quality.

- Provide alternative compositions featuring empty space that can be overlaid with text on magazine or book spreads.

- Consider hiring one or more models in order to shoot some stock lifestyle images, either on location or in the studio.

- Put as many images as you can online to increase your chances of a sale. A collection of several thousand is needed to guarantee a decent income

- Keywording is so important. See how similar images are keyworded, then improve on it.

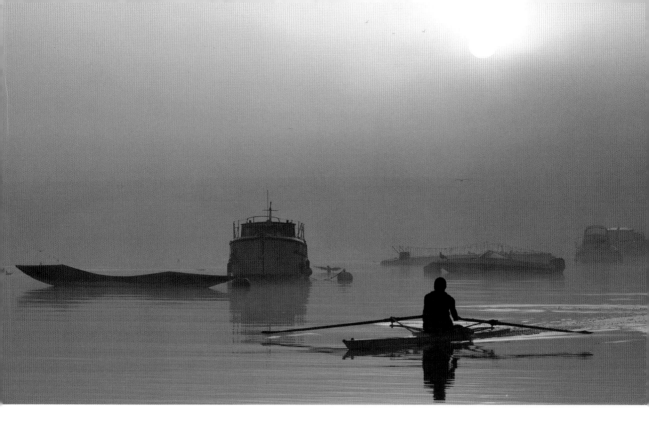

smoking in public places have almost certainly had magazines publishing stories on the topic, and these will have required supporting photography. A photographer anticipating this could have hired a couple of models and shot a series of 30 or so photographs showing people chatting and smoking in bars or restaurants, perhaps using a venue after hours. This type of thinking can make stock photography a successful and lucrative business.

Above: *This stock image was tagged with the following keywords, enabling it to be found in a variety of relevant searches: rowing, sculling, scull, boat, boating, dawn, fog, foggy, landscape, lone, mist, motor, oar, outdoors, peace, recreation, river, rower, rowing, small, solitude, sport, sunrise, Thames, tranquil, water, weather.*

Getty and Flickr

Getty Images, the world's largest image library, has formed a working relationship with the online social media tool Flickr to enable photographers to submit images from their Flickr accounts for consideration by Getty. Successful contributors will be able to sell photography through one of the largest, most competitive libraries in the world. More details can be found on the Flickr site at www.flickr.com/groups/callforartists.

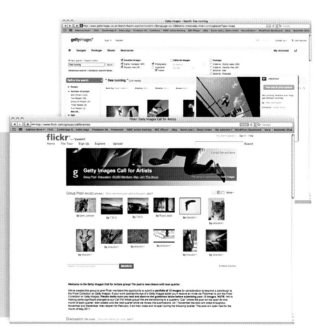

Glossary

Abberation
The process by which light is incorrectly focused by a lens, leading to image quality problems such as a lack of edge sharpness or coloured fringing.

Ambient light
Pre-existing, available light as opposed to that created by flash.

Aperture
A near-circular opening inside a camera's lens that lets light through to the sensor. The aperture is variable in size, so the amount of light transmitted can be varied in order to regulate brightness. Measured in f/stops.

Aperture priority
See exposure mode.

Artefact
Part of an image that does not exist in the scene in real life, but is rather generated by a problem with the lens, camera, electronics or software.

Aspect ratio
The rectangular proportions of an image, expressed as a ratio of the frame's width to height, eg. 3:2.

Back-up
A duplicate copy of a hard disk, made in case the original is damaged or stolen.

Blog
An abbreviation of web log, which is a kind of online diary that comprises words, images or both.

Buffer
A small amount of memory built into a digital camera that holds photographic information straight from the sensor, before it is written to a memory card.

Burning
The selective darkening of parts of an image in editing software, using a brush to define which parts should be darkened. Named after a traditional darkroom technique involving letting more light through to light-sensitive paper. The opposite of dodging.

Burning
Creation of a CD, DVD or Blu-ray disk.

Card reader
A device for reading memory cards when they are out of the camera. Many card readers accept more than one size and shape of card and connect to a computer via USB or FireWire cable.

CCD
A CCD (charged coupled device) is one of the two main types of sensor used in digital cameras. It is composed of pixels, which give out an electrical signal when they are struck by light. This electric signal is converted into a digital image file by the camera's image processor.

CD-R/CD-RW
A recordable or re-writable CD format.

CMOS
A CMOS (complementary metal oxide superconductor) sensor works in a different way to CCD-type chips, and can produce images with a lower signal to noise ratio.

CMYK
Cyan, magenta, yellow and black – the four main colours used by photo-quality inkjet printers. Some printers use more than this for a larger colour gamut, adding light cyan, green or grey inks, too.

Colour cast
The dominance of one colour over others in a photograph, giving an image an overall colouration. Often caused by coloured light sources or incorrect white balance settings.

Compact Flash
One of the main type of memory cards used in digital cameras. Larger than other types, they are also more robust and faster at transferring data.

Compression
The process of reducing the size of an image file, thereby maximizing storage space.

Contrast
The difference between the lightest and darkest areas of a photograph.

Copyright
Legal protection for the originator of a photograph that states an image may not be used, sold or reproduced without the photographer's consent. Arises automatically whenever a photograph is taken.

Depth of field
The distance between the furthest and nearest points that appear to be acceptably sharp in a photograph. Depth of field increases as the size of the aperture used becomes smaller.

Dodging

The selective lightening of parts of an image in editing software, using a brush to define which parts should be lightened. Named after a traditional darkroom technique involving the selective shading of light-sensitive paper. The opposite of burning.

Downloading

The process of transferring files from one place to another by requesting them from the remote location – memory card, hard disk or the internet.

Dpi

Dots per inch is the measurement of the resolution of an inkjet printer or a print made by such a device. It should not be confused with pixels per inch (ppi), which applies to the resolution of images before they have been printed.

DSLR

A digital single-lens reflex (DSLR) camera features a movable mirror that lets a photographer see directly through the camera's lens when looking through a viewfinder. Lenses are interchangeable for flexibility.

DVD

Digital versatile disk – a type of high capacity optical disk based on the CD. In its basic form the DVD can store 4.7GB of data. DVD-R and DVD-RW versions are recordable and re-writable respectively.

EXIF data

Exchangeable image file (EXIF) data comprises information about the equipment used (camera, lens, etc.), exposure settings (aperture, shutter speed, metering pattern, etc.) and other user-generated data (copyright, keywords, etc.). EXIF data can be read by different devices and software.

Exposure

The total amount of light allowed to fall on the camera's sensor as the photograph is made. The more light hits the sensor, the brighter the image will be. Exposure can be broken down into shutter speed (the time for which light is let through to the sensor), aperture (how much light is let through), and ISO (the sensitivity of the sensor).

Exposure mode

Digital cameras have several exposure modes, which govern how aperture and shutter speed are selected. Common exposure modes are manual (user sets both), program (camera sets both) and aperture- or shutter-priority mode (user sets one, camera sets the other).

Fill-in flash

A flash technique used to fill in (lighten) shadows in a photograph taken with ambient light.

Filter

A piece of glass or resin fitted to the front of a camera's lens in order to create a special optical effect.

Filter

A software-based special effect, applied using a computer and imaging application after the image has been captured.

FireWire

A type of connectivity used to transfer data from one electronic device to another very quickly via a cable. Often used with card readers and external hard drives.

Flash

A very short burst of bright light used to illuminate a scene when ambient light levels are too low. Flashes can be built in to the camera, be separate hotshoe units that attach to a camera, or be separate mains-powered or battery-powered units.

Flickr

A social networking and image sharing website.

Focal length

The distance between the centre of the lens and the camera's sensor. Conventionally measured in millimeters.

Formatting

The process of wiping a memory card or disk, replacing whatever is there with a brand new, blank file system.

F/stop

The size of a lens's aperture is expressed as an f/stop, which is defined as the focal length of the lens in use divided by the physical diameter of the opening (both measured in millimeters).

Gamut

The range of colours reproduced by a device, such as a camera, screen or printer.

GIF

Graphical interchange format – a type of image file comprising 256 colours, primarily used to show non-photographic diagrams on web pages.

Gigabyte (GB)

An amount of memory equal to 1,024 megabytes (MB) of information.

Greyscale

An image (or image mode) comprising a single colour channel and appearing as black, white and a range of greys in between.

HDMI

High definition multimedia interface (HDMI) is a connection type used to connect devices such as DVD and Blu-ray players, computers and digital cameras to TVs and displays.

Highlights

The brightest parts of a photograph.

Histogram

A graphical description of the range of tones in an image, with the brightness value plotted on the x-axis and the number of pixels corresponding to a particular brightness value on the other axis.

Hotshoe

A slot on the top of a camera where an external flash attaches.

Image processor

A microchip inside a digital camera that takes raw information from the sensor and turns it into JPEG images files that can be read and edited on a computer.

Inkjet printer

A type of printer commonly used by photographers to create hard-copy images. Tiny droplets of ink are fired from cartridges onto paper through tiny nozzles.

ISO sensitivity

A system used to describe the sensitivity of a digital camera's sensor, originally developed to describe the sensitivity of different films towards light. ISO sensitivity is user-adjustable, although it can often be set automatically. Much like shutter speed and aperture settings, ISO is increased in stops (or fractions thereof), with the sensitivity of the sensor increasing by one stop each time the value of the ISO sensitivity is doubled (100, 200, 400, 800, etc.). *See also* noise.

JPEG

JPEG (joint photographic experts group) is the type of image file used most commonly by photographers. Referred to as a lossy file format, since the type of compression used to make the file sizes small enough to store in quantity on a memory card involves some loss of image quality.

Kilobyte (KB)

An amount of memory equal to 1,024 bytes of information.

LCD

Liquid crystal display (LCD) technology is used in digital cameras for the display screens that show menu information and allow image review.

Lithium ion

Type of battery technology used in digital cameras.

Megabyte (MB)

An amount of memory that is equal to 1,024 kilobytes (KB) of information.

Megapixel

A count of the number of pixels on the surface of a camera's sensor (*see also* resolution). One megapixel is equal to one million pixels. A camera with more megapixels will capture more detail and produce files that be printed at larger sizes.

Memory card

A flash-memory storage device used inside digital cameras to store image files. Memory cards are available in different capacities, (usually measured in gigabytes) and physical types, including Compact Flash (CF), Secure Digital (SD), micro SD, xD, and Memory Stick.

Memory Stick

Type of memory card developed by Sony for use in its digital cameras as well as other consumer electronics products.

NiMH

An older type of rechargeable battery. Superseded by the much more advanced lithium ion (li-ion) technology.

Noise

Unwanted image artefacts taking on a random speckled appearance. Noise is exacerbated by high ISO shooting and heat, but can be reduced by digital processing, either by the camera's own image processor or in software during post-production.

Panning

A photographic technique involving shooting a moving subject with medium or slow shutter speed. The often tripod-mounted camera is moved to follow the subject on it's trajectory, keeping it in focus but blurring the background through the movement.

PDF
The portable document format (PDF) was developed by Adobe to enable sharing of images and text between computers using freely available viewing software. The PDF can now be written and viewed by many applications and is used extensively in the publishing and printing industries.

Pixel
Standing for picture element, pixels are the building blocks of all digital images. On a camera's sensor, pixels are tiny light-sensitive areas that together generate an electronic version of the image being projected onto them by the lens. In display screens each pixel gives out light, together forming the image that we look at on screen.

Pixelated/pixelation
When resolution falls to a level where image quality begins to drop, we often reach a point where we can see the individual pixels in an image – something we call pixelation.

Plug-ins
Extra software that enhances the functionality of other applications, such as Adobe Photoshop.

Ppi
Pixels per inch (ppi) refers to the resolution of a sensor or screen or an image in its electronic form. Not to be confused with dots per inch (dpi).

RAM
Random access memory (RAM) is the type of memory used by a computer to hold applications and images as they are being used.

Raw
An image-file format containing data as it came from the camera's sensor with no digital processing. Must be put through special raw-processing software in order to view it. Offers better quality and more versatility than the JPEG file format, but is much larger in size and requires extra digital processing.

Red-eye
An artefact whereby a person's pupils appear bright red when they are photographed with flash. Anti-red-eye software is available in-camera and on computer, and the effect is reduced by moving the flash off-camera.

Resolution
The ability of a lens or optical system to show detail. The higher the resolution of the lens or sensor (*see* megapixel), the more detail will be captured. A digital image containing many pixels is said to be of higher resolution than one containing fewer pixels.

RGB
An RGB image contains three colour channels, red, green and blue, which mix together to give a colour image (*see* greyscale).

Saturation
A measurement of how richly reproduced colours are in a photograph.

Sensor
The light-sensitive device in a digital camera that captures the image projected by the lens. Two types of sensor are in common use: CCD and CMOS. The more pixels a sensor has, the more detail it will capture and the larger the files from the camera will be.

Sharpness
The clarity of detail in a photograph, sharpness comprises two factors: resolution describes how much detail is seen; while acutance governs how sharp this detail looks by changing the contrast over lines and edges in the picture.

Shutter priority
See exposure mode.

Shutter speed
A measurement of how long the camera's shutter stays open to let light through to the sensor. Measured in seconds, or fractions thereof. *See* exposure.

Thumbnail
A small version of a photo shown for browsing and editing in imaging software.

TIFF
The TIFF (tagged interchange file format) file is commonly used by photographers who want the ultimate in image quality. Does not use lossy compression (*see* JPEG).

USB
USB (universal serial bus) connections are found in a computer system. They can be used to connect keyboards and hard drives, as well as digital cameras and card readers for transferring files.

White balance
A variable that corrects for (or introduces) colour casts.

WiFi
A method of connecting electronic devices together wirelessly.

xD card
A tiny memory card format developed jointly by Fuji and Olympus for use in digital cameras.

Index

The author

Ian Farrell is a photographer and journalist from Cambridge, UK. He is the former editor of the bestselling magazine *Professional Photographer*, and currently writes for numerous British photography titles including *Amateur Photographer*, *The British Journal of Photography* and *Digital Photographer*.

Ian has been shooting pictures since his parents bought him an SLR for his 12th birthday, and hasn't been far from a camera since. He uses a variety of cameras and formats (both digital and traditional) to photograph people and capture everyday life on the street. He works as a professional portrait photographer from studios in London and Cambridge.

You can see more of Ian's photography on his website at www.ianfarrell.org, and see regular updates of his personal work on his blog at www.ianfarrell.org/blog. You can follow him on Twitter as @eyefarrell.

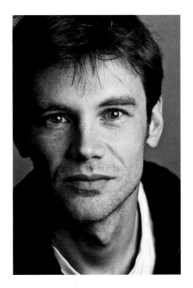

Acknowledgements

© **Ian Farrell Photography**: p15 all; p19 all; p21 all; p25 bottom; p27 all; p33 top right; p35 all; p36; p37 all; p42 all; p46 both; p48-49 all; p55 a, c, f, g; p57; p59 all; p60-61 all; p62 bottom right; p64; p65 top; p68-69 all; p70-71 all; p73 top right and left; p74-75 all; p77 all; p80-81 all; p82; p85; 86-87 all; p90-91 all; p93 b; p94; p95 top; p96 top; p97; p98-99 all; p104 bottom; p105; p108-109; p110 bottom; p111; p116-117; p124-125 bottom; p127 both; p142 top; p148-149 all; p150-151 all; p154 bottom; p164-165 all; p166; p170; p172 top; p173 bottom right; p174; p176 bottom; p177 top; p184-185 bottom; p218-219 both; p244; p255; p256; p259 top two; p260-261; p263; p264; 267; p282; p286 top, centre; p287; p288; p290; p292; p296-297 all; p304; p307; p308; p312; p314-315; p316; p318; p319; p320-321; p322-323; p327 right; p328-329; p332-333 all; p334-335 all; p338-339; p341; p343; p348; p350-351; p352-353; p358-359; p360-361; p362-363; p364-365; p366; p382 both; p383 bottom three.

© **Shutterstock:** p1 SlavaK/Shutterstock.com; p2-3 Camellia/Shutterstock.com; p4-5 X.D.Luo/Shutterstock.com; p6 Songquan Deng/Shutterstock.com; p8 zerra/Shutterstock.com ; p11 top Michal Ninger/Shutterstock.com; p13 top Valeria73/Shutterstock.com, p13 centre Irbiss/Shutterstock.com; p22 top stavklem/Shutterstock.com; p25 centre ssguy /Shutterstock.com; p26 top Shcherbakov Ilya Shutterstock.com, p26 centre jannoon028 /Shutterstock.com; p28 top Moreno Soppelsa/Shutterstock.com, p28 bottom left Serg64/Shutterstock.com, p28 bottom right S_E /Shutterstock.com; p29 bottom left 6493866629/Shutterstock.com; p30 bottom left Krzysztof Odziomek/Shutterstock.com; p31 top right Ungor /Shutterstock.com, p31 centre Colour/Shutterstock.com; p31 bottom Serg64/Shutterstock.com; p44 Lusoimages/Shutterstock.com; p47 bottom kzww/Shutterstock.com; p52 sint/Shutterstock.com; p54 Arsgera/Shutterstock.com; p55b Galyna Andrushko/Shutterstock.com, d Loskutnikov/Shutterstock.com, e bociek666/Shutterstock.com; p56 Gyuszkofoto/Shutterstock.com; p63 top Laurin Rinder/Shutterstock.com, p63 bottom Mark Yuill/Shutterstock.com; p65 bottom WDG Photo/Shutterstock.com; p67 bottom left Boerescu/Shutterstock.com, p67 bottom right Rechitan Sorin/Shutterstock.com; p72 bottom left Matej Kastelic /Shutterstock.com, p72 bottom right Tony Hunt/Shutterstock.com, p73 bottom Chistoprudov Dmitriy Gennadievich/Shutterstock.com; p78 George Burba/Shutterstock.com; p83 bottom leungchopan/Shutterstock.com; p88 bottom left Yellowj/Shutterstock.com; p89 bottom right Zurijeta/Shutterstock.com; p93 a cellistka/Shutterstock.com, c Tatiana Makotra/Shutterstock.com, d Aaron Amat/Shutterstock.com, e Nikola Spasenoski/Shutterstock.com; p95 bottom Cheryl Ann Quigley/Shutterstock.com; p96 bottom Surkov Vladimir/Shutterstock.com; p100 Mircea BEZERGHEANU/Shutterstock.com; p102 bogdan ionescu/Shutterstock.com; p103 bottom Renewer/Shutterstock.com; p104 top alias/Shutterstock.com; p110 top Mehmet Dilsiz/Shutterstock.com; p112 bottom Sergios/Shutterstock.com; p113 Nadezhda V. Kulagina/Shutterstock.com; p118 ULKASTUDIO/Shutterstock.com; p119 top supertramp88/Shutterstock.com; p119 bottom Dan Howell/Shutterstock.com; p120 top monticello/Shutterstock.com, bottom marema/Shutterstock.com; p121 top elena moiseeva/Shutterstock.com; p120 bottom wanchai/Shutterstock.com; p122 top Nailia Schwarz/Shutterstock.com, p122 centre Nailia Schwarz/Shutterstock.com, p122 bottom cozyta/Shutterstock.com; p123 all Nailia Schwarz /Shutterstock.com; p125 top Songquan Deng/Shutterstock.com, p125 centre Georgescu Gabriel/Shutterstock.com; p126 Avella/Shutterstock.com; p128-129 PHB.cz (Richard Semik) /Shutterstock.com; p130 Jessmine/Shutterstock.com; p131 top Ravis) /Shutterstock.com; p131 bottom Luiz Antonio da Silva/Shutterstock.com; p134 Richard Bowden/Shutterstock.com; p135 all vichie81/Shutterstock.com; p136 Artur Bogacki/Shutterstock.com; p137 top Artur Bogacki/Shutterstock.com, p137 bottom Yuriy Kulyk/Shutterstock.com; p138 top QUAN ZHENG/Shutterstock.com, p138 bottom Julie Lubick/Shutterstock.com; p139 top left Luciano Mortula/Shutterstock.com, p139 top right Luciano Mortula/Shutterstock.com, p139 bottom Jeffrey T. Kreulen/Shutterstock.com; p141 joyfull/Shutterstock.com; p142 bottom 72605554/Shutterstock; p143 top Elnur/Shutterstock.com, p143 centre Mishakov/Shutterstock.com, p143 bottom marekuliasz/Shutterstock.com; p144 Iv Nikolny/Shutterstock.com; p145 top Zzvet/Shutterstock.com, p145 bottom hunta/Shutterstock.com; p154 top Natalija Sirokova/Shutterstock.com; p155 Roman Sigaev/Shutterstock.com; p156 top Luciano Mortula/Shutterstock.com, p156 bottom Konstantin Visnevskis/Shutterstock.com; p157 top Pres Panayotov/Shutterstock.com,   p157 bottom left Neil Lang/Shutterstock.com; p159 bruno ismael da silva alves/Shutterstock.com; p161 bottom El Choclo/Shutterstock.com; p167 Insuratelu Gabriela Gianina/Shutterstock.com; p168 Christian Wilkinson/Shutterstock.com; p169 a Irina Fischer/Shutterstock.com, b Becky Stares/Shutterstock.com, c g215/Shutterstock.com, d charles taylor/Shutterstock.com, e Stephen Beaumont/Shutterstock.com, e Steve McWilliam/Shutterstock.com; p171 top left Annemien Mattheus/Shutterstock.com, p171 top right Sandra Gligorijevic/Shutterstock.com, p171 bottom left titov dmitriy/Shutterstock.com, p171 bottom right Brazhnykov Andriy/Shutterstock.com; p172 bottom niderlander/Shutterstock.com; p173 top Yana Godenko/Shutterstock.com, p173 bottom left Kotofot/Shutterstock.com; p175 Kapu/Shutterstock.com; p176 top stryjek/Shutterstock.com, p176 centre Sergey Ryzhov/Shutterstock.com, p177 bottom ronstik/Shutterstock.com; p178-179 both Blend Images/Shutterstock.com; p179 top left Stuart Jenner/Shutterstock.com; p180-181 Michael Klenetsky/Shutterstock.com; p182 Yurchyks/Shutterstock.com; p183 all sportgraphic/Shutterstock.com; p183 bottom left cjpdesigns/Shutterstock.com; p185 top Photo West/Shutterstock.com; p186-187 64279756/Shutterstock.com; p188 Ivonne Wierink/Shutterstock.com; p188 top right Yu Lan; p189 top left Gunnar Pippel/Shutterstock.com, p189 top right Steve Mann/Shutterstock.com; p190 Anna Omelchenko/Shutterstock.com; p191 all bjonesphotography/Shutterstock.com; p192 top Geanina Bechea/Shutterstock.com, bottom Netfalls/Shutterstock.com; p193 top Marcio Jose Bastos Silva/Shutterstock.com, p192 bottom niki2die4/Shutterstock.com; p194 Mark Bridger/Shutterstock.com; p195 JKlingebiel/Shutterstock.com; p196-p197 all sudalim/Shutterstock.com; p198 A v.d. Wolde/Shutterstock.com; p199 Brandelet/Shutterstock.com; p202 top left Evgeni Stefanov/Shutterstock.com, p203 top left Kletr/Shutterstock.com, p203 top right Judy Kennamer/Shutterstock.com, p203 bottom Wendy Sue Gilman/Shutterstock.com; p204-205 AndreD/Shutterstock.com; p206 dwphotos/Shutterstock.com; p207 top cinemafestival/Shutterstock.com; p208 TDC Photography/Shutterstock.com; p209 top J.Q/Shutterstock.com, p209 bottom Albo/Shutterstock.com; p212-213 all WH CHOW/Shutterstock.com; p215 Camellia/Shutterstock.com; p216-217 all mariait/Shutterstock.com; p217 a kavram/Shutterstock.com, b kavram/Shutterstock.com, c kavram/Shutterstock.com d Sergei Devyatkin/Shutterstock.com; p220-221 Luba V Nel/Shutterstock.com; p223 Jochen Schoenfeld/Shutterstock.com; p224 Ilia Dukhnovska/Shutterstock.com; p225 Seleznev Oleg/Shutterstock.com; p226 top left jadimages/Shutterstock.com, p226 top right Gordan/Shutterstock.com, p226 bottom Ke Wang/Shutterstock.com; p227 top Denis Babenko/Shutterstock.com; p229 top Wayneo216/Shutterstock.com, p229 bottom Loskutnikov/Shutterstock.com; p230 Warren Goldswain/Shutterstock.com; p233 top Fedorov Oleksiy/Shutterstock.com; p233 bottom Adi/Shutterstock.com;

p238 top ArjaKo's/Shutterstock.com, p238 Bottom ArjaKo's/Shutterstock.com; p245 Denis Babenko/Shutterstock.com; p247 top Hung Chung Chih/Shutterstock.com, p247 Bottom Hung Chung Chih/Shutterstock.com; p248-249 Knud Nielsen/Shutterstock.com; p251 both ArjaKo's/Shutterstock.com; p252-253 Will Thomson/Shutterstock.com; p257 all Hiep Nguyen/Shutterstock.com; p258 both Andrew F. Kazmierski/Shutterstock.com; p259 bottom three Andrey Bandurenko/Shutterstock.com; p262 both YuliaPodlesnova/Shutterstock.com; p266 shaferaphoto/Shutterstock.com; p268 Jeff Thrower /Shutterstock.com; p269 top and centre zhuda/Shutterstock.com; p271; p272-273 all voyloydon/Shutterstock.com; p274-275 all Zurijeta/Shutterstock.com; p276-277 all Merlindo/Shutterstock.com; p278 Samot/Shutterstock.com; p280 both Michael William/Shutterstock.com; p285 Carlos Neto/Shutterstock.com; p286 bottom left & right Dominik MichÃlek/Shutterstock.com; p299 both jaimaa/Shutterstock.com; p300-301 all gabczi/Shutterstock.com; p302 both Danylchenko Iaroslav/Shutterstock.com; p303 all Sam Strickler/Shutterstock.com; p306 Gurgen Bakhshetsyan/Shutterstock.com; p317 all Warren Goldswain/Shutterstock.com; p326-327 bottom Ruslan Nabiyev/Shutterstock.com; p330-331 Marcin Ciesielski & Sylwia Cisek/Shutterstock.com; p336 Daniel Prudek/Shutterstock.com; p337 paul prescott/Shutterstock.com; p340 Grischa Georgiew/Shutterstock.com; p344-345 all avian/Shutterstock.com; p355 Phillip Minnis/Shutterstock.com; p356 Jochen Schoenfeld/Shutterstock.com; p367 Konrad Bak/Shutterstock.com; p372 both befly/Shutterstock.com; p374 both Denis Babenko/Shutterstock.com; p376 Dean Mitchell/Shutterstock.com; p378 top left Fesus Robert/Shutterstock.com, bottom and p379 left-hand image Blend Images/Shutterstock.com, right-hand image Mana Photo/Shutterstock.com; p383 top Dja65/Shutterstock.com, centre nito/Shutterstock.com, bottom book violetkaipa/Shutterstock.com, bottom picture left Ingrid Petitjean/Shutterstock.com, picture right Itinerant Lens/Shutterstock.com; p386 all (comps) p386 top Picsfive/Shutterstock.com, p386 centre Givaga/Shutterstock.com, p386 centre right lavoview/Shutterstock.com; p386 bottom Brooke Becker/Shutterstock.com; p394 all (comps) nuttakit/Shutterstock.com; p398-399 Adriano Castelli/Shutterstock.com; p402 bottom left Pawel Papis/Shutterstock.com, p402 top right Galyna Andrushko/Shutterstock.com, p402 bottom right Matt Grant/Shutterstock.com, p405 top Tim_Booth/Shutterstock.com;

© **Casio**: p10; p11 bottom; © **Nikon**: p12 top right and left; p16 bottom; top right, centre right, p20; p33 top right; p103 top; © **Olympus**: p12 centre, p13 bottom right; p16 top; p17 top left; bottom right; p30 top right, bottom right; © **Canon**: p22 bottom; p26 bottom; © **Hoya**: p24 top; p25 top, © **SanDisk**: p28 centre, p232 bottom; © **Jobo**: p29 top; © **Sony**: p32 top; p39 centre right, p232 top; © **Apple**: p38; p39 top left; © **Adobe**: p40, p41 top centre, top right, centre right; © **Alien Skin**: p41 bottom centre; © **Corel**: p41 top left; © **HP**: p45 top right; © **Epson**: p45 bottom; p50 both; p227 bottom; p295 top; p377; © **Elinchrom**: p112 top; © **X-Rite**: p293 centre; © **Vanessa Green**: p62 bottom left; © **Hama GmbH & Co KG**: p31 top left; © **Ivo Marloh**: p347; © **Wolf Marloh**: p107 all; © **Annabel Williams**: p115 all; © **Joe Cornish**: p133 all; © **Chris Coe**: p147 all; © **Karen McBride**: p211 all; © **Morley von Sternberg**: p153 all; © **Siddhartha Lammata**: p158; © **Chris Lorimer**: p207 bottom; © **Laurent Geslin**: p200-201 both; © **Magnum Photos**: p160 top; p161 top; © **Getty Images**: p160 bottom, p163 both;

Quercus Publishing Plc
55 Baker Street
7th Floor, South Block
London
W1U 8EW

First published in 2011

A catalogue record of this book is available from the British Library

UK and associated territories: ISBN 978 0 85738 548 2
Canada: ISBN 978 1 84866 210 0

Printed and bound in China

10 9 8 7 6 5 4 3 2